THE GENERAL
HISTORY
OF THE VAST
CONTINENT and ISLANDS
OF
AMERICA

VOL. V.

AMS PRESS
NEW YORK

The five most famous men in Peru and Chile

RECEIVED
JUL 2 9 1914

THE GENERAL

HISTORY

OF THE VAST

CONTINENT and ISLANDS

OF

AMERICA,

Commonly call'd, THE

WEST-INDIES,

FROM

The FIRST DISCOVERY thereof:

With the beft Accounts the People could give of their

ANTIQUITIES.

Collected from the Original RELATIONS
fent to the Kings of SPAIN.

By *ANTONIO DE HERRERA,*
Hiftoriographer to His CATHOLICK MAJESTY.

Tranflated into *Englifh* by Capt. JOHN STEVENS.

VOL. V.

Illuftrated with CUTS *and* MAPS.

THE SECOND EDITION.

LONDON,
Printed for WOOD and WOODWARD in *Paternofter-Row.*
MDCCXL,

Library of Congress Cataloging in Publication Data

Herrera y Tordesillas, Antonio de, 1559-1625.
The general history of the vast continent and
islands of America.

An abridged translation of the first three decades
of Historia general de los hechos de los castellanos.
    1. Latin America—History—To 1600. 2. America—
Discovery and exploration—Spanish. 3. America—
Early accounts to 1600. I. Title.
F1411.H62132 1973   980'.01   70-169482
ISBN 0-404-07310-7

Reprinted with permission from a volume in the George Peabody
Department, Enoch Pratt Free Library, Baltimore, Maryland, 1973.

Reprinted from the edition of 1740, London
First AMS edition published, 1973
Manufactured in the United States of America

International Standard Book Number:
Complete Set: 0-404-07310-7
Volume V: 0-404-07315-8

AMS PRESS, INC.
New York, N.Y. 10003

THE

General HISTORY

Of the vaſt CONTINENT and ISLANDS of

A M E R I C A, &c.

❀❀❀❀❀❀❀❀ ❀ ❀❀❀❀ ❀❀❀❀❀ ❀❀❀❀❀ ❀❀❀❀❀❀ ❀❀

DECAD. IV. BOOK II.

❀❀ ❀❀❀❀❀❀❀❀❀❀ ❀❀❀❀❀❀❀❀❀ ❀❀ ❀❀❀❀❀❀❀❀

CHAP. I.

Pizarro *appoints the City of* Lima *to be the Capital of* Peru ; *founds that of* Truxillo ; *at variance with* Almagro ; *they are reconcil'd.*

IZARRO having founded the City of *Lima*, deſign d to make it the *Spaniſh* Metropolis of *Peru*, becauſe of its advantageous Situation and the Benefit of the Harbour, which he concluded wou'd be much reſorted to. He alſo ſettled another Colony, which he call'd *Truxillo*, in memory of his own native Town in *Spain* ; and endeavour'd to gain the Affections of the neighbouring *Indians*,

uſing

2 The H I S T O R Y of America.

ufing all poffible means to advance thofe two new
Towns. The Vale of *Chimo,* where this City of
Truxillo ftands, has its name from a potent Lord, and
when fubdu'd by the *Ingas,* they paid moft regard to
thofe Princes, and to the People, who had very notable burial Places, out of which much Gold has
been taken. The City of *Truxillo* was built near a
great and pleafant River, whence Trenches are drawn
to water the Gardens and Orchards, which are always green and frefh, and the Water runs by the
Houfes The Country is healthful, full of Farms,
and pleafant Houfes, abounding in Corn, Cattel, Fowl,
and all forts of Fruits ; and there is plenty of Fifh,
becaufe fo near the Sea. The City is in the Middle of a Plain, among delightful Groves of Trees ;
the Streets broad, and has a fpacious Market-Place,
whither the Mountain *Indians* came down to Trade,
and Ships fail d from thence, laden with Cotton,
Cloth, and other Things, carried to feveral Parts.

W·H I L S T *Pizarro* was at *Truxillo, Almagro* was
inform'd, that the King had given him the Government of all the Country to the Southward of *China,* which included the City of *Cuzco,* whereupon
he would not make ufe of the Commiffion given him
to that purpofe by *Pizarro,* who on the other Hand
was advis'd to read that Commiffion, as he did,
giving that Government to his Brother *John,* and
only impowering the Marfhal *Almagro* to go upon
the Difcovery of the *Cheriguanas.* Thefe Things
prov'd the Seeds of Difcord, fome fiding with *Pizarro,* and others with *Almagro* : The Brothers of
the former, who were grown haughty with their
Succefs, giving out that the latter intended to murder the Governour, whereupon being admonifh'd
by the Magiftrates to behave themfelves modeftly,
they grew more infolent, and had recourfe to Arms,
which

which might have caus'd much Bloodſhed, but that *Almagro's* Preſence ſtruck an awe upon the *Pizarros.* This was the Beginning of the Tumults in *Peru* between the *Almagros* and *Pizarros.* Advice of this Diſcord being carried to the Governour *Pizarro,* he haſted away to *Cuzco,* where *Almagro* met him in the Church, and they embrac'd, but each ſeem'd to blame the other. The Licenciate *Caldera,* a Man of a good natural Diſpoſition, well ſpoken, and excellently qualified in all Reſpects, undertook the Reconciliation, and having diſcourſed them both, with the Aſſiſtance of the Prieſt *Loayſa,* ſoon brought them to a Treaty, and meeting in the Governour's Houſe, they both ſolemnly ſwore faithfully, and without any evaſion, all that was contained in certain Articles there read, with the heavieſt Imprecations upon the Infringer of the ſame. The Subſtance of the ſaid Articles was 1. That their Partnerſhip ſhould ſubſiſt without any Infringement, through Intereſt, Ambition, or any other Motive. 2. That neither ſhould Plunder, Revile, or any way Offend the other 3. That they ſhould obſerve the Conditions ſtipulated between them long before. 4. That they ſhould jointly write to the King what related to thoſe Provinces, and neither of them any thing to the detriment of the other. 5. That all Profits ſhould be fairly produced and divided, and all reaſonable Expences allow'd on both Sides. This Oath was taken on the 12th of *June,* 1535. in the Preſence of many Perſons of Note, *F. Bartholomew de Segovia,* ſaying Maſs. All but *Pizarro's* Brothers rejoyced at this Reconciliation, being envious to ſee *Almagro* have ſo great a Share in what they coveted for themſelves, being already grown ſo arrogant, that ſcarce any could bear them. Notwithſtanding this ſolemn Reconciliation, there remain'd a difference of Parties, and the very *Indians,* who, till then, had been quiet, had their Share in theſe Diviſions, ſome incli-

ning

ning to *Pizarro*, and others to *Almagro*, but the moſt
applied to their *Ingra Mango*, whom they lov'd as
their natural Prince, Son to *Guaynacava* ; all thoſe
People following him whereſoever he went.

T H I S was the Poſture of Affairs, when *Almagro*
reſolved to lay aſide the former Project of the *Cheriguanas*, and to march into *Chile*, becauſe that Kingdom fell within the Government conferr'd on him by
the King, and the fame of the immenſe Wealth of
that Country had rais'd the Expectations of all Men.
Proclamation being made for ſuch as had no buſineſs
at *Cuzco* to prepare for that Enterprize, there was
much rejoycing, all being willing to ſerve under the
Marſhal, who was belov'd for his mild Temper and
Generoſity ; and he to the end that all might be furniſh'd with Arms and Horſes, brought out above one
hundred and eighty Loads of Silver, and twenty of
Gold, which he diſtributed to ſuch as would give
Bonds to repay the ſame out of what they ſhould get
in the Country they were going to ; and thus were
thoſe Kingdoms conquer'd for the Crown, the Conquerors ſerving for no Purchaſe, no Pay. *Almagro*
uſing all Diligence to ſet forward on his Enterprize,
deſir'd the *Inga* to appoint two *Indians* of Note to
go before him, to prepare and diſpoſe all Things for
the Reception of his Forces, and the *Inga*, accordingly aſſign'd him his Brother *Paul Topa* and the High-
Prieſt *Vilehoma*, whoſe Preſence was of much Moment
to keep the Country quiet, and it was thought that
the *Inga* ſent his Brother to take away all Occaſion of Jealouſy, and *Vilehoma*, as thinking him too
powerful, and of a turbulent Spirit. It was found
neceſſary for defraying the Expences of the Expedition, to have the Gold and Silver caſt at *Cuzco*,
to deduct the King's fifth, at which *Almagro* was
preſent, being very careful that the King ſhould have
his Due, and it was wonderful to ſee the vaſt Quantity

ty of thofe Metals. One *John de Lepe,* begg'd of *Almagro* one Ring, out of a Load of them that lay before him, who readily anfwer'd, he might take as many as he cou'd hold in both his Hands ; and being told he was a marry'd Man, gave him four hundred Pieces of Eight, to return to his Wife. To *l artho-lomew Perez,* who had been Jaylor at *Santo Domingo,* and prefented him with a Target, he gave four hundred Pieces of Eight, and a Silver Pot, weighing forty Marks, of eight Ounces the Mark, with two Lions Mouths of maffive Gold to it for Handles, which were found to weigh three hundred and forty Pieces of Eight. To *Montenegro,* who prefented him the firft *Spanifh* Cat that had ever been in tho e Parts, he gave fix hundred Pieces of Eight. It wou d be endlefs to recount the generous and charitable Acts of that Commander. He order'd *Paul Topa,* and the Prieft *Vilehoma,* to go before, and to halt at two hundred Leagues diftance, fending three *Spaniards,* with them ; and *John de Saavedra,* to follow thofe *Indians* with all the *Spaniards* that were willing to go, and at an hundred and fifty Leagues diftance to found a Colony, purfuant to what had been agreed with *Pizarro,* and upon this Commiffion was founded the Town of *Paria,* an hundred and thirty Leagues from *Cuzco,* to which all the People of *Collao* and *Los Charcas,* reforted. *Almagro* having fent away his Men, and fearing leaft *Pizarro* fhould fecure him, on Account of their late Differences, or, as was reported, being inform'd that there was fuch a Defign, to get him out of the Country the fooner, march'd with inconfiderable Forces, having order'd the Captains *Ruy Diaz* and *Benavides,* who were gone to *Lima* to raife Soldiers, to follow him, and *Roderick Orgoner* to ftay at *Cuzco,* and pick up as many as he could, to come after.

THE Day before he fet out from *Cuzco,* he advis'd *Pizarro* to fend away his Brothers into *Spain,* to avo d

all

all future Occasions of Discord, which would be very acceptable to all People, those Gentlemen insulting all Men on Account of his Authority, and in order to it said, he might give them what he pleas'd of his Treasure. This would have been wholesome Advice, if *Pizarro* had taken it, but he answer'd, That his Brothers lov'd and honour d him, as if he were their Father, and would never Occasion any Disturbance. *Almagro* being come to *Paria*, the Forces advanc'd, *John de Saavedra* having Orders to go along the High-Way to the Province of the *Chuchas*, the Capital whereof was *Topisa*, where *Paul Topa* and *Vilchoma* expected him. There he receiv'd Advice from *Cuzco*, that it was not proper for him to proceed on that Enterprize, but to halt, because a Person of Distinction was arriv'd at *Lima*, with a Commission from the King, to divide the Governments; but tho' this was most Expedient, he was so fully possess'd with the Ambition of disposing of such vast and wealthy Nations, as he had been inform'd of, and so intent upon bestowing much on those Gentlemen who follow'd him, that he valu'd not the Country he knew, and this gave Occasion to his conniving at many Crimes among his Soldiers, whence afterwards ensu'd much Desolation. The Lords of *Parcaz* visited, and made him considerable Presents, and tho they gave him bad Accounts of the Wealth of *Chile*, and much worse of the Deserts he was to pass through, neither he, nor his Soldiers would believe them, fancying they did it to save their passing through those Lands. Here we will leave them to proceed to other Affairs that belong to this Place.

Pizarro having sent away *Almagro* to *Chile*, return'd to *Lima*, leaving his Brother *John* to govern at *Cuzco*. At *Lima* he found, *F Thomas de Berlanga*, Bishop of *Panama*, who had the King's Commission to ascertain the Boundaries of the Governments of *Almagro*

gro and *Pizarro*, to prevent all Controverfies. *Pizarro* then began to Exercife much Liberality, giving two Gentlemen two thoufand Pieces of Eight each, a thoufand to a *Trinilarian* Fryar, to Portion his Sifters, and fo to feveral others. At this Time *Alonfo de Alvarado* came from *Truxillo* to *Lima*, and being a Man of Difcretion and good Management, *Pizarro* gave him Commiffion to go and reduce the Province of *Chachiapoyas*, and others to the Eaftward of them, with which he return'd to *Truxillo*, where he gather'd twenty Companies, and marching with them towards the *Chachiapoyas*, they arriv'd at *Cochabamba* and were well receiv'd, becaufe *Alonfo de Alvarado* being a good temper'd Man, would not fuffer any Perfon to be injur'd, by which means all the People came in to fubmit themfelves peaceably. He then told them, there muft be no more Idols nor Sorceries, nor fheding the Blood of Men, Beafts, or Birds, but that they were to adore the only G O D, the Creator of all Things ; they gave ready Attention to him, faying, they would be Chriftians, and then both Men and Women being drefs'd very gay, had a Dance in the Square, and laying down all the Jewels they wore in an Heap, prefented it to *Alvarado.* Having mention'd the Dances of the *Peruvians*, it is not improper here to obferve, that all Nations of the world living in Society, have their feveral Exercifes, by way of Recreation. In *Peru* there was a fort of Fight us d by way of Diverfion, which generally grew fo hot, that it prov'd dangerous. Thofe People have a thoufand Sorts of Dances, wherein they imitate feveral Profellions, as Shepherds, Hufbandmen, Fifhermen, Hunters, &c. with very leifurely Steps, Mufick and Meafure : Other Dances were of Perfons mask'd with hideous Vizors, and fome Men danc'd on the Shoulders of others, moft of thofe dances being fomewhat Idolatrous, becaufe they fo honour'd their Idols. At thefe Dances they play'd on

B 4 feveral

feveral mufical Inftruments, fome being little Pipes, like Reeds, others like Tabors, others like Snails, and they were all wont to fing, one or two repeating their Verfes, and the reft anfwering. Some of thofe Verfes were Hifto- rical, others Superftitious, and others Nonfenfical. Thefe Dances were call'd *Taaqui* ; and becaufe they are now only meant for Recreation, they are tolerated, the Pre- lates having contriv'd to put religious Matters into their Verfes, which they will liften to the whole Day. They have alfo introduc'd among them the feveral *Spanifh* Ways of Verfifying, which they are much taken with. *Alvarado* thinking thofe People were well-difpos'd to embrace whatfoever they fhould be taught, left fome *Spaniards* there, charging them to live peaceably and orderly, and having promifed to return fpeedily, went away to *Lima,* to give *Pizarro* on Account of what he had done, who thought fit that he fhould keep the Prefents that had been made him by thofe *Indians,* provided he wou'd immediately return into that Pro- vince to found a Colony there, and in order to it, he furnifh'd himfelf with all Neceffaries, and a Commif- fion to divide the Lands.

At *Lima* fome Soldiers joyned *Alonfo de Alvarado,* and though they did not approve of a Captain of fo much Moderation, however many follow'd him be- caufe he was good Natur'd. He went thence to *Trux- illo,* and having gather'd more Men there, march'd to *Cochabamba* where he mufter'd them, and found that the Foot had Crofs-Rows, Swords and Targets, and fhort Coats, ftuffed with Cotton, of good ufe by way of Armour in thofe Wars : The Horfemen had Swords, and Spears, and Morrions, with the fame fort of Armout. He named the Commanders, and prefcribed Laws for ftrict Difcipline, that the Natives might not be oppreffed, thinking fair Means the beft to reduce them to Obedience. The *Indians* were not pleafed to fee *Alvarado* return with fo many Men, but

he

he appeafed them with his courteous Behaviour, and having difpofed all Things to his Mind, marched away to the Eaftward, where he was inform'd, that the Inhabitants of the inner Provinces were incens'd at the others for having permitted the *Spaniards* to come in among them, whereupon, notwithftanding all *Alvara-do*'s Perfwafions, they began to affemble and threaten, declaring, that they would not fubmit, nor change their ancient Cuftoms, and therefore the *Spaniards* might depart and quit their Country. *Alvarado* fent Mef-fengers to advife them to return to their Houfes, and till their Lands, for he would do them no wrong, nor force them to quit their Religion, but only inftruct them to live as becomes rational Men. His Perfwa-fions not prevailing among thefe People, who were then in Arms, it was requifite to ufe Force, accor-dingly he advanc'd towards them, with fome of the Natives that had joined him. *Camacho* going before with twenty Men, at a League and half Diftance, came to a Stony Field, which was very bad for the Horfes, and then the *Indians* fent Meffengers to *Alva-rado*, with Prefents, fuing for Peace in an humble Man-ner, whilft they advanced towards the *Spaniards*. He returned an affectionate Anfwer, but as foon as the Meffengers were gone back the *Indian* Army appeared, and fell on with their ufual Cries, however being well received, they foon turned their Backs and fled.

Guayamamel, the Chief of the *Curacas,* or *Caziques,* perceiving that the *Spaniards* were not to be vanqu ih'd, perfwaded the reft to accept of Peace, alledging, it was vifible that the Sun favour'd the Strangers ; for which reafon it was better to be quiet in their Houfes and enjoy what they had, than to expofe themfelves to the dreadful Wounds thofe Men gave ; to endure Hunger, and deftroy their Wifes and Children. This he faid in the hearing of all his Army, and though *Guaman,* another powerful *Curaca* oppofed it, he in-
ftantly

ftantly ftripped himfelf of his fine Garment, and putting on a worfe, taking his old Wife along with him, went away to *Alvarado,* humbly begging Pardon, and offering to fubmit. *Guaman* follow'd his Example, as did the other Lords, except only *Guayamil,* who held out with a great Number of Men, and was a notable Juggler; but they found Means to feize and deliver him up to *Alvarado,* who condemned him to Death, as a Difturber of the publick Peace.

Alvarado proceeded to the Vale of *Vagua,* always taking care to do no harm, and found about eight thoufand *Indians,* guarding the Paffage of a River. Having readily made Floats, his Men being very Obedient upon all Occafions, they paffed the River near the Town, which they called *De la Cruz,* or of the Crofs, and met another Army, both which were attack'd, and foon routed. The Fame of thefe Succeffes, of *Alvarado's* Courtefy, and of the ftrict Difcipline obferv'd by his Forces, prevailed with all to fubmit to him, and he told them, That he would found a City in thofe Provinces, that fhould be as confiderable as that of *Cuzco,* where they might live pleafantly, and like Brethren. However he was inform'd, that there was another Army of *Chachiapoyas,* at Hand, whereupon, he fent to defire the *Curaca,* that they might be Friends, and avoid Effufion of Blood, of which no good could come. He anfwer'd, that having been told that the *Spanifh* Swords made great Wounds, and being defirous to fee one, he prayed him to fend it *Alvarado* accordingly fent one, with a Silver Hilt, which when he had obferv'd and try'd, he was aftonifhed, and went away to conclude Peace, fo that all the adjacent Provinces were reduc'd, and *Alvarado* apply'd himfelf to fettle the Government in Spirituals and Temporals. The *Ingas* had made a Road to this Province of the *Chiachiapoyas,* with whom they had

long

long Wars, and tho' vanquifh'd in one Battle, they
were at laft fubdued, and many of them tranfplanted
to *Cuzco,* where they fettled on the Hill called *Carmenga.* Thefe *Chiachiapoyas* are the whiteft and moft
graceful People of all the Nations in *Peru,* and the
Women fo beautiful, that they us'd to be carried for
the *Ingas.* They embrac'd the Religion, Habit and
Cuftoms of *Cuzco;* and when *Alvarado* reduc'd thefe
Parts, he then founded the City that was call'd *San
Juan de la Frontera,* that is, St *John on the Frontiers,*
on a Place call'd *Levanto,* an uneven Ground, which
they were forc'd to level for building of Houfes ;
but he foon remov'd it to the *Guancas,* becaufe it was
found to be an healthy Diftrict All the Province
of the *Chiachiapoyas, Guancas, Cafcayunga,* is within
the Territory of *San Juan de la Frontera,* in which
during the Reign of the *Ingas* there were Temples, Pa-
laces, and Royal Store-Houfes. In fome Towns there
are rich Gold-Mines, abundance of Cattel, and they
make fine Woolen-Cloth ; the Soil fruitful and producing all Things of the Growth of *Spain.* To the
Eaftward of this City is the great Ridge of the *Andes :* To the Weftward is the South-Sea, and beyond
the *Andes* is *Mayobamba,* and other great Rivers, with
other Nations more unpolifh'd, which the Natives fay
are the Progeny of the famous Commander *Ancoalla,*
who, on Account of the Cruelty practifed towards
him by the *Ingas,* abandon d his native Covntry, and
went away with as many of the *Chiancas* as thought fit
to follow him.

The Natives of the remoter Provinces difturbing
thofe that had fubmitted, *Alvarado* was oblig'd to
fend fome *Spaniards* to affift them in taking Revenge
of their Enemies, which they did accordingly, and
then he, by fair Means reduc'd the Territory of
Longua, whence he proceeded to that of *Charrafmal* to
to the Eaftward, taking with him a Number of the
Confe-

Confederate *Indians,* and halted in a Place near a Town
call'd *Gomora,* the Inhabitants whereof had fo great
a Conceit of their own Valour, that they fcoffed at
thofe who had comply'd with the *Spaniards* *Alvarado* having, according to his Cuftom, in vain endeavour'd to prevail on them by fair Means, fent *John
Perez de Guevara* againft them, with twenty Men,
but they fled and abandon'd their Town. Having
refted fome Days at *Charrafmal,* he march'd through
all thofe Eaftern Parts, without meeting any Oppofition, till he came to a Town, where they inform'd
him, that farther on, there were large Towns, and
the People were refolv'd to ftand upon their Guard,
and coming to a Town call'd *Corcon* found it abandon'd, and no Guides to be had, which put him to
fome Trouble, becaufe the Country was much cover'd. The *Indians* confiding in their multitude, and
being fenfible that fteep Hills were bad for the Horfes, whom they moft dreaded, waited an Opportunity
to attack the *Spaniards,* not thinking that *Alvarado*
knew any thing of their Defigns ; but he being vigilant, and acquainted with their Intentions, ufed
all means to fave the Effufion of Blood, which proving ineffectual, and underftanding that the Enemy
were drawn together on an high Mountain, he advanc'd againft them with all his Forces. The *Indians* were not idle, but coming down upon the *Spaniards,* wounded one Horfe, and ftruck a Dart through the
Pomel Part of a Saddle, tho' that Weapon had no
Iron Head : However the other *Spaniards* making
way to the Top of the Hill, thofe *Indians* were all
put to Flight, *Alvarado* not fuffering them to be purfu'd, to prevent the Slaughter, yet they, in the utmoft Defpair, for being, as they faid, forfaken by
their Gods, burnt their own Houfes, and deftroy'd
their Lands. To put a ftop to this Evil, *Alvarado*
fent *Camacho* with forty *Spaniards* and a thoufand *Indians*

dians to take fome Prifoners, who might go to offer Peace. At a few Leagues Diftance, *Camacho* met
five thoufand *Indians* of the Province of *Hafallao,* that
were marching to joyn thofe who had been defeated ; and it being ufual for Soldiers to obferve the
Methods of their Leaders, the *Spaniards* offer'd Peace,
which being rejeɛted, they ply'd their Crofs-Bows,
the Effeɛt whereof was fuch, that thofe *Indians* foon
fled, as did another Body that was following them.
Several other Skirmifhes happen d, which being much
alike in their Circumftances are not worth the mentioning in particular.

C H A P. II.

Of the Situation of the City of Lima ; *temperate Climate in the Torrid Zone ; difcoveries made by* Belalcazar, *he founds the
City of* Guayaquil.

THE City *De los Reyes,* or of the Kings, now
generally called *Lima,* is feated three hundred
Leagues from *Quito,* and at the like D ftance from
Los Charcas, whereas that of *Cuzco* is too far from
the firft of thofe Provinces and very near the latter.
The Harbour is very fafe and commodious, for the
great Trade carry'd on there from *New Spain,* and
all other Parts on the South-Sea, and therefore this is
the proper Refidence for the Vice-Roy, who is nearer
at hand than if he were in an inland Town to receive his Orders from the Court of *Spain,* and to
fee all that comes into and goes out of that Kingdom.
The Air is extraordinary healthful, the Heat being
moderated by the South Wind, and the Weather is
generally ferene and fair, becaufe the Sun being per-
pendi-

pendicularly over it, difpells all the Vapours that rife from the Earth. The Cold of the Night is not of it felf fufficient to temper the exceffive Heat of the Sun, whence it muft be concluded that the frefh Air alone renders the Torrid Zone fo moderate and delightful, that it is like a perpetual Spring ; whereas the Antients look'd upon it as not habitable, fuppofing it to be like an Oven, ever burning and fcorch'd up. That this Coolnefs is owing to the Wind appears in that fome Countries in one and the fame Latitude enjoying fuch Temperature as has been faid, others are fcarce tolerable for the Heat, as *Brazil Ethiopia*, &c. The fame is found in Places very little diftant from each other, ftill in the very fame Latitude, for *Potofi* is exceffive Cold and Barren, whereas *La Plata* is Temperate, Delightful, and Fertile, and yet the Diftance between them is but eighteen Leagues.

WHILST what has been faid above happen'd in other Parts of *Peru*, *Belalcazar*, removed the Colony he had founded at *Riobamba* to the City of *Quito*, giving it the Name of St. *Francis*, from whence he made many Excurfions, gaining feveral ftrong Holds thofe People had made. *John de Ampudia* upon one of thefe Expeditions, being inform.d where the *Indian* General *Zopezopagua* was with his Family, fent to advife him to be a Friend to the *Spaniards*, and not oblige them to Severity. He anfwer'd, that was what he defir'd, but that he dreaded their Cruelty, and Breach of Faith. *Ampudia* reply'd, he gave his Word that it fhould not be fo, but whatfoever was concerted fhould be obferv'd. *Zopezopagua*, on the one Hand, dreaded that they would prefs him for the Gold and Silver that had been hid, that being what the *Spaniards* hunted after, and was not fafe on the other, becaufe the Natives then had no regard to Friendfhip or Kindred, as only aiming to gain the good Will of the Conquerors, and confequently knew
what

what Courfe to take; but *Ampudia* knowing where he was, went thither with fix Horfemen and took him, tho fome fay he furrender'd himfelf; after which *Quingolamba* and other Commanders fubmitted themfelves, bringing confiderable Prefents of Cattel. Soon after *Yrruminavi* was alfo taken, which put an End to the War at *Quito. Belalcazar* cruelly wreck'd thofe great Men to difcover the Gold and Silver they had, but they were fo refolute as to difappoint his Covetoufnefs, and he inhumanly put them to Death.

AT this fame Time Captain *Tapia*, by Order of *Belalcazar*, fent one from the Province of *Chinto* to make Difcoveries Northward, and met with little Oppofition. At *Tacungæ Lewis Diaz*, took a ftranger *Indian*, who faid he was of a great Province call'd *Cundirumarca*, fubject to a potent Prince, who, fome Years fince, had fought a great Battle with certain very bold Neighbours he had, called *Chicos*, who having been much diftreffed by them, had fent this Man with fome others, to crave Aid of *Atahua'pa*, at the Time he was engaged in the War with *Guafcar*, and had been anfwer'd, that he would comply with his Requeft, as foon as the faid War was at an End, bidding thofe Meffengers to attend him till then, of all whom only this Man efcap'd, and went away to *Quito* with *Yrruminavi*. Being ask'd feveral Queftions concerning his Country, he talk'd of prodigious Plenty of Gold and other mighty Matters there were in it, which gave Occafion to fo many to attempt the Difcovery of *Dorado*, that has always look'd like an Inchanted Country. *Belalcazar* upon this Relation of the *Indian*, order'd *Peter de Anafco*, with forty Horfe, and the fame Number of Foot, to go with him to difcover his Country, which he faid was only twelve Days Journey diftant. In hopes of finding that mighty Treafure, they pafs'd thro' *Guallabanba*, and march'd between the Towns of the *Quillacingas*,

going

going over craggy, dreadful Woods and Mountains without finding any thing of what they fought after. A few Days after *Belalcazar,* who could never reft, fent *John de Ampudia,* with a confiderable Party of Horfe, after *Peter de Anafco,* who took all the other's Men under his Command, and attempted new Difcoveries. *Belalcazar,* in order to make a way from *Quito* to the 'Sea, and render it fafe for Trading, march'd out himfelf, and having reduc'd the Natives to Obedience, fettled a Colony, by the Name of *Santiago de Guayquil,* appointed *James Daza* Governour, and return'd to *Quito.* Thofe that were left at *Santiago* aforefaid made fuch hafte to grow rich, that the Natives being no longer able to bear their Diforders, confpiring together, kill'd them all, except four or five, with their Governour *Daza,* who return'd to *Quito,* and it was not without Difficulty that thofe People were afterwards fubdu'd. This City of *Guayaquil* was founded to the Weftward of *Puerto Viejo,* at the firft Entrance into which Territories are the *Indians* call'd *Guancavilcas,* who drew out their Teeth by way of Sacrifice.

WE left *Ferdinand Pizarro,* after his return from *Spain,* travailing through the Plains of *Peru,* to the City of *Lima,* where he heard by the way a vaft Quantity of Gold and Silver was to be melted down, whereupon he fent in hafte to his Brother the Governour, defiring to put off that Work for a few Days, as was accordingly done. Before his Arrival *F. Michael de Oronez,* Commendary of the *Mercenarian* Friers, founded a Monaftery, and the Bifhop of the Province of *Tierra Firme,* propos'd the affigning a Plot for a Cathedral, and then thinking there was no difference between *Pizarro* and *Almagro,* and confequently no Occafion for dividing their Goverments, as the King had order'd, or in reality perceiving that there was no good to be done among thofe
People,

People, he return'd home to his Diocefe, refufing to
accept of a great Prefent that was offer'd him ; feveral Gentlemen who were fatisfied with what they had
got, and forefaw the Mifchiefs that were like to enfue through the Ambition of the Governour *Pizarro's*
Brothers, took hold of that Opportunity to return to
their own Homes. *Ferdinand Pizarro* came at this
Time to the City of *Lima,* and the Governour his
Brother complaining that he had confented to the cutting off fo much of his Government for *Almagro,*
as would deprive him of the City of *Cuzco,* he ex-
cus'd himfelf by fhowing, that he had obtain'd the
Addition of feventy Leagues to his Government,
which would include the faid City ; adding, that the
King and Council were fo fully acquainted with the
great Merits of *Almagro,* as to think the Reward they
had affign'd him too little. The Governour had left
his Brother *John* to Command at *Cuzco,* as his Lieutenant, and, as was faid before, *Paul Topa,* and the
High-Prieft *Vilehoma,* were gone before on *Almagro's*
Expedition ; but before his Departure for *Chile,* the
faid *Vilehoma* had concerted with *Mango Inga,* who
was much honour'd and belov'd by the *Indians,* that
there fhould be a general Infurrection, for recovering
of that Empire, which had only a Shadow remaining
of its former Grandeur. Some Days after the departure of that Prieft, *Mango Inga* call'd to him many of
the Lords of the Provinces of *Condefuyo, Collafuyo,*
and *Chinchafuyo.* When they were come, after many
Sacrifices and Entertainments, *Mango* faid, He had
fummon'd them in order to declare, before his Kindred and Servants, what was expedient for them all,
in relation to thofe Strangers, whofe unbounded Avarice and Luft were not fatisfy'd, as appear'd by their
Plundering the very Temples, and taking their Wives
and Daughters for their Miftreffes. In fhort, he
reprefented all the Grievances they lay under, and

C

whatfo-

whatfoever elfe could excite them to deliver themfelves from that Bondage, before the *Spaniards,* who daily receiv'd Recruits, were grown too numerous. The firft Part of their Anfwer confifted in Cries and Lamentations, which being ceafed, they faid, he was *Guaynacava's* Son, and they pray'd the Sun and their Gods to be affifting to him in delivering them from that miferable Thraldom, and in order to it they advis'd him to make his Efcape privately from *Cuzco,* that they might all join him, and expofe their Lives in fo good a Caufe. This could not be done without the Knowledge of the *Yanaconas,* who having been Slaves before and made free by the *Spaniards,* if the Confpiracy fucceeded muft again return to their fervile Condition. They gave Notice to *John Pizarro* and other *Spaniards,* who, tho they did not give entire Credit to it, order'd thofe *Yanaconas* to obferve all the *Inga's* Motions in a cautious Manner, and to bring Advice of every Step he took, which they, being fo much concern'd, diligently perform'd. The *Inga* in purfuance of what had been concerted, was carried out of the City on his Bier, in the Night, attended by his Wives, his Servants, and fome of the *Orejones,* leaving fome People in his Houfe, and taking the way to *Chinchafuyo. John Pizarro* had Notice of it immediately, who went to the *Inga's* Houfe, where the Confufion and Diforder was fo great, that they plunder'd it, carrying off much Wealth, the greateft Part whereof the *Yanaconas* took. *John Pizarro* returning home defir'd his Brother *Gonzalo,* tho the Night was very dark, to purfue the *Inga,* as being fenfible of the Confequence, which he did with ten other *Spaniards,* on a large Trot, and at the Salt-Pits, half a League from *Cuzco,* they overtook the People that attended him, who being asked, where he was, anfwered, That he went another way. The *Inga* hearing the Noife, and perceiving they were *Spa-niards,*

niards, curfed thofe that had difcovered his Flight.
Gonzalo Pizarro laying hold of an *Orejon,* who was
near the *Inga,* preffed him to difcover that Prince, and
upon his not confeffing, caufed a Cord to be tied a-
bout his Genitals, and he tho much tortured, cried,
That the *Inga* was not there. Four Horfemen held
on their way, ftill inquiring for the *Inga,* who when
they were clofe by him, alighted from his Brier, and
hid himfelf among the Rufhes, but they hovering
about the Place where he lay, as believing they had
known him, he came out, and defired they would
not kill him, for he had departed the City to follow
Almagro, who had fent a Meffenger to him ; which
Lie raifed many Jealoufies that were the Occafion of
mighty Troubles and Slaughters. Thofe that had taken him, called out to *Pizarro,* who being come up,
they in a very courteous Manner, without giving one
ill Word, fet him up again on his Bier, and returned
to *Cuzco.*

John Pizarro was gone out another way, with a
great Number of Horfemen, in Queft of the *Inga,*
and being informed that he was taken, returned well
pleafed , knowing of how great Confequence the
fecuring of him was for preferving the Peace of the
Country, all the Natives paying him the greateft
Veneration, and told the *Inga ,* he was ungrate-
ful to his Brother in endeavouring to make his Efcape,
after that manner ; who again anfwered, his Defign
was no other than to follow *Almagro,* who had fent
to call him. Then going home, and finding his
Houfe plunder'd, he was the more incenfed, and fled
again, with a Defign to hide himfelf on the ftony
Mountains next to *Cuzco* ; but *John Pizarro* being informed of it, brought him back, and he was then
kept under a ftrong Guard. The *Indians* to excufe
him, faid, he was fo pefter'd with *John Pizarro's* Im-
portunity to give him Gold, that he went away to

C 2   evade

evade that Trouble. The Confinement of *Mango* was very grievous to the *Indians*, who cried to their Gods, fasted, offered Sacrifices, and begg'd Aid to set him at Liberty, making Songs, or Ballads, wherein they extoll'd the goodness of their Sovereigns, lamented their Misfortunes, and wish'd for some favourable Conjecture in order to find a Redress of their Grievances The Division of the *Spaniards* seem'd to offer an Opportunity, and those People being much inrag'd, and all not able to dissemble, as *Peter Martyr de Moguer* was in a Village that had been given him, the *Indians* killed him, thinking to keep it secret, but some of those that went thither with him, returning to *Cuzco*, discovered it, and the same being a Matter of great Moment in the Consequence, *Gonzalo Pizarro* marched with a Number of Men to chastise those *Indians*, who having Notice of it, retired with their Wives to a steep high Rock, carrying good Store of Provisions and Water, where they were besieged so long that their Water failed, and being ready to surrender, so much Water fell in the Night, that they repented saying, that GOD had commiserated their Condition, and sent them Plenty of Water. *Gonzalo Pizarro* sent advice to his Brothers, who marched to his Assistance, carrying a Wooden Galery to cover his Men in their approach to the Rock ; but the Defendants threw down so many Stones, that they broke it, wounding five Christians, and some *Yanaconas*. *John Pizarro* having often in vain summon'd them to surrender, and being disappointed of Success, by open force, tried many Artifices to as little Effect ; at length a Captain of the *Orejones*, who was at the Siege, by Order of the *Inga*, found means to speak to the besieged, bidding them to be of good Courage, for on a certain Night, all the Horses should be killed, when they were to sally to assist those that did it. One of the *Yanaconas* happening to hear the Discourse, gave advice to

John

John Pizarro, who caufed the *Orejon* to be burnt, becaufe he having been fent by him, to perfwade the
befieged to furrender, had told them what had been
faid, pretending to him, that they had demanded fix
Days to fubm t. At the fame time, he ordered Captain *Gabriel de Rojas,* whom he had left in his ftead
at *Cuzco,* to threaten *Mango Inga* for the Treachery
committed by his Servant *Rojas* after his natural mild
way, told the *Inga,* who excufed himfelf, faying, he
could not be blamed for the other's Offence ; and being afraid of his Life, commanded one *Pavaara Inga*
to go ufe his endeavours, that the Siege might foon
end. He coming to the Rock, difcourfed the Defendants, complain'd of the Confinement of *Mango Inga,*
added he was coming to their Affiftance, and that he
had the facred Axe of the Sun to take the Oath of Fi-
delity. They being well pleafed, contriv'd that he
fhould return the next Night, with only four Companions, to concert the Method for killing all the
Chriftians. The *Orejon* having well viewed the Fort,
the Gates, and the manner of fhutting them, return'd,
and told *John Pizarro,* that to the End he fhould be
kind to his Lord *Mango Inga,* he would do him a
fignal Piece of Service, which it was a great Hazard
would coft him his Life. He demanded four *paniards,* who being clofe fhaved, and daubed after the *Indian* manner with black or white, and cloath'd in their
Fafhion, with their Swords conceal'd, fhould go with
him at Night to the Rock, *John Pizarro* himfelf
being to follow them, with the reft of the *Spaniards,*
and the *Yanaconas.*

At the appointed Hour, the *Orejon* with the
four *Spaniards* began to climb the Rock with
much difficulty, the *Indians,* at the fame time, repenting the Agreement, for fear of fome double Dealing ;
but having offer'd to treat with only four, they would
not fail on their Part, directing that the firft Gate

C 3   fhould

fhould be open'd, if only four came, whereas if
there were more, they fhould be kill'd; but in cafe
they exceeded not that Number, the four fhould ftop
within the firft Gate, and the *Orejon* fhould pafs the
fecond Gate, till they faw the facred Axe, and took
the Oaths. None appearing but the four, and the
Orejon, who carried the little Copper-Axe, on which
feveral Oaths were taken, rais'd on a fhort ftaff and
a Club they ufe in fighting, concealed, as foon as
he came to the Top, he gave a call, fome armed Men
open'd the firft Gate, and the four being left there,
not a little Apprehenfive of fome Treachery, the fecond Gate was open'd, and as they were going to fhut
that again, the *Orejon* cafting off his Mantle, hand-
led his Club, and crying, *Viracocha Vecaramon*, that
is, *Spaniards or Chriftians, come quickly*, tho they made
all poffib'e hafte, the *Orejon* was kill'd ca'ling upon
the *Spaniards*, who fought defperately with their Swords,
the Darknefs of the Night, and the Narrownefs of
the Place, faving there Lives. *John Pizarro* came up
to their Affiftance, making good their Ground till it
was Day, when the *Indians* feeing the Enemy within
their Fortrefs, it was dreadful to hear the Cries and
Shrieks of Men, Women, and Children. Many of
them made Choice of a voluntary Death, cafting
themfelves headlong down the Rocks, and a dreadful
Slaughter enfu'd by the Hands of the *Yanaconas*, cutting off Arms and Legs, the *Spaniards* fhewing as little Mercy. One prime Man, of a good Prefence,
fhedding abundance of Tears, and often naming *Guaynacava*, tied together in one Rope, his wife, two
Children, fix Sheep, and many Bundles of Garments,
and fhutting his Eyes, caft himfelf headlong among
the Rocks, dragging a'l the reft after him. When
the heat of the Slaughter was over, the plunder enfu'd, which amounted to no more than five thoufand
Pieces of Eight, and thofe by the unanimous confent

fent of all, were given towards the Bu'lding of the Church of *Cuzco.* No fooner was this done, than News came, that *John Bozerril* had been murder'd at *Condefuyo,* by his own *Indians,* and *John Pizarro* refolv'd to march immediately to make another Example of them.

CHAP. III.

Ferdinand Pizarro *made Governour of* Cuzco, *fets* Mango Inga *at Liberty, who departs the City, and begins the War;* the Fort *of* Cuzco *taken;* Indians *routed;* Alonfo de Alvarado *marches to the Relief of the City.*

FErdinand Pizarro being come to the City of *Lima,* laboured to induce all the *Spaniards* to grant the King a free Gift, which they generally were averfe to, alledging, that the King already had the fifth of what they gain'd at the Expence of their Blood, and labour, without any charge to the Crown; and that they could expect no Advantage from any fuch Prefent, all the Benefits wherof would redound to the *Pizarros, Francis* being already created a Marquefs, and *Ferdinand* Knighted; however through their Influence a confiderable Sum was Collected, and the faid *Ferdinand* defir'd he might go to *Cuzco,* to carry on the Collection there, which his Brother granted, and to the End he might perform it with the greater Authority, appointed him his Lieutenant in that City, excufing himfelf to his Brother *John,* who was thereby remov'd from that Poft. Whilft this was in Agitation, Advice was brought that *Tizo,* Uncle to *Man go Inga,* had done fome harm about *Tarama* and *Bom-*

bon,

bon, for which the Governour order'd him to be taken into Cuftody; but he having Notice of it, made his Efcape into the thick Woods of the *Andes*, whence he fent to advife his Nephew *Mango*, to make his Efcape as foon as poffible, from the *Spaniards*, and commence the War, and he would come to his Affiftance. In the mean time the Governour vifited the Cities of *Truxillo* and St. *Michael*, eftablifhing good Rules and Orders in thofe Places, and every where perfwading the *Indians* to lay afide their Idolatry, and embrace the true Chriftian Religion. After which he returned to *Lima* to promote the Works and Eftablifhment of the new City.

Ferdinand Pizarro arriving at *Cuzco*, took Poffeffion of that Government, appointing his Brother *John* his Deputy, and then fet *Mango Inga* at Liberty, much againft the Will of his Brothers, whereupon it was reported, that the *Inga* had made him a very great Prefent of Gold. As foon as free, *Mango* began to contrive the Deftruction of the *Spaniards*, and for as much as it was requifite to make his Efcape from *Cuzco* he perfwaded *Ferdinand Pizarro* that he would go fetch a Statue of his Father all of Gold and Silver, that he faid, was four Leagues from *Cuzco*. Being permitted to go, with two *Spaniards* and his *Indian* Interpreter, *Ferdinand* was foon fenfible of the Error he had committed, and march'd out with feventy Horfe to bring back the *Inga*, who was then at *Colca*, and by the way met the two *Spaniards* he had fent with the *Inga*, who told him, they had been difmiffed by that Prince, faying he had no Occafion for them. However he advanced towards *Calca*, and coming to an high Ground, was attack'd by a multitude of *Indians*, whom he drove back to the Town, where he ftay'd that Night, in a very uneafy Manner, being alarm'd every Moment, and in the Morning he thought fit to return to *Cuzco*, not thinking that City fafe, the *Indians* in vaft Numbers charging him all the

way

way till he was in the Place. Tho *Ferdinand* was in *Cuzco*, the *Indians* did not draw off, but rather increased, till they amounted to two hundred thousand to carry on that Siege, the Defendants being no more than an hundred and seventy *Spaniards*, and about a thousand Natives that stuck by them, many of them *Yanaconas.* The Besiegers being come near to the Houses, *Ferdinand Pizarro* having given necessary Orders, made a Sally with all the Horse, whom the *Indians* suffer'd to advance till they had compassed them in; however they all fought their way out except one Gentleman, whose Horse falling, he was immediately kill'd, and they cut off his Head, and his Horse's, looking upon that as an extraordinary Success, whereupon they drew nearer to the City. The High-Priest *Vilehoma* possessed himself of the Citadel, whence they daily gain'd Ground, making Barricadoes in the Streets, by which means the *Spaniards* were confin'd to the Market-Place, and tho a Captain was put into a strong House adjoyning to secure it against the Enemy, they gained it that very Night, and by that means a great Part of the Square, throwing Stones with their Slings, so thick, that the *Spaniards* could find no Shelter, and being thus drove into two Houses, that were opposite to each other, they thought it better to sally out than to perish there, which accordingly they did, driving the *Indians* along the Streets, and throwing down their Intrenchments. The *Indians* to secure themselves against the Horses, made Ropes of the Sinews of Sheep, with three Nooses in each of them, and a Stone to every one, with which they so seiz'd their Horses and the Riders, that they were disabled from making use of their Weapons, when the Foot prov'd very useful, for cutting of those Gins, which they call'd *Ayllos*, with their Swords, tho' not without difficulty, those Cords being very tough.

Thus the *Spaniards* regain'd the Market-Place, with much difficulty, the Commander of the Foot being
wounded

wounded in the Head with a Stone. The Noise of the Horns and Drums, was hideous, and the Cries of the *Indians* nothing inferior, the *Spaniards* being in a Confternation, by Reason of the fmallnefs of their Number, and the Multitude that inclofed them ; whereupon confidering how much harm was done them from the Citadel, it was thought requifite to attack it, which was accordingly done, under the Conduct of *John Pizarro*, who, with his Men, drove the *Indians* before him, till he came to a Ditch the *Indians* had cut before the outward Wall ; there *Alonfo de Mefa* refolutely leap'd his Horfe over, and maintain'd the Fight till others got over, which brought them to that outward Wall in which there were two Inlets, one of which was gain'd with a mighty Slaughter of *Indians*. At the fame time there was an engagement in the City, to which the *Indians* fet fire, and all the Houfes being Thatch'd, it was foon burnt, which put the *Spaniards* upon the point of quitting it, and marching away to *Lima*. But they were not idle at that Place, for the Infurrection being general, a great Army of *Indians* was fate down before it ; however Supplies coming thither by Sea, and the Country being plain, where the Horfes were of moft ufe, the *Indians* could not ftay fo long before it as they did at *Cuzco*. The *Spaniards* there, being deftitute of all Hopes of Relief, upon feveral Confultations, were refolv'd to abandon the Place, having been nine Months befieg'd, but *John* and *Gonzalo Pizarro*, *Gabriel de Rojas*, and *Ferdinand Ponze* refolutely oppofed it, as a moft difhonourable Action, declaring they ought rather to die upon the Spot.

John Pizarro boldly carried on the Attack of the Citadel, and had gain'd all but the Towers ; when it was late, being much fatigu'd with the Labour of the Day, he took off his Helmet, and that very Moment he receiv'd fuch a Blow on his Head, with

a Stone,

a Stone, that it ftunn'd him, and he dy'd within a
Fortnight. The next Day *Ferdinand Pizarro* went
with twelve Horfemen to the Affiftance of thofe that
were carrying on the Attack, leaving *Gabriel de Rojas*
in his ftead, to defend the City. *Ferdinand Sanchez* was
one of the twelve that went with him, who applying
a Ladder to one of the Towers, and covering himfelf with his Target, nimbly ran up, notwithftanding
the many Stones caft at him, and leap'd in, others
following his Example, gain'd the other Towers, above
a thou and *Indians* being killed in this Action. Nor
were they idle in this City, where *Gabriel de Rojas*
was fhot through the Nofe into the Palate, and *Alonfo de Toro* knock'd down with two Stones. The Citadel being gain'd, *John Ortiz* was put into it with
fifty *Spaniards.* At the fame Time the Governour
Francis Pizarro finding himfelf clofe befieg'd, and receiving Advice from feveral Parts that divers *Spaniards*
had been kill'd in the Country, and that the Infurrection
was general, fearing to be again drove out of the
Country, fent Meffengers to the Marquefs *Cortes,* in
New Spain, to the Council of *Hifpaniola,* to *Guatemala, Nicaragua,* and other Parts, to demand fpeedy
Succours, which came afterwards, but late, when the Danger was over. He fent out, as foon as poffible, four
Commanders at feveral Times, with Parties of *Spaniards,*
who were all kill'd by the *Indians,* except eight or
nine, whom *Mango* fav'd to ferve him as Slaves; with
them he took fome Horfes. Arms, Muskets, and feveral Commodities, and the *Indians* fought with thofe
Weapons. Whilft they were thus preffed at *Cuzco,*
Ferdinand Pizarro, committing the Charge of the City to *Gabriel de Rojas,* march'd out with feventy
Horfe, fome Foot, and a Number of *Indians,* to *Tambo,* feven Leagues diftant, in the Vale of *Yucay,* where
the *Inga* refided. Being come near the Place, he rou-
fed fome Parties of the *Indians,* who all fled, faving
only

only two *Chiachiapoyas,* and they threw two Stones from the Wall, which broke an Horse's Fore Leg, whereupon he flung and plung'd fo furiously that the reft being difordered, were obliged to draw back to a Plain before the Gate of the Town, which fo encouraged the *Indians* that they returned to the Charge in fuch Numbers, as put the *Spaniards* almoft into Defpair of faving their Lives ; for at the fame Time the Enemy turn'd the River that runs by that Place, upon them, fo that the Horfes were boggled, and the *Canibal Indians* preffed on, fo that there was a great Slaughter of them, and thofe that fided with the *Spaniards.* At Night *Ferdinand Pizarro* retired with much difficulty, as frequently meeting with Bodies of Men, and being much perplexed with abundance of a Sort of Thorns or Thiftles, called *Cabuyo,* that were thrown in the way, and lamed the Horfes. When the Siege had lafted ten Months, they marched out for Provifions, and had a fharp Engagement, in which they took two Commanders, who informed them that the *Inga* defigned to raife a greater Army the next Summer, in order to complete the Expulfion of the *Spaniards,* and above three hundred of them having been kill'd during the War, all their Heads were carried to the *Inga,* and one of the *Spaniards* he had in Cuftody.

DURING this Siege it had been the Cuftom for fix Horfemen to go abroad once a Week, to fcour the Country, and fee whether there was any Relief from *Cuzco. Gonzalo Pizarro* going out in this Manner, with fix chofen Horfemen, after routing many fmall Parties, near *Xaquixaguana* , difcovered a great Multitude of *Indians,* and it being then the Cuftom with the *Spaniards* always to fall on, whether the Number of the Enemies were great or fmall, he did fo, the *Indians* preffing forward in a moft defperate Manner, fo that the Horfemen were oblig'd to retire fighting, and

yet

yet were so hard beset, that *Pizarro* was oblig'd to
send one to his Brother for Relief, which came so
opportunely, that it rescu'd those Men from certain
Death, they and their Horses being quite spent, and
the *Indians* despairing of Success, fled with Precipitation. Provisions growing very scarce in *Cuzco*, especially Flesh, *Gabriel de Rojas*, a very able Commander march'd out with seventy Horse, towards *Poma-
canche*, a Province fourteen Leagues from the City, and
returned with two thousand Head of Cattel: The
Indians, who appear'd on the Hills, not daring to attack him. After him *Ferdinand Ponce* performed such
another Expedition, towards *Condesuyo*, as did *Gonzalo
Pizarro*, who kill'd above a thousand *Indians*, and carried many Prisoners to *Cuzco*, who were all there set
at Liberty, but several of them had one Hand cut
off, which struck such a Terror among those People,
that they durst not afterwards come down into the
Plains, which gave an Opportunity to the friendly
Indians to go abroad as there was Occasion, and the
besieged were less streightned. Provisions falling short
again, *Gabriel de Rojas* marched with sixty Horse to
Xaquixaguana, where there was much *Indian* Wheat,
which he sent at several Times to *Cuzco*, under a Guard
of six Horsemen. After that, returning himself, he
was charged by a Body of *Indians*, who had several
Spanish Swords, Muskets, and other Arms, and some
Horses, all taken from *Spaniards* they had kill'd. A
Spaniard that was their Prisoner, having saved his Life,
taught them the use of those Weapons. *Rojas* would
not suffer his Horsemen to pickeer as they were wont,
but kept them in a Body whilst he sent to *Ferdinand
Pizarro* for some Cross-bows and Pike-men, which being come, he pour'd in several Flights of Shafts,
and then fell on with all his Horse, who soon put all
those Barbarians to rout, whom he would not suffer
to be far pursu'd, thinking it needless to shed the Blood
of

of the vanquiſh'd. Upon this Occaſion ſome *Indians* were ſeen on Horſeback, with Spears, behaving themſeives with much Bravery, and ſhewing that they had been inſtructed by Chriſtians.

T   Governour *Francis Pizarro,* being deliver'd from his Siege at *Lima,* as was ſaid before, becauſe the Horſe in thoſe Plains bore down the *Indians,* and the Mountain People had not their Health among the *Yungas,* that is, the Vales along the Sea Coaſt, he reſolv'd to ſend a Body of Troops to *Cuzco,* from whence he could get no Intelligence, the Diſtance being an hundred and twenty Leagues, and the *Indians* intercepting all Meſſengers. Accordingly he aſſembl'd five hundred Men, and gave the Command of them to *Alonſo de Alvarado,* ordering him to reduce the Country to Obedience as he went. *Alvarado* ſtay'd longer on the way than was convenient, which prov'd of very ill Conſequence, as we ſhall ſee hereafter. Whilſt he was on his march, *Ferdinand Pizarro* march'd out from *uzco* with eighty Horſe, and ſome few Foot, thinking to ſurprize the *Inga* at *Tambo,* but arriving there at Break of Day, found Things in another Poſture than he imagin'd, ſeveral Sentinels being poſted in the Fields and on the Walls, with proper *Corps du Garde,* who giving the Alarm with loud Cries and Comets, above thirty thouſand drew together, in good Order, waiting to make their Advantage of the *Spaniards.* It was ſurprizing to ſee ſome come forward with *Spaniſh* Swords, Targets, and Head-pieces, and ſome ſingle Men arm'd after this Manner, were ſo bold as to attack an Horſeman, thinking it an Honour to be kill'd with a Spear, to gain the Reputation of Bravery. The *Inga* himſelf was on Horſeback among his Men, with a Spear in his Hand, keeping his Troops in a Body, cloſe under the Town, which was fortify'd with a Wall, a River, good Trenches, and ſtrong Ramparts, at certain Diſtances.

Ferdinand

Ferdinand Pizarro confidering that no good was to be done there, refolv d to retire, which he did in good Order, the *Indians* purfuing and preffing hard upon him. In return for this Vifit, the *Inga* fent twenty five thoufand Men to make an Attack upon *Cuzco*, by the way of *Andefuyo*, who did it with fo much Refolution, that they were upon the Point of entering the Town, wounded feveral *Spaniards*, had once taken *Peter Pizarro*, but he was refcu'd, and kill'd two Horfes, after which they drew off. Another Party of them making an Attack by the way of *Carmenga* one of them being taken, gave Intelligence, that the Captains *Gaete* and *James Pizarro*, fent by the Governour to the Relief of *Cuzco* with a fmall Party, had been cut off by the way. Among other Things that happen'd, during this Siege, the *Indians* being very much bent upon burning the Church, believing that if they could do it all the *Spaniards* would perifh, caft abundance of red hot Stones out of Slings, and fhot fiery Arrows, till rhe Covering being Thatch'd, as is there ufual in the greateft Building, at length it took Fire, and it is certain that when once kindled there is no extinguifhing of it, for which Reafon they never attempted it; but all Men plainly faw that this Fire went out of itfelf, which both *Spaniards* and *Indians* looked upon as miraculous, and the latter were fo much daunted, that they never after came on with their former Fiercenefs upon the City of *Cuzco*, but flackned and left the *Spaniards* more at Liberty and Eafe.

CHAP.

C H A P. IV.

The Marquess Del Valle Cortes *upon the* South Sea; Don Antonio de Mendoza, *appointed Vice Roy of* New Spain; *what hapned at* Santa Marta, *and the River of* Plate.

THE Marquess *Del Valle Cortes*, was much offended at the Wrongs done him by *Nuno de Guzman*, and the more for that the Council at *Mexico*, neglected to do him Justice, and he could obtain no Answer to all the Letters he had writ to the King, whereupon, he resolved to raise Men, and go in Person to recover his Ship. Accordingly he sent three Ships he had fitted out, and marched himself by Land towards *New Galicia*, with a Body of Horse and Foot; which Motion of his put *Nunno de Guzman* into such a Consternation, as well answer'd the Expence the Marquess had been at. Being come to the Place where the Ship lay, he found it a Ground, and Plunder'd, the loss being computed at above twenty thousand Ducats. There the Marquess embark'd with all the Men and Horses his Ships could carry, leaving *Andrew de Tapia* to command the rest, sailing away to the Country where *Fortun Ximenez* had been kill'd, and arriv'd at the high Mountains call'd of St. *Philip*, and an Island three Leagues from the Continent, which he named *Santiago*. On the 3d of *May*, he entered the Bay, where the aforesaid *Ximenez* had been kill'd, which he call'd *Santa Cruzco*, being a safe Harbour against all Winds, lying in 23 Degrees and an Half of North Latitude. From that Place he sent for more Men and Horses, but the
Weather

Weather proved fo foul, that only the leaft Ships return'd. There the Marquefs ftay'd many Days in
great Want of Provifion, for the Country afforded
none, by Reafon that the Natives were Savages, having no Houfes, nor Tilling the Land, but only feeding upon Fruit, and the natural Product of the Fields,
and fuch Game as they kill'd with their Arrows,
Fifhing at Sea on Floats made of five Pieces of Timber, the Middlemoft longer than the reft, either ferving for an Head. The other Ships not returning,
the Marquefs went aboard that he had, with fixty Men,
carrying all Neceffaries for building a Ship, becaufe there
was no Timber in that Place. Having advanc'd fifty
Leagues on the Coaft of *New Spain*, one Morning
he found himfelf among a Parcel of Rocks, fo that
he knew not how to get out, or which way he had come
in. After plying about fome time, they fpy'd a Ship
at Anchor two Leagues from them, but could not
tell how to come at it, the Sea on all Sides breaking
upon the Flats. The other Ship having defcry'd
them, the Pilot come aboard in his Boat, and pretending to fteer the Marquefs's Ship, ran it aground,
but the Sea threw it into the Channel, fo leaky that
all they could do was to fave the Men and Goods;
however they brought it a Shore, and working Day
and Night, refitted and lanched it again. The Ship
found there being one of thofe that belong'd to the
Marquefs, had Plenty of Provifions, bought at St *Michael*'s in the Province of *Culuacan*, eighteen Leagues
to the Weftward of that Harbour, where the Marquefs was, call'd *Guayabal*; and the Men gave an Account that the other Ship going to *Xalifco*, and having taken in much lading of *Indian* Wheat and other
Provifions to return to the Marquefs, had met with
a Storm, that bore down its Mafts, fo that it was
drove afhore without any Sails, and Stranded, whereupon the Men went away by Land to *Mexico*, as
they

they defign'd to do themfelves, finding their Ship unfit for the Sea.

THE Marquefs caufed it to be fearch'd, and to fail with the other, but it ftruck and beat off the Rudder, whereupon he Imbarked aboard the other to return to the Place where he had left the Men. Two Days after a Yard fell and kill'd the Pilot, and then the Marquefs him'elf took charge of the Ship, till he arriv'd where his Men were, whom he found ready to perifh with Want, three or four being already Starved, for which Reafon he ordered they fhould have Meat given them by Meafure, left they fhould eat too much, and four or five dy'd. The other Ships he expected not coming, and be ng informed that *Don Antonio de Mendoza* was come to be V ce-Roy of *New Spain*, the Marquefs left his Men in that Place with Provifions for above a Year, and failing back for *Acapulco* met at feveral Times five of his own Ships, that were on their wav to joyn him, and brought them a l back to the aforefaid Port. There he receiv'd Advice of the Diftrefs *Pizarro* was in at *Lima*, and the danger of lofing that Kingdom, whereupon he immediately fent two of thofe Ships to his Affiftance, under the Command of *Ferdinand de Grijalva*, with a good Number of Men well Arm'd, and a confiderable Quantity of Muskets, Crofs-Bows, Spears, feventeen Horfes, fixty Coats of Mail, Linnen, Hangings, Silk Cufhions, Canopies, Veftments, for the Service of the Church, and many other Neceffaries, which tho they came after the Siege was rais'd at *Lima*, were very acceptable.

THE Prefident *Don Sebaftian Ramirez*, having Govern'd in *New Spain* for the Space of fix Years, with much Juftice and Moderation, and being defirous to return into his native Country, the King appointed *Don Antonio de Mendoza*, Brother to the Marquefs *De Mondejar*, Vice-Roy of that Kingdom, which Poft many, with good Reafon, thought ought to
have

have been beftow'd on the Marquefs *Del Valle,* who had perform'd fuch Wonders in the Conqueft of it The new Vice-Roy was in the firft Place charg'd to promote the Converfion of the *Indians,* and Propagation of the Chriftian Faith, taking Care in order to it, that the Service fhould be perform'd with the greateft Majefty and Decency, that the *Spaniards* fhould give good Example to the Natives, that vicious Perfons fhould be feverely punifh'd, and fcandalous Churchmen fent away into *Spain.* His other Inftructions were, that he fhould vifit all Parts of the Kingdom himfelf, or where that could not be, fend Vifitors of known Integrity ; that he fhould preferve the Regal Patronage over all Churches and Monafteries, not permitting any Perfon whatfoever to enjoy fuch Right ; that there fhould be a good Underftanding between the Spiritual and Temporal Courts ; that the People fhould be induc'd to contribute towards a free Gift to his Majefty ; that the *Indians* fhou'd not be permitted to live idle, but apply themfelves to Tillage, or other Employments ; that in regard the want of Money in thofe Parts was a great Obftruction to commerce, a Mint fhould be erected, to Coin Silver and Copper, but no Gold ; that fpecial Care fhould be taken not to opprefs the Natives in any Manner, but that they fhould be free ; that no Arms fhould be fold to *Indians* or Blacks, nor they fuffer'd to wear them ; that no Churches or Monafteries fhould be built without leave. Many more Inftructions there were for eftablifhing that Government, the moft of them according to the Laws and Cuftoms of *Spain,* and not neceffary to be taken Notice of in this Hiftory.

AT this Time the Adelantado of the *Canary If-*lands, *Don Peter Fernandez de Lugo,* contracted with the King of *Spain* to carry over fifteen hundred Foot, and two hundred Horfe, from *Spain,* and the *Canary* Iflands, to conquer the Province of *Santa Marta,* ly-

ing

ing between thofe of *Venezuela,* *Cabo de la Vela* and *Cartagena.* In purfuance to the faid Contract he landed there this Year 1535, and having refted a Fortnight, fent to offer Peace to the People of *Bonda,* which they refufing to admit, he made ready to fubdue them, having twelve hundred Men he had brought out of *Spain,* befides thofe he found in the Country. He marched from *Santa Marta,* and coming to *Bonda,* attack'd the Town, the Inhabitants ftanding upon their Defence, tho they had fent away their Wives and Children ; but after a long Conteft, they abandon'd the Place, having kill'd thirty *Spaniards,* through ill Management; for had that Affair been conducted as it ought, neither fo many *Spaniards* had been loft, nor the *Indians* gone off as they did. Several Parties were afterwards fent abroad, but perform d no Actions of Moment, whereupon the new Adelantado, or Governour, made all the neceffary Difpofitions for going up the River of *Santa Marta,* which being executed, in another Year fhall be then taken Notice of, as fhall the Expedition of *George Spire,* a *German,* in the Province of *Venezuela.*

AFTER the Encounter *Alonfo de Herrera,* before fpoken of, had at the River *Viapari,* with the *Indians,* who told him, that the Province of *Guayana* was behind, and that of *Meta* before him, he carried thofe *Indians,* who had given him that Information, as far as *Caburuto,* where he found the Country depopulated, by reafon of the War with the *Canibals,* yet fome Provifions were got, by means of the *Indians* he had with him. Being come to the Fall in the River, from whence *James de Ordas* had turn'd back, he caus'd the Veffels to be unladed, and with immenfe Labour had them drawn to the other Part where that River was again Navigable. Beyond that Fall they found large Plains, but abandon'd, and after feveral Days fail, came to the Mouth of the Creek of *Meta.* There feeing fome Tokens of Dwellings, and being in want of
Provi-

Provisions, they left their Veffels aground, well conceal'd among the Trees, marching through Moraffes,
with immenfe Labour, as carrying all they had on
their Shoulders, till they came to higher Lands, and
difcover'd till'd Ground, and the Houfes of the *Indians* called *Xaguas,* a war-like and bloody Nation, who
feeing the *Spaniards,* fent their Wives and Children into the Woods, and advanc'd to meet their Enemies,
well Arm'd with Darts, Lances, Macanas, and Shields,
attacking the *Spaniards* with great Refolution, but after a fhort Engagement they fled, the *paniards* purfuing them to the Town, where, to their great Satisfaction, they found Provifions. Having refted there
fome Days, and their Suftenance beginning to fail,
they were oblig'd to advance further, to find out
fome Place to Winter in, that Seafon drawing on.
Marching on up the Country, they came to a River,
which ten *Spaniards* fwam over, with their Swords and
Targets, and went on till they faw a large Town, returning then as they had been order'd, to give an Account of it, whereupon they made Floats, and all
crofs d the River. The *Indians* immediately left the
Town, and fled into the Woods; and the *Spaniards*
found Corn, and other Provifions, as alfo dumb Dogs,
by the *Indians* call'd *Mayos* and *Auries,* reckoning them
a great Dainty. Here they refolv'd to Winter, tho
frequently molefted by the *Indians,* who perceiving
that the *Spaniards* defign'd to ftay there, and went
out a Marauding, drew together from all Parts, thinking to furprize them. A Soldier that ftood Centinel,
at the Perfwafion of a Women, who offer'd to do
his Duty, quitted his Poft, to go cut a little Wood,
by which means the *Indians* were not difcover'd, and
fell upon the *Spaniards* unexpected, when many of
them were abroad. The Commander *Alonfo de Herrera* ran for his Horfe, which as ill Fortune would
have it, had been carry'd to Water, and he preffing

D 3   on

on for him, with Sword in Hand, receiv'd two Arrows, one in his Face, and the other in his Back, yet wounded as he was he mounted his Horse, and play'd his part courageously, as did all the other *Spaniards*, who tho hard press'd by that Multitude, at length put their Enemies to Flight, and they going off, were met by the other *Spaniards* who were returning with Provisions, and made a great Slaughter of them ; but coming to the Town found several of their Comrades wounded, three of them with poison'd Arrows, of which Number the Commander *Herrera* was one who died the 7th Day, to the great Grief of all his Men, because he was courteous and friendly to them all, brave as to his Person, and fit to manage any Enterprize.

Alvaro de Ordas succeeding *Herrera* in the Command of these Men, assembled them all, asking their Advice how to proceed, considering the Difficulties they laboured under, the small Number of Horses they had, the Multitude of *Indians* they were to deal with, and the badness of the Ways and Weather, offering, if they were willing, to lead them, as far as they should think fit. The Resolution was to return to their Vessels, which was done without any Opposition, but being oblig'd for want to eat their Horses, the Fish they could get, and Herbs, till they came into the Sea, where the danger was no less, the Wind proving contrary, and blowing hard one of their four Vessels ran aground, and was lost, only the Men being sav'd with their Arms. To add to their Misery, they met Abundance of *Canibals*, whom tho' they defeated, it was with the loss of four Men, and being taken aboard the other three Vessels, they sail'd to *Paria*, where they found the Fort ruin'd and the Country abandon'd. However advancing, they met Captain *Nieto*, with three Brigantins sent by *Jerome de Ortal*, to the Assistance of *Herrera*, which was a great
Comfort

Comfort to the diftreffed, and *Nieto* was aftonifh'd
to fee thofe Men in fuch pitiful Plight, ragged, and
confum'd with Hunger, and other Hardfhips, whereupon they all return d to *Jerome de Ortal,* who then appointed *Auguftin Delgado* to command inftead of *Herrera,*
ordering him to march to *Neveri,* and fettle on the Banks
of that River, which is two Leagues from *Maraca-
grana. Delgado,* purfuant to his Orders, began to build
a ftrong Houfe, to the great Regret of all his Men,
who found nothing to be got in that Place, and
fuffer'd very much. Neverthelefs he made an Incur-
fion far into the Country, and after fome Encounters
with the *Indians* came into a Diftrict where there were
many good Towns, and Plenty of Provifions, with the
Caziques, whereof he contracted Friendfhip, making them
Prefents of red Caps, Knives, and other Things they
valu'd, in return for which they gave him fome Gold.
Soon after a Party of Men fent by *Antony Sedenno*
landed within the Government of *Ortal,* and fupri-
zing fome of his Men, difarm'd and ftripp'd them,
in return for which *Auguftin Delgado,* fell upon them,
and ferv'd them in the fame Manner.

ABOUT this Time *Francis de Montejo,* Adelantado,
or Lord Lieutenant of the Province of *Yucatan,* having receiv'd no Succours, being continually prefs'd by
the war-like Natives of that Country, and finding it
yielded no Gold, abandon'd that Government, and
went away to *New Spain,* in hopes that the new Vice-
Roy there might put him into a Condition to retrieve
his lofs. Nor was it any better with *Andrew de Ce-
receda,* Controller of the Province of *Honduras,* who
for like Reafons, quitted the City of *Truxillo,* and
marching away with the Men that would follow him,
was fome Days after met by *Don Chriftopher de la Cueva,* who commanded a Party for *Don Pearo de Alvarado,*
Adelantado of *Guatemala,* to find out a way to *Puerto de Cavallos,* for carrying on the Trade of that Pro-

vinc

vince. Thefe two Commanders joyn'd their Forces,
having fign'd Articles to act unanimoufly, which *Cerezeda,* a wicked Man, foon broke, and fo they parted
again, and thofe Provinces were left in the fame Diforder as they had been before.

None having gone fince the return of *Sebaftian
Gabot,* to fubdue the mighty Provinces along the River of *Plate,* the King now granted that Government to *Don Peter de Mendoza,* upon Condition that he
fhould find a way by Land to the *South-Sea;* that
he fhould carry over a thoufand Men, and an hundred Horfes and Mares, with Provifions for a Year,
at twice, without the King's being oblig'd to contribute towards that Expence, only allowing him two
hundred Leagues in Length, towards the Streights of
Magellan for his Government, with a Salary of two
thoufand Ducats a Year, during his Life, and two
thoufand Ducats free Gift, to be receiv'd out of the
Profits of the Country. No fooner was this Enterprize nois'd abroad, than fo many Men flock'd to be
concern'd in it, that all poffible Expedition was us'd to
fet out upon it. *Mendoza* accordingly fail'd from *San
Lucar,* with eleven Ships, carry'd eight hundred good
Men, and well equipp'd, and had a good Voyage; for
thofe who are to fail for the River of *Plate,* fhould
not fet out after the Middle of *Auguft,* in order to
be there by the End of *November,* when the Summer begins in thofe Parts, and they have the Breezes
at North, and N.E. and if they go later, they cannot enter the River after the Month of *March,* when
the South and South-weft Winds prevail, and oblige
Ships to turn back to Winter at Port *Patos,* or in
the Ifland of St. *Catherine.* He came to an Anchor
at the Ifland of St. *Gabriel,* and difcover'd a litte River, on the other Side of the Ifland, towards the
Streights of *Magellan,* where he began to found a Town,
calling it *Nueftra Sennora de Buenos Ayres,* or, Our
Lady

Lady of good Air, on that Part of the Country call'd *Cabo Blanco,* or white Cape, where were none but *Canibal Indians,* who were always Enemies, and Cruel, as being barbarous Man-Eaters. The Provisions being insufficient for the Number of People, soon after their arrival, they were order'd to be allow'd only six Ounces a Man, which was their Sustenance, with Thistles, and other Herbs, so that the Allowance being short, and the Hardships many, they began to sicken and dye ; for which Reason, the Governour who was himself indispos'd, order'd his Brother *Don James de Mendoza,* to march with a Party, to find *Indians* to furnish Provisions, who met with a Nation call'd Qui-randies, dwelling in moveable Houses and Towns, like *Arabs,* with whom they encounter'd, and the *Indians* being very numerous and active, whereas the *Spaniards* were weak, kill'd *Don James de Mendoza,* and five more, taking hold of the Horses with Snares they carry'd, so that if the rest had not fled, and been supported by the Infantry, they had all perish'd. Next the Governour sent a Kinsman of his own, with four Ships, to discover certain Islands, where he had been told there were *Indians,* who spent so much Time in seeking those Islands, from one River to another, that the Allowance was reduc'd to three Ounces, so that the third Part of the Men aboard, being about sixty in all, dy'd, and they must have all starv'd, had it not been for some *Indians,* among whom they found *Indian* Wheat to support them till they return'd to *Euenos Ayres,* where the scarcity was so great, that many kept their dead Comrades three or four Days, that they might receive their Allowance, saying, they were sick, and others eat human Flesh, two Men that had been Executed, being devour'd from the Waste downward. The distress being so great, the Governour order'd *John de Ayolas* to sail with three Ships, and ninety Men in each of them, to look out for Provisions, and each Ship having but one Pipe of Meal, they

they were reduc'd to eat Herbs, Snakes, Alligators, Mice, and other Vermin, whereof many fickn'd and dy'd.

IT was now the Year 1536. when *Ayolas* ranging about, came to a Lake, where he found some *Indian* Fifhermen of the Nations of *Tambues* and *Carares*, who came in a peaceable Manner, whereupon the Soldiers were order'd to fit down, with their Weapons in their Hands, that the *Indians* might not perceive their Weaknefs. Thofe *Indians* brought some Fifh and *Indian* Wheat, which was a great Comfort, and therefore the Men repair'd to their Houfes, and took up their Quarters in one of them. *Ayolas* having got a good Quantity of Provifion, which the Natives freely furnifh'd by way of Barter, return'd to *Buenos Ayres*, promifing his Men he would be with them again within forty Days, and giving them leave, in cafe he did not, to march into the Country where they fhould think fit. Thofe *Spaniards*, who were left there having made Huts or Barracks, apart from the *Indians*, were reduc'd to very great Streights for want, when one *Gonzalo Romero* of the Number of thofe that had been left there by *Sebaftian Gabot* came to them, and faid, the Inland Country was very rich, and had good Towns, upon which Advice, they thought fit, fince *Ayolas* did not return, within the limited Time, and they were fomewhat recruited, to advance into thofe Parts. When they were upon the Point of fetting out *Don Peter de Mendoza*, arriv'd there in fuch diftrefs, that two hundred of his Men had dy'd with Hunger, fo that both *Spaniards* and *Indians* were forc'd to Fifh and take Pains to live ; and the *Spaniards* then beginning to be enur'd to the Food of the Country, the Captains advis'd *Don Peter* to fettle another Colony four Leagues below that Place where they were. However, they were divided among themfelves, fome for going to find the Country *Gonzalo Romero* told them of, and others for proceeding on the River *Paraguay*. Amidft
this

this Confusion, *Don Peter de Mendoza,* being very sick, resolv'd to go back to *Buenos Ayres,* in order to return into *Spain,* taking the sick along with him, and leaving the Treasurer *Alvarado* to command in that Place, which was call'd *Buena Esperanza,* or Good Hope, and ordering *John de Ayolas* with three Brigantins to make Discoveries on the River *Paraguay.* When *Mendoza* and *Ayolas* were gone, those that remain'd suffer'd so much, that they were forc'd to return to the Place where they had been before; *Ayolas* sailing up the River in great Want, because his Vessels were heavy, and could not fetch up the Canoes they saw. Here the Weather growing very foul they lost one of their three Vessels, but the Men were sav'd, and so they proceeded till they came into the Country of the *Ameguaes,* who supply'd them with a good Quantity of Fish and Canoes to carry the Men that march'd by Land. Thence they advanc'd to the Province of the *Carioes,* in other Parts of the *West-Indies* call'd *Caribes,* who met the *Spaniards* in a friendly Manner, giving them a great Quantity of *Indian* Wheat, Batatas, Fowl, and other Provisions, by way of Barter; and thus reliev'd they went on about an hundred Leagues to the *Payaguaes,* where they also found good Entertainment, and having rested some Days *Ayolas* thought fit to march up the Country, with an hundred and thirty of his own Men, and some of those *Payaguaes* assign'd him by their Chief, ordering *Dominick de Irala* to expect him there, with forty Men and the Brigantines, till he return'd.

IN the mean Time *Don Peter de Mendoza,* sent Captain *John de Salazar* with the Ships and eighty Men after the said *Ayolas,* from *Buenos Ayres,* where they began to live something better, necessity having taught them to Fish, Hunt, and find out Roots. Captain *Salazar* being come to *Buena Esperanza,* proceeded from thence at the Beginning of the Year 1537, in Quest of *Ayolas,* as far as the Territories of the *Cariores, rioes,* where he built a ſtrong Houſe, and gave it the Name of the *Aſſumption.* Whilſt he was on this Expedition, the Governour *Don Peter de Mendoza,* went away for *Spain,* leaving Captain *Francis Ruyz* to command at *Buenos Ayres,* till Captain *Ayolas* return'd from his Diſcoveries. *Don Peter* dying at Sea, the King confirm'd *Ayolas* in that Government, and ſent him Supplies of Men, Arms, and Proviſions, of all which more ſhall be ſaid hereafter.

The End of the Second Book.

THE
General HISTORY

Of the vaſt CONTINENT and ISLANDS of

A M E R I C A, &c.

DECAD. IV. BOOK III.

CHAP. I.

The march of Almagro *into the Kingdom of* Chile ; *two Commanders follow him with Recruits ; of the ſnowy and the burning Mountains,* and of the *Earthquakes in* Peru *and* Chile.

E left the Adelantado, or Lord Lieutenant, *Don James de Almagro,* marching towards the Kingdom of *Chile* about the beginning of the Year 1536, the High-Prieſt *Vilehoma* and *Paul Topa Inga* having been ſent before to keep the Natives in Quiet, becauſe no *Spaniards* had been yet in thoſe Parts. Whilſt they waited at *Topiſa,* the Capital Town of the *Chin-chas,*

richas, the three *Spaniards* sent with them by *Almagro,* and two others that had joyn'd them, exceeded their Orders, advancing as far as the Province of *Xuxui,* believing they should find good Entertainment, as they had till then, for the sake of *Paul,* and hoping to gain favour with *Almagro* for having discover'd the Country ; but they pay'd for their Presumption, for the *Indians* seeing so small a Number of Strangers, resolv'd to kill them, as they did, tho three of them sold their Lives very dear, and the other two flying, were sav'd by the Fame of the Army that was advancing. *Almagro* had at this Time march'd thro' the Countries of the *Canches,* the *Cannas,* and the *Collas,* and been inform'd, that there were great Mines of Metals at *Collasuyo,* and there was a talk of settling there, but he said that Country was too small for so many Men of Worth. At length he arriv'd at *Topisa,* and was well entertain'd by *Paul* and *Vilehoma,* who gave him ninety thousand Pieces of Eight in fine Gold, of the Tribute brought thither from *Chile,* and inform'd him of the Death of the three *Spaniards ;* he reprov'd the others that had escap'd, and dismiss'd several Lords to return to their own Homes. Soon after his arrival at *Topisa,* the High-Priest *Vielehoma* fled, in the Night, with some Men and Women, returning to *Collao* by ways unknown to the *Spaniards,* and being every where entertain'd, attended, and concealed, on Account of his Dignity, his Return, whilst the Troubles were at *Cuzco,* encouraging the *Indians* in their Revolt. Some *Spaniards* and *Yanaconas* were sent after him the next Day, but in vain ; however, they were inform'd that in his way, he had perswaded the Natives to have recourse to Arms, for recovering of their Liberty, representing the *Spaniards* as easily to be cut off by Reason of their small Number, and the People were well enough inclin'd to take his Advice, but that they dreaded the Horses, and

were

were daunted at the Sight of *Almagro's* Forces, which were fo well accouter'd, and made a fine Appearance, the Fame of their Valour being before fpread throughout all the Country.

Almagro, when he mifs'd *Vilehoma,* ask'd *Paul Topa,* why he had not given him Notice of his Defign, who anfwer'd, That he never knew any thing of it, which might be credited, becaufe he was very young, and well inclin'd; however, left he fhould happen to do the like, he order'd him to be guarded, and treated with much Refpect. Captain *Salzedo* was then fent with fixty Horfe and Foot to chaftife the *Indians* that had kill'd the three *Spaniards,* but they had fortify'd themfelves in fuch manner, that he could not come at them, whereupon more Men being fent him, under the Command of *Francis de Chaves,* the befieg'd fally'd, and fell upon the *Yanaconas* belonging to the latter, flew many of them, and carry'd off his Baggage, flying with all Speed along uncooth Ways, for fear of the Horfemen. *Almagro* having been joyn'd by fome *Spaniards* from *Cuzco,* and given the Natives all Satisfaction, defiring they would be kind to fuch as fhould follow him that way, march'd on to joyn *Salzedo* and *Chaves* at *Xuxuy,* where he ftay'd two Months, to pick up all that daily reforted to him. The Forces marching from thence advanc'd as far as *Chaquana,* where the Natives were in an Uproar, for which Reafon the Captains *Salzedo* and *Chaves,* were order'd to fcour the Vale of *Arruya,* with a Troop of Horfe, which prov'd of good ufe, for the People being amaz'd at the Swiftnefs of the Horfes, difpers'd; however, being recover'd of their Fright, they affembl'd fome Days after, in greater Numbers, fwearing by the high and powerful Sun, that they would either dye, or deftroy them all; fending out feveral Parties at the fame Time, to cut off the Blacks and *Yanaconas,* that went for Wood, Straw, and other Neceffaries; and becaufe
they

they did some Mischief, *Almagro* march'd against them,
and they kill'd his Horse. Going out again with
fifty Horse, he found the Towns abandon'd, the Inhabitants only shewing themselves on the Tops of the
Mountains, crying and howling after an hideous Manner. He left *Chaquana*, dismissing the Lords of
the Province of *Paria*, to return to their own Homes,
having with him two hundred Horse, and above
three hundred Foot, besides many *Indians* carrying
the Baggage, and guarded by the cruel *Yanaconas* and
Blacks, who us'd them so ill, that many dy'd by
the Way, for which the Commanders were much to
blame. After some Days march through the Country,
the Forces arriv'd at that which they call'd *Chile*, in
much want of Provisions, saw a small Fort, and tho
Plain, the Land seem'd to be barren. Some Horse
were commanded out to bring in Provisions, which
falling very short, and being inform'd that they were
to march some Days thro' a Desert, they were very
much cast down. *Almagro*, to encourage them, order'd some Sheep and Swine that remain'd to be distributed, and exhorted the Officers, Gentlemen and
Soldiers, to be of good Courage amidst their Sufferings, which martial Men were always expos'd to, and
the more, for that Honour and Interest were not to
be gain'd without Difficulty. They all chearfully
answer'd, that they would follow him, and bear with
all that should happen ; from which Time the Provisions were more cautiously distributed. Seven Days
they march'd thro' Lands of Salt-Peter, Dismal and
Barren, Hunger pressing, because the many Servants
they had with them, consum'd the Provisions, and
coming out of a Break, discover'd vast snowy Mountains, running a great Length, which were of necessity to be cross'd, without knowing the Extent of
them ; and the *Indians* said, there was much more
Snow than what appear'd, which would have daunted

ted any other People, that had not been, like them, enur'd to attempt such desperate Enterprizes, undergoing the greatest Hardships, and labouring at all sorts of Employments, from which when Occasion requir'd, the prime Officers and best Gentlemen were not exempted.

Almagro, who always endeavour'd to content his Soldiers, and was much concern'd at their Sufferings, being sensible of the Perplexity they were in, went before with a good Body of Horse, to pass the Mountains, and see whether he could find Provisions to relieve the Forces. Being come to the Passes, nothing was to be seen but deep Snow, and it then fell very thick, so that he endur'd very much that Day, till he came to some small Huts, where his Men stay'd that Night, very cold. Nor was their Fatigue less the next Day, the Wind blowing hard, and the Snow beating in their Eyes, besides they found, that from the Top of the Mountain there were twelve Leagues to the Vale of *Copayapo;* however, the next Day they reach'd that Vale, where they were well receiv'd, and supply'd with Provisions, which he desir'd the *Indians* to carry to his Forces, and they readily comply'd, carrying Sheep, Lambs, Wheat, and Roots. The Troops being got into the Snow, were in great Perplexity, the *Indians* complaining against those who had brought them out of their Countries, into such Distress, and the *Spaniards* comforting and helping them with much Compassion, because they were not able to move thro Weakness, and if they stood still were frozen to Death. In short, many dy'd with cold; there was no Wood to make Fire, and the Air was so sharp that it stifled them, and what was worst, at Night, there was no shelter. In short, thirty Horses perish'd, many *Indian* Blacks expir'd, leaning against the Rocks, and Hunger prevail'd so far, that the living *Indians* eat the dead, and the *Spaniards* would

VOL. V.   E   willing-

willing'y have eaten the Horfes, but that, if they
ftopp d, they were frozen to Death, and a Black who
led an Horfe, ha ting on Account of fome Cries he
heard, they were both ftarv'd. At laft, when quite
fpent, they began to fpy the good Countty, and paffing the Word from one to another, all took Heart,
efpecially when they faw the *Indians* bringing them
Provifions. When come into the Vale they all foon
recover'd. The Lord of that Place was a Youth,
who upon his Father's Death had been recommended,
together with the Government to a great Man, who
was his Relation, and not only ufurp d the Lordfhip,
but endeavour d to deftroy him ; but the loyaleft of
his Subjects having conceal d him, as foon as the
Spaniards came into the Vale, he apply'd to them for
Affiftance againft the Ufurper. *Almagro* having examin d into that Affair, and found him in the Right,
reftor'd him to his Eftate. Three *Spaniards* who had
Ignorantly advanc'd before the reft, pafs d through
many Parts, finding good Entertainment, till they
came into a Vale, the Lord whereof was call d *Mar-
candei,* who after a kind Reception, kill'd them and
their Horfes, when they were afleep, burying all
privately, after which he fell to facrificing, dancing,
and drinking to Excefs, with his People ; *Almagro*
always asking for thefe three Men, and being told,
that they went before. Departing from *Copayapo,* in
three Days he came to the aforefaid Vale, was well
receiv d and furnifh'd with Provifions and all other
Neceffaries ; but the *Yanaconas* fearching about for o-
ther Things, found fome Remains of thofe that had
been flain Being come from thence to the Vale of
Quimbo, Almagro order'd inquiry to be made into
that Affair, and Captain *James de Vega,* who was in
the Rear, to fecure *Mercondei* and his Brother, and to
fend fome *paniards* to *Copayapo* to feize the young
Man's Relation, that had ufurp d his Dominion, and
both

both of them to be conducted to *Quimbo,* where he
caus'd twenty seven of the prime Men to be burnt for
the Murder of the aforesaid three *Spaniards,* without
hearing what they had to say for themselves, which
was very unjust, and look'd upon as an extraordinary
Cruelty.

Almagro, at his setting out from *Cuzco* left *Roderick Orgonnez* there to pick up what Men he could,
and follow him, which he did with a few *Spaniards,*
and Blacks for their Servants, being well entertain'd
till they came into the Province of *Topisa,* where
wanting Provisions, and going out to furnish themselves, they met with arm'd *Indians,* who kill'd four
of them, which made them proceed on their Way in
much Distress. At *Chequana* they found better Accommodation, and took store of Provision, having
been inform'd of the Passage over the snowy Mountains, where the Cold was so excessive, that it kill'd
most of the Blacks and *Indians.* *Orgonnez* himself
helping to set up his Tent at Night, the Snow fell,
and the very Nails came off his Fingers, two other
Spaniards escap'd little better, and two others were bury'd in the Snow, with their Blacks, *Indians* and Horses. At length in four Days they made their way
thro', with the loss of twenty six Horses, all their
Furniture, and most of their Baggage; all which was
not valu'd for the Satisfaction of being out of that
Misery. The Lord of *Copayapo,* in Gratitude for the
favour shew'd him by *Almagro,* sent several *Indians*
laded with Provisions to meet them, which reviv'd
their Spirits, but they were forc'd to halt some Days
in that Vale, to recover Strength, the *Indians* being
very kind to them.

John de Rada, who had been sent by *Almagro* to
Lima, meeting there with *Ferdinand Pizarro,* after his
return from *Spain,* earnestly sollicited him to put into
his Hands the Dispatches he had brought from the King

for

for the said *Almagro,* but the *Pizarros* having no good
Intentions towards him, delay'd delivering the same
from Day to Day, till at last *Ferdinand* being importun'd, promis'd he should have them at *Cuzco,* which
was accordngly perform'd, the design having been to
gain Time. *Rada* then set out from that City, to
follow *Almagro,* and coming to *Chile,* found he had
eighty *Spaniards,* Horse and Foot, well Arm'd and
Accoutred in all Points, with sufficient Servants. The
Indians having every where convey'd away their Provision, those Men suffer'd very much, which oblig'd
their Commander to send out two Parties a marauding,
one of which by the Industry of the *Yanaconas* found
a considerable Quantity of Corn in a Cave, and the
other brought a Flock of Sheep, which being spent,
with much Difficu'ty and Danger, another supply was
procur'd, and then *Rada* sent to give *Orgonnez* Advice,
that he was marching to joyn him, desiring he would
send some Provisions to meet him on the snowy
Mountains. *Orgonez* did so, and by that means He
and his Men pass'd those dismal Ways better than the
others had done before.

There being often Occasion to speak of these and
such like dreadful Passes of Mountains, it will not be
improper to say something concerning them. It is
certain that different Airs have no less different Effects upon Bodies, not only of Plants, but of Animals, and even upon Iron, the hardest of all Metals,
for in some Parts of the *West-Indies,* Iron Bars have
been seen so eaten by the Air, that they would moulder away between the Fingers. It is well known,
that those who are not accustom'd to it, are generally
Sea-sick, when they go to Sea, which is occasion'd
by the watry Air which they are not us'd to, tho'
the Motion of the Ship, and the smell of Pitch and
Tar may add something to it; and this same Effect
is seen on the Mountain of *Peru,* call'd *Periacaca,* for
all

all that pass over it are troubled with extraordinary Qualms and Vomiting, till they come into a better Air, the same happening all along that Ridge of Mountains, for the Space of five hundred Leagues; and the only Remedy against it is to stop the Mouth, Nostrils, and Ears, and to keep the Stomach warm, because the Air is so cold, that it penetrates into the very Bowels. Something of the same Nature happens to Beasts, which are sometimes benumm'd to such a D gree, that they cannot stir. Those who have pretended to dive into this Secret, do believe that to be one of the highest Places in the World, which occasions the Air to be so thin, as not to be proportion d to Man s breathing, as requiring a thicker Air. The Co d on the Mountians in *Spain,* is outward'y painful to the Hands and Feet, and requires good cloathing on the Body ; but that in the *West-Indies,* tho not so smarting to the Hands or Feet, operates on the Bowels, as being more piercing than sensible, for which Reason that Ridge of Mountains is not inhabited, nor do any other Beasts breed there, besides the *Vicunas,* which have been before spoken of, and the Grass is always parch d. This Desert extended between twenty and thirty Leagues. There are other Deserts call'd *Punas,* where the Air insensibly consumes the vital Spirits, for which Reason, tho the *Spaniards* at first went over the Mountains into the Kingdom of *Chile,* they have since gone by Sea, or close along the Coast, to avoid the Danger of the Mountain Way, where so many have perish'd, and those who had the good Fortune to escape, were some of them maim'd and disabl'd by the Air, which tho not fierce, is so piercing that Men drop down dead insensibly, or else their Fingers or Toes drop off without any Pain. Thus when *Almagro* pass'd, the dead Bodies lay about extended, without any Corruption, or ill Scent ; and long after, a Boy was found there alive, who had

E 3   hid

hid himfelf in a Cottage, whence he us'd to go out to cut off fome of the Flefh of a dead Horfe, on which he liv d, fome Comrades he had at firft doing fo too, till they all dy'd one by one, and he faid he did not care to depart the Place, but die there, as the reft had done, becaufe he had no Inclination to go any whither, or take any Satisfaction.   Another who was paffing over thofe Deferts, being oblig d to ftay there at Night, heap d up the dead Bodies to fhelter him againft the Wind ; all which fhews that Cold to be fo penetrating, that it overcomes the vital Heat, and being extremely dry does not Corrupt the dead Bodies, Putrefaction proceeding from Heat and Moifture.

THIS Country is remarkable for many burning Mountains, and being fubject to Earthquakes.   The hot Exhalations rifing within the Bowels of the Earth, feem to be the principal Occafion of the former ; for thofe fetting Fire to the groffer Matter produce the Flame, Smoke, and Eruptions, and finding no way out, fhake the Earth, and make a dreadful Noife, till being reinforc'd by the Air, that Fire rends the very Rocks.   Thefe Earthquakes are moft frequent towards the Sea, and it has been obferv'd, that the greateft Earthquakes have happen'd between *Chile* and *Quito*, being a thoufand Leagues in Length.   In *Chile* there was one, that overturn'd Mountains, and turn'd Rivers into Lakes, by ftopping their Current, deftroy'd whole Towns, killing abundance of People, the Sea broke in for fome Leagues, and many affirm, that the Shock was felt three hundred Leagues along the Coaft. A few Years after happen'd the Earthquake at *Arequipa*, which almoft laid the City in Ruins.   In the Year 1586 happen d that at *Lima*, which ran along the Coaft an hundred and feventy Leagues, and fifty up the Inland.   Before the Earthquake a dreadful Noife was heard, which prov d a good Warning, for

the

the People ran out into the Streets, Squares, and o-
pen Places, and tho it threw down the principal
Structures in the City, not above twenty Perfons perifh d, and foon after the Earthquake ceas d, the Sea
had the fame Motion, as has been mention'd in *bile,*
running furioufly almoft two Leagues up the Country,
and rifing twelve Fathoms. The *Indians,* being us'd
to Earthquakes, in many Parts built their ittle Houfes
with Clay, looking upon it as lefs dangerous than
Brick and Stone. The next Year there was another
great Earthquake at *Quito,* and in fhort, all that Coaft
is fubject to that Calamity, inftead of the Thunder
and Lightning there is on the Mountains. The reafon
why the maritime Countries are fubject to thefe Earthquakes, feems to be, becaufe the Water ftops up the
Pores, and openings of the Earth, through which it
fhould difcharge the hot Exhalations ingender d in it,
and the Moifture condens'd on the Superficies of the
Earth, by the Drought of the Sun and Air, drives
back the hot Vapours, till taking Fire, they burft
out. Some are of Opinion, that when wet Years
follow two that have been very dry, there enfue fuch
Earthquakes. In the Year 1581, among the *Chiacha-*
poyas and at *Chuquiabo,* on a fudden a Piece of the
Mountain fell upon a great Part of the Town of
Angoango, killing many *Indians,* and the Earth that
fell ran a League and an Half, choak'd up a Lake, and
lay flat for all that Space.

E 4 CHAP.

CHAP. II.

Of the Atunlunas, Tindarunas, *and* Mitayos, *of the Tributes and personal Service* ; *the Description of the Province of* Quito.

IT is convenient before we proceed any farther, as we have before declar'd what the *Orejones Miti-maes* and *Yanaconas* were, to explain some Particulars that occur in this History. The *Spaniards* who had given them in Commendam, abusing the former Institution of *Yanaconas*, whom they had discharg'd from their State of Servitude, reduc'd into that Condition such others as were most for their Advantage, as Husbandmen, Handycrafts, and idle Persons, who serv'd sometimes one and sometimes another ; so that the paying all Tributes and Duties fell upon the *Atunlunas*. These Men, under the *Ingas*, became Tributaries at twenty five Years of Age, and so continu'd till fifty, not being oblig'd to pay before or after ; but the Number of *Indians* being decreas'd, they since pay from sixteen to sixty, the Wife bearing as much of the Burthen as the Husband ; because the Women spin and weave Cloth, and help to Till the Land, and perform other Labours. He that has no Wife is call'd *Guacha*, and is hard put to it to pay his Tribute. The *Mitayos Tindarunas*, are Tributary *Indians*, the *Curacas*, or native Lords have set apart to hire them out to work in the Mines, build Houses, and the like, and these are none of their Favourites ; for *Tindarunas* signifies Men that are under Compulsion. These they furnish to serve in their *Mitas*, or Turns, for the Space of two Months, or longer, according to the Custom of every Country. They are call'd *Mi-tayos*,

tayos, and the Magiftrates of every *Spanifh* Town order the *Curacas* of their Diftrict, to fend each of
them as many *Indians* as is ufual, according to the
Extents of their Lordfhips, to the Market-Place; for
the aforefaid Employments, and to look after the Cattel and Harveft. At the City of *Lima,* they give
every one of thefe *Tomayos* a Tomin, and a Quarter of
a Peck of Wheat a Day. At *Los Charcas* and *Potofi,*
becaufe the Country is richer and dearer, they give
two *Tomines* a Day; and at *Quito* they were wont
to give fix Tomines a Month, without Diet. This
ufe of *Nitayos* was brought up, when the King order'd perfonal Service to be abolifh'd, fo that they
are now pay'd for their Labour, which then they
were not. In the Territory of *Guayaquil,* there are
Indians call'd *Choros,* who carry on their Floats, on the
River *Doule,* all forts of Goods to *Quito,* and other
neighbouring Parts, and they cannot work afhore.

WHEN the *Ingas* fubdu'd thofe Provinces, they
made Roads thro' them for promoting of Commerce,
and for the more Conveniency of Travellers, built
Tambos, that is Houfes, with feveral Appartments, at
every four Leagues diftance, or lefs, to entertain Paf-
fengers, ordering the next Towns to place *Indians* there
to ferve them, with all forts of Provifions, and every
Curaca was appointed the Number of *Indians* he was
to furnifh, who were reliev'd in their Mitas or Turns,
and therefore call'd *Mitayos.* Thefe fupply'd every
Traveller with what he had occafion for, by way of Barter,
all of them carrying fomething of what their Country
afforded; the Soldiers and Meffengers of the *Ingas* had
alfo what they wanted at thofe *Tambos.* Befides all
thofe already mention'd, there were *Tamemes,* that is,
Porters to carry Burdens. Another fort of *Mitayos*
are oblig'd to furnifh Neceffaries for Repairing of
Bridges and High-Ways, as they were in the Days
of the *Ingas.* As to the Tributes, or Taxes, they
are

are every where moderate, and receiv'd in such Things as the Country produces, and every Person is able to afford. The personal Service was an unjust Usurpation among the first Conquerors, who were too intent upon their own Advantage and Authority, and on that Account would have brought those People into a sort of Servitude, which the Kings of *Spain* have entirely abolish'd, leaving the *Indians* as free as any of their other Subjects.

I r has been said before that *Sebastian de Belalcazar,* founded the City of *Santiago de Guayaquil,* after which his chief Care was to improve that of St. *Francis de Quito,* of which Province this will be a proper Place to give some Account. On the North it extends to *Carlusama,* which belongs to the Government of *Popayan ;* on the South to *Tiquizambi,* the Boundary of the City of *Cuenca ;* on the East to *New Baeza* in the Province of the *Quixos,* and on the West to *Puerto Viejo,* and the Foot of the Mountain being the Marsh Land of the South-Sea. The Climate of *Quito* is rather Cold than Hot, insomuch that they sometimes keep Fires in Winter. The Air is clear and serene, the Sun rising and setting very bright, never clouded, but only when it Rains. The Winter is from *October* to *March,* during which Months it commonly Rains, but never Snows, except only on some particular Tops of the Ridge of Mountains. Thus the Country is healthy, and the People live longer there than in *Spain.* In the Year 1558, the Small-Pox occasion'd a great Mortality among the *Indians ;* but generally both *Spaniards* and *Indians* dye of Colds or Defluctions, at the Beginning and End of the Summer. The chief Medicine here for the Pox and for great Colds is *Zarzaparilla* and *Guayacan,* and it is rare that any one misses of a Cure that drinks the Juice of the said *Zarzaparilla* when fresh. The City of *Quito* is seated at the Foot of the Ridge of Mountains

Mountains that rifes at *Puerto Viejo,* on the Coaft of the South-Sea, and runs Northward almoft to the City of *Cartagena;* to the Eaftward of it is the great Ridge of Mountains that runs to *Chile* Southward, and to *Santa Marta,* Northward On the other Ridge that lies to the Weftward, one League from *Quito,* is one Head above all the reft, being a burning Mountain, that often Smokes, and fometimes makes a great Noife, and cafts out Afhes; and on the 17th of *October,* 1566, it caft out Afhes, as if it had been Snow, from two of the Clock in the Afternoon, till ten the next Morning, the Quantity that fell in the City, and its Territory being fo great, that it cover'd all the Grafs in the Fields, which occafion'd fome Cattel to dye, and the reft fuffer'd much till the Rain fell. Thirty Days after it, fuch a Darknefs of Clouds hung over the City, paffing away to the Eaftward, that it put the *Indians* into fo great a Confternation that they fled to the Hills, with difmal Cries and Lamentations, faying, the univerfal Difollution was come. The Land between the two Mountains is good, fit for riding, tho there are fome rifing Grounds, yet it was hard to get Stone for building ; and at firft they made Lath and Plaifter Walls, afterwards they found a Quarry of Stone. In the Mountain to the Eaftward much Gold has been, and is ftill found, tho now lefs, becaufe it is forbid to make the *Indians* work. In the Territory of a Town call'd *Mira,* fifteen Leagues from the City, belonging to the Cazique *Otabalo,* there are Springs of Salt Water, of which they make a fort of grey and bitter Salt, valu'd by the *Indians* ; but the *Spaniards* carry theirs from the Sea, as was done in the Time of the *Ingas.*

GOOD Gunpowder is made there, and they have Plenty of Saltpetre, occafion'd by the Dampnefs coming from the Rivers, which in this Diftrict are as follows. The River *Guayaquil* has its Springs on the great

Ridge

Ridge of Mountains to the Eaftward, is joyn'd by feveral others, and is a League and an Half wide at the Mouth, when it fals into the South Sea. The great River of the *Magdalen* has its rife above *Timana*, on the Earftern Ridge of Mountains, runs away to the Northward, t'll it is loft in the North Sea, near the Town of *Santa Marta*, and near the Source of this River a Branch ftrik s off from the Mounta n, which ftretches away near this great River Weftward, where the *Paezes* and the *Pijaos* have their Dwellings. The River *Cauca* has its Oiginal in the Weftern Part of the Province of the *Coconucos*, nine Leagues from *Popayan*, keeps its Courfe on the Weft Side of the aforefaid Weftern Branch of the great Mountain, and falls into *Rio Grande*, nine Leagues below the City *Mopox*, which is in the Government of *Cartagena*. The River call'd *De los edros*, or of Cedar Trees, rifes in the Territory of *Quina*, appertaining to the City of *Pafto*, at the Foot of the great *Cordillera*, or Ridge of Mountains, having run nine Leagues, is joyn'd by the River *Mayo*, or of *May*, which crofses the Vale of *Putia*, cuts thro' the Weftern *Cordillera*, or Ridge, and falls into the South Sea, at a Mouth, a League wide. There are alfo the Rivers of St. *John*, of the *Paripazes*, of the *Piles*, and of *Buenaventura*, all falling into the South Sea, befides nineteen other Rivers, and many Brooks that fall into thofe already mention'd; and all of them are generally rapid Streams, efpecially that of *Cauca*. The great River of the *Magdalen* is Navigable for two hundred Leagues, almoft as far as *Tocayma*, thofe of *Cauca*, *Cedros*, *Buenaventura*, and *Guayaquil* are fome of them Navigable in Canoes, others in Floats. They commonly fwell in *October*, *November*, *January*, and *February*, by Reafon of the Rains; their Water is thin, and good to drink, but the Shores are not inhabited. At *Anciqueto*, half a League from the City of *Quito*, is
a Lake

a Lake a Quarter of a League in Compass, in which there are Geese, Herons, and other Fowl. Ten Leagues from the City, near to *Otabalo,* on the Top of an Hill, is a very deep Lake, a League about ; and close by *Otabalo,* is another two Leagues and an Half about. In the Territory of *Carangue,* is the Pool call'd *Yagualcocha,* signifying Sea of Blood, where *Guaynacapa* made the great Slaughter of the *Pastos,* tore out fifty thousand of their Hearts, and shed so much Blood that the Lake was dy d, as has been said in speaking of the *Ingas.*

In the hot Part of the Country in this Province, there is a sort of Fruit, call'd *Guaba,* two Spans long, the hind grey, and within it are Seeds or Kernels, with a white Pulp, sweet and cooling. There are *Guayabos,* that produce Fruit like Apples, with many Kernels, some white and some red, well tasted and wholesom. The Plantans have the Relish of dry Figs, but eaten green their Taste cannot be ascertain d. *Spanish* Fruit thrives well, but will not keep, for it soon rots. Vines thrive well in some Places, but not in others, and there is always Grass, higher in the hot Parts, than in the Cold, and withers in Summer. There is also much Wheat, Barley, and Maiz, and abundance of Cows, Horses, Sheep, and Swine, the Climate being very proper for them. The Turtle Doves, Sparrows, and other Birds, as also the Deer, do much harm to the Corn. The wild Beasts are Tygers, Leopards, Boars, and Bears. Of the Country Sheep there are but few, because the *Indians* generally load them ; but there are abundance of *Abras,* or *Gallinazas,* a sort of large Crows, very useful for cleansing the Land ; and in the Spring there are Multitudes of Swallows, Vulturs, Eagles, Hawks, Partridges, and other Birds, as Turkies, Pheasants, a sort of Back Birds like those we call by that Name ; but the Rivers yield little Fish, for which

Reason

Reafon they have it from the Sea. Within the Diftrict of this City there are fmall Snakes, Lizards,
Scorpions, and Vipers in the hotter Part, but not very
Venomous. In the River *Guayaquil* there are infinite
Alligators, and they fleep fo found, when they come
afhore to that Purpofe, that they do not awake, tho'
a Musket be fir'd at them ; it is eafy to k ll them
by wounding their Fore-Leg, or Gullet, but if touch d
in any other Part, they run into the Water, and all
the reft take the Alarm : Whence it is concluded, that
they take the Report of a Gun to be Thunder ;
they are very Mifchievous, and have done much harm
among *Spaniards* and *Indians*. A *Spaniard* wafhing his
Hands in a River, an Alligator ftruck him on the
Neck with his Tail, which made him fall into the
Water, where the Alligator feiz'd him by the Flank,
and carry'd him over the River above the Water.
Another Alligator feeing it, came up to take away
his Prey , whereupon the firft let go his hold,
to defend himfelf, and the Man, tho almoft fenfelefs
with the Fright, crawl d away, leaving the Alligators
engag'd, and the *Spaniard*'s Wounds did not prove
great or deep In the Territory of *Guayaquil*, there
are Bees, that fwarm, and make Honey in hollow
Trees ; they are little bigger than Flies, their Honey
and Wax is Ruddy, and tho' well relifh'd, is not fo
good as the *Spanifh*.

THE City of *Quito* lies under the Equinoctial,
fo that when the Sun is on that Line, a Man has
no Shaddow. Goods from the Sea are convey'd up
the River to the Landing-Place on Floats, and from
thence to the City, being forty Leagues, by Carriers.
The *Indians* keep Markets, where the *Spaniards* buy
what they have occafion for, and had formerly neither Weights nor Meafures, but barter'd by guefs.
Befides Tillage and Breeding of Cattel, the Product
and Trade of the Country confifts in Abundance of
Cheefe, made of the Milk of Cows, Goats, and Ews,
Cotton,

Cotton, Mantles, white, b'ack, and grey Cloth, Blankets, Hats, Serge, Sackcloth, Buskins, **Naval** Stores, Goat s Leather, pad and war Saddles, Cotton, and white Stuff; there is much Flax, but little of it spun, but there is much Wool, Sugar-Mills, *Spanish* Handycrafts of all forts. The City has little Land belonging to private Persons, the Fields and Pastures are in common, a great Break, or Slough runs thro' the Middle of it, and there are Bridges in all the Streets. The Land is fandy, but within the Depth of half a Fathom, there is Rock, the Situation not Moift, and *Belalcazar* made Choice of that Situation for the better Defence againft the *Indians,* who were numerous, and the *Spaniards* but a few. At firft they built fuch Houfes as they could, now they raife their Foundations three Spans above the Ground, make their Walls of Lime and Sand, with fome Peers of Brick, the Door Frames of Stone, and cover them with Tiles. There are in the City three large Squares, before the Cathedral, and the Monafteries of St. *Dominick* and St. *Francis ;* the Streets are wide and ftrait, containing above four hundred Houfes, the Number ftill increafing. The Cathedral is a good Structure, large, and has three Ifles. The Monaftery of St. *Dominick* built out of Alms, is a fumptuous Structure There is a Town-Houfe, a Court of Juftice, a Goal, and other publick Edifices. The Houfes of the better fort, and there are many of them, have generally two or three Appartments, with a Court, Garden, and Back-Yard. The Materials are to be had near by, the remoteft at three Leagues Diftance, carry'd on Carts, the Cuftom of Loading Men being entirely fupprefs'd; only at the Loading of Goods from the River *Guyaquil,* fome *Indians* of their own free Will get their living that way; for no Endeavours have been able to prevail with them to follow any other Employment, as Porters carry Burdens in all Parts of *Europe.* The City is well furnifh'd with all forts of Arms,

and

and there are Tambos, or Inns, at five or fix Leagues
diftance from it every way, well fupply'd w th Provifions, at reafonable Rates, according to the Price fet
by the proper Magiftrates. The firft B fhop *Don
Garci Diaz Arias,* began to build the Cathedral, and
it was finifh'd by the Bifhop *Don Fray Pedro de la
Ribera,* the King having order'd, that the City fhould
defray one third of the Expence, the *Indians* of its
Diftrict another, and his Majefty the other. There
are alfo two Parifh Churches, call d St. *Blafe* and St.
Sebaftian; the Bifhop's Palace ftands in the Square,
clofe by the Cathedral, which is well furn fh'd with
Veftments for the Divine Service, and has nothing
affign'd for Repairs, but when any thing is defec-
tive, the Inhabitants meet, and rate themfelves, without begging any Alms. Befides the Monafteries of
Dominicans and *Francifcans,* before mention'd, there is
one of *Mercenarians,* and in all of them there are *Indian* Friers, who live very religioufly. Several Languages are fpoken round about this City, but that of
Cuzco, which was introduc'd by the *Ingas,* is underftood by all, being eafily learnt, efpecially fince Rules
have been found for that Purpofe. In this Territory
there are above fifty thoufand Tributary *Indians,* and
the Number daily Increafes, becaufe they live very
eafy.

THESE Natives dwell together in Clans, or Tribes,
are fond of their native Country, which they never
forfake, unlefs ill us'd by their Caziques; they are
of a good Stature and Difpofition, learn any Handy-
craft that is taught them; not very ftrong, but floth-
ful, lovers of Novelty, inconftant, and giving to drinking, cunning in their Dealings, but muft be fometimes compell d to work, to maintain their Wives and
Children, many of them living to ninety or an hundred Years of Age. Thofe who live neareft to the
City are more polite, as is ufual in other Countries,
their

their Habit is a fhort Tunick, without Sleeves, as wide above as below, their Arms and Legs naked, with a fquare Mantle, a Yard and three Quarters every way, which ferves inftead of a Cloak ; they wear their Hair long, and that it may not hang in their Eyes, tie a String about their Heads. The Caziques and prime Men, as alfo the *Yanaconas* wear Hats, were formerly wont to have *Ojotas,* which only fav'd the Sole of the Foot, but now they ufe *Alpargates,* or Buskins. Their Bed is a Mat made of thick Rufhes, laid on Straw, and they cover themfelves with two Blankets. Their Jewels or Ornamenss are Necklaces of *Chaquira,* a fort of fmall Beads, or of Go'd or Silver, as alfo red Beads, and fome of white Bone, with Bracelets of the fame. The Houfhould Stuff confifts in a Grindftone for their Corn, Pottage-pots, and little Jars for their Liquor, which they call *Azua,* with oval drinking Cups, which hold above a Pint. Enough has been faid of their Religion, when Heathens ; the old Men were difficult to be brought to embrace Chriftianity at firft, as being hardned by their Education, but now they are all converted. The greateft Feftival among them is a general meeting of all the Neighbourhood, which lafts five or fix Days, during which time they do nothing but drink, fing and dance, which tires them to fuch a degree, that they muft have two Days to reft them. The Cazique was the Perfon moft refpected among them, and next to him the braveft Man, and he that till'd his Land beft, becaufe he fpending the Product in treating the reft, was moft belov d. The Meafure of Time is by Moons and half Moons; the *Cazique* s Houfe is the beft, where they affemble to their drinking Feftivals ; the other Houfes are fmall, about forty or fifty foot in length, with Mud Walls thatch'd, where they lay up nothing but what is abfolutely neceffary, either for themfe'ves, or for tillage, or for fuch Handycrafts as they practife.

VOL. V.   F   The

The Lands are divided among them, as they were formerly by the *Ingas,* no Alteration being made therein ; and when any Controverſy happens about them, it is immediately decided upon the Spot.

CHAP. III.

The Diſcovery and Planting of Popayan ; *of the Governments of* LOS Quixos, *or* Canela, *and of* Guarſongo, *or* Juan de Salinas; *the Diſcovery of the* New Kingdom of Granada.

IT was uſual among the Commanders, who had ſubdu'd one Province in the *Weſt-Indies,* to endeavour to extend into thoſe that were the next Borders, and accordingly *Sebaſtian de Belalcazar* having ſettled the Affairs of St. *Francis de Quito,* and its Territory, and ſent ſome ſmall Parties to diſcover what was about it, being inform'd that two Brothers, call'd *Calambaz* and *Popayan,* poſſeſs'd a large Province of a fertile Soil, and rich in Gold, to the Northward, thought it expedient, as he had found a way from *Quito* to the South-Sea, at the Bay of St. *Matthew,* to find out another to the North-Sea, and in order to it to begin with that Country of *Calambaz* and *Popayan,* notwithſtanding all the Difficulties that appear'd in that Enterprize. Having made the neceſſary Diſpoſition, he ſet out from *Quito,* with three hundred *Spaniſh* Horſe and Foot, without that Multitude of *Indians,* which other Commanders had been wont to take with them, having warn'd his Soldiers to furniſh themſelves with Arms and Cloathing, leaving all that was cumberſom, and only for conveniency, which he look'd upon as ſuperfluous for men who were to be

inur'd

inur'd to Fatigue, and whofe Succefs depended on
their Diligence and Induftry. In this manner he
march'd without any Oppofition, as far as *Otabalo,*
the firft Place in the prefent Government of *Popayan,*
and as foon as paft that Place, the Caziques of the
Paftos and *Patias,* who had been inform'd of his coming, met him with their Forces, refufing to give ear
to any Propofals, or to accept of Prefents, fo that the
Spaniards were oblig'd to truft to nothing but their Valour and Induftry, being foon reduc'd to want of
Provifions, all which thofe People had convey'd away.
They march'd feveral Days, continually skirmifhing
with the *Indians,* and gaining difficult Paffes till they
came to the Capital of the Province, being the Refidence of the Lord of *Popayan.* There *Belalcazar*
refolv'd to reft his Forces, perceiving that there were
many good Towns in the open Country, between
that Place and a Branch of *Rio Grande,* being fourteen Leagues diftant, all full of fine Meadows, Corn-
Fields, Groves of Fruit-Trees, and particularly *Agua-
cates,* which are very delicious, many Rivers that
come down from the *Andes,* whofe Water is very good
croffing the Country, in fome of which very pure
Gold has been found. Having met with a convenient Place, being a flat Eminence, which feem'd to be
healthy, he refolv'd to fettle there, tho' he had
little reft allow'd him by thofe war-like *Indians.* He
frequently fent Parties abroad to view the Country
and bring in Provifions, and thus he difcover'd the
Territories of *Xamundi,* the *Timbos,* who had much
Gold, the *Aquales, Guamba, Maluafa, Polindera, Palace, Tembio,* and *Colaza,* all of them war-like People,
and Man-eaters, having much low Gold, and liking
the Country that extends as far as *Cali,* being twenty Leagues in length, he caus'd that alfo to be difcover'd. However thefe Excurfions were not perform'd
free-coft, the *Indians* every where fighting defperately,

and

and endeavouring to expel thofe Strangers either by open Force, or want of Provifions, all which they withdrew, and conceal'd.

Belalcazar being in this Country, thought it proper to find out the Source of the great River of the *Magdalen,* which was generally believ'd to fall into the *North-Sea,* and he fuppos'd the Country about its Springs to be very Populous. He found it rife above *Popayan* from two Branches, the one five, and the other fourteen Leagues diftant from the City, and yet thofe two Sources are forty Leagues from each other, and there began certain Vales form'd by the *Cordillera,* well Inhabited by the *Coconuco Indians* and others. From the Country of the *Coconucos,* where one of the Branches of that River Springs, runs a little Brook, that ftretches through the wide Vale of *Cali,* where all the Waters of the two *Cordilleras,* or Ridges of Mountains meet, fo that when it comes to *Cali,* it is as large and rapid, as the River *Guadalquivir* at *Sevil.* One of the greateft Difficulties *Belalcazar* had to ftruggle with in thofe Parts, was the Variety of Languages, which requir'd fo many Interpreters, and fometimes it happen'd that three were employ'd to underftand what one faid. *Belalcazar* obferving the Extent of thofe Provinces, and their Diftance from *Quito,* refolv'd to build a City there, and to that effect labour'd to pacify the *Indians,* and though fome concluded a Peace they did not obferve it, but foon revolted, and convey'd away their Provifions, which reduc'd the *Spaniards* to great ftreights. Idols were found in fome Parts of thofe Provinces, but no peculiar Places of Worfhip; however they talk'd with the Devil, and did many Things by his Advice. Many of them had no full Knowledge of the Immortality of the Soul, tho' they believ'd that their Forefathers came to life again; and fome fancy'd that the Souls of fuch as dy'd went into the Bodies of thofe

that

that were born. They paid much honour to the dead, burying them with their Wives and Servants alive, befides Wealth and Provifions, as was practifed in *Peru.* In fome Parts they burnt them to Afhes, and in others parch'd them up at the Fire. They went naked and bare-foot, wearing nothing but little Mantles, but had notable Jewels or Ornaments, both Men and Women, and they had Numbers of Southfayers and Wizards.

Belalcazar was very well pleas'd with that Situation he had chofen, concluding it to be healthy, becaufe it is all the Year like the Month of *May,* the Nights and Days being almoft equal, as lying only forty Leagues to the Northward of the Equinoctial, fo that the Increafe or decreafe is not above ten Minutes, befides that a good River run through it; all that he miflik'd was that it rain'd there more than in other Places, and there was much Thunder and Lightning. The *Indian* Wheat there is the beft in *America,* and the *Spanifh* grows twice a Year befides there is abundance of Flefh of all forts, as black and white Cattel, Goats, and Swine, and Variety of Native and *Spanifh* Fruit. The Territory of that Government at this Time extends two hundred and twenty Leagues North and South from the Borders of the Province of *Quito,* to thofe of *Cartagena,* and an hundred in breadth to the Eaftward, from the *New Kingdom* of *Granada* to the South-Sea, wherein there are fourteen *Spanifh* Towns, part of them under the Jurifdiction of the Court of the faid *New Kingdom of Granada,* and the reft under that of *Quito;* the too much Rain hinders the Country abounding more in Corn, but it is rich in Gold Mines. The Towns in it are, the City of *Popayan,* where the Bifhop refides, in 2 Degrees and Half of North Latitude, the Towns of *Santa Fe de Antioquia, Santiago de Cali, Caramanta, Santiago de Arma, Santana de Anzerma, Guadalajara de Buga, Timana, San Sebaftian de* la *Plata, Almaguer, San Juan de Truxillo, Madrigal,* or *Chiapanchica, Agreda,* or *Malaga, San Juan de Pasto,* and *San Sebastian de los Paezes.* Thefe *Indians* were fo inhuman, that Fathers have been known to eat their Children, Husbands their Wives, and Brothers their Sifters, and they had publick Shambles of human Flefh

To omit nothing that falls under the Jurifdiction of *Quito,* we will proceed to the *Quixos, Canela,* and *Y-guarfongo,* or *Juan de Salinas. Belalcazar* fent feveral Commanders to difcover the *Great River of the Magdalen,* and other adjacent Parts, and among them that crofs'd the great *Cordillera,* or Ridge of Mountains, was Captain *Gonzalo Diaz de Pineda,* who enter'd the Country of the *Quixos* and *Canela,* and faid there were moft wealthy Provinces beyond it, which afterwards mov'd *Gonzalo Pizarro* to penetrate into thofe Parts, where he got nothing, but endur'd many Hardfhips, as fhall be mention'd in its Place. Afterwards in the Year 1557, the Marquefs *de Cañete,* fent *Giles Gonzalez de Avalos* to fubdue the *Quixos,* and make Settlements there, the fame lying to the Eaftward of *Quito,* and on the South of it is the Government of *Y-guarfongo,* otherwife call'd *Juan de Salinas;* on the North of it is *Popayan,* and on the Eaft the Countries of *Dorado;* the Latitude not one full Degree North, the Length about forty Leagues, and the Breadth under twenty. All the Country is very hot, and rainy, rough, yeilding little Corn, but has fome Trees like Cinnamon, which eaten in Powder has the fame Relifh, but lofes the Tafte any other way: In other Particulars it much refembles the other Parts of *Peru;* the Governour is appointed by the Vice-Roy, and there are in the Province four *Spanifh* Towns. The firft is *Baeza,* founded by *Giles Ramivez Davalos,* a Native of the City of *Baeza* in *Spain,* in the Year 1559; fixteen Leagues S. E. from the City of *Qui-*
to,

to, where the Governour refides. The next *Avila,* to the Northward of *Archidona,* which is the third, and the fourth *Sevilla del Oro.* The whole Government is in the Diocefe of *Quito,* the Natives readily embrac'd Chriftianity, have a Language of their own, and ufe that which is univerfal throughout *Peru*; their Habit, Religion, and Manners, were formerly like thofe already mention'd. They were troublefome to fubdue, and revolted feveral Times, but are now altogether peaceable, and fenfible of their Happ'nefs.

To conclude with the Jurifdiction of the Court of *Quito,* there is the Government of the *Pacamoros,* or *Bracamoros,* and *Yguarfongo,* otherwife call'd of *John de Salinas,* extending an hundred Leagues Eaftward, commencing twenty Leagues beyond the City of *Zamora,* which is the very Ridge of the *Andes,* and the fame Extent North and South, like the reft for Product, and has yielded much Gold; there are in it four *Spanifh* Towns founded by Captain *John de Salinas de Loyola,* when he was Governour; firft the City of *Valladolid,* in feven Degrees of North Latitude; twenty Leagues S. E. from the City of *Loxa,* beyond the Ridge of the *Andes*; fecondly, the City of *Loyola* or *Cumbinama,* about fixteen Leagues to the Eaftward of *Valladolid*; thirdly, *Santiago de las Montañas,* fifty Leagues from *Loyola* to the Eaftward, in whofe Territory more Gold is found than others, and it is very fine, but not equal to that of *Carabaya* in *Peru* and *Valdibia* in *Chile,* for this fometimes is above twenty three Carats and an Half.

It will be proper before he is quite forgot, here to obferve that *Jerome de Ortal* before fpoken of at *Maracapana,* attempting to carry on the Difcoveries up the Inland, and being a Man of little Conduct, all his Men but ten mutiny'd and forfook him, going away to *Venezuela,* where *Nicholas Federman,* Commanded, who receiv'd them. *Ortal* and his ten Compa-

nions

nions made their way to the ftrong Houfe he had built on the Sea Coaft, call'd St. *Michael de Neveri*, but being inform'd that *Antony Sedeño*, whofe Men he had before difarm d and ftrip'd, was landed with more Forces, he durft not ftay in that Place, and therefore fail'd away to the Ifland of *Cubagua*, leaving the faid *Sedeño*, in Poffeffion of the Counry. He made an In-road feveral Legues from the Sea, in a very diforderly manner, permitting his Soldiers to commit all Sorts of Infolences, which fo far provoked the Natives, that drawing together, they engag'd him with much Refolution, but they being routed with a very great Slaughter, *Sedeño* enter'd their Town, where he found much Gold, and many Women and Children, whom he fent to *Cubagua*, where Avarice prevailing, the King's repeated Orders for the Liberty of the *Indians* were not regarded, and thofe People cruelly reduc'd to Slavery. The Tygers were fo flefh'd on the Carcaffes of the *Indians* flain in the Battel above mention'd, that their Numbers being very great, the *Spaniards* were not fafe, for they wou'd by Night, without making any Noife, break into the Huts where they lay, and carry Men off into the Woods, where they were devour'd in a Moment ; and there was no fecurity but by keeping Fires, and defending themfelves with long Spears, when thofe ravenous Creatures affaulted them.

To proceed, now we are upon the Coaft of *Santa Marta*, the Adelantado of the *Canaries* having provided all Things for carrying on the Difcoveries along *Rio Grande*, or the great River of the *Magdalen*, appointed *Gonzalo Ximenez de Quefada* to Command in that Expedition, and to march by Land with above fix hundred Foot, and an hundred Horfe. Several Veffels were alfo fitted out to fail up the fame River, but being difperfed in a Storm, fome of them arriv d at *Cartagena*, where the Men refitted themfelves, and

went

went away to *Peru.* The other Veffels that return'd
were fent up the River after *Ximenez,* who was marching along the left Bank of it, enduring incredible
Hardfhips, without any muttering among his Men,
becaufe he was a Man of fingular Difcretion to manage them, and Partaker in all their Labours and Dangers, never fparing himfelf. When he had held on
his way fome Months, and pafs d an hundred Leagues
farther than any of thofe that had been a Year from
Santa Marta, whilft he was refrefhing his Men in a
Town call d *Tora,* or *Pueblo de los Bracos,* that is,
the Town of the Arms or Branches, becaufe fo many Rivers meet there, being about an hundred and
fifty Leagues from the Sea, the Veffels fent up the
River join'd him, to the unfpeakable Satisfaction of
all the Men, who then concluded their Enterprize
would prove Succefsful, *Ximenez* affuring them that
it could not fail of being fo. The Winter coming on, he refolv'd to take up his Quarters in that
Place, and the more becaufe the River overflow'd, and
there was no travelling along it. He therefore fent the
Brigantins to difcover, which advanc'd twenty Leagues,
and return'd as they went out, all the Country being
fo mightily overflow'd, that they could fee nothing
but Water. Before they came to *Tora,* they perceiv'd
that all the Salt in thofe Parts was carry'd from the
Sea, and Coaft of *Santa Marta,* by way of Barter,
and went up above feventy Leagues, being fo dear that
only the prime *Indians* could afford to eat it. Beyond
that Part where the Salt of the Sea reach'd, there
was another Sort like Sugar-Loaves, and the higher
they went the more plentiful it grew, which fhew'd
that it was brought down the River, as the other fort
went up it, and thence there was Reafon to conclude
that there muft be a very populous Country higher, the
Trade of Salt being fo great, and the *Indians* told
the

the *Spaniards,* that the Merchants who brought it said, there was extraordinary Wealth where it was made.

Gonzalo Ximenez, and *George Federman* coming in Time to meet in the *New Kingdom of Granada,* it is unavoidable to intermix their Progress, and therefore it is here requisite to say something of what was done by the Lieutenant of the latter. That Lieutenant was *Nicholas Federman,* who being inform'd, that some Men belonging to the Province of *Santa Marta,* had enter'd that of *Venezuela,* and were in the Territory of the *Coronados* hasted thither, and found that they had done much Harm, which had caus'd the *Indians* to Revolt, and though a Party he sent against them, had disarm'd those Intruders and taken their Captain, he sent them all away freely to their own Government. He had Orders to settle a Colony at *Cabo de la Vela,* but did it not, because the Country about it is Champion, without Wood, dry and barren, having no River that falls into the Sea, the Natives feeding on Fish and Venison, their Bread made of a mild Sort of Seed, and there being no Mayz, their Beds consisting of Deers Skins laid on the Ground, and there was no Appearance of any other than Seed Pearl. *Federman* having two hundred Horse and Foot, set out in *June* 1535. towards *Rio Grande,* the Fame being spread Abroad that there was much Wealth in those Parts. In order to it he pass'd the Lake of *Maracaybo,* and enter'd upon the Vale of *Tucuyo,* which stretches from North to South a League and Half in length, and half a League in breadth, enclos'd with Mountains on all Sides, taking its Name from a River that runs by. That District being thought fit for building a Town, one was afterwards founded there by the licenciate *Carvajal,* being healthy, leading to many Mountains, and abounding in Provisions. It is fifty Leagues from the Sea, seventy from *Leon,* n the Province of *Caracas,* eleven from *New Segovia,*
fourteen

fourteen from *Portillo de Corrora,* and twenty from *Truxillo.* In all this Territory there were no Lords, or Caziques, they paid Tribute to none, and they only adher'd to the greateft Men, to get Meat and Drink ; in other Refpects they were like the reft of the maritime Provinces, convers'd with the Devil, had many Wives, without any regard to Proximity of Blood, and were much given to fmoaking Tobacco. There were continual Wars between thofe that fpoke different Languages, to carry off each others Wives and Children ; their Weapons the fame that have been often mention'd, the Men put their Genitals into a Gourd, the Women had fome a Clout, others a large Leaf of a Tree, and others nothing to cover thofe Parts. Now they have Sugar-Mills, fow Cotton, and moft Things of the Growth of *Spain,* are all cloath'd. There are many Lions and Tygers, and fuch a Multitude of Deer, that a *Spaniard* ranging about with Horfes, *Indians,* and Dogs, has been known to kill five hundred in two Months, in fome of which the Bezoar-Stone is found. There are Gold Mines, but not much regarded, for want of Men, the *Spaniards* breeding abundance of Kine, Sheep, and Horfes. *Federman* at this Time alfo difcover'd *Bariquizemeto,* near a River fo call'd, becaufe when difturb'd it is of an Afh-colour, where the City of *Segovia* was afterwards founded. When he had Winter'd at *Tucuyo,* he proceeded on his Difcovery on the 13th of *December,* defigning to cro's the Mountains, tho' contrary to the Orders receiv'd from *George Spire,* which were to follow him, and, tho' he met with many Difficulties, as well from the bad Ways, as the Oppofition of the *Indians,* he at length arriv'd in the *New Kingdom of Granada*

Gonzalo Ximenez, who was intent upon the fame Enterprize, lay long at *Tora,* as has been faid, fending out Parties to extricate himfelf from that Place, where he had been enclos'd by the overflowing of the River,

ver, and in the End one of those Commanders return'd with an Account that he had run twenty
five Leagues up another River, and found some
Habitations, tho' not many, Tokens of a Road to the
Mountains, and a little Salt among the *Indians.* Upon this Advice *Ximenez* went himself, with most of
the Men, but he falling sick at the Place where the
other had been before, two Captains advanc'd with
twenty five Men, march'd twenty five Leagues over
woody Mountains, and came into a Plain Country
in which were great Towns, and good Tokens of
Plenty. *Ximenez* upon this Information, having brought
away all that had been left at *Tora,* set out with such
as were best able, their Number being much decreas'd
through the Hardships they had endur'd. Thus he
cross'd those vast and rugged Mountains, call'd of
Opon, fifty Leagues over, and though late, came into
the Plain, with only an hundred and seventy Horse
and Foot, and finding those great Loaves of Salt, before
spoken of, he enquir'd where it was made, and the
Indians admiring to see those strange Men, show'd him
a Salt-Water, from which they had it. Here he had
good Store of Provisions in Exchange for Hawksbels,
Sizers, and other Baubles, which made him stay the
longer, to recover his Men, for there was much *Indian*
Wheat, Venison, and excellent Fruit. This Plenty,
the good Buildings and Multitude of People being
Proofs that the Country was good, he advanc'd one
Days March farther, near to a Province subject to a
great Lord, whose name was *Bogota,* who having heard
of those strange People, was ready, with great Numbers of his Subjects to oppose the *Spaniards. Ximenez*
thinking it requisite to establish a Reputation in those
Parts, boldly charg'd that Multitude, who came on
with their usual Cries ; but as soon as they felt the
sharp Edges of the Swords, the Points of their Spears,
and the Force of the Horses, turn'd their Backs and
fled,

fled. This Lord *Bogota* was the greateſt in that Region, keeping many other great Men in ſuch ſubjection, that they rather fear'd than lov'd him, and the *Indians* ſaid, he had an Houſe of Gold, with a large Quantity of Emerauds ; but they perceiving the *Spaniards* much coveted that Metal, always magnify'd the Wealth, though it was really great in it ſelf. At this Time *Bogota* had finiſh'd a Town, the Houſes whereof were well built, encloſ'd with Bundles of Reeds, in very comly Order, and a Palace for himſelf, which was a ſufficient Specimen of his Grandeur, for it had ten or twelve Gates and Poſterns, with ſeveral Returns of Wall at each of them, and about it were two Encloſures at a conſiderable diſtance from each other.

THE *Spaniards* being Quarter'd in this Town found Proviſion enough, and many Sides, and large Pieces of Veniſon, dry'd with Salt. The next Day twelve *Indians* came, wrap'd up in black Mantles, with black Caps on their Heads, bringing Veniſon from the Lord, and a little Gold, ſaying, they were come to celebrate the Obſequies of thoſe that had been kill'd in the late Engagement. Then retiring into a Place of Worſhip, they ſung about two Hours and an Half, in a doleful Tune, the *Spaniards* being intirely Ignorant of what they ſaid, becauſe their Interpreters did not underſtand that Language. By them *Ximenez* ſent to adviſe the Lord to be his Friend, otherwiſe he would burn his Town, yet he did not comply. From thence he march'd to *Chia*, the uſual Reſidence of *Bogota*'s eldeſt Son, which he found abandon'd, however, ſome *Indians* came and brought Proviſions and Mantles, which was ſuppos'd to be done out of Curioſity, for the Lord put ſome of thoſe he could take, to Death, others he baſtinado'd, and others having torn their Mantles, and hung them about their Necks, which among them is a great Diſgrace, he turn'd out, bidding them

go

go to the new Men to revenge them, as they did, and *Ximenez* commanded Captain *Cardoſo* to take Guides that knew the Country, and repair with them to a Place, where abundance of Natives were, who had abandon'd their Dwellings, and ſurprize them at break of Day, which was perform'd ſo effectually, that he took about three hundred Men, Women and Children, and carry'd them to the Camp, where they prov'd of much Uſe, the *Spaniards* having none before to ſerve them ; beſides, ſome were ſent to adviſe *Chia* to appear, and be peaceable ; but neither he nor *Bogota* would comply, for which Reaſon it was reſolv'd to ſurprize them in the Morning ; and as they were upon their march a Cazique call'd *Subauſaque,* met them, with a Preſent of Fleſh and other Things, and then went away ; ever after ſending Proviſions to the Forces, tho' he durſt not appear abroad, for fear of *Bogota,* who was reputed to be very Cruel ; however, he was afterwards the beſt Friend the *Spaniards* had, who in all thoſe Towns found Gold and Emerauds.

CHAP. IV.

The Progreſs of Gonzalo Ximenez *in the New Kingdom* of Granada ; *he* Belalcazar *and* Federman *meet there unexpectedly* ; *they go down* Rio Grande, *and thence into* Spain ; Account of that Diſcovery.

CHia and *Bogota* refuſing any Accommodation with the *Spaniards,* as has been ſaid, *Ximenez,* reſolv'd to loſe no more Time ; but ſent the Captains *Ceſpedes* and St. *Martin,* with fifty Horſe and Foot, to ſeize the latter who the ſpies ſaid was three Leagues off. Theſe Commanders, tho' they us'd their utmoſt Diligence,

could

could not find him, and return'd with about two hundred Men and Women they took in another Town.
Notwithftanding that *Indians* came in daily, bringing
Gold, Emerauds, and Provifions to Barter with
the *Spaniards*, thefe were continually upon their guard,
becaufe the others had in the Night fet fire to fome of
their Quarters, and the Houfes being all thatch'd, if
they had not been very watchful, they might all have
perifh'd. *Ximenez* being far advanc'd into *Bogota's*
Country, order'd the Captains *Cefpedes* and St. *Martin*,
with thirty Men each, to march on feveral Ways to
fee what was beyond it; who returning faid, They
had fallen into a Nation, call'd *Panches*, which encompafs'd móft of *Bogota's* Lands, being parted by only
a little woody Mountain, tho' they us'd different
Weapons, and were continually at War. By this
Time the Interpreters began to underftand one another
better, and the *Indians* perceiving that the *Spaniards* were
fond of Gold and Emerauds, carry'd them greater
Quantities of both, and offer'd to fhew the Place
where thofe Stones were found, to the end that the
love of them might draw thofe People out of their
Country. *Ximenez* underftanding which way the
Country of the Emerauds lay, remov'd to the Vale
that was afterwards call'd *De la Trompeta*, and thence
fent Captain *Valenzuela*, with a good Party, to view
what the *Indians* talk'd of, which he did, and with
much Admiration found the Mine, about fifteen Leagues
from the Vale *De la Trompeta*, on an high and bare
Mountain, being a League in Circumference, and in
the Earth there were Veins of a fort of clammy Clay,
of a sky Colour, within which are the Emerauds, as
perfectly Octogonal, that Lapidaries could not make
them more Exact. They come out whitifh and
greenifh, and by Degrees turn to their natural Colour. Some are found in Clufters together, and o-
thers fingle. *Samaduco* was Lord of that Diftrict,

I   and

and others as well as his Subjects dig'd thofe Emerauds, at certain Seafons of the Year, when they offer'd great Sacrifices, bartering them away for Gold, Cotton Cloth, and a fort of Beads, much valu'd among them ; and tho' thefe Emerauds are very fine, thofe found in the Country about *Puerto Viejo,* have been more valu'd.

WHILST the *Spaniards* lay in the Vale *De la Trompeta,* feveral Parties going abroad, return'd with *Indians,* and among them Captain *Cardofo* brought two, who offer'd to fhew where the Lord *Tunja* lay, being a Man of great Fame, and particularly for his Wealth. *Cardofo* went in queft of him, and the *Indians* carry'd him about fourteen Days to perform one Days Journey, which was thought to be done to prevent *Tunja*'s receiving any Intelligence. Being come about Sun fetting to the Place where he was, they on a fudden befet his Houfe, took him, and fearching about, found a great Quantity of Gold, Emerauds, Cloth, and Beads, wherein his Treafure confifted. The Night was not fpent in idlenefs, the *Indians* labouring on all Sides to refcue their Lord, and the *Spaniards* maintaining their Ground ; but when Day appear'd, and the *Indians* faw the Number of their dead and wounded, they drew off, yet return'd again before Noon in great Numbers, and with much Fury gave the onfet, which prov'd as unfuccefsful as the former. The *Spaniards* amaz'd at the mighty Wealth they had found, tho' not fatisfy'd, offer'd *Tunja* his Liberty and their Friendfhip, if he would give them the reft of the Treafure he was faid to have hid, which he promis'd to do, but it never came to Hand. Captain *Valenzuela* having reported, that from the Top of the Emeraud Mountain he had feen vaft Plains, which extended as far as the Sight could reach, *Ximenez* went himfelf to view the Emeraud Mines, and order'd Captain St. *Martin* to go down into thofe Plains, faid to be defert, which tho' he endeavour'd,

vour'd, he could not perform, by reaſon of the
Thickneſs of the Woods, and the many Rivers, and
other Obſtacles he met with, which oblig'd him to
return to *Ximenez,* taking *Tunja* along with him, who
was not look'd upon to be ſo unpoliſh'd as *Bogota,*
and had many Towns under him, where they valu'd
themſelves upon their Gold and Emerauds, uſing their
Riches in their Funerals. The Interpreters growing
daily more expert, better Information was gain'd concerning the Country, ſo that a few Days after Intimation was given of two other Caziques, *Sagamoſo*
and *Duitama,* who were three Days Journey from them.
Ximenez march'd thither himſelf, but miſs'd of *Sagamoſo,*
who had withdrawn himſelf, and was in Arms, having
been acquainted that the *paniards* were coming. *Ximenez* having been diſappointed of *Sagamoſo,* return'd thro'
the Territory of *Duitama,* where in ſome Places of
Worſhip he found the Value of forty thouſand
Pieces of Eight in Gold, beſides Emerauds, and ſome
Part of the Gold was made into Crowns, Eagles, and
other Creatures. *Duitama,* with his Men ſeveral
Times furiouſly attack'd the *Spaniards,* but at length
retir'd with loſs to a ſtrong Poſt, where *Ximenez* not
thinking fit to moleſt him, return'd to *Tunja,* weigh'd
all the Gold and found 191294 Pieces of Eight in
fine Gold, and of the low 37283, beſides 1815 E-
merauds great and ſmall. A powerful Lord, neighbouring upon *Tunja,* who valu'd himſelf upon his
Bravery, threatned the *Spaniards,* and ſent to bid them
depart the Country, or elſe he would kill them, and
make Shields of their Horſes Skins, and Beads for his
Women of their Teeth, and accordingly when they
leaſt expected it, he came upon them with a Multitude of Men, arm'd with Pikes made of very hard
Wood, thirty Spans long, Swords of the ſame, Darts,
and Slings, and they advanc'd in ſuch good Order,
that had they not halted in a Plain, for want of con-

VOL. V.   G   ſidering

fidering the Harm the Horfes would do them, they
might have brought the *Spaniards* into jeopardy. The
Fight lafted long, thofe *Indians* omitting nothing that
became bold Men, but were at length oblig'd to give
way, by reafon of the great Havock the Horfemen
made among them.

Ximenez being inform'd that the Lord *Bogota* was
withdrawn to one of his Country-Houfes, and judging it abfolutely neceffary to fecure fo great a Man when
he had been perfectly acquainted with all Particulars relating to that Place, attack d it at Break of Day, yet
not fo fecretly but that the *Indians* had time to Arm and
ftand upon their guard, *Bogota* himfelf being among
them, who, being fenfib e of his danger, flipp'd out
the way that was leaft obferv d, two Soldiers who
knew him not, letting him pafs, to take away a rich
Mantle he had on, tho' he was ftruck with a Sword,
and fo bleeding he got into the Wood unobferv'd.
The *Indians* making diligent Search for him, perceiv'd
that thofe great Fowls they call *Auras*, which eat all
forts of Carion, made toward the Wood, and guef-
fing at the meaning of it, follow'd them, and found
Bogota dead, which was not known to the *Spaniards*
then As foon as he was dead, another Cazique call'd
Sagipa, poffefs'd himfelf of all the Dominion, on whom
Ximenez prevail'd to embrace his Friendfhip, upon
Condition, that he fhould affift him in his Wars a-
gainft the beaftly *Panches*, who were Man-eaters, which
was done, tho' thefe *Panches* came out in great Numbers to oppofe them ; they burnt two of their Towns,
killing many of them, which was very pleafing to *Sagipa*, and yet when return'd from the War, he kept
himfelf at a diftance, whereupon *Ximenez* fent for
him, and tho' with an ill Will, he came. *Ximenez*
told him, he knew *Bogota* had been an utter Enemy
to the *Spaniards*, and fince he had feiz'd all his Treafure he fhould give it him, and he would demand
nothing of what was his own. He demanded time,

2   and

and having produc'd only four thousand Pieces of
Light, the Men compell'd *Ximenez* to put him on
the Rack, to discover the rest, which was done so
inhumanly, that he dy'd without answering their Ex-
pectation.

At the same Time that these Discoveries were
made by *Ximenez, Federman* was carrying on his from
Venezuela and *Belalcazar,* from *Quito,* all of them directing their Course by several Ways, to the same
Place. In all this while the Adelantado of the *Canaries,* who had sent *Ximenez* upon the Expedition, had
heard no News of him, nor sent him any Supplies,
concluding he had perish'd, with all the Men, and
in this Perplexity he dy'd ; and the licenciate *Gallegos,* who had been left with the Vessels at *Rio Grande,* being much distress'd, return'd to *Santa Marta.*
Ximenez having in vain attempted to find a Passage
over the Mountains to the vast Plains he had been
told of, took a great Compass through the Country
of the *Panches,* reducing some of them by fair Means,
and others by foul, when being well pleas'd with the
Country he had discover'd, he call'd it the *New
Kingdom of Granada,* containing the Dominions of *Bogota* and *Tunja,* because he was a Native of the
City of *Granada* in pain , and then apply'd himself to found a City in the Province of *Bogota* ,
calling it *Santa Fe,* or St. Faith. Being thus
employ'd, and having divided the Lands, he resolv'd
to come himself into pain to give the King an Account
of his Discoveries, and the great Kingdom he had
subdu'd. In order to it he found out a new Way
to *Rio Grande,* through the Country of the *Panches,*
to avoid repassing the Mountains of *Opun,* which
would have been an intollerable Fatigue. Whilst he
was preparing to return, he sent his Brother *Ferdinand*
to take a view of the snowy Mountains, where he
had been told there was People serv'd in Gold and
Silver. *Ferdinand* having march'd six Days, was told

G 2

by

by some *Indians*, that there were Christians, both
Horse and Foot on the other Side of the River, and
not being able to imagine from thence they could
come, he cross'd the River with some few Men, and
soon understood that they came from *Quito*, under
the Command of Captain *Belalcazar*, who being also
inform'd, that there were *Spaniards* on the farther Side
of the River, pass'd it with an hundred and thirty
Men, and understanding that they were settled at *Bogota* march'd thither. When he was within six Leagues
of that new Colony of *Santa Fe*, advice was brought
that another Party of *Spaniards* had been seen towards
Pasca, which is to the Eastward, on the great Plains
that could not be come at and that they had many
Horses. Some Persons were sent to enquire who they
were, and brought word, that they came from *Venezuela*, under the Command of *Nicholas Federman*, who
directing his Course towards *Pana* through vast Plains,
struck to the Southward towards some great Mountains, and crossing very large Deserts, turn'd again
to the Northward, and fell into *Pasca*, where hearing
that there were Christians in the Country, he hasted
to refresh his Men, who were very much fatigu'd
and spent, for which he found good Conveniency
there, having only an hundred and fifty Men left of
those he brought from the Province of *Venezuela*.
These three Parties were now within six Leagues one
of another, and it was fear'd that they might fall at
variance about the Possession of the Country, each
of them claiming a right to it; but *Gonzalo Ximenez* discreetly reconcil'd those Matters, giving *Federman* a good Quantity of Gold, and a Tract of Land,
and offering to refer all farther Pretensions to the King,
if he would go with him into *Spain*; and *Belalcazar*
readily came into the same Measures, as desiring not
to return to *Quito* without the King's Commission.
Having concerted that the Men who came from *Venezuela* should remain in that new Kingdom, and that
half

half of thofe who came with *Belalcazar*, fhould go
back eighty Leagues to fettle a Colony in the Vale
of *Neiva.* The Commanders began to prepare for their
Voyage into *Spain*, and to build Brigant.nes to carry
them down the River, no one of them to fubmit to
the other, and each of them hoping to obtain his
Pretenfions at the Court. *Ximenez* having now four
hundred Foot, and fifteen hundred Horfe, refolv'd to
build two other Towns, for the better fecurity of
the Kingdom ; the one at *Tunja*, under that fame
Denomination, twenty two Leagues from *Bogota*, the
other at *Velez*, fomewhat above thirty Leagues from
Santa Fe, and twelve from *Tunja*, being the Entrance
into the new Kingdom, the way he went. All Things
being concerted and adjufted, and two Brigantins finifh'd, the three Commanders, with about thirty o-
ther Perfons fail'd down *Rio Grande*, and from thence
to *Cartagena*, where they got a Paffage into *Spain*, to
follicite their Affairs, and there we will leave them to
give a fhort Defcription of this Difcovery.

THIS *New Kingdom of Granada*, which Commen-
ces beyond the Mountains of *Opon*, is all a Champion,
with great Numbers of People, inhabiting diftinct
Vales, and all encompafs'd by the *Indians* call d *Panches*, who were Man-eaters, but the Natives of this
Kingdom were not The Country of the *Panches* is
hot, the new Kingdom co'd, or at leaft very temperate, and as the others are call'd *Panches*, fo thofe of
Bogota and *Tunja*, bear the Name of *Moxcas.* The
length of this Kingdom is about an hundred and thirty
Leagues,the greateft breadth thirty,and in fome Parts under
twenty ; the Latitude moftly in 3, 4, and 5 Degrees
Northward, divided into two Provinces call'd *Bogota*
and *Tunja*, which were the Names of their Sovereigns,
both of them Powerful, but *Bogota* the greateft, being able to bring fixty thoufand Men into the F.eld,
and the other forty thoufand. They were always at

variance

variance with their Neighbours the *Panches,* efpecially
thofe of *Bogota,* who'e Country is rich, but that of
Tunja much more in Gold and Emerauds. When
the *Spaniaras* firſt enter'd this Kingdom, the Natives
were in a great Conſternation, looking upon them as
the Children of the Sun and Moon, whom they a-
dor'd, ſaying, they ingender'd like Man and Woman,
and had ſent thoſe their Children from Heaven to puniſh them for their Sins, and therefore they call'd the
Spaniards Uchies, a Name compounded of *Uſa,* ſignifying the Sun, and *Chia* the Moon. Thus they
were wont to fly up to the higheſt Mountains, caſting down from thence their ſucking Babes for them to
devour, bel'eving by that means they ſhould appeaſe
the Wrath of Heaven, but above all they dreaded the
Horſes. Afterwards converſing with the *Spaniards,*
they began to be leſs afraid, and perceiving they were
Men like themſelves, reſolv'd to make trial of them,
whereupon enſu'd ſeveral Engagements with the *Bogotas,*
the *Tunjas,* and the *Panches,* till finding no Remedy
they ſubmitted ; tho' there was more Difficulty in
ſubduing the laſt of them, as being fierce, and their
Country rugged, where the Horſes could do leaſt Service. The People gave hideous Cries when they
fought, caſting Darts out of Slings above their Heads,
their Wooden Swords two handed, their Spears very
long, with ſharp Points, harden'd at the Fire. It was
their Cuſtom to carry with them to Battel the dead
Bodies of their braveſt Men, to ſerve for an Example to others, certain Men appointed for that Purpoſe
bearing them, all their Bodies daub'd with a ſort of Bitu-
men that never came off. The *Panches* went ſtark
Naked, except their Privities, uſing Bows, beſides
the other Weapons above mention'd, and large Bucklers, cover'd with Skins of Beaſts that defended the
whole Body from Head to Foot, and in the hollow
of the Lining all the Weapons mention'd, which
they

they take out to fight, and hang the Buckler a^t their Back, for it is light, and sometimes it hangs before to cover them. They fight silently, and always treat of Peace by means of the Women.

A L the People of this Kingdom are well shap'd, the Women have good Faces, not so tawny, or ill Featur'd as others in those Parts ; they wore black, white, or colour'd Mantles girt about their Bodies, reaching from their Breasts to their Feet, and others over their Shoulders , instead of Cloaks ; on their Heads Garlands of Roses and other Flowers, made of Cotton of several Colours. Some prime Women had Cotton Caps, all their Cloathing being of the same, and some of them Net Coifs. The Cold is not prejudicial, yet fire is agreable, which Temperature lasts all the Year ; for tho' there is a Summer, when the Earth is dry, the difference between it and Winter is not great. The length of the Day and Nights is equal, as being so near the Equinoctial ; the Country the healthiest in the World ; the Houses are of Timber, thatch'd, and those of the great Men built after a strange Manner, like Castles with several Inclosures about them, like a Labyrinth, having large Courts, with Mouldings and Painting. They eat *Indian* Wheat, Yuca, Pignuts, which they call *Yomas,* and Turneps, call'd *Cubias,* which they dress with Meat, and reckon them very Nourishing. They make a vast Quantity of Salt, and drive a Trade with it into several Parts, especially over the Mountains of *Opon,* to *Rio Grande.* The Flesh they had was Venison in great Plenty, and *Fricos,* like Rabbits at *Santa Marta,* call'd *Curies,* of which there are infinite Numbers. Birds are not so numerous, some Turtle Doves, and Ducks in the Lakes, in which and the Rivers they take excellent Fish.

I N Point of Morality these *Indians* were rational enough, punishing Crimes, and particularly Murder,

G 4   Theft,

Theft, and Sodomy, from which they are clear, and
there are many Gibbets along the Roads. They us'd
to cut off Hands, Nofes, or Ears, for other fmaller
Offences, and there were Penalties of Difhonour from
the greateft Men, as tearing their Garments, and cut-
ing off their Hair. The Subjects pay great Veneration to their Lords, never looking them in the Face,
tho' they difcourfe with them familiarly, and they
come into the Place where the Lord is, backwards.
In their Marriages they utter'd no Words, nor perform'd no Ceremonies, but only took the Woman and
carry'd her Home, having as many Wives as they could
keep, and the Lord *Bogota* had above four hundred.
Matrimony was prohibited within the firft Degree of
Confanguinity, and in fome Places within the fecond.
The Sons did not inherit, but the Brothers, and if
there were none living, the Sons of thofe that were
dead. Their Time was regularly divided into Months
and Years. The firft ten Days of the Month they
fed on an Herb, call'd *Hayo* on the Sea Coaft, which
is very Nourifhing and Purging; the next ten they
till'd their Grounds, and minded other Affairs, and
the laft ten they fpent in their Houfes among their
Wives, not living in the fame Appartment with them,
but the Man in one, and they all in another. They
kept thofe who were to be Rulers or Commanders, whether Men or Women, lock'd up for feveral Years,
when they were Children, fome of them feven Years,
and this fo clofe, that they were not to fee the Sun, for
if they fhould happen to fee it, they forfeited the
Lordfhip, eating certain Sorts of Food appointed, and
thofe who were their Keepers at certain Times went into
the Retreat, or Prifon, and fcourg'd them feverely.
When this Penance was over, they bor'd their Ears and
Nofes to wear Gold in, which was a great Honour,
they alfo wore Plates of it on their Breafts, Caps like
Miters on their Heads, and Bracelets on their Arms.
They

They were generally extraordinary fond of finging and dancing and have an indifferent talent for mechanick arts.

As to Religion they were very obfervant of it, and befides the Temples in the Towns, had others abroad in the Country, and abundance of little Chapels or Hermitages on the Roads, and in Woods, with much Gold and Emerauds in them all. They there offer'd Sacrifice with Blood, Water, and Fire, kill'd many Birds, fhedding the Blood about the Temples, and hanging them up, fprinkling the Place with Water, which was alfo a Sacrifice, and threw Sweets into the Fire. They had particular Prayers for all Occafions, which they fung, but did not Sacrifice human Blood, unlefs fome Boy were taken in War, whom they kill'd in the Temple with loud Cries. The Priefts were Children they bought thirty Leagues from thence in the Province of the *Mojas*, at the Houfe of the Sun, who the *Indians* thought did difcourfe with the Sun, held them in great Veneration, making very much of them, till they were grown Men, when they kill'd them and offer'd their Blood in Sacrifice. But if any one of them had happen d to touch a Woman, he was free from being Sacrific'd, alledging that their Blood was not pure enough for that ufe, nor a Propitiation for Sin. A Month before going to War, they fung Day and Night, except whilft they went to eat, praying to the Sun, the Moon, and other Idols, for victory, repeating the Caufes that indu 'd them to War, and if they return'd Victorious, thanks were return'd in the fame manner during fome Days; but if defeated, they fpent as much Time bewailing their Misfortune. They had Confecrated Woods and Lakes, where they Sacrific'd and were not to fell any Tree, nor take Water, but bury'd Gold and Jewels in thofe Woods, or caft it into the Lakes, as an offering, and never after touch'd it. The Sun and Moon were look'd upon

the

the univerfal Creators, befides which, there was a Multitude of Idols to intercede with the Sun and Moon, and the Temples were dedicated to thofe Idols. There were alfo Idols of Gold in the Houfes, and thofe who could not attain to it, had them of Wood, putting what Gold or Emerauds they could get into the Hollow of the Belly; being about half a yard in length, and fo great was their Devotion, that whitherfoever they went, the Idol was carry'd, holding it with one Arm and fighting with the other in their Battles; but thofe of *Tunja* were the moft religious of all. The dead were bury'd very tight bound up, firft taking out their Entrails, and putting Gold and Jewels into the Belly, with others about their Bodies, fhrouded with their fineft Mantles, and fo carry'd them to Chappels appointed for that Purpofe, where they were left for ever, from which Bodies the *Spaniards* at firft got much Treafure. Others were caft in deep Lakes, with Coffins, and Gold and Jewels in them. They had fome confufe Notion of the Immortality of the Soul, faying, that thofe who had been good here, afterwards enjoy d much reft, and the wicked endur'd much, being often fcourg'd. Thofe that dy'd for their Country, tho' they had been wicked, were thought to have Repofe among the Virtuous, and therefore Men dying in War, and Women in Child-bed went directly into Blifs, for their good Will to the Publick.

LITTLE can be faid of the Morality of the *Panches,* as being a Nation fo brutifh, that they worfhipp'd nor regarded nothing but their Pleafure and Vices, nor valu'd any thing but Eating and Diverfion efpecially if they could get human Flefh, and to that Purpofe alone they made Inroads into the Kingdom. Moft Part of this Country is fruitful, tho' there is fome Barren, for in conquering a Province on the Frontiers of the *Tunjas,* the Inhabitants were found to feed

feed on Pifmires, whereof there was Plenty, and being bak'd, they ferv'd inftead of Bread, fome being large, fome fmall, and kept in Yards, where they bred. This noble Kingdom was difcover'd, and the three Cities aforefaid founded in it, by the Licenciate *Gonzalo Ximenez de Quefada*, who fhew'd himfelf very difcreet both in War and Peace, for which his Name deferves to be honour'd He was born at *Granada*, and Son to the Licenciate *Ximenez*, and the Lady *Elizabeth de Quefada*. The conqueft was carry'd on in the Years 1536, 1537, 1538, and 1539.

C H A P. V.

The ftrange Adventures of fome Spaniards *left in* Florida, *after the unfortunate Expedition of* Panfilo de Narvaez, *with many Particulars of that Country.*

IT is now Time to give an Account of what became of the fmall Remnant of the Men *Panphilo de Narvaes* unfortunately carry'd into *Florida*, in the Year 1526, where moft of them perifh'd, only fome few being left in the Ifland of *Malhado*, or Ill-Luck, fo call'd for the Miferies they there endur'd. Thofe few *Spaniards* having efcap'd being deftroy'd by the *Indians*, who look'd upon them as the Caufe of a general Diftemper in the Stomach, that then prevail'd among them, and being perfwaded, that as there were fome among themfelves that pretended to work Cures by blowing and ftroaking the Parts affected, thofe Strangers might do the fame, they thereupon oblig'd them by Threats to practice that way of Healing, an *Indian* alledging, that fince there was a Virtue in Stones, there muft of neceffity be more in Men, and perhaps this was a particular Providence. The *Spani-*
ards

ards being thus compell'd to it began to practife upon their Patients, bleffing them in the Name of the Father, the Son, and the Holy Ghoft, breathing on them, and faying the Lord's Prayer, and the *Ave Mary*, begging of God to heal the Patient, and to infpire thofe Barbarians to ufe them well, whilft they continu'd there. It pleas'd the Divine Goodnefs, that all the People on whom they made the Sign of the Crofs, as has been faid, recover'd, for which Reafon they gave them Part of what they had, tho' both *Indians* and *Spaniards* were in great Want, which oblig'd them to part, that they might fubfift the better; but coming again together, fome Months after, they were fourteen in Number, and *Cabeza de Vaca*, being alone with his *Indians*, twelve of them repair'd to him, the two others not being able, becaufe of their great Weaknefs; and by the way thofe twelve met one more, and fo proceeded farther, becaufe *Cabeza de Vaca* did not come out to meet them. He did not follow them, as was faid, becaufe he was then fick, tho' it was not fufpected, that he imagin'd fo many together could not do well, and therefore he went away to the *Charruco Indians*, where he was in a better Condition, for he play'd the Doctor, and turn'd Merchant, and they wanting many of thofe Things which he brought them, by reafon of the War, he was well entertain'd and travell'd many Leagues up the Inland, and along the Coaft with his Commodities, being Sea-Snails, Shels much us'd among them, and other fuch Things, in Exchange for which he carry'd Deer Skins, Vermillion to paint their Faces and Hair, Flints to point their Arrows, Reeds to make them of, a fort of Glew, and Tufts of Deers Hair, dy'd red. *Cabeza de Vaca* lik'd this way of living, becaufe he was well entertain'd, and always travell'd Southward, to gain Ground, and get out of that Country, and enjoy'd his Liberty, tho' naked and
alone,

alone, enduring much Hunger and Cold, for the Space of fix Years he was there, having ftay'd fo long to bring away his two Comrades, *Oviedo* and *Alanis* who had been left in the Ifland ; but the latter of them dy'd, and the other detain'd him, fay- ing, they would depart in the Spring, which kept him, till at laft they fet out. Being come to a Creek that is a League over ; and by them fuppos'd to be the fame which they call Del *Efpiritu Santo,* or of the Holy Ghoft, they were inform d by fome *Indians,* that farther on they would find three Men like them- felves, whofe Names they told, as alfo that the *Indi- ans* before them had kill'd *Orantes, Valdiviefo,* and *Hu- elva,* for having remov'd from one Houfe to another ; and other *Indians* where *Orantes* was, had kill'd *Ef- quibel* and *Mendez* on Account of a Dream they had as they were wont to do by their own Sons, and to caft fome of their Daughters to the Dogs, as foon as born ; they added, that the living were very ill us'd, the Boys, who were very unlucky, beating, kicking, and fcoffing at them. At the fame Time they threw much Dirt at thofe two *Spaniards,* and cudgell'd them, for which Reafon *Oviedo* went back with fome *Indian* Men and Women, that had bore them Company, and *Cabeza de Vaca* ftay d there, and they two never met again.

T w o Days after what has been related, the *In- dians Orantes* was with, came to this Place to eat Nuts , on which they fed two Months in the Year, and fome Friends went to fee *Cabeza de Vaca,* who had been hid by his Favourers. It was a great Satisfaction to them to meet, and no lefs Trouble to fee themfelves naked amidft fo many Miferies, and having confulted together, they agreed to go farther on ; but firft to ftay fome Months till the Nuts being fpent the *Indians* remov'd to another Place, to eat *Tunas,* becaufe, if they thought they would go away, they would kill
them.

them. All the reft belonging to the Fleet above mention'd had perifh'd, fome fton'd to Death, and others
drown'd, which was the Fate of *Panfilo de Narvaez,*
as *Figueroa,* who was prefent, told *Cabeza de Vaca.*
Being among thofe *Indians* of the *Tunas,* they endur'd
Hunger, becaufe there were not enough for them all.
In that Country there were grey and black Cows,
with long Hair no bigger than thofe of *Barbary,* and
their Flefh coarfer than *Spanifh* Beef. When the
Time they had agreed on for making their Efcape was
come, the *Indians* had a Scuffle on Account of a
Woman, and parted, as thofe poor Chriftians were
forc'd to do, not being able to meet again till the
next Year, when they were again feparated by the *Indians* the very Day they were to have fled, and yet
they concerted to come together again the firft of
September, being the full Moon. The 13th the two
came, and *Orantes* the 14th, when they took their
Flight. Being come to the *Indians Avares,* they were
well receiv'd and Fed, thofe People being inform'd,
that they perform'd Cures. The fame Night three
Indians came, who were troubled with Pains in their
Heads, defiring *Caftillo* to cure them, and as foon as
blefs'd they were well, and carry'd him *Tunas* and
Venifon, reporting abroad the Cure that had been
made, whereupon many fuch Perfons came, bringing
fo much to eat, that they knew not what to do with
it, and the *Indians* for Joy of thofe Cures order'd a
Dance. The *Spaniards,* who had thought to have
proceeded further, being inform'd that the Country was
Defert, the *Tunas* being all eaten, and that it was
exceffive Cold, agreed to ftay and Winter among
thofe *Indians,* who went five Days Journey to feed on
a fort of Fruit, call'd *Yeros.* When they had fettled their Dwellings near a River, many *Indians* came
with five fick Perfons for *Caftillo* to cure them, he
blefs'd and all pray'd to God to heal them, fince that

was

was the only means for them to subsist, and the next Morning they were all in Health, to the great Astonishment of the *Indians*, for which those Christians return'd Thanks to God, confiding that he would deliver them out of that Misery.

THE *Spaniards* departed that Place and came to the *Indians* call'd *Maliconas, Susolas,* and *Atayos,* among whom their Cures were already known, so that many sick Persons were brought, but *Castillo* being a Man that fear'd God, despair'd of being able to do any good on Account of his unworthiness; which oblig'd *Cabeza de Vaca* to repair to a Place where many sick Persons were, one of them in a dangerous Condition, and took along with him *Orantes* and the Mulatto *Estevanillo.* They found the aforesaid sick Person almost dead, many lamenting him, the House pull'd down, which was a Sign of Death, his Eyes turn'd in his Head, and no Pulse. *Cabeza de Vaca* took off a Mat he had on him, and pray'd to God to restore him, and the rest that wanted it, to Health, and when he had been several Times bless'd and breath'd on, they carry'd him his Bow and presented it to him, with a Frail of *Tunas,* conducting him to cure others, and so those *Spaniards* return'd to their Quarters, being afterwards inform'd by the *Indians* their Friends, that the dying Man got up, spoke, and had eaten with them, and that all the rest were in perfect Health, which was so wonderful, that nothing else was talk'd of through all the Country, others coming to be heal'd and bringing Presents of their Provisions. According to the Account kept by the Moons, they stay'd eight Moons with those *Avares,* neither *Orantes* nor *Estevanillo* having yet perform'd any Cures, but they were so often importun'd to do it that they were forc'd to comply, being call'd the Children of the Sun. Being intent upon holding on their way, they fled one Days Journey from thence to the

Malicones,

Malicones, to feed among them on a fort of fmall
Fruit that lafted twelve Days, till the *Tunas* were
ripe, whither the *Arbadaos* that were fick reforted.
Having endur'd much Hunger there, they were directed to other *Indians* that fpoke the fame Language,
and to add to their Sufferings, they loft their way,
and it rain'd very much, which was no fmall Vexa-
tion to them that were ftark Naked. Refting that
Night in a great Wood, they roafted many *Tunas* to
feed on, and in the Morning going to feek out the
way they had loft, met with a Number of Women and Boys, who all ran away to call the Men, who
with much Admiration came to the *Spaniards* and
conducted them to a Village of fifty Houfes, where
they gaz'd on them with fear, and when fomewhat
recover'd from their Fright, touch'd their Faces and
Bodies, and then themfelves, after which the fick
were brought, and when cur'd, they freely forbore
eating, to give it to them, and were very forry that
they would go away. It was the Cuftom among all
the *Indians* from the Ifland of *Malbado* to this laft
Place not to lye with their Wives, from the Time
they appear'd to be with Child till two Years after
they were deliver'd, and to give fuck till twelve Years
of Age, which they faid was on Account of the great
want of Provifions, and they were fometimes three
Days without eating. If Man and Wife could not
agree it was ufual to part and take another, but not
if they had Children. None ever parted Men fighting but the Women, nor did they ufe the Bow in
private Quarrels, but only their Fifts or Cudgels. They
are all Martial Men, and as vigilant againft their Enemies as the beft in *Europe.* They dig Ditches, and
throw up Trenches, make Loop-holes, lay Ambufhes,
ufe extraordinary Stratagems, for the moft part killing
one another by furprize in the Night, being very cruel,
are ready upon any Alarm, watch their Opportuni-
ties

ties to take Revenge and make all Advantages of the
Failings of their Adverfaries. Their way of Pickeer-
ing is wonderful, skipping from one fide to another,
and fhoot ftooping to avoid being obferv'd.   There
is among them great Variety of Languages and Dwellings

T H E *Spaniards* coming to another Town, the Inhabitants carry'd their Children to touch their Hands,
giving them Meal made of a certain Fruit like Ga-
robs, that was eaten with Earth, and was fwe t and
agreeable, whereof they gave them fome Entertainments, with dancing. Depart ng thence, they arriv'd at a Town of an hundred Hou es after paffing a great River, with the Water up to their Brcafts,
the People advancing to meet them with Shouts,
clapping their Hands on their Thighs making a
fort of Mufick with hollow Gourds and Stones in
them, carrying them to their Houfes, without fuffering
their Feet to touch the Ground, abundance of People flocking to be blefs'd.   The next Day they he'd
on their Way, all the People bearing them Company ; and being come to other *Indians* found a good
Reception, had much Venifon brought them, and all
the fick that came to be cur'd went away found.
The fame happen'd among the next *Indians* they
came to, where there was fo much rejoicing, that
they could not fleep.   Another Cuftom they obferv d among thofe People, which was, that the *Indians* who went with the *Spaniards*, plunder'd the
Houfes where they came, and *Cabeza de Vaca* and his
Companions being much concern'd at it, thofe who
had loft their Goods comforted them, bidding them
not to be troubled, for they would farther on repay themfelves among others that were very rich.
Here they began to fee Mountains which they
thought ran from the North Sea, they made towards
them, and the *Indians* pillag d what they found,

VOL. V.   H   and

and when the Strangers were gone, the Natives prefented the *Spaniards* with what they had hid, being
Beads, Vermillion, and fome little Bags of Silver.
At this Place they agreed not to make towards the
Mounta'ns, becaufe they were near the Sea Coaft,
where the Peop'e are ill-natur'd, whereas up the Inland they are more courteous. Many Men and Women loaded with Water bore them Company, their
Authority being fo great, that none durft drink
without their leave. The *Spaniards* refufing to travel along the Mountains, the *Indians* turn'd back,
and they proceeded along a River and found two
Women, who gave them Meal of *Indian* Wheat,
and about Sun-fetting came to a Village of about
twenty Houfes, the Inhabitants lamenting, as knowing that the *Indians*, who came with them, would
plunder what they had ; but feeing them a'one,
they rejoyc'd. The next Morning when they were
about to depart, the *Indians* of the Town behind
them appear'd and pillag'd the Place, faying, that
thofe Strangers were the Children of the Sun, and
cur'd the fick, tho' they were able to deftroy them,
and therefore they fhould refpect them, and go a-
long to plunder the next Town, according to Cuftom. They travell'd three Days with thofe People, who conducted them to a Place of many Houfes,
fending fome before to give an Account of what
the others had faid of the *Spaniards*, adding much
more of their own Invention, being fond of Novelty, and addicted to lying, efpecially where any
Intereft is expected. The *Spaniards* were well receiv'd, the ftranger *Indians* plunder'd as much as they
could, and return'd. *Cabeza de Vaca* and his Companions advanc'd above fifty Leagues along the Side
of the Mountain, and in a Town of forty Houfes
found a large Copper Hawksbell, with a Face reprefented on it, very much valu'd, which thofe Peo-

I

ple faid they had of their Neighbours. Travelling feven Leagues over a Mountain, where the
Stones were Iron-Ore, at Night they came to fome
Houfes feated on the Bank of a River, where the
prime Men came out to receive the Spaniards with
their Children on their Backs, giving them little
Bags of fine Sand, and pounded Antimony, with
which they daub their Faces, as alfo Beads, and
Mantles of Neats-Leather. Their Food was *Tunas*
and Pine-Apple Kernels, better than thofe in *Spain*,
but fmall, as are the Trees.

I n this Place they brought *Cabeza de Vaca*, a Man
that had been wounded in the Side with an Arrow,
the Point whereof, he faid, reach'd to his Heart,
which put him to much Pain, and he was very fick.
Cabeza de Vaca with a Knife rip'd open his Breaft,
and though with much Difficulty, drew it out, and
ftich'd it up ; but the Blood running, he ftopp'd
it with the Scrapings of a Cow's Hide. The
Point of the Arrow, which was of a Deer's Bone,
was fent about all the Country, and there was much
dancing ; and the next Day he cut the Stitches, and
the Man was found, faying, he felt no Pain. This
Cure gain'd the *Spaniards* fo much Reputation, that
they could do what they pleas'd. Thofe People
fhow'd the Hawksbel, and faid there were many
Plates of that Metal bury'd in the Country from
whence they had it. From this Place they proceeded
through fo many Nations, that it is impoffible to
mention them all, and all the way they Plunder'd
one another, all being well fatisfy'd. The *Spaniards*
had always fo much Company, that they knew not
how to turn themfelves, and all the way they killed
Deer, Hares, Stock-doves, and other forts of Birds,
with their Arrows and Staves, which they prefented to the Chriftians, without touching them till
they begg'd leave. Sometimes there were above four
H 2   thou-

thousand Persons with them, which was very troublesome, because none would eat or drink till they
had bless d and breath'd upon it, and thus they travell'd above thirty Leagues, till they came to another sort of Reception without Plundering, tho' they
offer d all they had, and it was divided among those
that return'd Home, and those who went on attending the *paniards*, by that means recover'd what they
had presented of the others that were farther on.
They travell'd above fifty Leagues through desert
craggy Mountains, enduring much Hung r, till they
came into Plains, where they had a kind Reception,
and abundance of Goods were given to those that
were to return Home. The People farther on being their Enemies, they sent two Women to give
them Notice that the Christians were coming, it
being usual among them, tho' they be at War, for
the Women to Trade. No People coming out to
meet them, the *Spaniards* were for striking off to
the Northward ; but the Women said, there were
wicked People that way, and no Meat nor Water to
be had. The *Spaniards* being angry, they said, they
would go whithersoever they commanded, tho' they
were sure to perish, and many falling sick, eight Men
dy'd, which struck such a Consternation through
the Country, that they thought they should dye as
soon as they saw the *Spaniards.*

So great was the dread conceiv'd by those People, that they intreated the *Spaniards* not to be angry, imagining that they were the cause why the
Sick dy'd, whereupon *Cabeza de Vaca* and his Companions, apprehending that the Distemper would carry off too many, earneftly pray'd to God to put a
stop to it, and the Sick began to recover. Three
Days Journey from this Place they halted, and the
next Day *Orantes* and *Estevanillo*, guided by a Woman Slave, went to a Village where her Father liv'd,
and

and faw the firft Houfes that were any thing regularly built. Returning thence to *Cabeza de Vaca,* they acquainted him with it, and that thofe People did eat Kidney Beans, Pompions, and *Indian* Wheat. Being come to this Town, they di mifs'd the *Indians,* giving them what they had, and there began another Cuftom, for they came not out to meet the *Spaniards,* but expected them fitting in their Houfes, hanging down their Heads, their Hair before their Eyes and all their Goods laid in an Heap in the Middle of the Houfe, prefenting them with good Leather Mantles, and all they had. The People were wel fhap d and induftrious, eafi y to be underftood, and anfwering to the Purpo e, whom they call'd *De las Vacas,* or of the Cows, becaufe they ki l'd many up the River. The Women cover'd themfelves with Deer-Skins, as did the Men that were not fit for War, and ftaying there two Days, they got Information of the way they were to follow ; be ng told, that up a River to the Northward they would find many Cows to feed on, and to the Weftward there was Mayz. They agreed to hold on that way hoping it would lead them to what they defir'd, and crofs d the Country in thirty four Days Jouiney, till they came to the South Sea, having endur d much Hunger, paffing through a Nation that feeds on the Duft of Straw, one third Part of the Year, as they were forc d to do, being there at that Time. After the aforefaid Number of Days they came to fettled Houfes, where there was Plenty of Corn, Pompions, and Kidney Beans, and the People wore Cotton Mantles, thofe who had attended the *Spaniards* returned Home wel pleas'd, loaded with thofe Things. They travell d above an hundred Leagues through that Country, bleffing God for having brought them into a Country where there was fo much Store of Provifions,

H 3   for

for the Natives did eat much Venison and other
Game, and prefented the *Spaniards* with Mantles, Beads
of Coral, taken out of the South Sea, Turky Stones,
and four or five Points for Arrows made of Emerauds,
which they faid they had of another Nation in Exchange for Plumes and Feathers of feveral Colours.

In this Country the Women were more modeftly
clad than in others they had feen, were fhod, and
all in general, well or fick came to be blefs d, believing thofe Chriftians to be Men come from Heaven,
for which Reafon they had much Authority among
them, for they talk'd and eat little, and did not
fhow that they were tir'd, for to fay the truth they
were fufficiently try'd among fo many Nations, and
it pleafed God that all underftood them ; tho they
knew but fix Languages, which, if Providence had
not preferv'd them, would have been of little ufe,
where there was fuch great Variety of them. All
the way they travell'd thofe who were at War made
Peace, that they might have the Opportunity of
going to fee the Chriftians, and thus they left them
all in Amity, declaring every where, that they worfhipp'd one only God, who had created Heaven
and Earth, the Sun, Moon, and Stars, and all other
Things, from whom all Bleffings proceeded ; that
they ought to hurt no Body, nor take away the
Goods of others, with fuch like Inftructions, which
were well receiv'd. Thefe *Spaniards* believ'd that
the Country along the Coaft was well Peopled, and
abounded in Provifions, becaufe the Natives fow'd
Mayz and Kidney Beans thrice a Year, and in one
Town they found the People had Arrows poifon'd
with the Juice coming from a fort of Fruit, or of
the Tree that bears it. There they ftay'd three
Days, and in another a Days Journey farther, fifteen,
becaufe of the great Flood in the River, and there
Caftillo faw about an *Indian*'s Neck a Buckle belonging

ing to a Sword Belt, and an Horshoe ty'd to it.
Asking the *Indian* where he had them, he answer'd,
they came from Heaven, asking again, who had
brought them, he said some Bearded Men that
came from Heaven to that River, with Horses,
Spears, and Swords; and desiring to know where
those Men were, it was answer'd, that they were
gone to the Sea, where they and their Spears plung'd
under the Water, and afterwards, towards Sun-set,
they saw them above it again. They joyfully return'd Thanks to God for having heard some News
of Christians, and hasted on their Journey, to find
them the sooner, receiving better Information the
farther they went, telling the *Indians* that they were
going to bid those Men not to kill, or make Slaves
of, or do them any harm, at which they were much
rejoyc'd. They then pass'd through much Land
destitute of any Inhabitants, tho' it was fruitful
and agreeable, the *Indians* being fled to the Mountains for fear of the *Spaniards*, and at length came to
a Town on the Top of an Hill, whither abundance
of People were withdrawn, who presented them
with above two thousand Load of Corn, which
they gave to the poor, hungry People that had conducted them thither, and going on, many resorted to
them, and Tokens appear'd of the Places where *Spaniards* had lain. They return'd Thanks to God,
believing their miserable Captivity to be near an End,
and *Cabeza de Vaca* advancing with *Estevanillo* and
eleven *Indians*, overtook four *Spanish* Horsemen, who
were much surpriz'd to hear a Man in that strange
Garb, speak their Language. They gaz'd on him a
long Time, without asking any Questions or speaking a Word; he desir'd them to conduct him to
their Commander, as they did, and it was *James.
de Alcaraz*, who told *Cabeza de Vaca*, that they were
in *New Galicia*, and thirty Leagues from the Town

of

of St. *Michael*. *Caftillo* and *Orantes* then came with
above fix hundred of thofe that had fled on Account
of the War, who call'd others, and they came readily, returning peaceably to their Houfes, and fowing the Land. The four *Spaniards* having taken leave
of the *Indians*, and return'd Thanks for the Fatigue
they had undergone for their fake ; when they had
travell'd twenty five Leagues farther, arriv'd very
Hungry and Thirfty at *Culiacan*, where *Melchior
Diaz* was Captain and Alcalde of the Province, who
received them with fingular Humanity, giving Thanks
to God for having deliver'd them from fo long and
miferable a Captivity, praying them to appeafe the
Indians of that Country, who were in Arms, which
they undertook, fending other *Indians* to call them,
upon whofe Perfwafions three Caziques came with
about thirty *Indians*, bringing Prefents of Feathers and
Emerauds. *Cabeza de Vaca* asking them, in whom
they believed, they anfwer'd, in one they call'd *Aguar*, who they fuppos'd was Lord of all Things,
refiding in Heaven, and gave them Rain when they
pray'd for it, which they had learnt of their Fore Fathers. He told them, that *Aguar* was God the
Creator of Heaven and Earth, according to whofe
Will all Things were difpofed, and that after Death
he rewarded the Good and punifh'd the Wicked ;
that they fhould believe this, return to their Houfes,
live in Peace, build an Houfe to worfhip God as
the Chriftians did, and when any of them repair'd
to their Towns, they fhould come out to meet them
with Croffes in their Hands, and not with their
Bows and Arrows, and then they would be their good
Friends, ufe them well, and teach them all the reft
they ought to know, to the End that God might
reward them in the other Life, all which they promis'd to do.

THE

T HE four *Spaniards* then went on, with some few *Indians* towards the Town of St. *Michael,* the People by the way, who were peaceable, coming out in great Numbers to meet them, with Presents, whom they perswaded to become Christians, since they were Subjects to the Crown of *Spain,* they receiving them lovingly, and praying that their Children might be Baptiz'd. A few Leagues from thence they were overtaken by *Alcaraz,* above mention'd, who said, that all the Country they had found Desert, was then well peopled and peaceable, and the *Indians* going to sow their Lands. These Christians judg'd that the distance from Sea to Sea, where they had crofs'd might be about two hundred Leagues, as they declar'd in the Town of St. *Michael,* where they made Oath of the Truth of all that has been here related, before a Notary, on the 15th of ay, this Year 1536, and having rested there fifteen Days in order to proceed an hundred Leagues to the City of *Compostela,* where *Nuño de Guzman* then was, he there receiv'd them kindly, and cloathed them, in order to go on to *Mexico,* where they arriv'd on the 22d of *July,* and found all courteous Entertainment from the Vice-Roy Don *Antonio de Mendoa.* At *Mexico, Cabeza de Vaca* and *Orantes* parted from *Castillo,* and *Estevanillo* went away to *Vera Cruz,* whence they pass'd over into *Spain,* the following Year 1537. Of *Cabeza de Vaca,* we shall have more Occasion to speak hereafter.

T H E

THE
General HISTORY

Of the vaſt CONTINENT and ISLANDS of

AMERICA, &c.

DECAD. IV. BOOK IV.

CHAP. I.

A Word concerning the Provinces of Honduras *and* New Galicia; *the Adelantado* Almagro *returns from* Chile *to* Cuzco.

T H E *Spaniards* that had been left at *Honduras* by *Andrew de Cerezeda,* being reduc'd to the utmoſt Miſery, ſent to intreat the famous *Peter de Alvarado,* who had gain d ſo much Renown under *Cortes* in the Conqueſt of *Mexico,* and was then Governour of the Province of *Guatimala,* to come to their Relief, which he did, with all poſſible Expedition; and coming to

Naco,

Naco, was receiv'd with much Joy, and the Government refign'd into his Hands, after which he founded the Town of *Gracias a Dios,* or Thanks be to God, fo call'd, becaufe the Men having endur'd much in Travelling over barren Mountains, when they came into that Plain, faid, Thanks be to God that we are come into a good Country. This prov'd a good Situation, for foon after feveral rich Gold Mines were found, within four or five Leagues of it, which drew abundance of People, and the Colony throve. *Alvarado* founded another Colony at Port Cavallos, and having brought all Things into good Order, fail'd away into *Spain.* Soon after he was gone, *Francis de Montejo,* who had been oblig'd to quit *Yucatan,* as has been faid in its Place, having receiv'd the King's Commiffion to that Effect, went and took upon him the Government of *Honduras,* which *Alvarado* had with fo much Trouble and Expence fet upon a good Foot, when that Province was upon the Point of being loft.

At the fame Time a Judge was fent to try *Nuño de Guzman,* Governour of *New Galicia* for the many and heinous Crimes laid to his Charge, and tho' that Judge fent him Prifoner to *Mexico,* whence he was convey'd into *Spain,* he there found Favour enough to get off, without any Satisfaction made for the Wrongs he had done. Orders were now fent to Don *Antonio de Mendoza,* Vice-Roy of *Mexico,* to ufe all poffible Means for the converting and civilizing of thofe *Indians,* all which the faid Vice-Roy, being a Perfon of fingular Difcretion and Piety, took Care fhould be put in Execution, and met with all the Succefs that could be expected, abundance of virtuous religious Men being fent over to Inftruct thofe People, who inceffantly labour'd in that Function Some of them having learnt the Language to Perfection, compos'd Catechifes and
other

other Tracts fit for thofe People, and many of their
Children began to be educated among the *Spaniards*,
and taught the *Latin* Grammar, for which proper
Perfons were appointed, and maintain'd at the King's
Expence. Having hinted at thefe Things, we muft
now return to the Affairs of *Peru*, which were the
greateft Tranfactions then in thofe Parts.

THE Adelantado Don *James de Almagro* having
refted at *Copia*, becaufe there was Plenty of Provifions, remov'd to another Vale call'd *Copiapo*, in which,
and in another call'd *Coquimbo*, they found all he
had Occafion for whence he advanc'd an hundred
Leagues into *Chile*, and came to the chief Town
then nam'd *Concomicagua*, where abundance of the
Country People expected him, and among them a
Spaniard, who upon a Point of Honour was gone
where he might not be known, becaufe *Pizarro* had
affronted him. *Almagro* being well inform'd of
the Nature of the Country, repented his having undertaken that Journey, and would have return'd to
Peru, but for the fake of his Reputation ; however,
being defirous to do the King Service, and to fatisfy the Soldiers, he fent a Captain with eighty
Horfe and twenty Foot, to make Difcoveries as far
as he could, who return'd with a very bad Account,
as did others commanded out after him upon the
fame Errand. The Wealth that had been expected
not appearing, all advis'd *Almagro* to return to *Peru*,
and enjoy the Government the King had granted
him, fixing the Boundaries with that of *Pizarro*, and
fome told him, that if he fhould happen to dye
there, he would have nothing left him but the Title of *Don*. So preffing were thofe People to return
to the Enjoyment of the Comforts they had found
in *Peru*, that he was much perplex'd, and tho' he
would willingly have made fome ftay in *Chile*, and
founded at leaft two Colonies, they importun'd him

fo much that he was oblig'd to turn back, to the great Detriment of the People of thofe Nations. The more to induce him to return to *Peru*, his Friends urg'd, that fince the King had conferr'd on him the Government of *New Toledo*, he fhould take Notice that *Cuzco* was within his Limits, becaufe they knew he was defirous to live in that City. Setting out accordingly on their Return, fo took another Way, to avoid the fnowy Mountains, and difcover'd the Defert of *Atacama*, being all Sand for ninety Leagues, with little Water in it, and very little Green, unlefs in four or five Places, which occafion'd the Death of many Men and Horfes. As foon as pafs'd the Defert they heard of the War *Mango Inga* made at *Cuzco*, and that all the Country was in Arms, which inclin'd *Almagro* to make the more hafte back, to relieve the paniards in *Cuzco*, and accordingly they made no halt till they came to *Arequipa*, which is feventy Leagues from *Cuzco*, where they were well receiv'd and refted fome Days.

THE Defert of *Atacama* divides the Kingdom of *Peru* from that of *Chile*, to which there are two Ways, the one over the Mountains, and the other through the faid Defert, which, as has been faid, is near an hundred Leagues over, and dry, impaffable at fome time in the Winter, by Reafon of the great Snow that falls, in which Travellers perifh ; and in the midft of it is the River of Salt, the Water whereof is fo brakifh, that it prefently grows thick in the Hand, or any Veffel, and the Banks are all cover'd with Salt. There are few of the wild Sheep call'd *Guanacos* in this Defert, for they do not increafe by Reafon of the want of Grafs and Water. The Mountain way is more tedious, and Defert, there being no paffing the *Cordillera*, or great Ridge of Mountains without much Danger from the cutting Winds

Winds and Snows, which perish Men, when the
Paffage is not undertaken in the proper Seafon, the
Air being fo fharp, that it penetrates the very
Bowels.

Almagro having refted his Forces fome Days at
Arequipa, march'd for *Cuzco*, and in regard that he
had formerly contracted Friendfhip with *Mango Inga*,
fent him word, that he wonder'd at his Revolt, defiring him to be peaceable, and he would foon be
with him ; and asking what had induc'd him
to act as he did. The *Inga* anfwer'd, he rejoyc'd
at his Return, and fent word of the Motives he had
for taking Arms, complaining that no Refpect was
paid him in *Cuzco*, and that tho' he had given *Ferdinand
Pizarro* much Gold, he ftill importun'd him for more,
in fuch preffing Manner as had oblig'd him to with-
draw ; but ftill defir'd to be at peace with him,
looking upon him as a Friend, and therefore he might
fend him fome trufty *Spaniard* to treat with. *Almagro* fent two with a Prefent, whom the *Inga* receiv'd
favourably, and having told them that *Pizarro*'s Avarice had neceffitated him to take Arms, added,
that there fhould be a Sufpenfion till he faw *Almagro*, and gave Orders accordingly to his *Indians*. At
this Time Advice was brought to *Cuzco*, that *Alonfo de Alvarado* was with his Forces at *Xauxa*, and that
Almagro was advancing towards that City, holding
Intelligence with the *Inga*, to whom *Ferdinand Pizarro* fent a Mulatto Boy with a Letter to fignify
that *Almagro* was not Governour, but *Francis Pizarro*, which was the Beginning of Difcord. The *Inga*
gave the Letter fo fent him to *Almagro*'s two Meffengers, faying, he was fatisfy'd that the People of
Cuzco ly'd, for *Almagro* was the true Governour, and
therefore he would caufe that falfe Meffenger's Hand
to be cut off, but upon their earneft intreaty only
cut off one of his Fingers ; which done he difmifs'd
those

thofe Meffengers, bidding them defire *Almagro* to meet him in the Vale of *Yucay*, for he would be a Friend to none but him. However, thofe *Spaniards* told *Almagro*, that they did not think the *Inga* fincere, and fo it appear'd, for Captain *Ruy Diaz* being fent to him, he would not permit him nor his Companions to return, and the Adelantado advanc'd with his Forces to *Urcos*, fix Leagues from *Cuzco*.

THIS *Mango* was made *Inga* at eighteen Years of Age, and at firft feem'd to be well inclin'd, but afterwards prov'd very cruel. When the War broke out, all the *Indians* that were with the *Spaniards* went to ferve him, but underftanding that he order'd them to be hang'd, they return'd and prov'd very ufeful, for it is thought, that without them they could not have held out, becaufe they were inveterate Enemies to *Mango*. He put to Death all his Brothers, for fear they might fome way deprive him of the Empire, and therefore his Brother *Paul* kept always with *Almagro*, to fave his Life ; the *Inga* who generally had a Sword in his Hand, killing the *Indians*, when he was angry, which was the Occafion that the Country was the fooner reduc'd. *Paul* behav'd himfelf well upon all Occafions, being a Man of good Senfe, went through the Fatigues of the Expedition into *Chile* with much Courage, and when *Almagro* poffefs'd himfelf of *Cuzco*, he gave him his Brother *Guafcar*'s Houfe to live in, being the beft in the City, with a good Eftate ; he was always much refpected by the *Indians*, as being of the Royal Blood, and dy'd a Chriftian, having long before his Death built a ftately Chapel in the City, where he was bury'd, and much lamented by all the Country, being the laft of the *Ingas*, which has been taken Notice of here, tho out of its proper Place, that it may not be quite omitted.

FROM

FROM *Urcos, Almagro* went to the Vale of *Yucay* to confer with the *Inga* as had been appointed, whereupon *Ferdinand Pizarro* march'd out from *Cuzco* with a strong Party, to endeavour to discover the said *Almagro*'s Intentions, and coming near *Urcos* was met by a Body of *Indians*, with only two *Spaniards* among them, who had been sent out by *Saavedra, Almagro*'s Commander in that Place, to observe him. Those *Indians* railing at *Pizarro,* and casting many Stones and Darts, he attack'd, and made them retire, the two *Spaniards* doing the same. *Pizarro* then sent two others to endeavour to speak to them, who drawing near by Degrees, when they knew one another embrac'd, and *Pizarro*'s Men desir'd the others to go to speak to him, which they did, and he having embrac'd them, enquir'd after *Almagro* and his Intentions. They answer'd, his Design was to possess himself of *Cuzco*, which fell within the Government allotted him. The *Indians* observing how those *Spaniards* had been receiv'd, went to *Saavedra*, and told him, they plainly perceiv'd how little Confidence was to be repos'd in his Party, since they did not cut off those their Enemies, that were come from *Cuzco. Saavedra* was much concern'd to find those Barbarians so sharp, and that *Pizarro* was come out at a Time that might obstruct the Conclusion of the Peace that was in Agitation, and thereupon march'd out from *Urcos* to an Eminence in Sight of the *Pizarros,* whence he sent an Alguazil and a Notary to require *Ferdinand* not to offend those *Indians,* who were within *Almagro*'s Government, and under his Protection. Little Account was made of that Ceremony, the *Pizarros* answering, that since those *Indians* were under *Almagro*'s Protection, he should command them to lay down their Arms, and the same should be done on their Side ; but as to *Cuzco,* that *Ferdinand Pizarro* held that City for the
King

King and *Francis Pizarro*, and would not part with it, if it coft him his Life. Thus the *Alguazil* and the Notary return'd, *Ferdinand* charging them to defire *Saavedra* to come to a Conference, which he confented to, both of them being fubtle Men and defigning to impofe one upon another.

BEING met, after many Compliments, *Pizarro* reprefented how prejudicial Difcord among them would be to the Service of God and the King, advifing him to joyn his Forces with thofe of *Cuzco*, and promifing great Rewards for fo doing, in Hopes that Intereft would prevail on him. *Saavedra*, whofe Defign was to gain Time, which was requifite for advancing *Almagro*'s Affairs, perfwaded *Pizarro* not to break the Peace, but to quit *Cuzco*, which was well known to belong to *Almagro*, defiring a Treaty to be fet on Foot in order to it, and thus they parted, without coming to any Refolution. Both Parties advis'd their Commanders to attack their Adverfaries immediately, believing that a Victory on either Side would put an End to the Quarrel, but neither would confent, *Saavedra* becaufe he had no fuch Orders, and *Pizarro* becaufe he would not be the Aggreffor. *Almagro* was now much perpex d in the Vale of *Yucay* being inform'd, that Captain *Ruy Diaz* and his Companions, whom he had fent to treat with *Mango*, were ftripp'd, their Beards and Hair cut off, their Faces and Bodies daub'd with Vermillion, and they ty d to Stakes, where the *Indians* threw rotten Fruits at, and oblig d them to drink much of their Liquor, *Mango* not coming to the concerted Interview, till he enter'd the Vale with a numerous Army; befides being acquainted with what had pals'd between *Pizarro* and *Saavedra*, he order'd his General *Roderick Orgonez* to be upon his Guard, fince he had two Enemies upon his Hands. At the fame Time *Pizarro* fent out fix Horfemen to spy what was doing in the Vale of *Yucay*, which *Almagro* being inform'd of, he surpriz'd four of them, to enquire how Affairs stood at *Cuzco* and in other Parts. The *Inga's* Messengers seeing those four well us'd, ask'd leave to return to their Master, desiring the Prisoners should be deliver'd to them. *Almagro* answer'd, he would have the *Inga* come, that they might march together against those that were in *Cuzco*, and then he would deliver those and other Prisoners. The *Indians* repair'd to *Mango*, saying, the Sun had deliver'd him from falling into the Hands of his Enemies, who having taken those four Men, treated them like Brothers, whereupon the *Inga* and the High-Priest *Vilehoma* resolv'd not to trust *Almagro*, but to treat him as an Enemy, and accordingly sent fifteen thousand Men to attack him, who did it so furiously that the *Spaniards* were at first put to it, but by means of an Ambush they laid, repuls'd the *Indians*, who afterwards treated Captain *Ruy Diaz* and his Companions worse than before.

Almagro then resolv'd to march towards *Cuzco*, being invited by Letters from his Friends, for he had many by Reason of his Courtesy and agreeable Temper, whereas the *Pizarros* were much hated for their Pride, and all Men dreaded the Calamities of a Civil War. When come within half a League of *Cuzco*, *Almagro* represented to his Officers, how long he had serv'd the King, who had been pleas'd to confer that Government on him, wherein the City of *Cuzco* was certainly included, desiring they would assert his just Cause; but that rather than come to an open Rupture, if they thought fit, he would send Messengers to know what *Ferdinand Pizarro*'s Intentions were. They all approv'd of his Proposal, promising to stand by him faithfully, whereupon *Laurence de Aldana*, and *Basco de Guevara* were

sent

sent to tell *Pizarro* that *Almagro*, hearing of the Revolt of the *Indians*, was return'd from *Chile* to his Affiftance, and fince he was come, defir'd he would peaceably permit him to take Poffeffion of the Government the King had conferr'd on him, without interrupting the Friendfhip that was eftablifh'd between him and his Brother; with thefe Meffengers went the four *paniards* before mention'd to have been taken by *Almagro*, whom he then freely fet at Liberty. They met *Ferdinand Pizarro* marching with an hundred and fixty Horfe and Foot, and refolv'd to decide that Controverfy by Dint of Arms. Having deliver'd their Meffage, and contending that the City fhould be put into the Poffeffion of *Almagro*, *Pizarro* ftepping afide with *Aldana*, who was his Friend and Countryman, earneftly intreated he would tell him what *Almagro*'s Intentions were, and being by him affur'd, that there was no Defign to violate the Friendfhip eftablifh'd between him and his Brother, nor to raife any Commotions, *Pizarro* anfwer'd, that *Almagro* was very welcome, and might come into the City, one half whereof fhould be evacuated for him ; after which *Pizarro* return'd to *Cuzco*, and leave was given to carry Provifions to *Almagro*'s Camp, many at the fame Time writing to him, either for the ill Will they bore the *Pizarros*, or becaufe they expected that he was to become their Governour. *Almagro* having receiv'd *Pizarro*'s Anfwer, and knowing him to be a deceitful, double meaning Man, order'd *Chriftopher de Sotelo* to go to *John de Saavedra*, and bid him to be upon his Guard, fince he knew that *Pizarro* was a Perfon that had no regard to any thing fo he might carry on his Defigns. Juft as *Sotelo* was upon fetting out, Advice was brought from *Cuzco*, that a Party was going out from that City to intercept him. This and its being known that *Pizarro* always fpoke contemptibly of *Almagro*, mov'd

many

many to refolve to be reveng'd of him. *Almagro*'s beft Friends advis'd him not to fend *Sotelo*, but to order *Saavedra* to joyn, becaufe it was dangerous for the Forces to be divided, and at the fame Time to require thofe in *Cuzco* to receive him as their Governour, purfuant to the King's Commiffion. Accordingly he fent to *Saavedra*, and moving his own Camp, they met near the Salt-Pits, whence they return'd towards *Cuzco*, and halting near the City, he fent his Commiffion to the Magiftrates, requiring them to admit him as their Governour. *Mango Inga*, who was at *Tambo*, had Notice of all that pafs'd, in Hopes that the *Spaniards* would fight at the Salt-pits, and to that Effect, the High-Prieft *Vilehoma* offer'd many Sacrifices, looking upon the ill ufage of Captain *Ruy Diaz*, and his Companions as no fmall one. *Ferdinand Pizarro* feeing *Almagro* fo near the City, made all the neceffary Difpofitions for the Defence of it, and then came the licenciate *Guevara* and *Ferdinand de Sofa*, demanding to have the Magiftrates affembled, before whom they prefented his Commiffion, and requir'd he fhould be receiv'd as Governour. After many Debates they faid that it was a Matter of great Confequence, and as fuch they cou'd not give an Anfwer to it till the Morrow, to which Effect it was requifite that a Sufpenfion of Arms fhould be concluded for fome Days, which *Almagro* would not confent to, fuppofing it to be an Artifice of *Ferdinand Pizarro*, to gain Time, till *Alonfo de Alvarado* and the Marquefs came to his Affiftance.

Pizarro fearing to be attack'd that Night, was in much Perplexity, and the more for that he perceiv'd the Inhabitants were lefs firm to him than he had expected; yet on the one hand, declar'd he would defend the City, tho' it coft him his Life, and on the other faid, he would deliver up the City, if any

fuch

such Order from the King could be produc'd. *Almagro,* who had Intelligence of all that was done, by the Advice of his Friends, refolv'd to expect the Anfwer of the Magiftrates, and in cafe it was not to his liking to enter the Place by Force. His Meffengers returning, the Sufpenfion of Arms was agreed to, upon Condition that *Almagro* fhould continue on the Ground where he then was, and that *Pizarro* fhould not proceed in fortifying the City. Moft of the Soldiers in *Cuzco,* being difgufted at *Pizarro's* harfh Temper, were inclin'd to *Almagro,* who was generous and mild, fo that they began to fpeak their Minds, and being tir'd with watching many Nights under Arms, and that Night being cold and rainy, they all went away to their Quarters, only twenty ftaying at *Pizarro's* Houfe, with fome Muskets ftanding on Refts at his Door. The Men that came from *Chile* were very uneafy on Account of the Sufpenfion of Arms, alledging it was only a Contrivance of *Pizarro,* who having only two hundred Soldiers with him, of which the one half were difcontented, only gain'd Time to be joyn'd by *Alonfo de Alvarado,* who was come to *Abancay,* and that having broken down the City Bridge, which was next to them, he had violated the Sufpenfion of Arms, and therefore it was lawful to attack and poffefs themfelves of the City of *Cuzco,* which would put an end to that Difcord, others were of a different Opinion; but the firft prevailing, General *Orgoẽe* in a Moment drew up the Forces, and advanc'd towards the City, *Almagro* having given ftrict Orders that no Man fhould be kill'd or plunder'd, his Intention being no other than to take Poffeffion of what the King had granted him. When they enter'd the City, fome within it might have given Notice to *Pizarro,* but thought fit to wait the Event, fo that the Night being dark and rainy, *Almagro*

magro with one Party advanc'd to the Church, and his General *Orgonez* with another to *Pizarro's* Houfe, to prevent any Succour coming to him, *Bafco de Guevara* taking Poft in another Street to the fame Effect. *Orgone* befet *Pizarro's* Houfe, and fecur'd the Muskets, when *Ferdinand Pizarro* hearing the Noife, arm'd himfelf, and with half his Men, went to make good a Door, fending his Brother *Gonalo* with the other half to defend another, railing at *Almagro* for making that attack. *Orgonez* bid him furrender and he fhou'd be well us'd, which he refus'd, and *Orgonez* to fave Effufion of Blood, fet fire to the Houfe, by that means obliging them to run to him to avoid being burnt in it. *Almagro* would not then fee the *Pizarros* till his Paffion was over, but order'd the Magiftrates to meet, and pay Obedience to the King's Orders, which they did, and he promis'd not to make any Alteration in the Government, but to treat them with Generofity and Affection, and accordingly offer'd to make *Gabriel de Rojas* his Lieutenant in the City, who, tho' concern'd or the ill Fortune of the *Pizarros*, accepted of it. Thus the Affairs of *Cuzco* feem'd to be in a peaceable Pofture, but the *Indians* bringing Advice that *Alonfo de Alvarado* was at the Bridge of *Abancay*, or *Apurima*, Confultations were held how to deal with him. This Difcord among the *Spaniards* was very pleafing to the *Indians*, in Hopes that thofe Strangers deftroying one another, they fhould recover their Empire, to which purpofe they offer'd frequent Sacrifices, and tho' a confiderable Part of their Army was disbanded, yet a great Number lay ftill at *Tambo*, with the *Inga*, waiting to fee the Event of thofe Diforders.

C H A P.

CHAP. II.

What pass'd between Almagro *and* Alonso de Alvarado, *till this latter was defeated; Treaties between* Almagro *and* Pizarro *concluded and violated.*

A *Lonso de Alvarado* advancing with his Forces to relieve *Ferdinand Pizarro,* when he had pass'd the Vale of *Andaguailas,* was told, that *Almagro* had possess'd himself of *Cuzco,* and seiz'd the *Pizarros,* but would not give Credit to it, and therefore proceeded to *Cochacaxa,* a Days Journey from *Auramba.* At *Cuzco, Almagro* being inform'd, that *Alvarado* was advancing against him, sent a Party of twenty Horse to bring some better Intelligence about him, and receiv'd Advice, that he had five hundred *Spaniards* with him, whereupon he order'd his General *Orgonez* to write to *Peter de Lerma,* perswading him to come over to his Party, with as many Friends as he could. *Lerma,* being disgusted with the *Pizarros,* upon receipt of the letter, gave out that *Cuzco* had submitted to *Almagro,* which made many ready to declare for him, some in Hopes of Reward, others for the sake of Peace, and others in Hatred to the *Pizarros. Lerma's* Answer being brought to *Cuzco, Almagro* consulted with his Friends what was best to be done, and it was resolv'd to send to require *Alonso de Alvarado,* since he was in *Almagro's* Government, to submit to him, or in case he would not, to go back into *Pizarro's* District. *Ferdinand Pizarro,* tho' confin'd, being inform'd of this Design, found means to convey a Letter to *Alvarado,* exhorting him to adhere to his Brother, and to secure the Messengers that went to

require

require him to fubmit, who fent that Letter to the Governour *Pizarro*, and to fign fy to *Almagro* that he had done fo, and expected the Governour's Orders thereupon. In the mean Time he fortify'd his Camp, and plac'd Guards on the Bridge of *Abancay*, to prevent being furpriz'd. Whilft thefe Things were tranfacting about *Cuzco*, the Governor *Pizarro*, who had, as has been faid, long before fent for Succours to all Parts of the *Weft Indies*, receiv'd a Reinforcement of above two hundred and fifty *Spaniards* from the Ifland *Hifpaniola*, which making up four hundred Horfe and Foot, he march'd from *Lima* to reduce the Country that was Revolted Being come to the Vale of *Guarco*, where a noble and ancient Fortrefs ftood, he there receiv'd *Alvarado*'s Letter which put him into a great Confternation, for the taking of *Cuzco* and his two Brothers; and by the Advice of his Friends, order'd *Alvarado* to endeavour to keep his Ground, and avoid engaging with the other Party. It was alfo decreed to write in very courteous manner to *Almagro*, putting him in mind of their former Friendfhip, of the Service of God and the King, and defiring to have the difference between them amicably adjufted ; making all the neceffary Preparations at the fame Time, in cafe it fhould be neceffary to come to a Rupture ; tho' fome faid, there was no neceffity for thofe Struggles, fince it were fufficient to enquire whether *Cuzco* really was within *Almagro*'s Covernment ; but Ambition prevailing above Juftice, that Advice was not regarded.

James and *Gomez de Alvarado*, with fome others, were fent by *Almagro* to *Alonfo de Alvarado*, to advife him to embrace his Party, and in cafe of refufal, to fhow him the King's Orders, and require him to fubmit to them, all which he refus'd, and inftead of it caus'd thofe Meffengers to be difarm'd, and put into Irons, notwithftanding their upbraiding him with Breach of Faith, and violating the

Law

Law of Nations, which protects all such Messengers. No Answer returning to *Cuzco* from them in eight Days, *Almagro* concluded they were detain'd Prisoners, and consulting with his Friends what to do in that case, his General *Orgoñez* plainly told him, he did not Question their being made Prisoners, which being a manifest Breach of Peace, he should put to Death the two *Pizarros*, and march out against *Alvarado*, in whose Forces he had many Friends that would immediately come over to him, so to rescue those Gentlemen who were confin'd for serving him. Though this Advice was generally approv'd, *Almagro*, who only aspir'd to get his Government without Effusion of Blood, being naturally averse to it, and unwilling to do the King any Disservice, or disoblige *Francis Pizarro*, whom he still lov'd, tho' he hated his Brother *Ferdinand*, would not consent to put those two to Death. *Orgoñez*, told him, he might be as merciful as he pleas'd, but should be assur'd, that if ever *Ferdinand Pizarro* gain'd his Liberty, he would be reveng'd to the full, without any Remorse, as plainly appear'd by his natural Temper, so well known by Experience. *Almagro* then order'd the Forces to be in readiness, and the next Day march'd with them out of the City, leaving *Gabriel de Rojas* there for his Lieutenant, with Orders to take special Care of the *Pizarros*. In three Days he arriv'd at the Bridge of *Apurima*, where being told that *Alvarado* was march'd another way to *Cuzco*, he made so much haste back, that tho the Distance was twelve Leagues, he arriv'd there in one Day before Sun-set. *Orgoñez* there telling him, that if he would not put to Death the two *Pizarros*, he might thank himself for whatsoever the Consequences of sparing them might be, he could not be prevail'd with to consent ; and having rested eight Days he return'd towards *Alvarado*,

rado, to refcue his Meffengers, who tho' Prifoners, fent him Advice of all that happen'd in *Alvarado* s Camp, and among other Things, that *Peter Alvarez Holguin* was gone out with thirty Horfe, to get Intelligence of him. *Almagro* thereupon fent *Francis de Chaves* with a ftronger Party, to feize thofe Men, which he perform'd fo dexteroufly, that only three of them efcap'd by means of their good Horfes. This troubled *Alvarado,* who having pofted Guards at the Bridge, and a Ford, expected the coming of *Almagro,* to whom *Peter de Lerma* and others deferted, being conniv'd at by others, that were no lefs inclin'd to follow his Example.

Almagro being come to the Bridge of *Abancay,* his General *Orgoñez* defir'd the *Inga Paul,* who always adher'd to *Almagro,* and was much Refpected to order his *Indians* to throw up a Trench near the Ford, againft the Enemies Artillery, and to make two hundred Floats for croffing the River. *Almagro's* Forces confifted of about four hundred and fifty brave and hardy Soldiers, enur'd to Labour, divided into three Bodies, one at the Bridge, another at the Ford, and a third for a Referve. Three Hours after Night fell, *Orgoñez* made a Faint, as if he would pafs the River, by which he kept the Enemy on the other Side, upon their Guard all the Night. The next Day *Almagro* would have fent again to require *Alvarado* to releafe the Prifoners, but his General *Orgoñez* would not hearken to it, alledging, that fuch Delays were prejudicial. When Night came on, *Orgoñez* again made fhow of paffing the River, and when he thought it a proper Time, boldly enter'd it with eighty brave Horfe, and finding it deep and dangerous, cry'd, Courage Gentlemen, make hafte, for this is the Time. As foon as fome were pafs'd, they alighted, and preffing hard upon *John Perez de Guevara,* who defended that

Poft,

Poft, wounded him in the Thigh, fo that he fell. *Orgonez* then fir d fome Muskets, which were a Signal to *Almagro* that he had pafs d the River, he then attack d the Bridg?, with fixty Horfe and fome Foot, who gaining their Point, feveral of *Alvarado*'s Men deferted to them, whilft he made Head againft his Enemy with much Refolution. *Orgonez* prefs'd forward defperately, crying, God fave the King and *Almagro* ; the other Party praying for the King and *Pizarro* ; and tho' *Orgonez* was hurt in the Mouth with a Stone, and bled much, he rufh d with Sword in Hand among the thickeft of the Enemy, declaring, he would either conquer or dye, and bidding his Men kill and wound without Mercy, for it was a Shame that thofe infolent *Pizarros* fhould oppofe fuch brave Men. *Alvarado* perceiving he was undone, retir d to a rifing Ground, whither *Orgonez* purfu d with a Party of Horfe, took and fent him Prifoner to *Almagro.* Next he order'd *Francis de Chaves* to go and fecure his Camp, which he d d, fixty Soldiers that had been left to guard it, peaceably fubmitting with their commanding Officer; however, it was plunder'd and much Treafure found, but *Almagro* caus d a great Part to be reftor'd, and treated the Conquer'd with much Courtefy, faving *Alvarado*'s Life, whom *Orgonez* would have Executed. This Victory was gain d on the 12th of *July*, 1537, after which *Almagro* difcours d *Alvarado* very affectionately, offering him his Friendfhip, if he would embrace his Party ; and to fhow that he had never intended to rob any Man, commanded all that had been taken from the Vanquifh d, and could be found, to be reftor d, making good all that was wanting out of his own Treafure, by which and fpeaking them fair, he gain d all *Alvarado*'s Soldiers, appointing *Peter de Lerma* their Commander.

A Coun-

A COUNCIL being then call'd to advise wha^t
was next to be done, the General *Orgonez* was for
sending *James de Alvarado* to govern at *Cuzco,* with
Orders to behead the *Pizarros, Alonso de Alvarado,*
and *Gomez de Tordoya,* and to march the Army to
Lima and secure the Governour *Pizarro,* all which
Almagro then confented to, but was prefently after
diffwaded from putting it in Execution; whereupon
Orgonez again prefs'd him to it, urging, that if he
did not at leaft put the two *Pizarros* to Death, as
Ufurpers of his Right, and Difobedient to the
King's Orders, they would prove the ruin of him
and all his Friends. *Almagro* defir'd him to be pacify'd, for tho' his Jurifdiction extended to the Vale
of *Lima,* he had rather be a lofer, than incroach upon another, and to fave bloodfhed, if he could manage his Affairs without it. They return d to *Cuzco* on the 25th of the fame Month of *July,* 1537,
when *Ferdinand Pizarro* being much dejected, his
Friend *James de Alvarado* often vifited him, and he
won eighty thoufand Pieces of Eight of him, but
would not receive them when fent to him, which fav d
his Life, for *Alvarado* ever after ftood his Friend.
The General *Orgone*, an able Commander, and of fingular, worldly Prudence, being convinc d that there
could be no lafting Peace, provided Arms, and made
Gunpowder, which was then done to Perfection in
Peru, all the necessary Ingredients for it being found
in that Kingdom. The Governour *Pizarro* on the
other Hand, fent to *Almagro,* defiring he would fet
his Brothers at Liberty, and amicably adjuft the
Limits of their Governments; but he, being advis d not to truft any of the *Pizarros,* anfwer'd, that
he had feiz'd thofe Brothers for having difobey'd
the King's Orders, and therefore would not difmifs
them till all that belong'd to his Government was
quitted, fince they had dealt unjuftly with him;

befides

befides that he could not put up the wrong done him by *Ferdinand* railing at him both in *Spain* and the *Weft-Indies*. Whilft the e Meffages were paffing, the Governour *Pizarro* advanc'd to *Nafca*, where he receiv'd the News of the Defeat of *Alonfo de Alvarado*, which very much perplex'd him, as fearing that *Almagro* being fo ftrong, would march againft him, and therefore advifing what to do with the Commendary *Bovadilla*, of the Order of the *Mercenarians*, and 'ome others, it was generally a-greed that he fhould march on, and endeavour to have an Interview with *Almagro*, hoping that as they had been long Friends, all Things would be adjufted; but two others oppofing it, and urging, that he ought not to put himfelf into the Power of his Enemies, and had better return to *Lima*, he approv'd of their Counfel, refolving to gain Time and impofe upon *Almagro*, to which Purpofe he fent Commiffioners to treat at *Cuzco*, and one with them, who had full Power to undo all that they fhould conclude on. *Almagro* receiv d them in friendly Manner, but his General *Orgonez* ftill urg'd, that he ought to have march'd to *Lima*, to make himfelf Mafter of that City, and behead all the *Pizarros*, which he did not Queftion but the King would approve of; but this was oppos d by *James de Alvarado*, by whom *Almagro* was entirely govern'd, and after fome Debates, it was propos'd to the Commiffioners that *Almagro* fhould remain poffefs'd of all the Provinces to the Eaftward of *Guarco*, and and all to the Weftward fhould remain to *Pizarro*, till fuch Time as the Bifhop of *Panama*, who was appointed for that Purpofe by the King, fhould come to fettle the Limits of their Governments. Yet all thefe Propofals came to nothing, *Almagro* being af-fur'd that the *Pizarros* did not deal fincerely, and would certainly

certainly infnare him, if he rely'd upon them, whereupon it was refolv'd to take the Field immediately.

Pizarro, in the mean Time, hafted back to *Lima*,
fome Soldiers joyning him by the way, and he
fpreading abroad falfe Reports againft *Almagro*, to
deftroy the good Opinion generally conceiv'd of him.
At *Lima*, he caus'd the Drums to beat, and proclaim'd War, making all the neceffary Difpofitions
for it. *Almagro*, tho', as has been faid, he had refolv'd to march againft *Pizarro*, did not think fit
to leave *Mango Inga* with fo great a Power behind
him, and therefore fent General *Orgoñez*, with two
hundred Horfe and Foot to diftrefs that Prince.
The *Inga* being fenfible that he could not ftand his
Ground at *Tambo*, where he had lain fome Time,
remov'd to the Vale of *Amayabamba*, taking Captain
Ruyz and his Companions along with him, and
fending to intreat *Paul Inga* to quit the Party
of the *Spaniards*; but *Paul* being well pleas'd with
the ufage he found among them, anfwer'd *Mango*,
he would have him confider how little he had gain'd
when he befieg'd *Cuzco*, with 200000 Men, a-
gainft only 200, where he had loft 50000, and
therefore pray'd him to be reconcil'd to *Almagro*,
for tho' he had declar'd him *Inga*, he would freely renounce that Dignity, to reftore him to Peace
and Quietnefs, which *Mango* regarded not, inveigh-
ing againft *Paul*, and fortifying himfelf in the beft
Manner. General *Orgoñez* marching againft him with
the utmoft Diligence, was inform'd by fome *Indians* of the Preparations that were made to receive him;
but being a Man of invincible Courage, he over-
came many Difficulties, and tho' fome Horfes were
loft, he enter'd the Vale, and furprifing a Fort, the
Indians after fome Refiftance fled, and were purfu'd
to a River, on the bank whereof *Orgoñez* lay that
Night, and there Captain *Ruyz* and his Companions,

ons, having made their Escape in that Confusion of the *Indians* came to him, and were receiv'd with much Joy, all Men condoling the ill usage they had gone through. *Orgonez* still pursuing the *Inga*, as he fled over Mountains and Vales, being in much Danger to be taken, he had Thoughts of suing for Peace, but was hinder'd by his People, and at length made his way into another Province that was more difficult of Access, twenty five Leagues from *Cuzco*, *Orgonez* still pursuing so close, that he took many of his People, and the *Inga* escap'd, with only one Woman. This done *Orgonez* return d to *Cuzco*, releasing all the Prisoners he had taken, some whereof went away to their own Homes, and others return'd to the *Inga*. When he came to the City, *Almagro* dismiss'd *Pizarro*'s Commissioners, with this Answer, that two Arbitrators should be appointed on each Side who might settle the Boundaries so much contended for. After which *Almagro* set out from *Cuzco* with five hundred and fifty Horse and Foot, taking *Ferdinand Pizarro* along with him Prisoner, and leaving *Gonzalo Pizarro*, and *Alonso de Alvarado* Prisoners in the City; but they having corrupted their Guards, and drawn others into their Party, to the Number of thirty, made their Escape and got safe to *Lima*.

Almagro advancing in his March to the Province of the *Lucanes*, it was there resolv'd to secure the Sea-Coast, that Supplies might be receiv'd from other Parts, as well as the King's Orders, in case of a War, and to that Purpose to found a Colony in the Vale of *Chincha*. At *Nasca* Advice was brought, that the Prisoners at *Cuzco* had made their Escape, which much troubled *Almagro*, whereupon *Orgonez* told him, he would be undone for not having taken his Counsel to put them to Death, and therefore he ought immediately to Execute *Ferdinand Pizarro*

zarro, which he would have done had not *James de Alvarado* diffwaded him. Being come into the Vale of *Chincha* in *October,* this Year 1537, a Town was there founded, with the ufual Formalities, and call'd *Almagro, Pizarro's* Commiffioners returning to him from *Cuzco,* with the aforefaid Propofals for an Accommodation, he declar'd he was ready to come into thofe Meafures, and to refer the Adjufting of the Controverfy to Arbitrators. Not long after thofe who had made their Efcape from *Cuzco* arriv'd at *Lima,* having been forc'd to fight their way through the Mountains, where they had been attack'd by the *Indians.* From his new Colony *Almagro* fent the Commiffioners to *Pizarro* to fettle the Limits of their Governments, till the King fhould order otherwife.

FOR the better underftanding of this Controverfy it is requifite here to mention what follows. It has been before obferv'd, that F. *Thomas de Berlanga,* Bifhop of *Tierra Firme,* went to *Lima,* in the Year 1536, with a Commiffion from the King to fettle the Limits of the Governments of *Pizarro* and *Almagro,* allowing the former of them two hundred and feventy Leagues in a direct Line, North and South upon the fame Meridian, to commence at the River of *Santiago* in the North ; and to the latter two hundred Leagues to commence where the other ended, and fo to proceed Southward in the fame Manner, thefe diftances to be adjufted by the Latitude, according to the Number of Leagues allow'd to every Degree ; and each of them to extend Eaft and Weft to all Provinces within the faid Latitude. The Bifhop coming to *Lima* with this Commiffion, *Pizarro* found means to perfwade *Almagro* to undertake the Expedition to *Chile,* without knowing what the King had granted him, and obftructed the Bifhop's going to *Cuzco* to execute

4   his

his Commiffion, which he perceiving, return'd to his Bifhoprick, refufing the Prefents offer d him by *Pizarro.*

HE now underftanding that *Almagro's* Commiffioners were coming, fent *Alonfo Alvarez,* with thirty Horfe to the Vale of *Mala,* to intercept all Perfons and Letters which came that way ; purfuant to which the faid *Alvarez* feiz'd the Commiffioners, and all they had, as well Treafure as Papers. *Pizarro* advifing with his Confederates how to proceed in this Cafe, fome of them declar'd it was an open Act of Hoftility, and therefore all ought to be reftor'd, becaufe *Almagro* had not done fo by his Meffengers that went to *Cuzco,* and accordingly it was refolv d, that private Letters fhou'd be ftopp'd, but the Difpatches reftor'd, with a Compliment of Excufe. However, *Alvarez* took away their Horfes, and having mounted them on Mules, they were conducted under a Guard to the *Azequia,* or Trench, a League from *Lima,* whither *Pizarro* came to confer with them, and after feveral Meffages backward and forward it was concluded, that F. *Francis de Bovadilla,* Provincial of the *Mercenarians,* fhould be added to the four Commiffioners, to decide all Controverfies, as abfolute Umpire, which was very difagreeable to *Almagro's* General *Orgoñez,* who always advis'd him for the beft, yet his Counfel was never taken. *F. Bovadilla* entering upon his Mediatorfhip at *Mala,* order'd, that *Pizarro* and *Almagro* fhould both appear before him giving Hoftages for the Security of their Perfons, but *Pizarro* refufs d to give any Hoftage, as never intending to come to an Accommodation, whereupon the Arbitrator requir'd that thofe two Governours fhould meet upon the Security of their own, and the Oaths of moft of their prime Officers. Upon this Refolution *Orgoñez* again, told *Almagro,* that he

VOL. V.   K   was

was certainly a loft Man, if he rely'd on the *Pi-zarros*, who would never keep Faith with him, advising him again to Execute *Ferdinand Pizarro*, and retire to *Cuzco* along the Plains, whither *Pizarro* would follow him over the Mountains, which would fo harrafs his Men, that they would not be fit for Service, afluring him, that whoever came off Victorious would be juftified at Court. *Almagro* was deaf to his Advice, which afterwards prov'd his ruin; for as *Orgonez* faid, *Pizarro* would not at firft take the Oath, tho afterwards he did, without any defign to keep it; and therefore going to *Mala* with only twelve Horfemen as had been order'd, he was follow'd foon after by his Brother *Gonzalo* with feven hundred Men, and laid a Party of Mulketiers in Ambufh to furprize *Almagro* when he came to *Mala.* He on the other Hand would not in the leaft Tittle tranfgrefs his Engagement, tho he had many Warnings of the Treachery of his Adverfaries, but left ftrict Orders that the Forces fhould not ftir without his Directions. Being come to *Mala*, he went up with Hat in Hand to falute *Pizarro*, who had an Helmet on his Head, which he touch'd, and receiv'd him coldly; and prefently began to difcourfe him in an haughty Manner about his feizing of *Cuzco*, and imprifoning his Brothers; to all which he anfwer'd very difcreetly. Whilft they were in this difcourfe *Francis de Godoy*, a Man of Honour, who could not bear with the intended Treachery againft *Almagro*, gave him Notice of the Defign to feize him, as did fome others, whereupon he pretended to go down to eafe himfelf, and an Horfe being ready at the Door, mounted and rode away with all his Company, his General *Orgonez* having at the fame Time, for fear of fuch falfe Dealing, march'd his Forces towards the River *Lunaguana.*

THE

THE *Pizarros* were in a rage to fee that *Almagro* had broke through all their Snares, and the Mediator *Bovadilla* having examin'd divers Pilots as to the Latitudes of the divers Places on which the Decifion of the Controverfy depended, and finding them vary, at length on the 15th of *November* 1537, pronounc'd Judgment in this manner, *viz.* That for as much as the Pilots did not agree in the Latitude, particularly of the Town of *Santiago,* the Governours fhould fend a Ship, with two Pilots for each Party, as likewife a Notary, and two other Perfons that knew the Town of *Santiago,* who all upon Oath fhould take the faid Latitude afhore becaufe of the Motion of the Ship, which fhould be attefted by the faid Notaries, in order to put the King's Orders in Execution. That for as much as *Pizarro* being in Poffeffion of *Cuzco*, *Almagro* had feiz'd it by Force, without any Commiffion from the King, for fo doing, he enjoyn'd him to reftore it to *Pizarro* within thirty Days, and to releafe the Prifoners there taken within fix; that *Pizarro* fhould furnifh *Almagro* with a Ship to fend his Difpatches to the King, and allow Merchants to trade with him; that within fifteen Days they fhou'd both difperfe their Armies, fending out Parties to reduce the Natives, *Almagro* retiring from the Vale of *Chincha* to that of *Nafca,* and *Pizarro* not to depart the Vale of *Lima*; that there fhould be perpetual Peace between them, without offending one another, and all this under the Penalty of 200000 Pieces of Eight, and forfeiture of their Commands. *Pizarro,* as well he might, declar'd he was content with this Sentence, but *John Rodriguez Barranga, Almagro's* Attorney appeal'd from it to the King and Council. When this Judgment was known among *Almagro's* Forces, they were all ftruck dumb at firft; but when recover'd, cry'd out in furious manner, that the Injuf-

tice

tice of that Frier was not to be born with, adding, that *Almagro*'s Ignorance, S oath, and old Age, would occasion the *Pizarros* to triumph over then, and possess the richest Provinces, sending them to l ve among the *Charcas* and *Collas*, reflick People, who had not so much as Wood The Mut ny grew so high, that *Imagro* knew not how to quell it. His General *Orgonez*, seing him in that Perplexity, bid h m not be concern'd, tho' it was his own Fault, in never taking his Advice; but that he should still behead *Ferdinand Pizarro*, and march to *Cuzco*, where they would fortify themselves, for he was sure that *Francis Pizarro* never design'd to be at Peace with hm.

ON the other Hand, the Governour *Pizarro's* Men were for marching immediately to rescue his Brother *Ferdinand*, and possess themselves of *Cuzco*. However, another Treaty was set on Foot, *Francis Pizarro* resolving to comp'y with any Composition, provided he might set his Brother at L berty, and to observe none of it afterwards. The main Articles were, that *Almagro* should remove the n w Colony of his own Name to *Zangalla*; that he should have a Ship to send his D spatches to the King; that he should hold the City of *Cu co*, till the King might decide the Controversy; that no Alteration should be made in other Particulars; that both Armies should break up within twenty Days, and that *Ferdinand Pizarro* should be set at Liberty, taking an Oath, and giving Security that he wou d appear before the King, and neither directly nor indirectly act in any Manner to the Prejudice of *A magro*. Both Parties took a solemn Oath to observe these Articles. This was the Posture of Affairs, when Captain *eter Anzures*, whom *Pizarro* had sent into *Spain*, return d to *Lima*, with Orders from the King, that the two Governours should keep within the Districts assign'd them for avoiding of Discord, but in case either of them

at

at the Time when thofe Difpatches came to their
Hands, had poffefs'd himfelf of any Provinces that the
other pretended did appertain to his Government, the
fame fhould continue to him that had the Poffeffion
for the prefent, and he who thought himfelf injur'd
fhould apply to the King and Council of the *Indies,* who upon the Examination of the Right would
fee Juftice done. Notwithftanding this Order was fo
much in Favour of *Almagro, Pizarro* writ to him fignifying, that he could not ftand to what had been concerted between them, by reafon there were frefh Difpatches arriv'd from *Spain,* and he muft obey the
King's Commands. To avoid tedious Repetitions
of Things much to the fame Purpofe, another frefh
Agreement was concluded between thofe two Governours, by which *Ferdinand Pizarro* was to be fet at
Liberty, and *Almagro* to retain *Cuzco* till farther
Orders from the King, *Pizarro* at the fame Time
refolving to break through all Capitulations, when he
had once recover'd his Brother, and *Almagro,* whofe
Intentions were always fincere, ftill complying after
fo much Breach of Faith on the Part of his Adverfaries, to avoid Effufion of Blood, and the other fa-
tal Confequences of a Civil War. Having concluded this Agreement without the Knowledge of his
General *Orgoñez,* when he acquainted him with it,
that Commander laid hold of his Beard with his left
Hand, and with the Right made a Motion of cutting his Throat, faying, *Orgoñez, Orgoñez,* this Head
of yours will be cut off for your Friendfhip to *Don
Diego de Almagro.* There were others befides *Orgoñez*
who concluded, that not only *Almagro's,* but the
lives of all his Friends were like to be brought into
much Danger by fetting *Ferdinand Pizarro* at Liberty, for he was known by long Experience to be
revengef, bafe, and of a perverfe Difpofition. How-
eve., *Almagro* fet him at Liberty, and then march'd

K 3   away

away to the Va'e of *Zangalla*, to which Place he remov'd the Colony he had before founded at *Chincha*.

C H A P. III.

Falſho⌐d of the Pizarros ; *all Accommodations rej.ɛted ; the Civil War begun ;* Almagro's *Forces d feated ; he put to* Death ; Peter de Candia's *unfortunate Expedition.*

IT is very Remaikable that the *Pizarros* being full of Rancour, and all they had done mere Fiction and Diſſimulation, as ſoon as ever *Ferdinand* was ſet at Lberty, without any Regaid to their ſeveial Promiſes and Capitulations, not only under their Hands, but the moſt ſolemn Oaths, they immediately began to make all Preparations for War, as if it had been already declar'd. In order to it, a Gentleman, a Lawyer, and a Notary, were ſent to require *Almagro*, who was then in the Vale of *Zangalla*, to quit all that had been conquer d and ſubdu'd by *Francis Pizarro*, and upon h s refuſal to lay to his Charge a'l the Effuſion of Blood, and other Calamities that were like to enſue. This bare-fac'd Perfidiouſneſs of the *Pizarros*, caus'd *Almagro* to ſend away *James de Alvarado* as his Lieutenant, to ſecure *Cuzco*, which *Orgonez* did not approve of, ſaying, That *Alvarado's* fair Words were very pleaſing, but nothing to the Purpoſe at that Time. Then the Forces march'd by the way of the Mountain of *Guaytara*, *Orgonez* leaving Guards to ſecure the two Poſts. After this ſame, Skirmiſhes happen'd between the Parties on both Sides, but as they were inconſiderable, do not deſerve to be particularly mention'd tion'd. *Imagro* then order'd *John de Guzman,* who was the King's Controller, and as such had special Licence to go and come when he pleas'd, to take a Journey into *Spain,* to acquaint his Majesty with the Posture of Affairs in *Peru,* but *i arro,* notwithstanding his Royal Commission, seiz'd and kept him Prisoner. Having then resolv'd to make himself Master of *Cuzco,* he march'd towards the Mountain, of which a Deserter gave *Almagro* timely Notice, and yet two Parties advancing in the Night, gain'd both the Passes, without any Resistance, which, as has been said, had sufficient Guards upon them to have made the same good. *Orgone* hearing the Noise, and advancing with an hundred Horse to relieve those at the Posts, being told that they were lost, curs'd *Francis de Chaves* and himself, for having intrusted him, and so he retir'd to joyn *Almagro,* as he did the next Day, when it was by some advis'd to turn back and attack the *Pizarros,* their Men being then in Disorder, sick and almost Starv'd with the Cold of the Mountain ; but this Advice was rejected, through the ill Fate of those Forces, and so they held on their march towards *Cuzco. Pizarro* now puff'd up with Pride beyond all Measure, without any regard to all his Oaths, or to the King's Orders, publickly pretended that all the Country from *Pasto* at the Equinoctial to the Streights of *Magellan,* was within his Government, and intended to confer all that Part about the Line, which as has been said, had been subdu'd by *Sebastian de Belalcazar* on his Brother *Gonzalo.* In order to this he Commission'd *Laurence de Aldana* to repair to *Quito,* and by all means, fair or foul to possess himself of those Provinces, and if possible, to secure *Sebastian de Belalcazar.*

Francis Pizarro having now appointed his Brother *Ferdinand,* Superintendent and Governour, and his

K 4 other

other Brother *Gonzalo* Captain General, becau'e he was so old himself that he could not undergo the Fatigue, his Forces consisting of seven hundred Horse and Foot began their march towards *Cuzco.* Several well minded Persons, perceiving that there was nothing but Malice and Revenge in this undertaking, which was so prejudicial to the Service of God and the King, and likely to end in much Effusion of *Spanish* Blood, considering the Rancour of those Brothers, endeavour'd to dissuade them from pursuing that wicked Course, but all in vain, their Pride and Fury rendering them incapable of listning to Reason, or paying any regard to the Commands of their Sovereign. *Almagro* in the mean Time having rested thirty Days at *Bilcas,* where there was Plenty of Provisions, and being sensible that a Battel was unavoidable, consulted what was best to be done. General *Orgones* advis'd to turn back over the Mountains, and surprize the City of *Lima,* where he would be ready to receive the Recruits that arriv'd from all Parts, and might send an Account to the King of the Posture of Affairs. This Advice was seconded by others, and certainly was the best, but Fate had decreed the ruin of *Almagro,* and therefore he always adher'd to the worst Counsel. He was then very sick, and there were Apprehensions of his Death, however he recover'd, being reserv'd for a more miserable End. Intelligence being now brought him, that *Ferdinand Pizarro* was marching over the Mountains to *Cuzco,* he hasted away, and took Possession of that City, where he made all necessary Dispositions for War, whilst the *Pizarros* advanc'd to the River *Apurima,* where they might have been easily defeated, had their Adversaries made their Advantage in securing that Pass. That Opportunity being lost, tho' it had been advis'd to defend the City, as being inferior in Number to the Enemy, who

who drew near, about five hundred *Spanish* Horse and Foot march'd out with six little Field Pieces, and the *Inga Paul Topa* leading six thousand *Indians*, *Almagro* himself was carry'd out in a Bier being so weak that he could not ride, but as he spoke to his Commanders, declaring the Justice of his Cause, and that they would be all ruin'd in case the Enemy prevail'd. The Forces were drawn up by *Orgonez* among the Salt-Pits, contrary to the Opinion of several Commanders, who insisted that they should fight in the open Plain, as being strongest in Horse, whereas the other Party had much the Advantage in Foot.

Pizarro's Army drawing so near *Cuzco* that the News was spread through all the Country, that a Battel would ensue; whereupon the Natives from all Parts cover'd the adjacent Hills to behold that Action, wishing both Parties might be destroy'd, and all the Servants and Women in the City flock'd to see that Spectacle. Some Horsemen going out from both Sides upon Discovery, came so near as to speak to each other, and then return'd to give an Account of what they had seen. *Almagro*'s Officers again press'd *Orgonez* to advance into the open Plain, for the Advantage of his Horse; but he persisting in his Opinion, drawing up the Infantry in one Body, with the Musketeers, and Crofsbow-men in the Front; the Horse were also in one Body, *Orgonez* and *Peter de Lerma* being on the Flanks, disposing their Field Pieces as seem'd most convenient. This was their Posture when Advice was brought that their Enemies were at hand, and about Sun-setting *Ferdinand Pizarro* drew very near, and then halted, only a little River parting them, and it was remarkable, that tho' they lay there all that Night, neither Side made any Overtures towards an Accommodation, so great was the Aversion of both Parties to each other. The
next

next Morning *Pizarro*'s Forces march'd towards the
High-way of the *Ingas*, call'd *Collasuyo*, taking a
Compass to fall upon them from the upper Ground,
at about half a League's distance. There *Ferdinand
Pizarro* encourag'd the Commanders with fair Promises,
and finding them chearful, order'd Captain *Castro*, with the Musketeers and Crossbow-men, to pass
the River and advance towards the Enemy, which
he did, and taking Post on a rising Ground, began
to play upon his Enemy, whereupon both Armies
push'd forwards, crying, God save the King, and
the one side *Almagro*, and the other *izarro*. As
soon as ever they engag'd, the *Indians* set up an hideous
Cry, and Captain *Salinas* was kill'd with a Musket
Shot. *Francis Hurtado*, Ensign General to *Almagro*,
basely deserted to the *Pizarros*, many of the Horse
fled, without striking Stroke, and the Foot hid themselves among the Ruins that were about the Fields.
Pizarros's Fire-arms did much Execution, and *Peter de Lerma* spying *Ferdinand izarro*, ran full tilt
at him, calling him perjur'd Wretch and Traytor,
giving him such a Shock, that his Horse came down
upon his Knees, and had not his Armour been very
good he had been kill'd. The Order of the *Chile*
Men being broke by those that fled, the Advantage
appear'd on the Part of the *Pizarros*, one of whose
Soldiers cry'd Victory, but *Orgoñe* run his Sword
into his Mouth and kill'd him. The longer the
Fight lasted the more Advantage the *Pizarros* gain'd
for want of Order among the *Almagros*. *Orgoñez*,
who had perform'd the Part of an able Commander
and Soldier, endeavouring to bring back some that withdrew from the Battel, was wounded with a Musket
Ball, and his Horse kill'd, yet he got up, and being
beset, fought manfully, wounding many. Being
call'd upon to yield himself, he ask'd, whether any
Gentleman was there to whom he might yield, and
one

one *Fuentes,* a Servant to *Pizarro,* anfwer'd, yes, he might fubmit to him, which when he did, the faid *Fuentes,* like a Vil'ain, having been inftructed by his Mafter, murder'd him, after Quarter given. Upon his Death no Oppofition was made, and *Almagro* feeing his Forces routed, made off on a Mu'e to the Citadel of *Cuzco.* The Soldiers, who had been formerly defeated as was faid in its Place, at *Abancay* or *Apurima,* in Revenge for that D'fgrace, barbaroufly kill'd the wounded Men. *Ferdinand Machicao* look d out for *Peter de Lerma,* and finding him wounded on the Ground, ftabb'd h'm in fev ral Places, and then went away, thinking he had been dead, which he proclaim d about as he went. A great Shower of Rain fell then, whereupon the Victors march d into the City. This Battel was fought on the *Saturday* before *Palm-Sunday,* in the Year 1538, and lafted two Hours. Of *Almagro's* Men an hundred and twenty dy d in the Battel, and afterwards of their Wounds, many of them being kill'd in cold Blood ; of *Pizarro's* very few.

Alonfo de Alvarado underftanding that *Almagro* had withdrawn himfelf into the Citadel of *Cuzco,* went and took him out from thence, and *Ferdinand Pizarro* being told of it, declar'd he could have wifh d he had been k:ll'd, ordering that he fhou'd be kept in fafe Cuftody. Thus the Adelantado *Don Diego de Almagro,* fell into the utmoft Diftrefs, yet he loft not the Affection of his Friends. The Soldiers Plunder'd the City, and there were Quarrels about it, the Prifoners were many ; and *Peter de Lerma* was found with feventeen Wounds about him, and laid in a Bed, with little Life in him, where one *Samaniego,* bafely ftabb'd him, as was believ'd by the Inftigation of *Ferdinand Pizarro,* for his charging him in the Battel, as was there faid. This Victory being thus gain'd, all who had an hand in it, expected

ted to have Lands given them, taken from those that
were in Possession; but *Pizarro* was afraid of raising
new Commotions by depriving those Possessors, and
and therefore held the Soldiers in hand, telling them,
that Colonies were to be settled at *Los Charcas* and
Arequipa, where they should have Lands, but that
did not satisfy them. *Alonso de Alvarado* ask'd leave
to return to *Lima*, in order to go to his Government of the *Chiachiepoyas*, where he would build a
City, which was granted, and with him was sent the
young *Almagro*, Son to the Adelantado, to be deliver'd to *Francis Pizarro*, that he might not be a-
mong his Father's Soldiers, whom we shall hereafter
call the Men of *Chile*. *Francis Pizarro* receiv'd the
News of the Victory with much Joy, being sole
Lord in that Empire, and from that Moment his
Temper alter'd, and he became more Insolent and
Haughty, resolving at the same Time to go to *Cuzco*.
Ferdinand Pizarro stood upon his guard, because making no Distribution of Lands, and the Soldiers not
being enrich'd as they had expected, not only mut-
ter'd, but threatned; making no Account of the
richest Country in the World, *viz. Los Charcas*, where
he gave out he would build a Town; and therefore
he was under some Apprehensions from his own Men,
and those of *Chile*, telling them he expected his Brother, and would then provide for them all.

Peter de Candia, who was very rich, and an old
Friend to the *Pizarros*, wanting to lay out what he
had got, and being inform'd by an *Indian* Woman
he had, that beyond the Mountains *Andes* there was
a very wealthy and populous Country, call'd *Ambaya*,
and secretly begg'd he might have the discovering of
it, which was readily granted by *Ferdinand Pizarro*,
who thought it an Happiness to rid himself of some
of those turbulent People, that kept him in continual fear; there being at that Time above one thou-

sand

fand fix hundred *Spanifh* So'diers in *Cuzco. Peter de
Vergara* defir'd he might have the reducing of the
Prov nce of the *Bracamoros,* thought to be no lefs
rich and populous than the other, which was likewife eafily obtain'd, for the fame Reafon of fending away fo many idle and trouble´ome Perfons. *A-
lonfo de Mercadillo* obtain´d the Conqueft of the
Chupachos. Peter de Candia began to make ready for
his Enterprize, and to that End made ufe of eighty five thoufand Pieces of Eight he had of his own,
and run into Debt as much more, by wh:ch means
he gather'd three hundred Soldiers, well equip'd,
they concluding that fince he laid out fo much,
he knew what he was going about, and confequently, that they fhould be all rich, or in cafe the Undertaking did not anfwer, they fhould lofe nothing,
which made them willing to go ; fome being alfo
compell'd to it by *Pizarro,* becaufe they had been
of *Almagro's* Party. *Peter de Candia* having march'd
as far as the Va e of *Paqual,* ten Leagues from *Cuzco,* and five from the Mcuntains *Andes,* ftay'd there
above fix Weeks, whereupon *Pi arro* fent him Orders to proceed on his Enterprize, and not ftay to
burden the Province. At the fame T me to Exercife his Cruelty, and juftify his Proceedings, he
dec'ar'd he would proceed againft *Almagro,* and as
thofe in Power never want Flatterers to carry on
their Defigns, many immediately flock'd in to inform againft that unfortunate Gentleman, fo that
the Notaries foon fill'd up much Paper with Depo-
fitions.

Peter de Candia made his way over the Mountains
Andes to the Eaflward, by the way of *Tono,* and at
Opotari found a large and populous Town, three
Leagues from *Tono,* and thirty from *Cuzco,* whence
proceeding farther, the ways prov d fo bad, that the
Horfes

Horses tumbled headlong from the Rocks, and the
Men suffer'd much, and yet they went on, tho'
their Commander was not so discreet as was requisite for such an Undertaking, and might have tak-
en a better way. Being reduc'd to these Streights,
never seeing the Sun, and infested with continual
Rain and Storms, he advis'd with his Officers,
what was best to be done, but they knew not
what to resolve on, in regard that it seem'd impossible to advance, and scarce practicable to turn back;
however, it was resolv'd to proceed, and thus they
came to a more difficult Pass than any they had
yet met with, being a solid Rock, yet cover'd
with thick Trees, with such Boughs or Twigs
shooting from them, that the Horses could not penetrate. In this Distress Providence inspir'd them to
cut abundance of those Twigs, with which they
made Cables, and fastning them to the Trees
and the Bodies of the Horses, with incredible labour, drew them up. Having overcome this immense Difficulty, they arriv'd in the Country of
Abisca, being hot Vales, where they halted, got
Provisions, and whilst they rested, the Commander
sent some to discover the Country, who returning
some Days after, said, they could find no better
way than that they had already come through,
which was a great Affliction, yet they advanc'd
four Days, and met with *Indians* that had Bows,
were Man Eaters, and came up boldly to discharge
their Arrows. The Mountain grew still more impassable, and the Men weaker, but having no other
Remedy, they still went on, and as they were
making way with the Boughs of Trees over a
Morass, were set upon by some *Indians,* on whom
they fir'd several Muskets, and took one. He being ask'd, how long they should be passing that
                                        Mountain,

Mountain, said there was nothing else all the way
before them, and as to their way of living, that they
had little Houses, cover'd with the Boughs of those
Trees, their Weapons were Bows and Arrows, and
they fed on *Yuca* Roots, which they sow'd and
were satisfy'd with, hoping they should never have
seen their Faces; that in those Woods there were
Monkeys, wild Cats, and some *Dantas,* which they
kill'd with their Arrows, he then advis'd them to
go no farther, because they would perish. Notwithstanding all he could say, they advanc'd, travel-
ing every Day about a League, little more or less,
suffering much by the Thorns that ran into their
Feet and Legs, crossing Rivers, Quag-Mires, and
Stony Places, with much Difficulty, and the more
because many were sick and wounded, besides that
Hunger began to pinch, and they fed on the Horses that dy'd. Being reduc'd to this Extremity,
Peter de Candia, order'd they should turn towards
the left, and it pleas'd God, that in a few Days
they got out of that Misery, which they had labour'd under three Months, and at length came out
at *Collao,* to some Towns belonging to Captain *A-
lonso de Mesa,* a *Canarian* and *Luke Martin,* which
was a mighty Comfort to them.

THE Governour *Francis Pizarro* was so over-
joy'd at the Advice brought him of the Victory
obtain'd over *Almagro,* that not being able to conceal it, he set out in a triumphant Manner from
Lima, on his way to *Cuzco,* and arriv'd at *Xauxa,*
declaring, that he would not consent to the putting
of *Almagro* to Death, tho' at the same Time he
meant otherwise. The new Bishop, F. *Vincent de
Valverde,* intreated him to rest satisfy'd with the
Blood that was already shed, not to forget his former Friendship with *Almagro,* and the Favours receiv d

ceiv'd of him, with many more very Pious and
Chriftian Perfwafions, to which *Pizarro* return'd a
civil Anfwer, but the Venom lay at his Heart. The
Captains *Vergara* and *Mercadillo* fetting out upon
the'r intended Enterprifes, met *Francis Pizarro* at
Xauxa, where they deliver'd to him the young *Almagro,* Son to the Adelantado, and other Prifoners;
with an Account of the Battel, and that his Brother was forming a Procefs againft *Almagro,* defigning to execute him, as foon as Judgment fhould be
given; putting him in mind of the Inftability of
worldly Affairs, and that God would not permit
Sinners to efcape unpunifh'd. *Peter de Candia* being
with Captain *Mefa,* as was faid above, the latter per-
fuaded the former to march back to *Cuzco* with all
his Men, having form'd a Confpiracy among them
to kill *Ferdinand Pi arro,* and being on their march,
fome of thofe Confpirators writ to *James de Alvarado,* inviting him to joyn with him in that Defign,
which he refufing, they fear'd he might betray
them, and to prevent it made the Difcovery themfelves. Whilft thefe Things happen'd, *Almagro* was
very fick in his Confinement, and fent to defire *Ferdinand Pizarro* to fee him, which he did, and pro-
mifs'd him his Life, but as foon as come out from
him, order'd the Lawyers to conclude the Procefs
againft him with all fpeed, wherein he was charg'd
with having ufurp'd the Regal Authority in *Cuzco,*
and imprifon'd the Governour; befides the fighting
of *Alonfo de Alvarado,* at *Abancay,* or *Apurimo* and
other Matters that are always alledg'd againft thofe
that are down. Tho' *Pizarro* had refolv'd to deftroy him, he fent him many Compliments, and
Prefents of Sweet-meats, and other Dainties, but as
foon as the Procefs was clos'd, he pafs'd Sentence
of Death upon him, and then fent a Frier to prepare

pare him for Execution. *Almagro* much furpriz'd
at that Intimation, defir'd to fee him again, he
came, and tho' the unfortunate Gentleman reprefented the Injuftice of his Proceedings, the many good
Offices he had done him and his Brothers, and the faving of his Life, when he had been often importun'd
to put him to Death, with many other powerful Arguments, nothing was of Force to move him from
his Purpofe, but he went away bidding him prepare
for Death.

Almagro accordingly made Chriftian Difpofitions,
with much Zeal and Fervour, appointing his Son
Don James, Governour, by Virtue of the King's
Commiffion fo Authorizing him, and *James de Alvarado* his Guardian, till he came to Age, and by
his laft Will, made the King his Heir, declaring there
was a great Sum of Money in the common Stock
of Partnerfhip, between him and *Pizarro*, which he
defir'd might be brought to Account, and that his
Majefty would be pleas'd to fhow Favour to his
Son. A Body of Men was drawn up in the great
Square, Parties at the End of the Streets, and the
Guards doubled upon all *Almagro's* Friends, by which
it appear'd, that they Defign'd to put him to Death,
to the unfpeakable Sorrow of his Soldiers and Adherents, whom they call'd the Men of *Chile*. They
exclaim'd againft *Pizarro*, calling him Tyrant, and
threatned to Revenge their Commander, as they afterwards did. The *Indians* wept bitterly, declaring
they had never been mifus'd by him. For thefe
Reafons *Pizarro*, tho' he defir'd it, durft not put
him to Death in publick, but order'd him to be
ftrangled in Prifon, after which he was brought out
and beheaded, *Pizarro* himfelf, like a falfe Hypo-
crite, afterwards attending his Funeral. The Lamentation was univerfal among the *Spaniards*, and

particularly *James de Alvarado* seem'd inconsolable, publickly exclaiming against *Pizarro* for killing the Man that had sav'd his Life. *Almagro* was sixty three Years of Age, small of Stature, his Countenance disagreeable, especially after he had lost one Eye in the Wars. He was bold, adventurous, much inur'd to Fatigues, discreet, generous, a Friend to good Men, of a gentle and sweet Disposition, zealous in the Service of his King, and had a great Share in subduing of those Kingdoms; born at *Aldea del Rey,* and of mean Parentage. *Francis Pizarro* was much blam'd on Account of his Death, because, having been near four Months in Prison, he could not but know, and might have prevented it, by which it appear'd to have been done by his Consent and Approbation ; and his Brother *Ferdinand* often declar'd as much, to clear himself from the Imputation of Inhumanity and Perjury ; and all Men reflected on their Barbarity towards a Man who had been so great a Support to them upon all Occasions.

A soon as *Ferdinand Pizarro* had dispatch'd *Almagro,* he sent Advice of it to his Brother *Francis,* and endeavour'd to ingratiate himself with *Gabriel de Rojas, John de Saavedra, Basco de Guzman,* and others of the *Chile* Commanders, that they might forget their old Friend, which they never did. Next he march'd out with above four hundred Men, to meet *Peter de Candia,* and having drawn him, with his prime Officers into his Tent, secur'd his Person, and those of the Captains *Messa* and *Villagran. Messa* was presently Executed for the Conspiracy before mention'd, but *Villagran* was begg'd off, many admiring that *Pizarro* could be prevail'd on to spare him, and concluding he did it to take off the Imputation of Cruelty. *Peter de Candia* being found
innocent,

The HISTORY of *America.* 147

innocent, was also difmifs'd, and the Command of his Men given to *Peter de Anzures,* who was joyn'd by feveral Gentlemen and Perfons of Diftinction, and march'd away to the Vale of *Caravaya,* about the latter End of *September,* this Year 1538, whence with much Difficulty they proceeded to the Province of *Zama,* and fo held on their way over the Mountains, fometimes coming into Flats, but very woddy and clofe. Such were the Difficulties and Hardfhips they met with, that many of their Blacks and *Indians* perifh'd in thofe Deferts, and in this manner they came to the great River of the *Omapalcas,* which rifes to the Eaftwards and runs away to the North Sea, the Spring being on the Mountain of the *Mojas.* When they had pafs d the Country of the *Cheriabonas,* perceiving that it was abfolutely neceffary to crofs that River, they made Floats, all the Country abounding with Wood. When thofe Floats were ready, they fpent eight Days in paffing the River, tho' fome of the Nation call'd *Marquires,* living on its Banks, attempted to obftruct them ; to quell whom *Peter Anzures* himfelf, with thirty Soldiers on twelve Floats, made towards thofe *Indians,* who receiv'd them with loud Cries, and vaft Flights of Arrows, but as foon as the *Spaniards* came afhore were put to the rout. That Difficulty being overcome, *Anzures* fet out with a Party and able Guides, to feek for Provifions, and and after fix Days march came into a plain open Country. This is what happen'd in *Peru* till the End of the Year 1538, we muft now look back to what was doing in other Parts.

L 2   CHAP.

C H A P. IV.

Difcoveries from the Province of Venezuela ; *actions in that of* Honduras, *and
the Defcription of it* ; *of two Men that
liv'd eight Years in a defert Ifland* ; *fome
Ordinances of the King, fearch into the
burning Mountain of* Mafaya.

ANtony Sedeño having been left upon his Difcovery in the Province of *Venezuela*, it is
now Time to return to him. On his march to
find out the Province of *Meta*, he was overtaken
by the licenciate *Frias*, fent by the Council or
Court of *Hifpaniola*, to proceed againft him for having
quitted the Ifland of the *Trinity*, which he was
commiffion'd to fubdue, and enter'd upon the Limits of another's Government. *Frias* governing
himfelf indifcreetly, *Sedeno* fecur'd him, and fent
back an hundred Men he had brought with him.
This done he held on his way to the Provinces of
Anapuya and *Orocomay*, where he was friendly receiv'd and entertain'd ; but proceeding to the Country of *Gotoguaney*, found the People in Arms, and
at the Entrance into it a wooden Fort, the Timbers faftned together with Ropes of Withes, having Loop-holes at proper diftances, and well mann'd
which being an Obftacle to their Defigns, it was
refolv'd to attack, as they did, but the *Indians*
fhooting poifon'd Arrows, the Men that happen'd
to be hurt were forc'd to burn their Wounds, or
elfe they dy'd raving Mad. The Heat being exceffive, *Sedeno* drew them off, and gave another onfet

set the next Day, when the *Indians* seeing many
kill'd by the Fire-arms and Crossbows, march'd out
at Night, in good Order with their Wives, Children, and Goods, in the Centre, to retire to a
Mountain a League from thence, which was thick
wooded , whither they made their way in Safety,
tho' the *Spaniards* pursu'd, and endeavour'd to break
them. Having rested in this Place a few Days, to
cure the sick and wounded, they advanc'd in twelve
Degrees of North Latitude, crossing spacious desert
Plains, where were many Rivers, but well furnish'd
with Venison, which they kill'd in those Plains.
The Men grew tir'd and uneasy, seeing no Hopes
of finding what they sought for, which occasion'd
something of a Mutiny ; but *Sedeno*, being a Man
of ready Wit, and Bold, immediately hang'd Captain *Ochoa* and a Soldier, which quell'd the Commotion ; and tho' sick himself, took Care of all
Things, the Soldiers, tho' they had Flesh enough,
as has been said, wanting Bread, wherefore he sent
out several Parties, all of them returning with little Relief, till *Bonilla* entring upon the Mountain,
fell into the Province of *Cataporaro*, and finding
Plenty of *Indian* Wheat, and some Tokens of Gold,
they agreed to Winter there. Soon after *Antony
Sedeno* dy'd, and *John Fernandez* was chosen Commander in his stead, but he did not long survive,
the Forces marching back when they had consum'd
the Provisions, steering their Course by the Compass, as is done at Sea. The Country they were
then in was low, the Inhabitants thin, without any
Houses, only little Sheds, and the Floods prevailing
in Winter, they withdrew into the Hills, using
Canoes in the lower Grounds, having no Tillage,
nor any Government, and feeding on Dantas, Swine,
and Deer, with some little Meal made of Roots.

L 3 The

The *Spaniards* here suffer'd very much, being, besides all their Wants, often attack'd by those savage, fierce People, to add to all their Sufferings they came into spacious sandy Plains, where they were like to perish with Thirst. After many Days travelling over those Sands, Zabanas and Marshes, the Scouts found a Path, and having advanc'd far along it, spy'd a Village, which they thought to have surpriz'd the next Morning, but the Country being all flat and open, the *Indians* perceiv'd them, and arm'd, being much surpriz'd to see those strange Men in their Country, so that they made some Resistance, till their Wives and Children were got into Places of Safety, and then retir'd themselves, abandoning the Town. There the *Spaniards* found much Corn, and some white Salt, and having rested some Days, held on their March, till they mutiny'd, divided themselves into two Parties, fought among themselves, and after that they stole away in small Numbers to return to the Sea, whereupon *Reynafa,* who had then the Command, made the best of his way to *Venezuela,* one *Lofada,* with thirty of the Men taking his Course for *Cubagua,* and both of them, after many Sufferings arriv'd at those two Places. These Things happen'd in the Years 1537 and 1538.

THE Adelantado *Montejo* being quietly possess'd of the Province of *Honduras,* took away all the Lands from those on whom *Don Peter de Alvarado* had conferr'd them ; banish'd all the *Indians* that were come of their own Accord from *Guatimala,* and brought all the Town that had Revolted into Subjection ; but when he thought all the Country was in Peace, as he had writ to the Vice-Roy of *Mexico,* a bold *Indian* rebell'd in a Territory call'd *Cerquin,* in the District of the City of *Gracias a Dios,*

Dios, lying among the Mountains, and of difficult Access. This *Indian,* whose Name was *Lepira,* signifying Lord of the Mountain, summon'd all the neighbouring Lords, with whose Assistance he drew together thirty thousand Men, whom he perswaded to recover their Liberty, saying, it was a shame, that so great a Number of brave Men should be held in miserable Servitude by a few Strangers; offering to be their Leader, and to expose him'elf to the greatest Dangers, and assuring them of Victory, if they would be united. They promising to stand by him, some for Inclination, and others for fear, the War was begun, and some few *paniards* kill'd, that were surpriz'd about the Country. The Adelantado *Montejo,* sent Captain *Ca eres* from *Gracias a Dios,* with some *Spanish* Soldiers, to reduce *Lempira,* who was then fortifying a very noted ock, call'd of *Cerquin,* where he stood upon his Defence, doing some harm to the *Spaniards,* who suffer'd much at the Siege, which lasted six Months, being oblig'd to Winter in the Field, and perhaps might not have ended so soon, had not *Lempira* happen'd to dye after this manner. Many prime Men were engag d with him in this War, some again st their Will, that they m ght not be look'd upon as Cowards, others out of Respect to *Lempira,* and others advis'd him to give over the War, and make the *paniards* his Friends, for that in the End he wou'd prove the loser; but he was so resolute as never to regard any Overtures of Peace made him by the *Spaniards,* but on the contrary rail'd at them from his Fort. Hereupon Captain *Cazeres* order'd an Horseman to draw as near as the Point Blank of a Musket, and whilst he was making some Proposals, another behind him to shoot *Lempira.* Accordingly, whilst he was in Discourse with the

Horse-

Horfeman, the other Soldier took his aim fo well, that he fhot him in the Forehead, the Head-piece he had on nothing availing him. *Lempira*'s Body came tumbling down the Hill, having that Sort of Cotton Armour on, that was then us'd by the *Spaniards*, as being of much ufe in thofe *Indian* Wars.

THE *Indians* had heard of the *Spaniards* long before they came into the Parts about *Nombre de Dios*, and yet they did not put an End to the Wars among themfelves; becaufe the Inhabitants of *Cerquin*, in particular, thought it impoffible that they fhould come at them, becaufe of their own great Numbers, and that they were firft to pafs through many Countries, and conquer feveral Nations, and particularly the *Cares* and the *Potones*, with whom *Lempira* was then at War, and the Fame of his Valour was fo great, that they affirm'd he had in one Battel kill'd an hundred and twenty Men, with his own Hand, and old *Indians* reported it had been pofitively affirm'd, that *Lempira* was inchanted, becaufe having been in many Battels, he was never wounded. He was of a middle Stature, broad Back'd, ftrong Limb'd, Bold, Daring, of good Senfe, never had any more than two Wives, and dy'd between thirty eight and forty Years of Age. *Alonfo de Caceres* having fent him a Meffage, offering Peace, advifing him to fubmit to the King of *Spain*, and promifing he fhould be honourably treated, he kill'd the Meffengers, declaring he would own no Superior, nor admit of any other Religion or Cuftoms than thofe he had already. When he was dead *Cazeres* fent the other Lords a Prefent of Shirts, Buskins, Cocks, *Mexican* Cloth, and four Spears, threatning, that if they did not fubmit they fhould dye as well as their Chief. They return'd another Prefent of Cocks, faying, they would be fubject to the great King of *Spain*, whom they call'd *Acapuca*, which imports

ports the great Christian; and thus they made their Submission with much Musick and Rejoycing.

THE Province of *Honduras,* on the one side borders upon that of *Guatemala,* at the Cities of *San Salvador* and *San Miguel,* and the Town of *Nueva Xeres*; an another upon the Province of *Nicaragua* about *New Segovia,* and on the third upon the Province of *Taguzgalpa,* call'd *New Estremadura,* and has two Sea Ports, one of them the City of *Truxillo,* the first *Spanish* Town in the Province, and the other *San Juan del Puerto de Cavallos,* where Ships trading thither unlade. Most of the Province is full of Woods and Mountains, tho' there are some Vales, the Land being very spacious. There are in it four *Spanish* Cities, and two Towns, *viz. Truxillo,* which gives the Title to the Bishops; *New Valladolid,* otherwise call d *Comayagua,* in a temperate Situation, healthy, and the Country abounding in Cattel; where the Cathedral is, and the Government resides, and some Silver Mines have been found in its Territory; the City of St. *Peter* founded in the Year 1536, by the Adelantado *Peter de Alvarado,* is hot and sickly, once had the best Trade, but lost it upon the Discovery of *Golfo dulce,* whither the Goods are convey'd in Boats. The City of *Gracias a Dios* stands between Hills, the Territory very woody, produces Corn, and has good Breeds of Mules and Horses. The Town of St. *George* stands in a spacious Plain call'd *Ulancho,* ill seated near the River *Guayape,* whence much Gold has been taken, the whole Extent of the Province is about three hundred and seventy Leagues. The City of *San Juan de Puerto de Cavallos,* being afterwards much infested by Pirates, was remov'd to the Place formerly call'd *Amatique,* eighteen Leagues distant from the other, and call'd *Santo Tomas de Castilla.*

THIS

THIS fame Year 1537, the fupreme Council of the *Indies* in *Spain,* made fome Ordinances for thofe Parts, the Heads whereof were, That as Hofpitals had been founded for the Sick, in the Cities of *Nombre de Dios* and *Panama,* the like fhould be done at *Vera Cruz* and *Puebla de los Angeles* in *New Spain;* that the Prelates fhould fee the Children of the mixt Race between *Spaniards* and *Indians,* inftructed in the Chriftian Doctrine and good Manners; that the Vice-Roy fhould not permit the *Indian* Youth to live idly, but to learn fome Trades; that the Colledge founded by the *Francifcan* Friers at *Mexico,* for teaching *Indian* Boys the *Latin* Grammar, fhould be finifh d; that no Cloth of Gold, or Silver Brocades, nor Laces, or Embroideries, &c. fhould be worn; that Pieces of E ght, of Four, of Two, and fingle Royals fhould be coin'd in the Mint; that Roads fhould be made; that *Indians* who did not underftand *Spanifh,* appearing before any Court, fhould be allow'd a Chriftian Friend of their own, to affift them, left the common Interpreters call'd *Naguatatos,* fhould not explain things fairly, and thofe People be thereby wrong'd; that Alcaldes fhould be cho en yearly in Corporations, as in *Spain,* and that Appeals from them fhould lye to the Royal Courts, except in fuch Cafes, as according to the Laws of *Spain,* were to be referr d to the Council of the Place; that thofe who were Alcaldes fhould not be chofen again into the fame Office till two Years after they had ferv'd it before; that no Officer of the Crown fhould be chofen into that Employment, &c.

IN *April* 1538, a Ship commanded by *Peter de Cifuentes,* fail'd from *Santo Domingo,* in the Ifland *Hifpaniola,* laden with war-like Stores, and other Goods for the Ifland *Margarita,* and having touch'd

at

at *Puerto Rico,* proceeded to another Port in the Ifland of *Santa Cruz,* to water, where two large Canoes full of *Canibal* Archers came out to oppofe
them, and fhooting poifon'd Arrows purfu'd them
two Leagues. The Wind being fcant, five Days
after they arriv'd at the Ifland *Piritu,* thirty Leagues
to the Leeward of the Pearl Coaft, where the Pilot not being able to get a diftinct View of the
Land, ftood away to Weftward, coafting along the
Continent, and thus they came to the Ifland of *Gua-
iamacoran,* but finding no Water there, ftruck over
to a Port on the Continent, where the *Indians* were
in Arms; however they put into a Creck, where
they lay all Night, and in the Morning eleven Canoes came out, asking for Axes. A *Genoefe* Sailor
thinking the *Indians* had been Friends, unadvifedly
went into one of the Canoes, which immediately
made away, the *Indians* fhooting their Arrows ; the
few Sailors aboard the Ship fir'd at them with two
Muskets they had, loaded with Flints, and kill d one
that feem'd to be their Chief, and two others, which
made them keep aloof, many of them for fear of
the Muskets, leaping into the Water, but the *Genoefe*
Sailor was never more heard of. Thence they fail'd to
another Port, where finding no Inhabitants, they
water'd, and perceiving that their Pilot was ignorant, and knew not where he was, they refolv'd to
return to *Santo Domingo,* and touching at an Ifland
higher up, belonging to the Factor, *John de Am-
pues,* their Pilot ran away from them, whereupon it
was refolv'd to hold on their way for *Santo Domingo,* without any body to direct them, being all un-
skilful in the Art of Sailing. Being in this Confufion, and in the midft of their Paffage, a Storm
came up that bore away both their Mafts, with the
Sails, the Ship at the fame time taking in much
Water,

Water, and thus they drove a head, as the Wind and Sea would carry them, till fix Days after, they came at Night upon *Cape de la Serrana*, the Storm never ceafing, where the Ship beating on the Flat, becaufe they had not yet feen the Ifland, by reafon it is very fmall, they at length difcover'd it by the whitenefs of the Sand, and one of the Men bethought himfelf to take a Flask of Powder and a Steel in his Mouth, and fwam to the Ifland, where having left the Powder, he return'd to the Ship, which he found fplit into four Parts, and the Men in one of them. He then took what Ropes he could find, and making them faft to one another at their length, carry'd one end Afhore, along which the other Men got off, the next Flood in the Night carrying away all the Ship, fo that in the Morning nothing of it was to be feen, nor any thing fav'd out of it but the Powder and the Steel, fo that for want of a Flint, they fed near two Months on the raw Flefh of Sea Calves and Cormorants, drinking their Blood. That courfe of Life being fo miferable, they made a Float of fome Pieces of Timber the Sea had thrown on the Ifland, binding them together with Thongs made of the Skins of the Sea Calves. Three of the Men got upon it, two and a Boy ftaying behind. Four Days after, one of thofe that remain'd, whofe Name was *Moreno,* there being no Water nor Fire on the Ifland, and the Month of *Auguft* being come in, began to eat his own Arms, and dy'd raving of thofe hurts. The other having no Company left but the Boy, confider'd what he fhould do to live, began to fcratch the Ground with the Shells of Tortoifes, where he found the Water as Salt as that in the Sea, becaufe there was no Depth, for which reafon he drank it mix'd with the Blood of Sea Calves,

for

for it had never rain'd in all that Time, to make
any Advantage of it, tho' he had dug Pits in the
Sand, lin'd with the Skins of the faid Sea Calves,
and when it pleas'd God that the Rain fell, which
was in *October,* they drank out of Sea Shel's ; but
that fupply was not lafting, the Sand fucking it up.
The Winter coming on, and no Poffibility of living
without Fire, they made a Float, and went over to
the Place where the Ship had perifh'd, and duck-
ing feveral Times, it pleas'd God that they found
a Pebble, with which they ftruck Fire, looking upon it as the faving of their Lives, and therefore
made Fire every Night, that it might be feen by
the Ships paffing that way.

THERE were two other Men in the like defperate Condition on an Ifland two Leagues from thence,
who feeing the Fire, repair'd to it on a Float, after having liv'd in that manner five Years. They
all agreed to make a Boat of the Timber the Sea
brought Afhore, to which purpofe they made Bellows of the Sea Calves Skins for their Forge, and
found a Saw and fome Iron where the Ship funk.
Having made their Boat, and Sails of Skins they
embark'd, defigning for the Ifland of *Jamaica,* but
when put to Sea, a Sailor call'd Mafter *John,* being
the fame that had been on the Ifland from the firft
with the Boy, confidering that the Boat was made
of odd Pieces, without any Pitch or Tar, or Calk-
ing, but only daub'd with the Greafe of the Sea
Calves, mixt with Charcoal Duft, for which reafon it was impoffible to be fav'd in it, he refolv'd
to return to his Ifland, with one of thofe that came
from the other ; the other Man and the Boy
going on in that Boat, who were never more heard
of. The other two returning to the Ifland, as
has been faid, made two little Boats of thofe Skins,
and

and fcour'd all over that Shore, being twelve Leagues
in length, the greateft Depth not above a Fathom,
in which Space there there are feventeen fmall Iſlands, all of them fometimes overflow'd by the Sea,
except five, which is proper to be known for Ships
that may happen to paſs that way. The two Men
being in that Diftrefs, fed on the Tortoifes Eggs
they found on thofe Iſlands, being cloath'd in the
Skins of Sea Calves, and agreed to build two little
Towers of dry Stone, fixteen Fathoms about, and
four in height, with Stairs to go up, one on the
North, and the other on the South Side, where
they went up to look out, and made Fire to be
feen by any Ships paffing by, in hopes of being
reliev'd out of that mifery. They alfo made an
Enclofure of twenty two Fathom, to take Fiſh, the
Stones whereof coft them much Trouble, being o-
blig'd to fetch them out of the Sea, becaufe the
Iſland was all Sand, of which they made Salt, by
cafting it into Pits, with Water, which turn d into Salt. They built an Hut, cover'd with Skins;
five Months in the Year they fed on Tortoifes
Eggs, which were good Suftenance, for they waſh'd
and fet them out a drying, and being bury'd in the
Ground a Fortnight, the White of them turn'd into Water, and was good to drink. At other Times
they would eat Cormorants, when to be had, making them caft up the Fiſh they carry'd for their
Young, which they eat, and a fort of Roots like
Purflane. Three Years after the others went away,
being eight they had been there, it pleas'd God to
relieve them in their Diftrefs, for one Day they
fpy'd a Ship under Sail, made a great Smoak on
their Towers, which being perceiv'd by thofe a-
borad, they lay by, hoifted out their Boat, the
Mafter went Afhore with a Notary, who took an
Account

Account of all thofe Particulars here mention'd, and then they carry'd thofe two Men to the *Havana* where their Habit and manner of living was much admir'd. Thofe Men farther declar'd, that the Sea Crabs and Snails tormented them much, breaking their reft in the Night, for which reafon they were often forc'd to turn the Day into Night. Mafter *John* alfo confefs'd, that making his complaint one Day to God, for that he had been eight Years in that Defert, naked, bare-footed, and in fuch want of Suftenance, he pray'd he might either be taken out of the World, or carry'd to fome Chriftian Country; after which in a Paffion of Defpair, he faid, fince God will not, let the Devil take me hence, and I fhall end my Days; and that rifing in the Night, he faw the Devil ftanding clofe to his Hut, more hideous than he is painted, his Nofe very flat, cafting out Smoak at it, and Fire at his Eyes, his Feet like a Grifon's, and Tails like a Rat's, his Legs like a Man, his Hair very black, with two little Horns. Seeing that frightful Spectacle, he faid, he had call'd his Companion, and that taking a Crofs they had, they walk'd all over the Ifland, praying, and never after faw any thing, but a Fortnight after he was much frighted, thinking he had heard Footfteps, but faw nothing. During the aforefaid eight Years, the fame Mafter *John* faid, he had been twice Sick, both times about *Auguft*, and that he had let himfelf Blood.

NEWS being brought into *Spain* of the Battel before fpoken of, fought at the Salt Pits near *Cuzco* in *Peru* the King fent Orders into thofe Parts, enjoyning both Parties to live in Peace, till their Governments were limited by regal Authority, with other Directions moftly in Favour of the *Pizarros*; but at the fame Time a Court was erected at *Panama,* whofe
Jurif-

Jurifdiction was to extend over all Parts of *South America*, that Appeals from all Governours might be brought before it, and thofe in Power might not oppre's all others by obftructing their having Recourfe elfewhere for Redrefs of their Grievances. That Court was alfo to promote the Converfion of the *Indians*, and their being brought to live politely, that they fhould not be compell'd to pay any Impofitions but fuch as they had before paid to their Lords, when Pagans; and that no *Indians* fhould be put to work in the Mines, but Blacks carry'd over for that purpofe. Many more Powers and Inftructions were given to the Judges of that Court, relating to particular Perfons, which are not neceffary to be taken Notice of; but among the reft they were enjoyn'd to caufe fearch to be made into the burning Mountain of *Mafaya*, in the Province of *Nicaragua*, of which one *Francis Sanchez*, Inhabitant of the City of *Granada*, in that Province, had writ to the King, that he had been let down into it with fome others two hundred and thirty Fathoms in Depth, to an open fpacious Place there was within, having another Mouth, from which there were an hundred Fathoms more to the Place where the Fire lay, burning continually in moft furious Manner, the which the faid *Sanchez* did believe to be either Silver or Gold, but that having with a Chain let down a Bucket, made of a Piece of a great Gun, the fame broke by the way, not being fo well made as it ought to have been, and fo the intended Difcovery was difappointed. Upon this Information and Order, fome Perfons were with much Peril let down into the faid burning Mountain, being furnifh'd with a proper Utenfil to bring up fome of that burning Matter, and what came up prov'd

to

to be some burnt Dross, till at last their Chain either broke, or was melted by the violent Fire ; upon which Trial the most knowing Men and Founders in those Parts declar'd, that what had been brought up was nothing but calcin'd Stones, or at most Sulphur.

The End of the Fourth Book.

THE
General HISTORY

Of the vaſt CONTINENT and ISLANDS of

AMERICA, &c.

✿✿✿✿✿✿✿✿✿✿✿✿✿✿✿✿✿✿✿✿✿✿✿✿✿✿

DECAD. IV. BOOK V.

✿✿✿✿✿✿✿✿✿✿✿✿✿✿ ✿✿✿✿✿✿✿✿✿✿✿✿

CHAP. I.

Actions of Lawrence de Aldana, *in the Provinces of* Quito, Paſto, *and* Popayan; *his Colony of* Anzerma; *Deſcription of the Mountain* Abibe.

HAVING left *Peru* for ſome Time, we muſt now return to ſee what was done in theſe vaſt Dominions. *Laurence de Aldana,* who, as has been ſaid before, had been ſent in the Year 1538, againſt *Belalcazar,* who was making the Diſcoveries already mention'd, in the Province of *Popayan,* being

ing come to *Quito,* fent away two of *Belalcazar*'s
Friends Prifoners to *Lima,* and then proceeded him felf to-
wards *Popayan,* which was eighty Leagues diftant, the
Soldiers muttering for being carry'd away againft their
old Commander. Being come to *Pafto,* he ftay'd
there two Months, reducing all the Lords of that
Country, that had revolted. There was at this
Time great Scarcity of Provifions at *Popayan,* the
Indian Wheat being brought twenty or thirty
Leagues, becaufe the Natives would not till the
Ground, hoping to ftarve out the *Spaniards,* who
were forc'd to feed on fuch Herbs as they found
in the Fields, and both they and the *Indians* did
eat Alligators, Snakes, Locufts, and many other
loathfome Things, which occafion'd much Sicknefs,
and the Famine was fo great all about, that the Natives did eat one another, ranging about in Parties to
take Prifoners, and devour them. The *Spaniards*
ask'd them, why they would be fo inhuman, when
they might avoid that Calamity, by fowing their
Corn ; and they anfwer'd, They were fatisfy'd to
confume one another, and be bury'd in their own Bellies.
This Calamity was follow'd by another no lefs de-
ftructive, being a Plague of fuch a pernicious Nature, that Men dropp'd down dead on a fudden.
Ferdinand Sanchez Morillo, Inhabitant of *Popayan,*
reported that he met an *Indian* upon the Road, carrying feven Hands ty'd up with a Cord, and ask-
ing what they were for, he anfwer'd, to eat them,
Ten or twelve Boys being in a Corn Field, twenty
Indians fell upon, cut in Pieces, and devour'd them.
Many more fuch Barbarities happen'd, during this
Famine, when above fifty thoufand *Indians* were eat-
en, and above an hundred thoufand dy'd of the
Plague, tho' *Francis Garcia de Tovar,* the Deputy
Governour, us'd all his Endeavours to obftruct that

inhuman

inhuman way of Feeding, and to apply Medicines
to the Peftilence. *Aldana* coming to *Popayan,* conceal'd his moft important Commiffion in Hopes to
get *Belalcazar* into his Hands ; but he, as has been
faid, was gone into *Spain,* and *Aldana* taking all poffible Care for the Prefervation of the *Indians,* went
away to *Cali,* from whence he fent Provifions for
the Relief of thofe at opayan, who therefore call'd
him their Father, and Reftorer ; and the *Indians*
feeing the *Spaniards* were not to be ftarv'd out, fell
again to fowing of Corn.

BEFORE this in the Year 1536, the licenciate
John de Badillo, had been fent to *Cartagena,* as Judge,
to fit upon Trial of *Don Peter de Heredia,* Governour of that City. Captain *Francis Cefar,* a Man
of Valour and Difcretion, was then gone out with a
Party upon Difcovery, in which Employment he
fpent about ten Months, travelling over almoft impaffable Mountains, call'd of *Abibe,* till he came into the Vale of *Goaca,* where the *Spaniards* being but
fixty three in Number, defeated an Army of twenty thoufand *Indians.* After this Victory they found
a fmall Temple, or Place of Worfhip, and near it
a large Tomb, out of which they took the Value
of thirty thoufand Pieces of Eight in Gold, and
were told there was a confiderable Number of fuch
Graves in the fame Vale. *Cefar* having loft feveral Men
in that laborious Expedition , thofe that remain'd
being few, and the Horfes quite fpoilt, he refolv'd to
turn back, and it pleas'd God that they arriv'd at the
City of St. *Sebaftian of Uraba,* whereas they had
fpent ten Months on their Journey outward. Advice hereof was foon carry'd to *Cartagena,* where
the licenciate *Badillo* had imprifon'd *Don Peter de Heredia,* and being allur'd by that Quantity of Gold,
hoping much more might be found , refolv'd to
go

go himfelf upon that Expedition, that in reality his
Defign was to crofs over the Country to *Peru,* for the
great Fame of the Wealth of that Country, and in
his way to fearch thofe Tombs he had heard of. In
order to it he fent by Sea, up the Bay of *Uraba,*
to the City of St. *Sebaftian,* three hundred and fifty *Spaniards,* with five hundred and twelve Horfes,
a great Number of Blacks and *Indians,* and all other
Neceffaries, on which he expended above an hundred
thoufand Pieces of Eight. He fet out from that City in *February* 1537, and fpent a Year upon the
Progrefs, enduring many Hardfhips, in hopes of finding an immenfe Treafure, and at length having loft
ninty two *Spaniards,* and an hundred and nineteen
Horfes, arriv'd with the Remainder at the City of
Cali, having always aim'd at making for the South
Sea, for otherwife he had fallen into *Bogota,* which
had enrich'd them all, without paffing through fo
many Difficulties. There *Laurence de Aldana,* order'd the Men to be well Quarter'd and Entertain'd.

HAVING here mention'd the Mountains of *A-
bibe,* it will be proper to give fome Account of
them This Ridge runs to the Weftward, the Length
of it is not certainly known, but the Breadth of it
is in fome Places twenty Leagues, in others more,
and in others lefs. The ways the *Indians* had on it
were fo very uncouth, that the Horfes could not pafs.
Captain *Cefar,* the firft *Spaniard* that crofs'd them,
marching Eaftward, arriv'd in the Vale of *Guaca,* thro'
ways, that befides their Steepnefs, were full of Bufhes
and Roots of Trees, that entangled the Feet of Men,
as well as Horfes. Towards the Top the Afcent
is very Steep, and when *Badillo* pafs'd it, a Paffage
was made of Timber and Earth, and yet many
Horfes broke their Necks, others were left behind

M 3   alive,

alive, not being to go farther, and many Men perifh d miferably. On the Top of the Mountain
there are no Towns, but in the Vales there are
many *Indians*, rich in Gold, which is found in the
Rivers that run down from the Mountain to the
Weftward. The Rain falls moft part of the Year
on the Mountain, and the Trees are continually
dropping with that Rain, yet there is no Grafs for
Horfes, and the *Spaniards* muft have perifh'd had
they not always made Fires of a fort of Trees like
Afhes, the Timber whereof within is white and
dry, was foon kindled, and then burnt like dry
Fir, till quite confum'd. In the *Indian* Towns
there was Plenty of Provifions, Fruit, and Fifh ;
they wore Cotton Mantles of feveral Colours ; their
Weapons were Darts, Spears, and *Macanas*; they
had Bridges over the Rivers, made of long tough
Roots growing among the Trees, of which they twif-
ted Cabels, faftned to the Trees on each Side, and
laid Timbers acrofs them. Moft of the *Indians* about
that Mountain were fubject to a Cazique call'd *Nu-
tibara*, who was carry'd about on a golden Bier,
and had many Heads of his Enemies before his
Houfe, for they were wont to eat their Bodies ;
they Worfhip'd the Sun ; the Devil appear'd and
fpoke to them in feveral Shapes. An *Indian* Woman,
who went away with *Badillo*'s Men, told them, that
when Captain *Cefar* return'd to *Cartagena*, the prime
Men of thofe Vales affembled, and having offer'd
extraordinary Sacrifices, the Devil appear'd to them
in the Shape of a Tyger, and told them, that thofe
Men were come from beyond the Sea, and would
foon return to fubdue the Country, therefore they
fhould prepare for their Defence, and then he vanifh d ; after which Preparations were made accordingly,

dingly, and all the Gold being taken out of the Graves was hid.

ALL that was got by *Badillo's* tirefome Expedition, amounted to two thoufand fix hundred Pieces of Eight in Gold, which had been ftolen out of a Bundle in his Tent, eight Leagues fhort of *Cali*, and was taken upon the Thief, and being divided among the furviving *Spaniards*, came to five Pieces of Eight and an half a Man, after having gone through fo many Hardfhips. *Badillo* having refted his Men at *Cali*, was about fending Colonies to fettle in the Province of *Burutica*, ; but *Aldana* knowing that he had incens'd all the People in his Paffage thither, would not permit it, whereupon *Badillo* went away, with fome of his Men to *Popayan*, in order to proceed towards the South Sea, and *Aldana* produc'd his Commiffion to be Governour in thofe Parts, which was well receiv'd in *Quito, Cali, afto,* and *Popayan*, and he began to apply himfelf to the Converfion of the *Indians*, being a modeft, difcreet, and good Chriftian. He next divided the Lands among thofe he thought moft deferving, and fent the reft to fettle in the Province of *Anzerma*, which *Belalcazar* had difcover'd, confirm'd *Peter de Anafco* in his Poft, he being then founding a Colony at *Tumana*. *George de Robledo* was order'd to lead the new Colony to *Anzerma*; and to call it *Santana de los Cavalleros*, otherwife nam d *Anzerma*; four Leagues to the Weftward whereof is a good Town, and a League from that again is the River of *Santa Marta*. The *Indians* of the aforefaid Town, were fubject to a Lord call d *Cirichia*, who liv'd in a good Houfe, with a Court before it, enclos d with a fort of very thick Reeds or Canes, that grow in that Country, and on the Tops of them many Heads of the *Indians* that had been eaten, and he had feveral Wives. When *Badillo's* Men pafs d through this Town, the

M 4

Indians

Indians having hid all their Provisions, there was no *Indian* Wheat, or other Food to be found ; and those *Spaniards* for a Year past had eaten no Flesh, but of the Horses that dy'd, or some Dogs, whereupon thirty Soldiers ranging abroad for Meat, lighted near the great River on some People that were fled, who had a Pot full of Flesh ; those *Spaniards* being violently hungry, thought of nothing but eating, and when they were well satisfy'd, one of the them took out of the Pot a Man's Hand, with the Fingers and Nails, which quite turn d their Stomachs, but their hunger being quell'd, they return'd to their Quarters much out of Countenance. Many Brooks have their Sources on a Mountain near this Town, and Gold is found in them. The Natives went bare-foot and Naked, the Women wearing little Mantles, and some of them are Beautiful. They bury d their dead in their Houses ; had no Idols, nor was there any Worship found among them ; but they talk'd with the Devil ; marry'd their Nieces, and some of them their Sisters ; the Son of the chief Wife was Heir. This Province borders on that of *Cartama*, through which *Rio Grande* runs, and beyond it is the River *Pozo* ; to the Eastward of it are other great Towns, abounding in Provisions and Fruits, and the Inhabitants are not fond of human Flesh. The Lords were carry'd on Biers, and wore fine Cotton Mantles of several Colours ; the Women wore their Hair curiously comb'd, rich Gold Collars and Rings in their Ears, making Holes in their Noses to fix little Pellets of Gold in them ; and had large Vessels of the same Metal for use in their Houses. They had there many Sorcerers; no regard was had to Women's being Maids when they marry d ; dead Bodies were parch d at the Fire, with much Lamentation, after which
they

they drank, and repeated a fort of Pfalms they had learnt of their Forefathers, and then bury'd them in their Houfes. In other Parts they bury'd them on Hills, with their Cloaths, Arms, Wealth, Meat, and fome Women alive.

AT the End of the third Chapter of this Book, we left *Peter de Anzures*, marching on his Difco-very with the Men that had belong'd to *Peter de Candia*, entering upon a Plain in which there were fome Groves and Rivers, at the Conclufion of the Year 1538. Hoping to have found fome Towns there to quarter his Men, he found only Fields where the Root Yuca had been planted, but all pull'd up, and hid by the *Indians* upon Advice that the *Spaniards* were coming. After much ranging about, nothing could be found but a Place that feem'd to have been Inhabited, whereupon he fent Captain *Alonfo Palomino* to look out farther, and re-turn to him at a Place appointed. *Palomino* having travell'd twelve Leagues, and feen nothing but fome fmall Towns, without any Provifions, return'd with fome *Indians*, who affirm'd, there was nothing elfe to be feen for many Leagues farther ; but that five and twenty Days Journey from thence, there was a mighty River running from Eaft to Weft fo wide that the Sight could not reach from the one Bank to the other, and in it many Iflands inhabited ; and that at the end of thofe five and twenty Days Journey, there were large Provinces, inhabited by many Nations, fpeaking feveral Languages, where there was Plenty of Sheep, Deer, and other forts of Food, with delicious Fruit, and that the People there were cloath d. This Information much con-founded *Anzures*, who was covetous to fee thofe Countries, but confider d that it was impoffible to carry his Forces through thofe Deferts, and back to

Peru ;

Peru ; besides that, he knew not whether those *Indians* spoke Truth, and instead of twenty five there might not be fifty Days Journey, wherefore he resolv'd to return to his Men, without finding any thing but those great Plains, with the Towns in them burnt, which the Natives said had been done by their Enemies the *Juries.* The Winter drawing on, when the Rivers welling would become impassable, it was resolv'd to turn towards the Provinces of the *Moxos* and *Cotabamba,* to come out at *Chuquiabo,* and accordingly they went up the River with much Toil ; for besides the want of Provisions, they were oblig'd to hew their Way through the thick Woods, having no other Food but the Cores of tall Palm-Trees, growing in those Parts, and Herbs ; and to add to their Affliction, the continual Rains rotted their Cloaths on their Bodies, whilst at the same time they were making Passages over Quag-Mires with Boughs of Trees, and to cross the Rivers on Floats ; the *Indians* and Blacks dropping down dead as they went, and the survivers feeding on the Bodies of the dead. Having thus travel'd sixteen Days up the River, without finding any Town, when about three thousand Men and Women were dead, they came to a Town where some sustenance was found, yet but little in that great Distress.

THE Inhabitants of the Place informing them, that the way on the Left, would carry them to *Collao,* they enter'd upon it, with continual Rain, and no Provisions, so that they kill'd their Horses by Degrees, thinking them great Dainties, and yet there was not one indecent Word, or the least muttering among those Men against their Commanders. Having with much Difficulty surpriz'd one of four Blacks that had cross'd the River, by whose Direction they resolv'd to pass the same, and made

Floats

Floats in order to it, a great Number of *Indians*
ftood ready on the other Side to oppofe them,
who wounded eight *Spaniards,* three whereof dy'd,
yet were they put to Flight. On that Side of
the River they found a large Field, whence the
Indian Wheat had been carry'd in, and a Town
call'd *Setelingra,* where was great Store of Yuca,
Agis or Batatas, and other forts of Food, with
which they loaded three Floats, and fent them to the
Forces. Upon the Encouragement of this good
Fare, they ftay'd there fix Weeks, without any
Salt or Flefh. When all the Food was devour'd,
they fet out from thence without any, and after
three Days march through Woods, met with fome
Cacao, and three Days after came into a Field of *Indian* Corn. Notwithftanding thefe fmall Recruits,
they were fo much fpent, that not being able to
carry the Veftments for Divine Service, they bury'd them near an *Indian* Place of Worfhip, and by
them a *Spaniard* that dy'd. Being come in this
Diftrefs into the Province of *Tacama,* a Country as
impaffable as they reft, they threw away their Arms
and all they had, refolving to return to *Peru,* after
five Months of Diftrefs, fifty *Spaniards* being fick,
and the reft carrying them what they could get to
eat, three or four Leagues. Eight Days they waited
to be able to crofs the River *Tacama,* becaufe it
was much fwell'd, and yet feven *Spaniards* were
drowned in paffing it when fallen. The Ways
were ftrew'd with *Spaniards, Indians,* and Blacks,
that dy'd for Hunger, and when an Horfe was kill'd,
each Quarter was fold for three hundred Pieces of
Eight, and the reft proportionable, for Payment
whereof the Buyers gave Notes under their Hands.
Much Treafure was thrown away during this Expedition, and coming to a Town call'd *Quiquixano,*
there

I

there was nothing in it to eat, which oblig'd them
to kill fourteen Horses, for by this Time an hundred and forty three *Spaniards* were dead, and above
four thousand *Indians* and Blacks, two hundred and
twenty Horses had been eaten, each of which had
cost five or six hundred Pieces of Eight. Three
Days after they came to the Town where they
had enter'd upon their Progress, call'd *Ayabire,*
where they found *Gaspar Rodriguez Enriquez,* Brother
to *Peter Anzurez,* who like a Man of Honour, was
going to his Assistance, with seventy *Spaniards,* and
a great Quantity of Provisions. It is to be observ'd,
that the Leagues mention'd in all these Expeditions
are computed from the Degrees of Latitude and
Longitude, and that this Ridge of Mountains which
parts *Peru* from the Countries to which the said
Expeditions were undertaken, extending from *Otopari* on the *Andes* of *Tono,* to the Vale of *Cochabamba,* North and South, is sixty two Leagues in
Length, according to the Latitude, but much more
in the Course of Travelling, and *Otopari* is in thirteen Degrees of Latitude, and *Cochabamba* in seventeen. There are four ways to pass that Mountain,
the first of *Opotari,* along the River thirty Leagues
from *Cuzco;* the second in the Territory of *Caravaya,* by *Sandia* and *San Juan del Oro,* little above
thirty Leagues to the Southward from the first Pass
of *Opotari;* the third at *Camata,* eighteen or twenty Leagues beyond *Sandia,* and the fourth at *Cochabamba,* twenty three Leagues by the Latitude above
Camata; for tho' Attempts have been made behind
Pueblo Nuevo, and at *Sangavan* to find a Passage,
none have been able to do it, so that these four are
the only Ways.

To continue the Discoveries at this Time attempted from *Peru,* Captain *Mercadillo,* formerly mention'd,

tion'd, having gather'd an hundred and eighty five
Spaniards, Horfe and Foot, march'd along the River of the *Chupachos,* and being told by the Guides,
that he ought to keep on the Right Hand of the
River, for that the other Side would lead him into
the Diftrict affign'd *Alonfo de Alvarado,* he would
not be advis'd ether by the *Spaniards* or the Natives,
becaufe befides being of a pofitive Temper, he was
Rough and ill Natur'd, fo that adhering obftinate-
ly to his own Conceit, he advanc'd to the Eaftward, over vaft high Mountains, and fuch uncooth
Ways, that all the Horfes perifh'd, and in this manner, the Men being all diffatisfy'd with his ill Management ; they came to the Province of *Mama,*
a war-like Nation, where finding good Store of Provifions, they refted about fix Weeks ; and fending
out Men, with Native Guides to view the Ways,
were inform'd, that if they march'd to the Weftward, they would come into rich and populous Provinces ; yet he would hold on his Way to the
Eaftward, becaufe, being fenfible that he was ill belov'd by his Men, he concluded, that if he happen'd
to come near to *Alvarado,* who had gain'd the Affections of moft People, his Soldiers would defert
him ; and therefore he advanc'd over almoft impe-
netrable Mountains, with the ufual Difficulties from
Rivers, Moraffes, and Hunger, his Men muttering
and declaring, that no good was to be expected under fuch a Commander. Being come to the moft
difficult Part of the Mountain, after feven Days
march, Parties were fent out feveral Ways, which
returning, brought Advice that there were no Roads,
Habitations, or Provifions to be found, which was
a great Mortification to them all, and Confufion to
the Commander *Mercadillo,* who in his Tent advis'd with fome Friends and Natives about the
Method

Method that might be us'd to penetrate through
that wretched Country, to the Province of the
Ycayzingas, which Name fignifies, double Nofes, becaufe thofe People us'd to fplit theirs. They all told
him, it was impoffible to pafs that way, where they
muft all perifh, yet was he fo indifcreet as to reject
their Council, and much more to communicate it
to thofe that did not keep the Secret; for when
the Advice thofe he had confulted with had given,
was made known, a *Spaniard* whofe Name was *Ca-
calla*, confidering the Folly of the Undertaking, difcours'd *Ferdinand Gafcon*, the Colonel, and other
prime Men, reprefenting, that their Commander was
refolv'd to lead them to evident Deftruction, whereupon thofe Gentlemen, repairing to *Mercadillo*, in a
very courteous and fubmiffive Manner as was due to
a Superior, intreated him, as their Chief, and a Chriftian, not to caft away fo many brave Men, but to
return to the Province of *Mama*, where they would
confult about finding a fafer way to the Province
of *Ycayzinga*. He anfwer'd, he was refolv'd not to
turn back, but to hold on the fame way, whereupon they left him very much diffatisfy'd. This
being known, all the Men repair'd to the Colonel,
and other prime Perfons conjuring them not to lead
them to manifeft Deftruction in compliance with
the Madnefs of *Mercadillo*; whereupon, they in
the Prefence of a Notary, requir'd him to turn
back, and he refufing, they requir'd him again, when he
bid thofe that did it, to give it under their Hands.
No fooner were the Words out of his Mouth, than
they all drew together to Sign; yet he ftill perfifting, commanded him to defift, or he would punifh them, whereupon the Colonel and other prime
Men laid hold of him, faying, It was no differ-
vice to God or the King, to prevent thofe Forces
perifhing

perifhing through his Rafhnefs, fince they were all unanimoufly agreed in that Point. His Obftinacy nothing abating, they drew up a formal Procefs a-gainft him, and fo return'd to *Xauxa.*

CHAP. II.

The Governour Pizarro *comes to Cuzco ; defeat of* Indians ; Ferdinand Pizarro *goes away to* Spain ; *the Towns of* Arequipa *and* Pafto *built* ; Defcription *of the Province of* Pafto.

FRancis *Pizarro,* Governour of *Peru,* being at *Xauxa,* receiv'd Advice of the Defeat of *Almagro* before fpoken of, near *Cuzco,* and with it that Gentleman s Son *James,* was deliver'd to him, whom he fent away to the City of *Lima,* ordering him to be well treated, and promifing that his Father fhould not be put to Death, which none of *Almagro's* Friends gave any Credit to, becaufe *Pizarro* was then too much puff'd up to return to his former Partnerfhip. He proceeding thence to *Cuzco,* at the Bridge of *Abancay* had the News of the Death of the Adelantado *Almagro,* which fome faid he had receiv'd before, and conceal'd it, and that at this Place the Trumpets founded for Joy of it ; tho' his Friends affirm'd, that he was concern'd and fhed Tears. At *Cuzco* he was receiv'd with Tokens of Joy, and willingly gave Ear to Flatterers, who applauded the defeating and putting to Death of *Almagro.* The Account here given of the Proceedings a-gainft that unfortunate Gentleman, and the Behaviour of his Adverfaries is exactly the fame that was
                                         tranfmit-

tranfmitted to the King, and deliver'd by the Sons
of many that were prefent at all thofe Tranfactions;
tho' others reprefented them as directed by Affection or Prejudice. When *Pizarro* came to *Cuzco,*
his Brothers were at *Collao* ; *Ferdinand* who defir'd
to return into *Spain,* endeavouring to amafs much
Gold and Silver, either by fair or foul means, as
concluding, that the more he carry'd, the better he
fhould fuceed in his Bufinefs. The *Indians* in thofe
Parts under ftanding that there were very many
Spaniards at *Cuzco,* and believing they would come
thither, affembled in great Numbers upon Advice
brought them that *Ferdinand Pizarro* was mov'd to
Ayabire, pofted themfelves along the Drein that was
from the Lake *Titicaca,* where that Commander underftood, that they expected him, and had taken a-
way the Bridge that us'd to be there. The *Spaniards* being in Sight of thofe *Indians,* who fhouted
at them on the other Side of the Water, fome Horfemen ventur'd into it, of whom four were drowned,
and one that got over was taken and facrificed. Captain *Gabriel de Rojas* return'd to the Town of *Ce-
pita,* and carrying Timber, made a way over ; whereupon the *Indians* fled, and were purfu'd to *Collao,*
where feveral Skirmifhes happen'd with them ; and
Ferdinand Pizarro fuppofing his Brother *Francis* to
be then at *Cuzco,* went away to that City, leaving
his other Brother *Gonzalo,* to command in thofe Parts.

THE Soldiers of the Party of the *Pizarros,* that
did not go upon the Difcoveries before mention'd,
were difpers'd about the Provinces of *Condefuyo,* and
Chinchafuyo, living after a libertine Manner, thinking
they might do what they pleas'd, and when the
Indians complain'd to the Governour, he receiv'd
them after a ftern Manner, telling them they ly'd,
which Encouragement of his made the Magiftrates
and

and Officers of Juftice, connive at all their Villanies. On the other hand he publickly fhow'd his Aver- fion to the *Spaniards* of *Chile*, which incens'd them, and accordingly they only waited an Opportunity to fhow their Refentment, and raife new Troubles. *James de Alvarado* whom the Adelantado *Almagro* had appointed his Executor, and as fuch Governour of the New Kingdom of *Toledo*, till his Son was of Age, being willing to perform the Truft repos'd in him by his late Friend, very civilly intreated the Governour *Pizarro*, that laying afide the City of *Cuzco*, till fuch Time as the King fhould decide that Controverfy, he would evacuate the reft of that Province, in Excution of what the King had directed by his Commiffion. *Pizarro* anfwer'd him very rudely, faying, That his Government had no Bounds, but extended as far as *Flanders*. Thus it appear'd that the Troubles were not at an End, that his good Fortune had made him lay afide all the Sedatenefs he before pretended to, and that he was entirely poff.fs d by Ambition. *James de Alvarado* taking with him fuch Evidences as he thought re- quifite, went away to *Lima*, where he embark'd for *Spain*, tho' the Governour endeavour'd to ftop him.

THE *Ingo Manga* having withdrawn himfelf, as was faid before, with his *Orejones* and old Com- manders to the Mountains *Andes*, his Head Quar- ters being at *Viticos*, his Men made Excurfions on the High Ways to rob, to the great Difturbance of the Country, for they impal'd all the *Spaniards* that fell into their Hands, or elfe rack'd and facrific'd them, which ftruck fuch a Terror, that they durft not not go to *Cuzco*, unlefs it were in confiderable Numbers. *Francis izarro* appointed the Factor *Il- lan Suarez de Carvajal*, to put an End to that War. He march'd with a good Power from *Cuzco* to

Bilcas, whence he proceeded to the Province of *Gua-manga,* and encamp'd at *Uripa,* four Leagues from *Cubamba.* Upon Advice thereof, *Mango* thought fit to retire farther back into the Mountain, whence he had before advanc'd a little, for the better making of his Excursions ; and the Factor being inform'd of the Place where he lay, which was not far dis-tant, order'd Captain *Villadiego,* with thirty of the most active Soldiers, being Musketeers, Crofs-bow, and Target Men, to march to a Bridge three Leagues from his Quarters where the *Inga* was said to be, and endeavour to feize him by surprize. *Villadiego* fet out at the fecond Watch of the Night, pro-ceeded to the Bridge, and having juft paft it, was inform'd by fome *Indians,* that the *Inga* was on the Top of a Mountain, with about eighty Men, ha-ving fent away all his Forces before, upon Intelli-gence of the Approach of the *Spaniards. Villadiego* being eager to take or kill the *Inga,* for the Ho-nour and Profit he expected to gain by it, began to climb a very fteep Hill, without firft viewing it, or examining the Place where the Enemy lay, and the harm they might do him, and this later than was proper, for the Sun rifing, its Height and the Steep-nefs of the Afcent was fo fatiguing, that meeting with no Water, they fainted away, and yet encou-raging one another, advanc'd a League and an Half. The *Inga* underftanding that thofe *Spaniards* were making towards him, almoft fpent, and without any Horfes, mounted one of four he had, with an Horfe-man's Spear in his Hand, commanding three of his Relations to mount the other three Horfes, and en-courag'd his eighty Men not to let flip that fa-vourable Opportunity they had in their Hands. *Vil-ladiego* being come to the Top of the Hill, fent three or four of the ableft Youths to get Sight of the *Indi-ans,*

ans, who had not gone far before they heard the
Noife of the Horfes, and Men making towards them.
The *Spaniards* being drawn up, the *Inga* appear'd
leading his Men, all in length to enclofe them, who
difcharg'd their Muskets and Crofs-bows, and tho'
they kill'd fome *Indians*, they clos'd with loud
Cries, broke one of *Villadiego* s Arms, letting fly
great Numbers of Arrows and Darts. *Villadiego,*
tho' his Arm was broken, did Wonders till he fell
down dead, as d:d twenty three more, being quite
fpent; the other fix efcap'd, and convey'd the News
to the Factor, by the Help of the friendly *Indians,*
who reliev'd and carry'd them in Hammacks. The
Inga, when he had flain the *Spainards,* and fent their
Heads to the Vale of *Vuticos,* caus'd the Hands, Nofes, and Ears of many of the *Indians* that were there
to be cut off, and their Eyes put out, fending for
more Forces to defend him, if attack'd.

   Ferdinand Pizarro returning to *Cuzco,* and leaving
his Brother *Gonzalo* at *Collao,* he went away to the Vale
of *Cockabamba,* where the Natives not being fubdu'd, affembled to cut him off, his whole Force being but fixty Men among whom were feveral Commanders of Note. The *Indians* to the Number of
thirty thoufand, having offer'd their Sacrifices, and
vow'd they would make a drinking Cup of *Gonzalo Pizarro's* Skull, drew near to the *Spaniards,* and
encamp'd, making many Fires, and fpending the whole
Night in drinking their Liquor call'd Chicha, and
crying out to the *Spaniards,* that they fhould foon
feel the Weight of their Hands, for they now knew
how to deal with them. In the Morning *Gonzalo
Pizarro,* by the Advice of his Officers, divided his
Men into three Squadrons, two under the Command of the Captains *Garcilaffo* and *Onate*, with
whom was *Paul Inga*, and the th:rd he headed
himfelf.

himfelf. Captain *Gabriel de Rojas* was commanded with a few Horfemen to cover the Foot that were in the Town. *Garcilaffo* charging the *Indians*, they redoub'ed their Cries in fuch manner, that there was no hearing what was fa:d, and both Parties fought intermix'd without any Order, the *Spaniards* making a wonderful Slaughter with their Swords and Spears, and the Horfes trampling abundance under Foot. Then *Gonzalo Pizarro*, and Captain *Oñate*, charg'd, and tho' the Lords of *Confara* and *Pocona*, came on with eight or nine thoufand *Indians*, they could not prevail. The Lord of *Chichas* fell upon *Gabriel de Rojas*, but found fuch Oppofition, the *Inga Paul*, and his Men behaving themfelves bravely, that he fled, and the *Spaniards* with their *Indians* purfu d them, fo that in the F:ght and Purfuit, near a thoufand of thofe People were kill'd. That Multitude being thus difpers'd, Captain *Gartilaffo* went with thirty Men to the Vale of *Pocona*, where he routed a thoufand *Indians*, and then the *Spaniards* having been reinforc'd from *Cuzco*, remov'd to the Va'e of *Andamarca*, and the Lord of *Confara*, feeing no Hopes of prevailing, fu'd for Peace. Thus the Country of *Collao* and *Los Charchas* was fubdu'd by Degrees, fome *Spaniards* being of Op:nion that Settlements ought to be made there, which others oppos'd, undervaluing the richeft Country in the World, for fome Mines began to be difcover'd, whereupon *Gonzalo Pizarro* went away to *Cuzco*, to advife with his Brother, leaving Captain *James de Roxas* in the Territory of *Los Charcas*, with a'l the Men, being an hundred and forty *Spaniards* Horfe and Foot.

THE Governour *Francis Pizarro* being inform'd of the Difafter befallen the Captain *Villadiego* and his Men, march'd out himfelf with feventy Men to joyn the Factor *Yllan Suarez*, fending out three Parties

ties several Ways to surprize the *Inga,* who having
Intelllgence by his Spies of all that was done, retir d
to *Viticos,* whereupon *Pizarro* considering it was impracticable to pursue him over the *Andes,* and the
Damage the *Inga* and his People did in obstructing
the Trade between *Lima* and *Cuzco,* concluded that
the only Remedy was to found a new Colony. To
this Purpose he pitch'd upon the Territory of *Guamanga,* assigning its Jurisdiction from *Xauxa* to the
Bridge of *Bilcas,* with the Provinces on both Sides
thereof. All that Country being divided already between the nhabitants of *Cuzco* and *Lima,* they urg'd,
it was unjust to take the same from them to give
it to others ; in Answer to which, he presently requir'd all those who had Lands in the Territories of
Cuzco or *Lima,* to declare where they would fix
their Residence, and he would there assign them
Lands, by which means the Colony was founded,
by the Name of *San Juan de la Vitoria,* in the Province of *Guamanga,* where Captain *Francis de Carde-
nas* was appointed Governour, and so *Pizarro* return'd
to *Cuzco.*

THE City of *Guamanga* was then founded at an
Indian Town of the same Name, near the great
Ridge of the *Andes,* and afterwards, the War with
Mango Inga being at an End, it was remov'd to
the Place where it now stands, being a Plain, near
a Ridge of small Hills, to the Southward, a Rivulet of good Water running by it, and there the
best Brick and Stone Houses in all *Peru* have been
built. The Situation is very healthy, because neither the Sun, the Air, nor the Dews are offensive,
nor is it hot or damp, but perfectly Temperate.
The *Spaniards* have built many Country Houses, keeping their Cattel about the adjacent Rivers and Vales,
the greatest River in the Country being *Vinaque,*

N 3   where

where are fome large Structures that feem to be very ancient, and the *Indians* fay were built by white Bearded People, who were in the Country before the Time of the *Ingas,* and they are of a different Form from thofe of the *Ingas.* All along the Banks of *Vinaque,* and in other Places near the City as good Wheat grows as the beft in *Spain,* all forts of Fruit anfwer very well, and it is wonderful to fee what Numbers of Pigeons there are. The Avenues to the City are delightful, as is all the Country, which was full of *Mitimaes,* becaufe of its being a Frontier to the *Andes,* which lye to the Eaftward. To the Weftward is the Coaft of South Sea, the *Indian* Towns fubject to it have a fruitful Soil, abounding in Cattel, and the People are all cloath'd. They had publick and private Places of Worfhip, their Funerals were like the reft defcrib'd in other Places ; before their being fubdu'd by the *Ingas* they were a war-like Nation, and after Conqueft of the *Soras* and *Lucanes,* which are within this Jurifdiction, a great Number of them fortify'd themfelves on a Rock, which they defended above two Years againft the *Inga Yupangui.* They all wore Marks of Diftinction on their Heads, as their Anceftors had done, and were formerly moft extravagantly Superftitious, and given to Soothfaying.

THE Governour *Pizarro* took Care upon all Occafions to fend Meffengers into *Spain,* with fuch Accounts of all Affairs as were moft for his Advantage, and confiderable Prefents to the Kings and all his Friends, having at the fame obftructed the Paffage of thofe that had been fent by *Almagro.* One *Zavallos* being the laft fo employ'd by him, return'd at this Time, and among the Difpatches brought over a Patent creating him a Marquefs, with Authority to fettle on himfelf and his Heirs as much
Land

Land as was inhabited by sixteen thousand *Indians.*
As an allay to this Joy, a few Days after Advice
was brought that the Commotions of *Peru* being
known in *Spain,* a Judge had been appointed to come
into *Peru* to enquire into those Affairs. Captain
Peter Anzures being return'd from his tedious and
fruitless Expedition, before spoken of, was now
Commission'd by the new Marquess *Pizarro* to go
settle a Colony in the Province of *Los Charcas,*
which he did calling it *La Plata,* in the District of
Chuquisaca, a temperate Country, and fit for Wheat,
Barley, Vineyards, all sorts of Fruit, and Breeds of
Cattel, all which bears a great Price, on Account
of the immense Wealth afterwards found there. Its
Territory is very large, through which some Rivers
of good Water run, where when those *Indians* were
subdu'd by the *Ingas,* they built regular Towns,
were cloath'd, worshipp'd the Sun, had Temples to
offer Sacrifices; the Natives and the *Carangues* were
war-like People, and report that the *Ingas* kept Men
there to dig Silver for them, especially on the Hill
of *Porco,* besides which several other good Mines
have been found near the Town of *La Plata,* and
all the Country is thought to be full of Mines,
from which the new Town had the Name of *La*
Plata given it ; and *Ferdinand Pizarro* order'd a Mine
to be wrought, which he took for himself, and if
he had continu'd it, would have yilded him above
200000 Ducats clear, but of the prodigious Wealth of
these Mines we shall speak in another Place.

Alonso de Alvarado set out about this Time upon
his intended Discovery, to the Southward for a
Province the *Spaniards* call'd *Los Motilones,* where he
found large Rivers, little Store of Provisions, and the
Houses at a great Distance from one another, and being come to a great River that runs away to the

North-

Northward, he was told that there was a good Country beyond it, whereupon he refolv'd to pafs, and there being no Probability of Fording, fet his Men to build a Boat, and in the mean Time was inform'd that fifteen Days Journey from thence, beyond a great Mountain, there was a Plain, where on the Banks of a Lake refided an *Orejon*, of the Race of the *Ingas*, whofe Name was *Ancoallo*, and that befides him there were feveral other great Lords. Having finifh'd the Boat and crofs'd the River, they attempted to pafs the Mountains, but after all their Endeavours could never find any Way, and the *Indians* faid they knew none, and that what they knew concerning *Ancoallo* and his Country, they had received from their Forefathers; fo that either they knew not the Way, or would not fhow it. The Country of *Mayabamba* is unwholfome, by reafon of the many Rivers, Mountains, and Woods, for which Reafons *Alvarado* refolv'd to repafs the River, and fo this Expedition came to nothing.

THE Marquefs *Pizarro*, after having given the neceffary Orders for founding the new Towns of *Guamanga* and *Pafto*, ftay'd fome Days at *Cuzco*, endeavouring to bring *Mango Inga* to Obedience by by fair means, but being difappointed, he directed his Brother *Gonzalo* to carry on the War againft him. The other Brother *Ferdinand*, having by hook or by crook gather'd a vaft Treafure for the King, and for himfelf, and taking a Copy of the Procefs, and all other Evidences that he thought might juftify the murder of *Almagro* before the King, thofe Writings being drawn up as he would have them, which was eafy to be done there, he fpoke to the Marquefs, his Brother, about his intended Journey into *Spain*, and being both of them haughty and ill Natur'd, they differ'd fo much about it, that *Ferdinand* went away from *Cuzco* in a Rage; but as they
had

had both need of each other for carrying on their Defigns, they were foon reconcil'd. By this Time *James Nuñez de Mercado,* and *James Gutierrez de los Rios,* both Friends to the late Adelantado *Almagro,* were gone into *Spain,* and they, in Conjunction with *James de Alvarado,* gave an Account to Dr. *Robles,* the eldeft of the Counfellors for the *Indies* of all that had happen'd in *Peru,* proving by dint of Argument, and undeniable Evidences, that the *Pizarros* had been to blame for all the Differences between them and *Almagro,* and that what they had done was the Effect of Ambition, Revenge and Cruelty, whereupon the Doctor propos'd to fecure *Ferdinand Pizarro,* knowing he would foon be at *Panama,* in order to pafs over into *Spain.* The faid *Ferdinand* being ready to fet out for *Spain,* advis'd his Brother the Marquefs to be always upon his Guard, apprehending that the *Chile* Men would do him fome Mifchief, and at leaft to fend young *Almagro* into *Spain,* becaufe thofe People were very fond of him, which the Marquefs did not much feem to regard. *Ferdinand* then embarking at *Lima,* fail'd away for *New Spain,* landed at *Guatulco,* near *Tecoantepeque,* and travelling through the Country was arrefted near *Guaxaca,* and carry'd to *Mexico;* but the Vice-Roy having no Orders from Court to detain him, let him proceed on his Journey; as he did, and arriving at the Iflands *Azores,* ftay'd there till he could hear from his Friends, whither he might go fafely to Court, and having receiv'd their Anfwer, repair'd thither, but met not with fo good a Reception as he had expected. The Marquefs, his Brother, going from *Cuzco* to *Collao,* at *Chucuito* receiv'd a Letter from *Ferdinand Machicao,* advifing him to take fpecial Care of his Perfon, becaufe the Men of *Chile* defign'd to kill him. Many Gentlemen and Soldiers of Note, who had ferv'd and fought for him,

him, being in his Company at that Time, whom
it was requisite to reward and provide for, he resolv'd to found the City of *Arequipa*.

BEING gone about that Affair, he was inform'd
that *Mango Inga* was for Peace, tho' it prov'd not
true, for that Prince being much distrefs'd, us'd many
Artifices, by which he avoided several Dangers, and
so he twice escap'd falling into the Hands of *Gonzalo Pizarro*. The Marquefs, upon that Advice,
thinking he had done with the *Inga*, order'd his Brother *Gonzalo* to go take upon him the Government of the
Provinces about *Quito*, and he accordingly set out with
a Number of Men along the Mountain great Road,
declaring he defign'd to make some Difcovery, particularly in the Province of *Canela*, which was reported to be very rich. The Marquefs at the same
time made Choice of *Peter de Valdibia*, who had been a
Colonel, a difcreet Perfon, and had ferv'd in the
Wars in *Italy*, to go upon the Difcovery and Conqueft of the Kingdom of *Chile*, ordering him to be
ready by the Beginning of the next Year, which
would be fifteen hundred and forty. Then the
Marquefs being come to the Vale of *Yucay*, in
hopes to conclude an Accommodation with the *Inga
Mango*, the more to gain his Affection, sent him a
fine Pad, some Silk Garments, and other Prefents;
but that Barbarian met two Servants of the Marquefs's, who carry'd the Prefent, and kill'd them,
which made the Marquefs repent his Credulity, and
to begin his Revenge, he caus'd one of the *Inga*'s
Wives he had in his Hands, to be kill'd in the
fame Place where his Servants had been flain, which
was look'd upon as an indifcreet and unchriftian Action. Returning then to *Cuzco*, he gave the neceffary Orders for founding the City of *Arequipa*, and
went way to *San Juan de la Victoria*, otherwife call'd
Guamanga, and thence to *Lima*,

To

To return to the Provinces about the Equinoctial. *Gonzalo Diaz de Pineda,* who was Deputy Governour at *Quito,* having obtain'd a Commiſſion for founding a Town in the Country of the *Paſtos,* perform'd it this Year 1539, in the Vale of *Guacanquer,* but it was afterwards remov'd to the Vale of *Tris,* where it continues by the Name of *Villa Vicioſa de Paſto.* The diſtance between *Popayan* and *Paſto* is forty Leagues, in which laſt Province are the Towns of *Aſqual, Mallama, Tucurres, Capuis, Lles, Gualmatal, Funes, Chapal, Piales, Papiales, Turca,* and *Cumba,* and from it the Town of St. *John de Paſto* was ſo call'd. Of the other adjacent Provinces nothing occurs to be ſaid, but that near a Town call'd *Paſtoco,* there is a Lake on the Top of the higheſt of all that Ridge of Mountains, the Water whereof is exceſſive cold, and tho' it is eight Leagues in length and four in breadth, their are neither Fowls nor Fiſhes in it, nor does the Land produce any Trees, or other Thing whatſoever; and not far from it is another Lake of the ſame Nature. Near the *Paſtos* are the *Indians* call'd *Quillacingas,* but differing in Cuſtoms, for the *Paſtos* did not eat human Fleſh, they were ill countenanc d, both Men and Women, ſlovenly and rude; void of Religion, no Idols being found among them; yet they believ'd, that after Death they were to live again in ſome very delightful Places; their Habit was ſhort Tunicks and Mantles. The *Quillacingas* convers'd with the Devil, bury'd their Wealth with the Dead, and ſome living Perſons with them, to the Number of fifteen or twenty, with the prime Men. In the Country of the *Paſtos* little Mayz grows, but there are great Breeds of Cattel, and much Barley, Papas, and Fruit. Among the *Quillacingas* grows much Mayz, the Natives are well made, war-like, and hard to be brought under; they have large Rivers of good Water, one of them lying between *Pasto* and *Popayan*, call'd *Rio Caliente*, or the hot River, is dangerous, and they pass over it with Cables, the Water of it is the finest in all those Parts. In this same Province is the River of *Angasmayo*, whither the *Inga Guaynacava* extended his Dominion. The Town is seated in a delightful Vale, thro' which runs a pleasant River of good Water, and it produces Plenty of Wheat, Barley, and Mayz. All those Plains abound in Deer, Rabbits, Partridges, Pigeons, Turtles, Pheasants, and Turkeys, the Country is very cold.

C H A P. III.

Discoveries made by George de Robledo ; *the Provinces of* Picara, Paucura, Pozo, Quinbaya, *&c.*

GEorge de Robledo setting out from *Cali,* march'd along a Vale, through which the great River of the *Magdalen* runs, the Baggage being carry'd along it on Floats, and a large Canoe, to a Town call'd *Del Pescado,* or of Fish, on the Bank thereof, nothing of Note happening by the way, but that a Soldier having stabb'd a Black Woman he was marry'd to, fled towards *Timana,* and was taken and eaten by the *Indians,* a just judgment for the Wrongs he had done those People. *Robledo* entering upon that Province, found no Provisions, the Natives being fled, upon Advice of his coming, but he sending out Parties after them, they brought above two hundred Prisoners, whom he treated courteously, promising they should not be molested, if they would return to their Houses, and so dismis'd them. The Report of this good usage being spread abroad, some of the Caziques

ques began to submit, and People the Country, and some of them told him, that towards the North Sea, there were Men with Horses, who did much harm where they came, for which Reason *Robledo* immediately gave Orders to find out a proper Place to settle his Colony, because those might be People from *Cartagena*, and if they happen'd to found a Town first, it might occasion Trouble. The Adelantado *Don Peter de Heredia* having complain'd to the King of the Injury done him by the licenciate *Badillo*, the licenciate *Santa Cruz* was sent to call him to Account, who understanding that *Badillo* was gone from *Uraba* up the Country, sent *John Greciano* as his Deputy, with a Party to bring him back to *Cartagena*, at the same Time appointing *Levis Bernal* to command those Men. They set out from *Cartagena* in the Year 1538, and were not gone far beyond *Uraba*, before they cavill'd about the Command, each making what Friends he could. They cross'd the Mountain *Abibe* without much Difficulty, because *Badillo* had made the Way, and there some young Men kill'd such a large Snake, that they found a whole Deer, Horns and all in its Belly; at length after many Hardships and Contentions they came upon the Frontiers of the Province of *Anzerma*, and finding Plenty of Provisions, stay'd there some Time; but the Discord still continuing, they proceeded so far as to draw out in Arms to engage one another; but just then Captain *Ruy Vanegas*, who was going with twenty Horse, by Order of *George de Robledo* to seek out a proper Place to build a Town, appear'd on a Ridge, call'd of *Umbra*, whence he spy'd the Men of *Cartagena*, and they upon Sight of him held their Hands. *Robledo* being inform'd of what had happen'd, plac'd his Colony on another Hill, call'd *Guarina*, to which those of *Cartagena* resorted, and submitted themselves

to

to him ; however, the Town was remov'd to the Hill of *Umbra,* where it now ftands.

Robledo made it his Bufinefs to reduce the *Curacas,* or Lords, by fair means, and fent *Suer de Nava* with fifty Men to view the Province of *Caramanta,* and bring him an Account of it, whift he went himfelf to *Ocuzca,* and perfwaded the *Curaca,* fo call'd, to come to him, but he, tho' well us'd, finding himfelf under a Guard, made his efcape, and could not be had again. *Suer de Nava* returning, faid he had perfwaded thofe People to whom he went to live peaceably. *Robledo* going about to vifit his Diftrict, Captain *Ruy Vanegas* happen'd upon a Temple, into which many *Indians* were withdrawn, with abundance of Goods, and the Value of twelve thoufand Pieces of Eight in Gold, moft of which was reftor'd to the Owners, to keep them in good Temper. Having thus concluded Peace with the Inhabitants of the Vale of *Apia,* and being inform'd that *Ocuza* and *Umbruza,* another confiderable Lord were joyning to attack the new Town of *Anzerma,* he return'd thither, and by fair means pacify'd thofe People, promifing to do them no harm, fo that he had leifure to difcover the Countries beyond the *Cordillera,* or Ridge of Mountains to the Northward of *Anzerma,* and accordingly fent *Gomez Hernandez* with fifty Men, to difcover the Province of *Choco,* and going with him as far as the Vale of St. *Mary,* he was there met by an *Indian,* who pretended to be the Lord *Umbruza,* whom he treated very courteoufly, but being fatisfy'd that he was not that Lord, he caus'd him to be burnt. *Gomez Hernandez* came to the Mountain *Cima,* which is very uncooth, but much wooded ; fubject to continual Rain, and full of wild Beafts, Monkeys, and fuch Creatures, the Inhabitants going naked, and very brutal, living in Houfes on Trees, where a Soldier call'd *Alonfo Perez,* entering
one

one of thofe Houfes, feiz'd an *Indian* Woman, who took her Captivity fo much to heart, that fhe caft herfelf down headlong from thofe vaft Rocks. *Hernandez* travell'd fome Days with much difficulty, about that wild Place, till he came to a River, which they all fuppos'd to be that of *Darien*, becaufe it ran to the Northward, finding nothing to eat but the Fruit call'd *Pixibaes*, which ftood them in much ftead. Afterwards they found many Turkeys, Pheafants, and Dantas, as big as Mules, and being come to the Top of a Mountain Ridge, they faw the Country all about feem'd to be flat, but much wooded, without any Champion ; all about the Hills the Houfes were large built on the Trees upon great Forks. The *Indians*, who were naked and well fhap'd, as foon as they fpy'd the *Spaniards*, beat many little Drums, and play'd on Pipes, whereupon a great Number drew together, fhooting abundance of Arrows, and cafting Darts at the *Spaniards*, who had the misfortune that feveral of their Crofsbow Strings broke, and having no Horfes, they were hard prefs'd, but keeping their Order, they made a wonderful Retreat, thofe Mountainiers purfuing them a whole Day, when being fatisfy'd with having drove them out of their Country, they defifted, and the *Spaniards* got fafe to *Anzerma.* On the other hand Captain *Ruy Vanegas* was endeavouring to reduce *Pirfa* and *Sopia* ; the People of *Pirfa* were in Arms, and had made great Pits very artfully cover'd with Grafs, and within them fharp pointed Stakes of hard Wood, and when the *Spaniards* purfu'd them, they ran to skulk in the Brakes. One Horfe happen'd to fall into a Pit and was kill'd, which difcover'd the Contrivance, and after fome of thofe People had fuffer'd, Peace was offer'd them, and they fubmitted.

Robledo having fettled his Affairs, as has been faid in the Year 1540, was very intent upon croffing the great River of the *Magdalen*, to difcover the Provin-

ces

ces on the other Side of it; and tho' the Enterprize
seem'd difficult, he resolv'd to venture upon it, to
which Purpose he distributed the Lands among those
that were to remain as Inhabitants of his new Town,
which done, he set out from *Anzerma,* with few
above an hundred Horse and Foot. When come to
the Town of *Irra,* near which the great River of the
Magdalen, otherwise call'd of *Santa Marta,* passes with
a rapid Stream, Floats were made which carry'd over
the Horses and the Baggage which was small, Experience having shown that Forces going upon Discoveries ought not to be encumber'd. The Soldiers
plac'd themselves between two Canes as thick as a
Man's Thigh, fastned at the Ends with two great
Pieces of Timber, an *Indian* swimming before drew
the Canes by a Withy, other *Indians* going behind
to steer and keep the Machine steady, and in this
difficult and dangerous Manner, the Soldiers crofs'd
that rapid River, the like whereof has never been
seen. When over the River, *Robledo* sent Messengers to the Province of *Carrapa,* which is large and
very rich, desiring they would admit of him as a
Friend, which the Lords being desirous to live in
Peace agreed to, and brought Presents of Jewels and
Provisions. Here the *Spaniards* stay'd above a Month,
and the *Indians* told them, that beyond the Mountains *Andes,* there was a plain and wealthy Country,
call'd *Arbi,* aud gave some Information of the Provinces of *Picara,* *Paucura,* and *Pozo,* all rich and populous, at War among themselves, as those of *Cara-
pa* then were with the People of *Picara.* *Robledo*
judg'd it proper to proceed, and desir'd some Persons
of Distinction to go with him, and to furnish Men
to make War on such as would not admit of his
Friendship. The Lords of *Carrapa* comply'd, and
furnish'd four thousand fighting Men. They march'd
to *Picara,* a larger Province than that of *Carrapa,* and
more

more wealthy, where the Natives were in Arms, but after many Threats and much Noife, they fled, the *Carrapas* purfuing, taking fome Prifoners, and killing others, and devour'd both the living and the dead. Meffengers were fent to offer them Peace, and being afraid of the Horfes, the Dogs, and the panifh Weapons, feveral Lords came to make their Submiffion, bringing a confiderable Quantity of Gold. Having in twenty Days adjufted all Affairs at *Picara,* they proceeded to *Pozo,* where the Houfes of the Lords were fortify'd with Enclofures of thick Canes, on which were Scaffolds and Breaft Works to offer Sacrifices and look out. Thefe *Indians* are the braveft of any in *Peru,* were wont to carry their Arms with them when they went to till the Land, were dreaded by their Neighbours, and would be at Peace with none, their Habitations reaching to *Rio Grande.* Being inform'd of what had happen'd in the other Provinces of their Neighbourhood, and making no Account of the *Spaniards,* after many Vows and Sacrifices offer'd up to their Gods, above fix thoufand of them affembl'd to to make good the Paffage through a Wood.

T H E *Spaniards* were marching at their Eafe down a River, along which were many Trees and much Fruit, the Country pleafant and delightful, without thinking of any Enemies. *Robledo* and fome others being foremoft, heard the Noife of thofe Barbarians, and calling fome others, they all went up the Hill that was in the Way, without expecting any Oppofition. The *Indians* of *Carrapa* and *Picara,* amounted to eight thoufand, and were very fearful, thofe of *Pozo* made much Noife, calling the *Spaniards* Women, with other fuch like Expreffions. When up the Hill, which was fomewhat difficult of Afcent, *Robledo* fpurr'd on, crying St. *James,* and the reft follow'd him, the *Indians* cafting their Darts; he gave a Target he had to the Trumpeter, and with a Crofs-

bow kill'd three or four *Indians*, and then taking his
Spear, fell in with the Enemy, till an *Indian* taking
good Aim, pierc'd his Right Hand with a Dart,
and he alighting to save his Spear, another Dart ran
deep into his Back; however the *Spaniards* play'd
their Parts so briskly that they gain'd the Top of the
Hills, and the *Indians* flying were pursu'd, by which
means those who were with the *Spaniards*, had a good
Supper of the Prisoners they took. The Men were
much concern'd to see *Robledo* wounded, for they
lov'd him entirely, by Reason of his Affability and
good Behaviour.

THE Customs of the *Indians* of *Paucura* and those
of *Anzerma*, were almost the same, tho their Languages were different. They us'd every *Tuesday* to
Sacrifice two Men to a wooden Idol they had, as big
as a lusty Man, facing to the East, and his Arms
extended; Prisoners taken in War were shut up and
well fed, and when fat, on their Festivals they were
brought into the Market-Place, and there kill'd, making them kneel and hold down their Heads to have their
Brains dash'd out with a Club, and they went to this
Execution very merrily, without speaking a Word or
suing for Mercy. On the one Side of the Province
of *Pozo*, is the great River, and on the others the
Provinces of *Carrapa*, *Picara*, and *Paucura*. Those
People said they deduc'd their Original from the Province of *Arma*, and they resemble it in their Language
and Customs: Their principal Lord was call'd *Pima-
raque*; both Men and Women are large of Body, and
their Countenances disagreeable; in their Houses they
had great wooden Idols with Wax Faces, in such
Shape as the Devil appear'd to them, and he gave them
Answers by the Mouths of those Idols. The Graves
were in their Houses, and when the Lords dy'd, they
did put into them Meat, Women, Boys, Jewels, Arms,
and all the best Things they had. They are good
Husband-

Husbandmen, and Brave, and when they went to War, were wont to carry Cords to bind the Prisoners. There are great Gold Mines in this Province, which extends to certain Mountains, whence good Rivers flow ; the Language is like that of *Pancura*; the Soil yields much Corn and Fruit ; the Men went naked, only wearing little Clouts to hide their Privities; in all other Respects like those of *Pozo* ; had some Bows, but no poison'd Arrows, using Slings, and strewing sharp Thorns about the Roads to offend their Enemies. In the Province of *Carrapa* they had little low Houses ; The Country full of naked Hills ; the Men large and strong, long visag'd, as are the Women ; very rich in Gold, wearing Jewels, and using Gold Vessels to drink out of, wherein they were vicious, and little eaters, but excessive drinking was practis'd throughout the *West-Indies.* They had no Temples nor Places of Worship, tho' the Devil spoke to them ; their Graves and Burials like their Neighbours ; the prime Men marry'd their Nieces, some of them their Sisters and had many Wives ; they were Men-Eaters ; went to the Wars with many Ornaments of Gold, and Crowns on their Heads, carying large Colours ; knew there was but one God, but after a very confuse manner ; the Sick offer'd many Sacrifices for Recovery of their Health ; the Country abounds in Fruit, Venison, and much Variety of other Provisions, and very agreable Roots.

THE *Spaniards* were so much incens'd at their Commander's being wounded, that they resolv'd to be severely reveng'd on the *Indians* of *ozo,* and marching beyond the Ridge of the Hill, where the Engagement had been, the Colonel receiv'd Advice, that the *Indians* had fortify'd themselves on a Rock, with many Women and Children ; but as soon as the *paniards* approach'd, their Hearts fail'd them. The Confederate *Indians* encompa's'd the Foot of the Rock,

whilst

whilst the *Spaniards* gain'd the Top, setting on their Dogs, which were so fierce that they tore out the very Bowels of those wretched People, who to shun that Danger, cast themselves headlong down those Craggs, dashing themselves to Pieces, and if they happen'd to escape that Peril, fell into a worse, being the Hands of their Enemies of *Picara* and *Carrapa,* who treated them inhumanly, killing Men, Women, and Children, and devouring them raw ; and returning to their Quarters with about two hundred Loads of human Flesh, sent great Presents of it into their own Countries. The News of this horrid Slaughter being spread about the Country, to avoid the continuance of that Calamity, they su'd for Peace, bringing Presents of Gold and other Things. The same being concluded, and *Robledo* somewhat better of his Wounds, he dismis'd the *Indians* of *Picara* and *Carrapa,* and with those of *Pozo* proceeded to *Paucura,* where *Pinoma,* an Enemy to *Pozo,* was Lord, who hearing how they had far'd, submitted, and brought good Store of Provisions. A Soldier then complain'd that the *Pozo Indians* had stolen some Swine, and whether it was true, or that they had been lost, *Robledo* charg'd them with Breach of the Peace, and order'd *Suer de Nava,* with fifty *Spaniards* to chastise them for the Theft. The *Paucura Indians* rejoycing to see those Men march against *Pozo,* that no Opportunity of doing harm to their Enemies might slip, assembled to the Number of three thousand, and march'd with the *Spaniards.* As soon as enter'd the Province of *Pozo,* without ever examining into the Matter, they fell to plundering, burning, and destroying all before them, and the *Paucura Indians* carry'd off two hundred Men, cut into Quarters, to their own Country to feast on, that beastly Custom being so establish'd among them, that for the sake of eating one another, there was no Peace between Parents and their Children, or Brothers and Brothers At last the Swine
were

were found, and the Peace being again eftablifh'd, wh.ch needed not to have been broke, *Suer de Nava* return'd to their Quarters.

THERE being no more to do in *Paucura,* upon Advice that there was near by, to the Weftward, a large and wealthy Province, call'd *Arma,* the greateft in *Peru,* and where much Gold might be found, in cafe the Natives were fubdu'd, *Robledo* mov'd that way. The Natives had been inform'd, that the *Spaniards* were brave, that they cou'd cleave a Man down at once with their Swords, that their Spears went clear through the Body, that their Shafts flew like Lightning from the Crofsbows, and that their Horfes were wonderful fleet ; hereupon they held a Confultation about War or Peace, and offer'd Sacrifices. When the *Spaniards* drew near to a Mountain, they heard a great Noife of Drums and Horns, the *Indians* having fent away their Wives, Children, and Goods, and being come to that Place to oppofe them, who immediately began to mount, the Enemy rowling down great Stones upon them ; yet after all they fled, and in the Purfuit fome were taken, who had ftately Ornaments of Gold, Plumes of Feathers, Crowns, large Plates, and their Colours ftrew d with Stars and other Figures of the fineft Gold, and fome of them were cover'd with Plates of it from Head to Foot, from which Time that Pafs was call'd the Mountain of the Men in Armour. The Province appear'd there large, plain, and populous, the Fields fow'd with Mayz and *Yuca,* and large Groves of the Fruit-Trees call'd Pizibaes. Their Towns were feated on the Tops and Sides of Hills, the Houfes round and fpacious, fit to contain fifteen or twenty Inhabitants Being farther advanc'd, the *Indians* guarded the Pafs of another Mountain more difficult of Accefs for the Horfes, *Robledo* fent feveral Times to offer them Peace, to which they anfwer'd, asking them why they went to rob what did not be-

long

long to them? Bidding them go home to their own
Country, since they liv'd peaceably in theirs; at the
same Time casting their Darts and Stones, with great
Cries. The Sun beginning to grow hot, *Robledo* order'd his Foot to attack them with their Targets, Cross-
bows, and Dogs, till the Horse searching all about,
found a Place to go up, tho' with much Difficulty,
whilst the Foot kept the *Indians* in play, who seeing
the Horses fled, and in the Pursuit much Gold was
taken, and that Pass call'd *De los Cavallos*, or of the
Horses. The Lords then, not thinking fit to run any
farther Hazard, begg'd Pardon, bringing Presents of
Gold in Net Baskets, the *Indians* at the same time giving the Soldiers extraordinary Pieces of Gold, and when
they carry'd Water to their Horses, threw some of them
into the Buckets, being well pleas'd to see them drink,
and all the Gold was twenty one Carats fine. The Lord
of *Maytama*, who was the greatest in the Province,
being on the other Side of a Mountain, and not having made his Submission, the Commander sent thither the Commendary *Sosa*, with fifty Men, who
coming at break of Day to the Top of the Mountain,
found the *Indians* standing upon their Defence; but
they soon fled. The next Day *Robledo* himself came
and took up his Quarters in *Maytama*'s House, which
being known about the Province, all the Lords came
in, bringing Plates, Crowns, Bracelets, Plumes of
Feathers, and other Things of Value, hanging on
Poles, carry'd on the Shouldiers of Men by two and
two. The Country being thus reduc'd, *Robledo* thought
fit to settle a Colony there, and sent the Commendary *Sosa* down the River to seek a proper Place, and
having found a large Town, he resolv'd to keep the
Feast of *Easter* there, for which Reason it was call'd
El Pueblo de la Pasqua, that is *Easter Town*, after which
he discover'd the Towns *Blanco* and *Zemisara*, and the
Province *De la Loma*, then proceeded to another Town
call'd

call'd *Pobres* which is oppofite to *Buritaca,* from whence he return'd. In the mean Time all the Province of *Arma* had confpir'd to make War on the *Spaniards,* began to flacken in furnifhing Provifions, and kill'd the Blacks and Confederate *ndians* they cou d furprize abroad defigning to attack the *Spanifh* Quarters, but did not put it in Execution by reafon of fome Differences among themfelves. *Robledo* then march'd out of the Province, leaving it as much at Enm ty as when he firft came in ; and fome *Indians* appearing on the Top of a Mountain, he call'd them, they came to him, he cut off the Hands of fome, the Ears of others, and wounded others, and fo held on his way through the Territories of *Pozo, Picara,* and *Carrapa* to that of *Quimbay* .

B E F O R E we conclude with the Actions of *George de Robledo,* it is requifite to fee what was doing in the Parts adjacent, till he and other *Spanifh* Commanders came to meet. So great was the Fame of the Wealth of the *New Kingdom of Granada,* that all Men defir'd to Trade there, and accordingly one. *Peter Lopez,* a Merchant fet out from *Popayan,* in Company with Captain *Offorio,* towards *Bogota,* fufpecting no harm from the *Indians* who were then at Peace, and thus came into the Province of the *Yalcones,* bordering on that of *Paez.* Captain *Peter de Anafco,* was at the fame Time fet out from *Timana* for *Popayan,* and was come into the fame Province, where the Natives revolting, kill'd him and all his Companions, exceping only two who made their Efcape to *Timana*; the like they did to Captain *Offorio* and his Party, exercifing the utmoft Cruelties upon them al', and devouring their Bodies, and refolving to defend themfelves againft any that fhould pretend to revenge their Quarrel, to which Purpofe they made all the neceffary Difpofitions, cutting Trenches, and rendering the Ways almoft impaffable. This News being brought to *Popayan, John de Ampudia* march'd out with fixty Horfe and Foot, to chaftife

thofe

thofe Barbarians. Thrice he engag'd and routed them, but they ftill coming on in greater Numbers, he was kill'd in the fourth Battel, and his Men oblig'd to fteal away by Night to *Popayan.*

The Adelantado *Pafcual de Andagoya,* having obtain'd a Commiffion from the King to fubdue the Country about the River of St. *John,* on the South Sea, Landed his Forces in a Bay, whence he directed his Courfe to the City of *Cali,* through fuch Ways as kill'd all his Horfes, and much harrafs'd the Men, and was readily receiv'd in that City, without confidering that there is no River of St. *John* in all that Country. Being admitted there, he receiv'd Advice that *Robledo,* above fpoken of, had made confiderable Difcoveries, and founded the City call d *Santana de los Cavalleros,* in the Province of *Anzerma,* whereupon he fent *Michael Munoz* to take Poffeffion of it in his Name, and call it St. *John.* He alfo Poffefs'd himfelf of *Popayan,* and fearing that *Belalcazar,* who had built thofe Places would return, and call him to Account, he conniv d at all the Crimes that were committed, to ingratiate himfelf with the Inhabitants, that they might affert his unjuft Caufe. *Robledo* coming into the Province of *Quimbaya,* would have founded a Colony there, but his Men not liking it, as feeming to be nothing but Moraffes full of Reeds, and praying he would Reward them with fome better Country, he fent out to fearch the Woods, and other adjacent Parts, and the Lords there being luxurious and floathful Perfons, hoping that the *Spaniards* were only paffing through, one of them call'd *Tacurunbi,* carry'd him a Gold Cup, weighing above feven hundred Pieces of Eight, with other fmaller, but very valuable Pieces, and thofe that had been fent out to difcover, returning, reported there were many good Towns, and the Country was rich and plentiful all the way to the great Vale of *Cali.* Other Lords came in from all Parts, with abundance of Gold,

all

all which that Commander took to himſelf. Upon this good Account of the Country, he founded a Town, and gave it the Name of *Cartago,* becauſe all the Men that went with him upon the Diſcovery were of *Cartagena,* and call'd the *Carthaginians.* The Colony being eſtabliſh'd, *Robledo* went away to *Anzerma* and *Cali,* to ſee *Paſcual de Andagoya,* to prevent what he apprehended from *Belalcazar,* his Ambition prevailing on him to hope he might ſecure to himſelf the Dominion of what he had diſcover'd. At *Cali* he indiſcreetly ſubmitted himſelf to *Andagoya,* preſenting him with four thouſand Pieces of Eight he had receiv'd in his Progreſs, and *Andagoya* the more to ſecure him to his Intereſt, contriv'd to marry him to a Kinſwoman of his Wife's; ſo that having eſtabliſh'd his Affairs, he return'd to *Santana* and *Cartago,* where he reduc'd ſome Diſtricts diſcover'd, and ſent *Alvaro de Mendoza* to ſee what was beyond the ſnowy Mountains, or the Ridge of the *Andes,* who from the Top thereof, ſaw Ways that led to the other Vale, or River of *Neyva,* when thinking it unadviſable to proceed any farther without Horſes, he return'd, and *Robledo* diſtributed the Territory of *Cartago* among his Men.

THIS Province of *Quimbaya* is fifteen Leagues in length, and ten in breadth, from *Rio Grande,* to the Mountains *Andes,* very populous, and not uncooth. No Part of the *Indies* produces ſo many thick Reeds, with which they build their Houſes. On the Top of the great Mountain is a Mouth that Smoaks very much, and from it ſeveral Rivers run down that Water the Country, over which there are Bridges of Reeds or Canes, bound together with Withes, and they yield much Gold. The Men and Women are comly; there is Plenty of *Spaniſh* and Native Fruit; the Lords are very dainty, and had many Wives; did not uſe to eat Man's Fleſh, unleſs upon ſome great Feſtival; they made Gold Ornaments in the Shape of all Things they ſaw, and well
wrought

wrought; their Weapons were Spears, Darts, and Slings; they are very underſtanding, and ſome were notable Sorcerers. When they met at their Merriments, after having drank plentifully, a Party of Women drew up on one Side, and another on the other, and ſo the Men and Boys, and making a Noiſe, they aſſaulted one another caſting Rods and Darts, and for this Sport, at which many were wounded and ſome kill'd, they made large Targets of their Hair, which they us'd in War. In their Dances one led, ſinging to two little Drums, and all the reſt anſwer'd, every one holding a Cup of Liquor, ſo that they danc'd, ſung, and drank, at the ſame Time. In their Songs they repeated their preſent Difficulties, and the Actions of their Anceſtors; as for Religion they had none, but convers'd with the Devil, and ſaid they ſaw frightful Apparitions; the Cure of their Diſeaſes was frequent Bathing. They believ'd there was ſomething Immortal in Man, tho' they knew nothing of a Soul, imagining it was a Tranſmutation, and that the Bodies were to come to life again, for which Reaſon their manner of interring was like the others before mention'd, expecting to be convey'd into very delightful Places. The Climate is very healthy; where *Spaniards* live to a great Age, without any Diſtempers, or being troubled either with Heat or Cold.

CHAP. IV.

Francis Vazquez de Cornado *appointed Governour of* New Galicia ; *diſcoveries made by* F. Mark de Niza, *to the Northward of* Culiacan, *as far as* Cibola.

NUno de Guzman having been remov'd from the Government of *New Galicia,* as has been ſa d before, *Francis Vazquez de Cornado* was put into his Place in the Year 1538, and in the Year 1539, finding the
Spaniſh

Spanish Colony of St. *Michael* in *Culiacan,* to be so much distress'd by a powerful Cazique, call'd *Ayapin,* that the Inhabitants were upon the Point of abandoning it, he march'd to their Assistance, and having drawn off many of the Natives from the Party of *Ayapin,* pursu'd, took, and hang'd him, whereupon all the *Indians* of those Parts came down from the Mountains, to enjoy the Plenty and Fertility of their Lands. The Vice-Roy of *Mexico,* being a Person of Piety, and great Friend to F. *Bartholomew de las Casas,* was by his Advice, for reducing the *Indians,* rather by the preaching of Religious Men, than by force of Arms, and to that Effect had sent several of them into *New Galicia* with the Governour *Cornado,* among whom was F. *Marc. de Niza,* of the Order of St. *Francis,* whom he order d, with a Companion and proper Guides, to penetrate from the Town of St. *Michael* in *Culican* into the Country. In order to it the Governour sent to the Towns of *Petatlan* and *Cuchillo,* sixty Leagues from *Culiacan,* six *Indians* of that Country, who had been kept among the Friers at *Mexico,* that they might learn *Spanish,* and be well affected to Christiany. Those Natives having inform'd their Countrymen, that there was no Design to make War on, or reduce them into Slavery, but only to convert them to the Christian Religion, return'd with above eighty Men, to whom the Governour gave the same Assurances, and desir'd they would take F. *Mark de Niza* with them to make the same Declaration to others that were farther off. The Frier accordingly set out with them, his Instructions from the Vice-Roy being to this Effect, That he should charge the *pantards* at *Culiacan* to use the *Indians* well; or else they should be punish'd; that he should assure the *Indians* the King had been concern'd for the

Wrongs

Wrongs done them, and would take Care for the future to prevent the like, and that none fhould be made Slaves, but that they in return muft ferve God, and be loyal to his Majefty ; that he fhould make all neceffary Obfervations relating to the Country, and fend Advice of all that he found, and particularly if he met with any large Town, fit to build a Monaftery in, to give Notice, or come back himfelf, for Religious Men for the fame, with many other Particulars of lefs Moment, and too tedious for this Place. He began his Journey on the 7th of *March* 1539, with his Companion F. *Honoratus* and *Eftevanico* the Black, who came out of *Florida* with *Cabeza de Vaca* and the others, as was faid in its Place, befides the abovemention'd fix *Indians* that fpoke *Spanifh,* the others they had brought with them, and thofe of *Petatlan,* to which Place they directed their Courfe, all of them very well pleas'd , meeting confiderable Prefents of Flowers and Provifions on the Way. Having travell'd the fixty Leagues to *Petatlan,* they refted three Days, and then F. *Mark,* leaving his Companion there fick, held on his Journey, abundance of People joyning him as he went on, but with little Provifion, becaufe there had been three Years of Scarcity, as they alledg d. In thirty Leagues Journey from *Petatlan,* he met with nothing worth Obfervation, only that fome *Indians* came to him from the Ifland the Marquefs *Del Valle Cortes* had difcover'd, who affur'd him that the fame was an Ifland, which had been queftion'd before, for he faw them pafs over to the Continent on Floats, the Diftance of about half a League. Some other *Indians* of another larger Ifland farther on, came alfo to him, who inform'd him, that there were thirty more fmall Iflands, inhabited by poor People, who had Mother of Pearl hanging about

bout their Necks, but fhow'd none. He held on his Way through a Defert, four Days Journey over, leaving behind many *Indians* of the Country and Iflands, and then came upon others, who were furpriz'd, heaving heard nothing of the *Spaniards*, becaufe they had no Communication with thofe that were left behind, by reafon of the Defert. They gave the Father much Provifion, touch'd his Habit, call'd him a Man come from Heaven, and by means of the Interpreters, he preach'd to them the Knowledge of the true God. Thefe faid, that four Days Journey up the Country, where the long Ridges of the Mountains ended, there was a flat fpacious open Plain, where the People were cloath'd, had Veffels of Go'd, he fhowing them fome, and they had Ornaments of it hanging at their Ears and Nofes. That Plain being at a D.ftance from the Coaft, and his Orders being to keep along it, he left it till his return, and advanc'd four Days among thofe fame People, till he came to a Town call'd *Vacapa,* which is forty Leagues from the Sea, where he was well entertain'd, and ftay'd till *Eafter* ; fending People in the mean Time to the Sea three feveral Ways, one of them being *Eftevanico,* from whom Meffengers came four Days after, praying F. *Mark* to follow him, becau'e he had receiv'd Information of a large Country call'd *Cibola,* thirty Days Journey from the Place where he then was, and this was affirm d by one of the *Indians Eftevanico* had fent.

THE *Indian* declar'd, that in the faid Country there were feven great Cities fubject to one Lord, the Houfes of Stone, one or two Stories high, regularly built, the Doors adorn'd with Turkey Stones ; and the Inhabitants all cloath d. The Father did

not

not set out immediately, because he waited for the Messengers that were gone to the Sea, who return'd on *Easter-Day*, with the aforesaid Account of the Islands, being thirty four in Number, and with them came some of the Islanders, who presented the Father with large Bucklers made of Cows Hides, well dress'd, which cover'd a Man from Head to Foot, having Holes at the Place for the Hand to pass through. This Day came three *Indians* of those call'd *Pintados*, their Arms and Breasts wrought, their Dwellings being to the Eastward, and extending almost to the seven Cities, of which they gave some Information. Having dismiss'd the *Indians* that came from the Coast, F. *Mark* set out on *Easter-Monday*, with two of the *Indians* of the Islands that would bear him Company eight Days, and three *Pintados*, taking his Way towards *Estevanico*, and the third Day met other Messengers coming to hasten him, confirming the Relation sent before of those large and wealthy Regions of *Cibola*, which was the first of the seven Cities, and was told, that beyond the seven Cities there were three Kingdoms call'd *Marata*, *Acus*, and *Tontecu*, where the People had Turky Stones hanging at their Ears and Noses. These *Indians* receiv'd F. *Mark* very kindly, presenting him Store of Provisions, and bringing their Sick to him to be cur'd, over whom he read the Gospels. They gave him Skins brought from *Cibola*, very well dress'd. In other Places, the *Pintados* still following him, he was well receiv'd, and had the same Account of *Cibola*, and he found a great Cross *Estevanico* had erected, as a Token that the News of the good Country held, and those People said he had left Word, that he would stay at the Entrance upon the first Desert. Here he took Possession, and went about

five

five Days, finding People and good Entertainment every where, many Turky Stones and Cows Hides; and was inform'd, that in two Days, he would come to a Defert that was four Days Journey over, without any Food, for which they had provided, as alfo for Shelter. Before he came to the Defert, he met with a pleafant Town, where they water'd their Fields with Trenches, and abundance of Men and Women came out to meet him, cloath'd in Cotton and Cows Hides, which they look upon as the better Habit. With them came the Lord of the Town and two of his Brothers, very well cloath'd in Cotton, with Collars of Turky Stones, and prefented him with Cups, *Indian* Corn, Turky Stones and feveral other Things, of all which the Father never receiv'd any. They touch'd his Habit and told him, there was much of that fort in *Tonteac,* and that it was made of the Hair of certain fmall Creatures, about the bignefs of fome *Spanifh* Greyhound *Eftevanico* had with him.

THE next Day F. *Mark* enter'd upon the Defert, and in four Days found Provifions and Cottages to lie in, and then came into a populous Vale, where all the Inhabitants of the firft Town came out to meet him, clad like thofe before mention'd, with Necklaces of Turky Stones, and fome of them in their Ears and Nofes; and there the Father heard as much talk of *Cibola,* as there in *New Spain* of *Mexico,* many of the People having been there. Here he had alfo an Account of the Wollen Cloth of *Tonteac,* and becaufe the Sea Coaft ran far to the Northward, he thought fit to fee it, and found that in the Latitude of thirty fix Degrees it turns off to the Weftward. Then holding on his Way, he travell'd five Days

through

I

through the great Vale, well inhabited by fightly People, plentiful and agreeable, all water'd, and thofe People went to *Cibola* to earn their living. Here he met with a Native of that City, who fled from the Governour plac'd in it by the Lord of the feven Cities, whofe Refidence was in that they call'd *Abacus*. He was a Man of good Senfe, would go with F. *Mark*, that he might obtain his Pardon for him, and gave a Defcription of the City, faying the others were like it ; that *Abacus* was the Capital, and that the Kingdom of *Matara* lay to the Weftward, where there had been great Towns with Houfes of Lime and Stone, as at *Cibola*, but was much decay'd, by reafon of the War with the Lord of the feven Cities ; that the Kingdom of *Tonteac* was very rich and populous, the Inhabitants wearing Cloth, and very polite ; and that there was another very great Kingdom, call'd *Acus* ; but that *Abacus* was one of the feven Cities. In this Vale they brought the Father an Hide, above as big again as a Cow's, and faid it was of a Beaft that had only one Horn in the Forehead, bowing down towards its Breaft, and that from it came a ftrait Point, in which that Creature had much Strength ; the Colour of it was like a Goat, and the Hair as long as a Man's Finger. Here he receiv'd Advice from *Eftevanico*, who fent him Word, that ever fince he had travell'd apart, he had never found the *Indians* in a lie, for which reafon Credit might be given to them as to what they faid of the fine Countries there were ; and the Father himfelf affirm d, that having Travell'd an hundred and twenty Leagues from the Place where he had the firft Notice of *Cibola* , he had always found every thing exactly true that they told him.

THE

THE Natives of the Vale intreated F. *Mark* to ſtay with them three Days, becauſe from the entring upon the Deſert to *Cibola,* there was full fifteen Day's Journey, and ſince above three hundred Men went with *Eſtevanico,* carrying Proviſions for the Deſert, they alſo would go to wait upon him, hoping they ſhould return very rich. He ſtay'd the three Days, and ſetting out, enter'd upon the Deſert on the 9th of *May* 1539. The firſt Day they found a very broad Road, and the Tokens of the Fires Travellers that went to *Cibola* were wont to make, and thus advanc'd twelve Days, always well furniſh'd with Proviſions, and Game, as Hares, and Partridges, like thoſe in *Spain* for Colour and Savour, but ſmaller, and there an *Indian* of *Eſtevanico's* Company came to F. *Mark* very melancholy, and tir'd, and ſaid, that one Day's Journey ſhort of *Cibola, Eſtevanico* had ſent before his Gourd, or Calabaſh by Meſſengers, to give Notice that he was coming. About that Gourd were ſome Rows of Hawks-bells, and on it two Feathers, one White, and one Red; and that having deliver'd the Gourd to the Governour of *Cibola,* he ſeeing the Hawks-bells about it, threw it on the Ground in a great Paſſion, telling the Meſſengers, that he knew thoſe People, and bid them be gone, and not come to *Cibola,* for he would kill them all; that *Eſtevanico* telling his Companions, that ſignify'd nothing, for he had found the beſt Reception where they ſaid ſo, held on his Way, and came to *Cibola,* where he was not admitted, but put into a great Houſe, and all he had, Goods to Exchange, Turkey Stones, and other Things given him by the Way, taken from him, all of them being kept up a Day and a Night without any thing to eat; that he who gave this Relation being compell'd to it by Thirſt, went out to drink at a River near by, where he ſaw *Eſtevanico* running away, and ſome of his Companions kill'd, whereupon this *Indian* hid himſelf, and made his Eſcape up the River. This

Account made many of thofe that were with the Father weep, and he comforting them, faying, that ought not to be credited, they affirm'd, that the *Indian* did not lye, whereupon he went afide, to pray to God to direct him, how to proceed as might be moft for his divine Service. Then returning to the *Indians*, he open'd the Petacas, or Baskets in which were the Commodities for bartering, which he diftributed among the Prime Men, encouraging them to follow him. One Day's Journey from *Cibola*, they met two more of the *Indians* that had been with *Eftevanico*, very bloody, and wounded, upon Sight of whom there was a forrowful Lamentation among them. When the Father, who could not forbear weeping, had pacify'd them, he order'd thofe two to relate what had hapned, who faid, That above three hundred of their Parents, Children, and Brothers had been kill'd, and there was no going to *Cibola*, and agreed in all the other *Indian* had faid, adding, that the next Morning *Eftevanico* went out of the Houfe, with fome Prime Men, when many from the City fell upon them, and they flying tumbled one over another, being above three hundred, befides Women, when they themfelves were fhot with Arrows, and wounded, as appear'd, whereupon they lay down among the Dead till Night, when they fled, and in the Day faw Abundance of People looking at what was done, from the Tops of the Houfes in the City; and that they had not feen *Eftevanico* any more, but believ'd he had been fhot as well as the reft. F. *Mark* was much furpriz'd at this News, not knowing what Courfe to take, but faid *Cibola* would not efcape unpunifh'd. The *Indians* anfwer'd, that there were none able to do it, becaufe the Nation was very powerful, and thus they continu'd their Weeping and Wailing, The Father went afide to pray, and returning about an Hour after, found a *Mexican Indian*, whofe Name was *Mark*, weeping, who faid to him, Father,

the{e

thefe People have agreed to kill you, becaufe you and
Eftevanico have been the Occafion of the Death of
their Relations, and will bring them to Deftruction.
F. *Mark* diftributing what remain'd of the Goods
brought to trade, told them, That it would be no Advantage to them to kill him ; but he fhould be a great
Gainer by it, for that dying in the Service of God he
fhould go to Heaven, and as foon as the *Spaniards*
could receive the Advice they would make War upon them. With thefe and other Arguments he appeas'd them, but their Lamentations did not ceafe ; however he pray'd fome one of them to go fee what was
become of *Eftavanico,* which none would ; yet, he
declar'd, he would not return, without having a Sight
of *Cibola,* and only two of the Chiefs agreed to go
with him. With them, his own *Indians,* and the Interpreters he went on till he came in Sight of that
City, which he faid was feated in a Plain, near the Side
of a round Hill, affording the beft Profpect of any
Town in all thofe Parts, the Houfes of Stone, having
upper Floors, and flat Roofs, as appear'd to him from
an Hill, whence he took his View, and that it was
larger than *Mexico;* affirming, that he had a great Mind
to have enter'd the City, but that he alter'd his Refolution, confidering, that if he fhould happen to
be kill'd, there would be no Body to bring back
an Account of that Country, which he look'd upon
to be better than any as yet difcover'd.

F. *Mark* having made all the Obfervations he thought
neceffary, with the Affiftance of the *Indians,* laid together an Heap of Stones in that Place, and erected a
Crofs on it, taking Poffeffion for the King of *Spain* of
the feven Cities, and the Kingdoms of *Totonac, Acus,*
and *Marata,* and fo return'd to thofe he had left behind. Being paft the Defert, and come again into the
Vale, there was a mighty Lamentation for thofe that
had been kill'd, he took his Leave, and travelling ten

Laegues

Leagues a Day, to pass over the second Desert, reach'd
the *Abra*, or Opening, where it was said before the
Mountains terminated, and was there told, that the said
Opening extended many Days Journey to the Eastward. He would not go into it, for fear of Danger, but
from the Mouth of it saw seven handsome Towns,
in a pleasant Vale, the Soil very good, and much
Smoak rising from them, the *Indians* telling him there
was much Gold among those People. There he e-
rected two Crosses, took Possession, and then held on
his Journey, till he arriv'd at St. *Michael* of *Culiacan*,
hoping to have found the Governour *Francis Vasquez
de Cornado* there; but not finding him, proceeded to
the City of *Compostela*, and thence sent Advice to the
Viceroy, and to his own Provincial of what he had
discover'd. The Fame of F. *Mark*'s Relation, tho'
not believ'd by all Men as to the Magnificence, and
Wealth of those Countries, excited the Viceroy to
undertake that Conquest. The Marquess *del Valle
Cortes* was for undertaking the same, alledging, that
it belong'd to him, as Captain-General, and pursuant
to what he had contracted with the King, besides
that he had been at great Expence in building seven
or eight Ships to carry on Discoveries by Sea. The
Adelantado *Don Peter de Alvarado* also claim'd the
same, saying, it was his Right in Virtue of his Agreement with the King, and that he was fitting out a
Fleet, with a considerable Number of Men. The
Marquess and the Viceroy were at Variance upon this
Account, and the Marquess sent out three Ships to discover, under the Command of Capt. *Ulloa*, as shall be said
hereafter, and came away himself into *Spain*. The Viceroy
apply'd himself to gathering of Money, to raise Forces a-
gainst the next Year, with other Ships under the Command of Capt. *Alarcon*, sending at the same Time for *Alvarado*, to adjust that Affair with him. We must now
leave those Expeditions till their proper Time, to see what
was doing in other Parts.   C H A P.

CHAP. V.

The Colony of Comayagua *in the Province of* Honduras *founded ; Agreement between* Alvarado *and* Montejo *; Provision for Defence of the* Indians *; Affairs in the Province of* Popayan, *and the New Kingdom of* Granada.

I T is Time to fee what was doing in the Province of *Honduras,* where the Adelantado *Don Francis de Montejo,* having put an End to the War of *Cerquin,* before fpoken of, thought it requifite to build a Town between the two Seas, the Country there being moft populous, and ought to be kept in Subjection. Accordingly, he fent Capt. *Alonfo de Caceres,* who founded it twenty-fix Leagues from the North, and the fame diftance from the South-Sea, where there is a River that runs twelve Leagues from Port *Cavallos,* and is Navigable for Canoes, as far as an *Indian* Town, from which to the Place call'd the Town of St. *Mary* of *Comayagua* is twelve Leagues more, the Way fit for Carts. Capt. *Caceres* and the Inhabitants fignify'd to the King, that this would be a very commodious Place for the Trade between the two Seas, alledging, that fewer People would dye, and there would not be fo many Difeafes, and Difficulties as in the Paffage between *Nombre de Dios* and *Panama,* fhowing that the Country was healthy, plentiful, and agreeable for the entertaining of the many People that were to pafs that Way, and affirming, that the Navigation from the Place to be pitch'd upon on the South-Sea to the Port of *Lima* was better than from the City of *Panama.* They

P 3   faid

said the Country was rich in Gold Mines, and produc'd *Spanish* Wheat, Vines, and other Fruit, besides Abundance of Cattle, the Climate being temperate, and well water'd, and the Town seated in a delightful Vale, almost four Leagues in Length. Whilst the Adelantado *Montejo* was intent upon these Projects, *Don Peter de Alvarado* arriv'd at Port *Cavallos*, with a Fleet from *Spain*, and proceeded with his Wife, a good Number of Men, and Store of Provisions and Ammunitions, having made a new Contract with the King about undertaking Discoveries, to the Town of St. *Peter*. *Montejo* hereupon consulted with his Friends how to behave himself, and *Alvarado* taking no Notice of him, tho' he had been landed a Month, they advis'd to send him a Compliment, and in a courteous manner enquire into his Intentions; because there was no other way of proceeding since he was so strong. *Alvarado* answer'd, that having been inform'd of his coming into that Province, which he had conquer'd, and taken away his Lands, and those given to the Conquerors, the King had order'd them to be restor'd, which Orders he would cause to be notify'd to him. *Montejo* did not like this Answer, because the King's Orders, and the Power to back them were not to be withstood. The Bishop of *Honduras* Elect, to prevent Mischief went away to *Alvarado*, who show'd him a Commission he had from the King directed to the said Elect, for restoring him, and all that had been dispossess'd of their Lands by *Montejo* to the same, and all the Profits that had occur'd since their being so dispossess'd. The Elect hereupon intreated him to endeavour to adjust that Difference amicably without coming to an open Rupture, which *Alvarado*, who was of a generous Disposition, consented to, and the same being approv'd by *Montejo*, he came to wait upon him, and his Lady *Dona Beatrix de la Cueva*. *Montejo* seeing the King's Commission, and

Alvarado's

Alvarado's Power, confented to quit *Honduras* to him, only defiring he would give him the Government of *Chiapa,* belonging to *Guatemala,* and the Town of *Suchimilco,* which was granted him, and the Bifhop having rated the Profits of the Lands he had receiv'd fince his taking Poffeffion thereof at twenty-eight thoufand Ducats, *Alvarado* immediately remitted him the one Half, and was two Months after eafily prevail'd upon to forgive him the other Half. This Accommodation was afterwards confirm'd in *Spain,* and from that Time forward the Province of *Honduras* was peaceable under the Government of *Alvarado,* whereas before it had always been full of Broils, and under Oppreffion, through the Wickednefs of the Governours.

AFFAIRS being thus adjufted, *Alvarado* proceeded to the Province of *Guatemala,* where, upon his Arrival, there began to be a noife of Arms for fubduing the Coaft of *New-Spain,* which very much troubled the Bifhops, and Religious Men of the Order of St. *Dominick,* who had done Wonders by their Preaching in thofe Parts, without the Affiftance of any Military Power; whereupon F. *Cafas* and F. *Roderick de Andrada* were fent into *Spain* to defire more Religious Men might be fent over, and other Things advantageous to the *Indians,* in order to carry on their Converfion more fucceffively. Thofe two Fathers, tho' the King was not then in *Spain,* were much favour'd by the Council, and on their Account the new Laws were afterwards eftablifh'd, which will be fpoken of in their Place, and the Viceroy of *Mexico* was reminded of fome Inftructions before given him, tending to the Honour of God, and the Eafe of the Natives, as firft, that all *Spaniards* who had *Indians* in *Commendam* fhould be oblig'd to marry, for obviating of fome Sins that were difcernable; that an Univerfity fhould be eftablifh'd in the City of *Mexico,*

for

for the Improvement of all People, and to save continual
sending so many from *Spain,* which has succeeded so
well, that it is now inferiour to none in *Europe* ; that
the Proclamation for regulating Exorbitance in Appa-
rel should be suspended, *&c.*

THIS same Year 1539, two Ships sail'd from *Cadiz,* under the Command of Captain *Alonso de Cabrera,*
who arriving safe at *Buenos Ayres,* produc'd the King's
Commission for the Commanders and Soldiers to choose
a Governour, in Case none had been appointed by the
former Governour Don *Peter Mendoza,* and it appearing that *Francis Ruyz Galan* had been appointed to
Command at *Buenos Ayres* till *John de Ayolas* should
return from the Expedition he was gone upon, Captain *Cabrera* aspiring to that Post, occasion'd a Controversy with the said *Galan,* which was compos'd by
appointing them both to govern. At this time a Ship
that had design'd to pass through the Streights of *Magellan* for *Peru,* having been forc'd back came into *Buenos Ayres,* which put those two Governours into a
better Condition to sail up to the Town of the *Assumption,* as they had before intended. The *Franciscan*
Friers, who went over in those Ships to serve God,
took their Way up into the Country, and beginning
to preach, with the Assistance of able Interpreters, till
they could learn the Language themselves, found a
considerable Harvest, converting and baptizing those
People. The two Governours *Cabrera* and *Galan* coming to the *Assumption,* found, that when *Ayolas* went
out upon his Discovery, he had substituted *Dominick
de Irala* in his Stead, whereupon *Galan* by the Contrivance of *Cabrera,* who would have been join'd with
Irala, was remov'd from the Government ; but *Cabrera* not being admitted himself, prevail'd so far as to
be sent out with nine Vessels and four hundred Men
in Quest of *John de Ayolas.* Being come to the Place
where *Ayolas* had left *Irala,* and hearing no Tidings of
him,

him, it was refolv'd to proceed with a Part of their own Veffels, and fome *Indian* Canoes to the Country of the *Payagoaes*, where after fix Days, they took a Canoe with fix *Indians* in it, for underftanding of whom they had no Interpreter ; however by Signs, and in the beft manner it could be done, they came to underftand, that the *Spaniards*, and the *Indians* who went with them, were up the Country, in a ftrong Houfe they had built, digging Gold and Silver. Here-upon it was refolv'd, that two hundred and ten Men, with fome light Guns, taking thofe *Indians* for their Guides, fhould go find out that ftrong Houfe. The firft Day, the Way prov'd good, and the next grew bad, and feveral Days they found no dry Land to reft on, but Water up to their Middles, and fometimes deeper ; whereupon they return'd to their Veffels, much fatigu'd and harafs'd, having fpent a Month on that fruitlefs and toilfome Expedition. That vaft Quantity of Water thofe *Spaniards* met with, was the Inundation of the great River of *Plate*, otherwife call'd *Paraguay*, which has the fecond Place among the greateft in the World, coming down from the Moun-tains of *Peru*, and falling into the *North-Sea*, in thir-ty-five Degrees South Latitude, for like the *Nile* in *Egypt*, though much farther in Extent, it overflows all the Country about for the Space of three Mouths, and then returns to its Channel, which put a Stop to the Progrefs of thofe *Spaniards*. Two Days after their re-turn to the Brigantines, when they were upon their return to the *Affumption*, came an *Indian*, who had made his Efcape from fome Canoes of the *Payagoaes*, and faid, he was a Native of the upper Country, of a Nation call'd *Chanes*, and that *John de Ayolas* being come into his Country, where he was receiv'd in peaceable manner, faid, he was going farther to know where the *Chemeneos* and *Carcaraes* had their Gold and

Silver,

Silver, they ufing much of thofe Metals, and that finding them in a warlike Pofture, he obferv'd their Wealth, and return'd to the *Chanes,* faying, he retir'd in order to come again with a greater Power ; that the Chief of the *Chanes* gave him much Gold, and Silver, with *Indians* to carry his Baggage and Provifions, of which Number he was one, and having pafs'd through Deferts, becaufe they wanted Arms, they came, very much fatigu'd, to the Port, where they had left their Brigantines with *Dominick de Irala,* where having ftay'd feven or eight Days, fome Friends of the *Payagoaes* went to fee him, carrying Prefents of Fifh and Venifon, inviting him to go to their Houfes, which he confenting to, becaufe the Brigantines were not there, and confiding in the *Payagoaes,* they on the Way kill'd him and all his *Indians* in a Morafs, through Covetoufnefs of his Gold and Silver. This was a great Affliction to thofe *Spaniards,* who could not at that time attempt to revenge that Maffacre, and recover the Treafure, by reafon of the great Inundation, being themfelves at that time in a poor Condition, and five hundred Leagues from the Sea ; whereupon they return'd to the *Affumption,* and foon after to *Buenos Ayres,* which Place they entirely abandon'd, and carry'd all away to the *Affumption,* thinking it moft advifeable that they fhould be all together, in order to make their Excurfions into the Country.

Belalcazar, who, as was faid in its Place, had made the great Difcoveries in the Province of *Popayan,* and then went into *Spain* to procure a Commiffion from the King, fucceeded well there in his Negotiation. His Majefty, in Confideration of his good Service, and to put a Stop to the unbounded Ambition of the *Pizarro's,* giving him the Government of all *Popayan, Guacallo,* and *Nejba,* as far as the Frontiers of St. *Francis de Quito,* with all the adjacent Parts, by the Name of

of the Provinces of *Popayan,* becaufe he had difcover'd
them, and with it the Title of *Adelantado,* or Lord
Lieutenant, and all other Prerogatives ufually granted
to other Governours and Difcoverers in thofe Parts,
fo that he was independent of all but the King, and
the Court of *Panama,* and had Orders, that *Gonzalo Pizarro* fhould not intrude into that Province,
notwithstanding any Authority given him by the Marquefs his Brother, and the Court of *Panama* was directed to expel *Pafqual de Andagoya,* if he had enter'd
the fame, under Colour of the River of St. *John.*
Belalcazar lofing no time, foon came to *Panama,* where
embarking again, he landed in the Port of *Buenaventura,* and proceeded thence to *Cali,* at which Place
they had before receiv'd Advice of his coming. *Andagoya* was thereupon making Preparations to oppofe
him, but his Title being precarious, and Men generally fond of Novelties, they wifh'd for his coming,
fending Letters to meet him, with Promifes of their
Affiftance, whereupon *Andagoya* fecur'd fome Perfons he fufpected, and fent others to oppofe him at
the narrow Pafs on the Mountains. However he arriv'd fafe at *Cali,* and the two Parties having recourfe
to Arms, were upon the Point of engaging, till fome
Religious Perfons interpofing, it was agreed, that *Belalcazar* fhould produce his Commiffion before the
Magiftrates, and if they thought fit to admit him, the
Government fhould be put into his Hands, or elfe *Andagoya* to remain in Poffeffion, and though many of
the Soldiers at *Cali* were gone over to *Belalcazar,* he
wifely concluded it beft to ftand to this Accommodation, that being the Way to be put into Authority
without Force of Arms. The Magiftrates having feen
Belalcazar's Commiffion, own'd him, excluding *Andagoya,* whom he prefently fecur'd, and fent to *Popayan,* as an Intruder into another's Right, ordering all
Things

Things to his own Mind ; and then appointed *Peter de Ayala* to repair to *George de Robledo,* to require him to own his Authority, and order that the Town of St. *Anne* of *Anzerma* fhould not be call'd St. *John,* as *Andagoya* had nam'd it. *Robledo* went away from *Cartago* to *Anzerma,* whence he writ to *Belalcazar,* as his Superior, intreating him not to give Credit to his Enemies, for he was very ready to ferve him, and then went away again with one hundred Men to proceed on his Difcoveries, to diftribute Lands to thofe who had ferv'd, and had none, and having crofs'd *Rio Grande* at the Town of *Yrra,* the Report prefently flew about, that he was revolted, which was occafion'd by his afpiring to be Commander in Chief.

WHILST thefe Things hapned in the Court of *Spain,* and at *Popayan, Jerom Lebron,* who was Governour at *Santa Marta,* pretending that the *New Kingdom of Granada* appertain'd to his Jurifdiction, march'd thither with Forces, the fame Way that *Quefada* had gone before, and having loft many Men on that difficult Way, fome of thofe that went with him gave fo ill an Account of his Behaviour to the People there, that the greater Number refolv'd not to admit of him for their Governour. However being come to *Belez,* with two hundred Foot, and above one hundred Horfe, he fhow'd his Commiffion, and was receiv'd by the Magiftrates. Captain *Ferdinand Perez,* who govern'd that Kingdom before, underftanding that *Lebron* was come into it, fent for Captain *Cardofo,* who was then two Leagues from *Santa Fe de Bogota,* and fearing left he on Account of his Friendfhip with *Lebron* might occafion fome Difturbance, left him at *Santa Fe,* with fome Men, and with the reft of the Forces proceeded himfelf to the City of *Tunja;* whence he fent two Captains to difcourfe *Lebron,* who advis'd him to retire, becaufe he would not be admitted to govern there, till

till such time as the King had signified his Pleasure, as had been agreed among the three Conquerors; but *Lebron* still advancing with his Forces, and being come near to *Tunja*, without receding from his Design, both Parties came in Sight of each other, and were upon the Point of coming to Blows; but some Religious Men and Commanders interposing, and representing how prejudicial such a Breach would be to the King's Service, a Treaty was set on Foot, and *Lebron* produc'd his Commission before the Magistrates of *Tunja*, upon Condition, that if they admitted him as Governour, he should remain in that Quality; but they refusing, he enter'd his Protestations, and began to form a Process against those that refus'd to submit to him. They all went together to *Santa Fee*, where he also produc'd his Commission, and was again rejected, and though he appeal'd, they still persisted, alledging, that the Country was very unsettled, and therefore it was prejudicial to the Service of God, and the King to blow up the Coals, or make any Innovation. *Lebron* finding that after all his Positiveness *Ferdinand Perez* had enjoin'd him to desist, under the severest Penalties, commanding him not to make any Uproar in the Country, desir'd they would let him go on to make Discoveries, with as many of his own Men as are willing to follow him; but they would not grant even that, whereupon he resolv'd to return to *Santa Marta*, and pray'd Captain *Cardoso* to go with him, promising not to take Notice of what was past, and he being then upon his Departure for *Spain* embrac'd that offer, together with Captain *John de Junco*. Being come to *Santa Marta*, when they were ready to embark, *Lebron* seiz'd them both, saying, he would not obstruct their Voyage, but that they should be carry'd over as Prisoners, because he had condemn'd them all in the *New Kingdom of Granada* to Death,

and

and Forfeiture of their Eftates, as Traytors; however, after much contending, he confented that they fhould upon their Parole of Honour, appear before the King and his Council; fuch was the Arrogancy of thofe Governours, that they concluded all Things juft, which were agreeable to their Notions.

The End of the Fifth Book.

THE

THE

General HISTORY

Of the vaſt CONTINENT and ISLANDS of

A M E R I C A, &c.

❋❋❋❋❋❋❋❋❋❋❋❋❋❋❋❋❋❋❋❋❋❋❋❋❋

DECAD IV. BOOK VI.

❋❋❋❋❋❋❋❋❋❋❋❋❋❋❋❋❋❋❋❋❋❋❋❋❋

CHAP. I.

Ferdinand de Soto *contracts with the King for the Conqueſt of* Florida ; *his Arrival and Actions there.*

ERDINAND *de Soto,* born at *Villa-nueva da Barcarota,* a Commander of Renown in the *Weſt-Indies,* who having ſerv'd in *Caſtilla del Oro,* and *Nicaragua,* was one of the firſt that went upon the Conqueſt of *Peru,* and being a Man of Worth, and Valour, was by *Francis Pizarro* appointed his Lieutenant-General, and the firſt *Spaniard* that ſaw

the

the mighty Prince *Atahualpa Inga*, Sovereign of so many Kingdoms and Provinces, observing the Discord that began to appear between the *Almagros* and *Pizarro*'s, resolv'd to go away into *Spain*, not so rich as his Service and good Qualities deserv'd, considering the immense Wealth then found in *Peru*. This Gentleman aspiring to undertake great Actions, suitable to his lofty Genius, begg'd of the King the Conquest of *Florida*, which was readily granted him upon his own Terms, because he was a Person of Experience, of a good Presence, and Mien, and for his Age and strong Constitution, fitted to endure Hardships. Since the Time that *Panfilo de Narvaez* had been ruin'd in that Country, till then no one had offer'd to go upon that Enterprize, looking upon it as very dangerous and chargeable. Among other Things granted to *Soto* was the Government of the Island of *Cuba*, because it was to be the Place of Arms for carrying on that Conquest. The Design being made publick, near one thousand Men were soon rais'd, the Reputation of the Commander, and the Hopes of gaining much Wealth being a great Encouragement, and among them were many Gentlemen of Birth. Ten Ships being fitted out to carry those Men, with all necessary Stores, they sail'd from *San Lucar* on the 6th of *April* 1538, in Company with the Fleet for *New Spain*, all under the Command of the Adelantado *Ferdinand de Soto*, as far as he was to go, that is to the Island of *Cuba*, the Factor *Gonzalo de Salazar*, being appointed to command the *New Spain* Feet afterwards, who to show his turbulent Temper every where, the first Night they were at Sea, went away a Cannon-Shot a-Head of all the Fleet, to plague the Admiral, for which Reason a Cannon being fir'd at him, the Ball went through all his Sails, from the Poop to the Head, and the second tore all the Side of the Ship above the Deck, Then the Admiral pushing forward, *Salazar*'s

Ship

Ship being ungovernable for want of her Sails, they ran foul of one another, and were both in Danger of being caſt away, in the dark, had not the Admiral cut all the Rigging of the other which was foul of his, and ſo got clear. *Soto,* underſtanding that what *Salazar* had done proceeded from Pride, would have cut off his Head, but upon his Submiſſion, and many Intreaties, he forgave him.

THIS Fleet arriv'd ſafe at *Santiago* in the Iſland of *Cuba,* where not long before, a *Spaniſh* Ship commanded by *James Perez* had fought the whole Day with a *French* Privateer ; parting very courteouſly at Night, and returning furiouſly to the Engagement in the Morning, they continu'd it four Days, till at length the *French* Man ſlipp'd away in the Night. *Soto* as ſoon as arriv'd in *Cuba* ſent Orders for repairing the *Havana,* which had been burnt by *French* Privateers, and built the firſt Fort in that Place. Having ſent to diſcover the Ports along the Coaſt of *Florida,* and appointed his Lady Governeſs of *Cuba,* he put aboard three hundred and thirty Horſes, and nine hundred Men, beſides the Sailors, and ſailed from the *Havana* on the 12th of *May* 1539. The laſt Day of the ſame Month he came to an Anchor in the Bay of *Eſpiritu Santo,* or the Holy Ghoſt, and landed three hundred Men, who lay there that Night, without ſeeing one Native, but about break of Day, an infinite number of thoſe People attack'd, and oblig'd them to retire to the Sea. *Baſco Porcallo de Figueroa* went to their Relief with a Party, for the *Indians* preſs'd hard with their Flights of Arrows on the *Spaniards,* who being new rais'd Soldiers, were not come to their Fighting, but upon *Porcallo's* appearing, the *Indians* were forc'd to retire, having firſt kill'd that Commander's Horſe with an Arrow, that pierc'd thro' the Covering of the Saddle, and penetrated a Span deep into the Body. All the Forces landed, and march'd

VOL. V.　　　　　Q　　　　　TWO

two Leagues to a Town belonging to the Cazique *Harribiagua*, who was fled to the Mountains, fearing to be call'd to Account for the Cruelty he had exercis'd on some *Spaniards* that came thither with *Pamphilo de Narvaez*, of which number none had escap'd but one *John Ortiz*, by the Assistance of that Cazique's Wife, who abhorr'd his Cruelty, he fled to the Cazique *Mucozo*, who protected, and us'd him well. The Adelantado understanding where that Man was, sent a Gentleman call'd *Baltasar de Gallegos* with sixty Horsemen to bring him, because he wanted him for an Interpreter, and this was at the time that the Cazique was sending *Ortiz* with fifty *Indians* to offer Peace. Those *Indians* were stark naked, having only Clouts, and great Plumes of Feathers, their Bows in their Hands, and their Quivers full of Arrows. As soon as they saw the Horsemen, they were for running into the Wood, apprehending they should be attack'd ; but *Ortiz* would not take the good Advice of those People, and his raw *Spaniards* were impatient to run full speed upon them, in despight of their Commander. All the *Indians* got into the Wood, none but *Ortiz* remaining on the Plain, whom *Alvaro Nieto* assaulted with his Spear ; and he giving a Leap backward spoke the *Indian* Language, having forgot his own, but remember'd to make the Sign of the Cross, and *Nieto* ask'd him, whether he was *John Ortiz* ? He said, he was ; and the other took him up behind him on his Horse, and carry'd him to his Captain, who was drawing together his Men that were dispers'd after the *Indians*. Some never stopp'd till they came to the Town, the rest were appeas'd, but when they saw one of their Company wounded, they exclaim'd bitterly against *Ortiz*, because that had hapned through his Inadvertency.

THE Adelantado was much pleas'd that he had got *Ortiz*, whom he carefs'd, as also the *Indians* that went

with

with him, order'd him that was wounded to be dress'd, and sent to thank the Cazique *Mucozo,* for his good Usage of that Man, offering him his Friendship. Ortiz could give very little Account of the Country, because under his first Master his whole Business had been carrying Wood, and Water, and he never would be out of the others Sight, for fear of giving a Suspicion that he would run away, when his Usage was good; but said, he had been told, that the Country farther in was good, and fruitful. *Mucozo* then went to visit the Adelantado, who entertain'd, and gave him some *Spanish* Baubles, thanking him for his Friendship. That Cazique's Mother came next, weeping, demanding her Son, and begging that they would not kill him, the Adelantado endeavouring to pacify her; and though she did eat, it was with much Precaution, asking *Ortiz,* whether she might eat with Safety, fearing there might be Poison, and yet would not eat unless *Ortiz* tasted first. *Mucozo* staying a Week among the *Spaniards* diverting himself, and enquiring about the Affairs of *Spain,* the Adelantado endeavour'd to learn some Particulars of that Country, the Forces continuing in the Cazique *Harrihiagua's* Town, because it was nearest to the Bay of the *Holy Ghost.* During that time he dismiss'd the Ships, that his Men might have no Hopes of getting out of that Country, as many antient and modern Commanders had done before, and among them *Cortes* in *New Spain* ; ordering, that only Four should stay, to serve upon Occasion. He discreetly labour'd to gain the Friendship of the Cazique *Harrihiagua,* taking Care that no Mischief should be done in his Country, not thinking it proper to offend him that was the first in his Way, lest it should prove of ill Consequence, but nothing would prevail with him. Some Men went out every Day under a strong Guard to bring Forage for the Horses, and on a sudden a Multitude of *Indians* fell upon them, with

Q 2 such

such hideous Cries as scar'd them, and before they could come to themselves, those People laid hold of a Soldier, whose Name was *Grajal*, and carry'd him off very well pleas'd without doing any other Harm. More *Spaniards* coming out upon the Alarm, twenty Horsemen pursu'd them two Leagues by the Track, till they came to a Piece of Ground that was all overgrown with Reeds, where the *Indians* were eating, drinking, and singing very merrily, without any Fear, or Concern, having their Wives with them, and bid *Grajal* eat, for they would not use him ill as they had done *Ortiz*. Upon hearing the Noise of the Horses the Men fled, leaving the Women and Children with *Grajal*, he having been stripp'd, came out stark naked to meet the *Spaniards*, who return'd well pleas'd with their Booty, to the Quarters, and the Adelantado to pacify those People, order'd the Women and Children, and some Men that had been taken to be dismiss'd.

WHEN the *Spaniards* had lain three Weeks in that Place, the Adelantado sent Captain *Baltasar de Gallegos*, with sixty Horse, and a like Number of Foot, to discover the Country beyond the Lordships of the Caziques *Harrihiagua* and *Mucozo*, which was that of *Urribarracuxi*, and asking Guides of *Mucozo*, he refus'd to give them, saying, It was a Piece of Treachery to guide any that would do harm to his Friend and Brother-in-Law. The *Spaniards* answer'd, That they must needs go, and that it were better to send him Word, that they would do him no Injury. This he said, he was willing to do, and having march'd seventeen Leagues, they found *Urribarracuxi*'s Town abandon'd, and that Cazique would never come out of the Woods, or contract Friendship with the *Spaniards*, or offend them. In this Country they saw wild Vines, Walnut, Mulberry, Plum, Oak, Pine, and other such Trees as grow in *Spain*, and the open Fields were

were very agreeable. Captain *Gallegos* sent back five Horsemen to acquaint the Adelantado with what he had seen, and that there was sufficient Provision in the Town. *Soto* desiring to take the Cazique *Harrihia-gua,* one Day his Lieutenant *Vasco Porcallo* would go out with a Resolution to search him by fair or foul Means, though the Adelantado advis'd him rather to send another. The Cazique being inform'd of it, sent him Word, not to Labour in vain, for he would never be able to come at him, by reason of the bad Ways. He still holding on, they came at last to a deep Morass, which all refusing to enter; *Porcallo,* to set his Men an Example, spurr'd on his Horse, but soon fell, and had like to have been stifled, which was such a warning to him, that considering he was in Years, and had a great Estate, he desir'd Leave to return to *Cuba,* and give over that dangerous and fatiguing Enterprize, fitter for young Men than for him, and having obtain'd it, distributed several Horses he had, his Arms and Provisions among the Forces, leaving a Son he had, call'd *Gomez Xuarez de Figueroa,* well equipp'd, to continue that Undertaking, in which he behav'd himself like a Man of Honour.

UPON the Intelligence sent him by Captain *Gallegos,* the Adelantado resolv'd to advance, leaving Captain *Calderon* in that Place, with forty Horsemen, to secure the Ships, and Provisions, ordering him not to give the *Indians* any cause of Complaint, but rather to connive at the Injuries they might offer him. He would not halt in *Mucozo's* Town, for fear of being burdensome to him with so many Men, though that Cazique offer'd to entertain him ; only he recommended to him the *Spaniards* that were left at the Bay of the *Holy Ghost.* He held on his Way North-North-East, without taking Care to mark down the Country, which was a great Fault, and coming to *Urribarracuxi,* us'd all Endeavours to gain the Friendship of

Q 3 that

that Cazique, but to no Effect. Being to pass a Morass which was three Leagues over, with much Industry a Way was found, though it held them two Day's March, and the next Day the Fore-runners return'd, reporting, that it was impossible to proceed any farther, by reason of the many Rivers that ran out from the great Morass. Three Days were spent in searching out some Way to pass, the Adelantado, being always the first that went abroad upon Discovery, during which time the *Indians* made Excursions out of the Woods to shoot the *Spaniards* with their Arrows, but were generally disappointed, and some of them taken, who to get their Liberty, offer'd to show the Passes, and maliciously led the *Spaniards* to such Places as were impassable ; but some, when their Knavery was discover'd, being torn by the Dogs, one of them undertook to Conduct them, and easily brought them out into a clear Country. However they came to another Morass, which had two large Timbers, and some Boughs of Trees laid over the narrowest Part of it, as a Bridge. The Adelantado sent two Soldiers, that were good Swimmers to repair that Bridge, who were set upon by many *Indians* in Canoes, but, though wounded, made their Escape. Yet the *Indians* appearing no more, the Bridge was repair'd, and the Forces pass'd over into the Province of *Acuera,* the Cazique whereof being offer'd Peace, answer'd, That he had rather be at War than Peace with Vagabonds. The Forces continu'd here twenty Days, during which time the *Indians* kill'd fourteen *Spaniards,* whose Heads they carry'd to their Cazique, and though the *Spaniards* bury'd the Bodies as they found them, they were dug up again by the *Indians,* who quarter'd, and set them up on the Trees. The *Spaniards* all that while kill'd only fifty *Indians,* because they were always upon their Guard. The Forces march'd from *Acuera,* without doing any Harm in the

the Country, marching Northward, a little to the Eaftward for *Ocali,* free from Moraffes, and the Land fruitful. Having march'd twenty Leagues, they came to *Ocali,* a Town of fix hundred Houfes, abounding with *Indian* Wheat, Pulfe, Acorns, dry'd Plums, and Nuts. The Cazique and the Inhabitants were withdrawn into the Woods, and upon the firft Summons return'd a civil Anfwer ; but came at the fecond, tho' under much Apprehenfion, and the Adelantado *Soto* going with him to view a Part of a River, over which a Bridge was to be laid, there appear'd on the farther Side of it about five hundred *Indians* fhooting their Arrows, and crying, Away Vagabond Robbers. The Adelantado ask'd, Why he permitted his Subjects to do fo ? To which he anfwer'd, That many of them had caft off their Obedience on Account of his being in Friendfhip with the *Spaniards.* The Adelantado reply'd, That if it was fo, he might go his Way, which he did very well pleas'd, promifing to return, but did not. The Bridge was made by laying feveral Cables a-crofs, and Planks over them, for there was Plenty, and the fame proving good, the Men march'd over, with much Satisfaction, they being after the old *Roman* manner Engineers and Pioneers to build Bridges, and make Ways.

THE Guides being fled, thirty frefh *Indians* were taken, who being well treated, and prefented, conducted the Forces fixteen Leagues over a good Country to the Province of *Vitacucho,* which was about fifty Leagues in Compafs, and divided between three Brothers. On the Way was a Town call'd *Ochile,* which being attack'd about Break of Day, the *Indians* alarm'd by the Drums and Trumpets ran out, and finding all the Avenues fecur'd, ftood upon their Defence, and tho' the Cazique was courted to be friendly, he would make Refiftance, till his Men perceiving that the *Spaniards* releas'd the Prifoners, and did

no

no Harm, acquainted him with it, and he, making a Virtue of Necessity, submitted, was well treated by *Soto,* and bore him Company, with many of his People, to a spacious Vale that was inhabited, but the Houses scattering. This Cazique sent to acquaint his Brothers, that the *Spaniards* were only passing through to other Countries, and did no Harm, requiring nothing but Provisions, and to be Friends. One of them return'd a favourable Answer, treating the *Spaniards* affectionately; but the eldest, who was most powerful, would not let the Messengers return, and afterwards sent a Reproof to his Brothers, saying, They had acted like foolish young Fellows, and that they might tell those Strangers, that if they offer'd to set their Feet in his Country, the one Half should be roasted, and the other Half boil'd. However, the Adelantado returning very kind, and courteous Answers, *Vitacucho,* for that was the greater Cazique's Name, had a mind to be acquainted with the *Spaniards,* and went to see the Adelantado, with five hundred Men very gaily adorn'd after their Manner. He was well pleas'd at the Sight of their Forces, begg'd Pardon for the harsh Expressions he had us'd, promising to make amends by his future Behaviour, and the Adelantado made much of, and presented him, as did the Officers, which he was very fond of; being about thirty-five Years of Age, strong limb'd, and of a fierce Aspect. The next Day the Troops enter'd *Vitacucho's* Town in good Order, those Towns having no particular Names but those of their Lords, and this consisted of about two hundred Houses, besides many scatter'd about the Country. There the *Spaniards* stay'd two Days, making merry, when the other two Lords ask'd Leave to return to their Homes, which was granted, and the Adelantado making them some Presents, they went away well satisfy'd. *Vitacucho* went on slily two Days, contriving to destroy
the

the *Spaniards*, to which Purpose he had summon'd all
his Neighbours, perswading them that it was abso-
lutely requisite to destroy those wicked People. He
imparted his Design to four *Indians* the Adelantado had brought with him for his Interpreters, telling them, he had ten thousand *Indians* well arm'd
to put it in Execution, and that some of them should
be roasted, others boil'd, others hung up on the tallest
Trees, and others poison'd that they might live to see
themselves pine and rot away ; desiring they would
keep the secret, and tell him their Opinion. They
said, they approv'd of it, and that it was an Exploit
beseeming his Valour, and nothing could be better contriv'd than what he had done. *Vitacucho* thus encourag'd,
warn'd his Confederates to be in a Readiness ; but the
four *Indians*, being convinc'd of the Difficulty of putting that Design in Execution, by reason of the good
Discipline observ'd by the *Spaniards*, discover'd it to
John Ortiz, that he might acquaint the Adelantado,
who having advis'd with his Officers, it was thought
fit not to take Notice as yet, but to contrive to punish *Vitacucho* in the same manner as he had projected
to execute his Design, standing upon their Guard in the
mean Time, yet as if nothing were known. When
the appointed Day was come, *Vitacucho* desir'd the
Adelantado to march out his Forces, to see his Subjects, whom he had drawn out in order, that he
might be acquainted with his Power, and Manner of
making War. The Adelantado, a discreet Man, and
well skill'd in the Art of War, as having gradually
ascended to that Degree, courteously answer'd, He was
willing, and that it being customary among the *Spaniards* to march out in Order of Battle, to honour their
Friends, it would also be a Satisfaction for his *Indians*
to see their Method of fighting ; and the better to pal-
liate his Intentions, the Adelantado walk'd out a-foot
with the Cazique. The *Indians* were drawn up with
a Wood

a Wood on their Left, and two Lakes on their Right, being about ten thousand, well equipp'd after their Manner, and adorn'd with Plumes of Herons, Swans, and Cranes Feathers, besides several other Sorts, which rising at least half a Yard above their Heads, made them look the taller. Their Bows lay on the Ground, the Arrows cover'd with Grass, to look as if they were unarm'd, there being two Wings on the Sides of their main Body.

THE Adelantado, and the Cazique, with each of them twelve chosen Men, advanc'd, both having the same Design. The *Spaniards* mov'd on the Right of their Commander, the Cavalry was in the midst of the Plain, the Infantry close to the Wood, and when come to the Place, where it was known that *Vitacucho* intended to give the Signal, for executing his Design, the Adelantado being sensible that his Men were willing and ready, took the Advantage, and order'd to fire a Musket. Upon that Signal, the twelve *Spaniards* seiz'd *Vitacucho*, as he had design'd to do by their General, who being privately arm'd, mounted his Horse, and fell in with the *Indians*, being always the first either at Fighting, or hard Labour. The *Indians* having taken up their Arms, prevented his penetrating through many of their Ranks, by killing his Horse with their Arrows, for they always level'd at the Horses, being sensible of the Harm they did them. The Adelantado's Page brought him another Horse, at such Time as his Cavalry was breaking the main Body of the *Indians*, who thereupon betook themselves to Flight, some into the Wood, and others into the Lake, those who fled along the Plain being overtaken, and either kill'd or taken. Those that were in the Van far'd worst, about nine hundred of whom took into the lesser Lake, where the *Spaniards* attack'd them with their Fire-arms and Cross-bows, only to scare them, that they might surrender, but they shot as long as
they

they had Arrows, and to be able to do it the better one would ſtand upon four that were ſwimming, ſtaying there till all his Arrows were ſpent. This continu'd from Ten in the Morning till Night, when the *Spaniards* incloſ'd the Lake, none ſurrendring till Midnight, tho' they were promis'd their Lives, but when they had been fourteen Hours in the Water, Neceſſity oblig'd the feebleſt to ſubmit. The reſt ſeeing that no Harm had been done them, ſurrender'd the next Day at Noon, when they had been above twenty-four Hours in the Water, and it was obſervable to ſee them come out tir'd, hungry, ſleepy, and ſwollen, becauſe they had drank much Water; only ſeven obſtinate Fellows ſtaying behind, till Seven in the Evening, when the Adelantado thinking it a Piece of Cruelty to ſuffer thoſe reſolute Men to periſh, order'd twelve *Spaniards* to ſwim to them, with their Swords in their Mouths, who dragg'd out ſome by the Hair, and others by the Arms, half drowned, but Care was taken to recover them, and being aſk'd, why they were ſo obſtinate? They ſaid, that being Commanders, they would ſhow their Lord, that they were worthy of their Poſts, by dying for him, and leave a good Name behind them, wiſhing they had been permitted to end their Days where they were. Four of them were about thirty-five Years of Age; the other three being about eighteen, and Gentlemen's Sons, came from Home to gain Honour, upon *Vitacucho*'s Call, and unwilling to return Home vanquiſh'd, the Adelantado gave them Looking-glaſſes, and other Baubles, and ſo diſmiſs'd them; but told the four Commanders, in the Preſence of *Vitacucho*, that they deſerv'd Death for having broken their plighted Faith; but that he forgave them, in Hopes that they would amend for the future, and then invited *Vitachuco* to dine with him every Day, being ſenſible, as a Man of Experience, that more was to be gain'd in thoſe

Countries

Countries by bearing, and forbearing, than by Severity, unless it could not be avoided.

THE *Indians* taken amounted to above one thousand, who were employ'd in the Service of the Forces, and *Vitacucho* order'd them to destroy all the *Spaniards* as they were at Dinner, which was concerted to be perform'd the 7th Day after the former Skirmish. The Adelantado, and *Vitacucho* dining together that Day, the latter on a sudden started up, gave a loud Cry, which was the Signal, and laying hold of the Adelantado, gave him such a Cuff with his Fist as knock'd him down, and he fell upon him, to kill him ; but the other Gentlemen that were at Dinner, in a Moment kill'd *Vitacucho*. Upon the aforesaid Signal given, every *Indian* attack'd his Master, some with Firebrands, others with the Pottage-Pots, others with the Pitchers, or whatsoever came to hand ; among which the Firebrands did most Harm ; but in Conclusion, all the *Indians* perish'd. Four Days after the Troops march'd for *Osachile*, when it was propos'd to make another Bridge like the former, over a River, but by reason of the Opposition of the *Indians* six Floats were made, which carry'd over one hundred Musketeers and Cross-bow-men, thirty Horse swimming over. The *Indians* then fled, and the Bridge was made, without the Help of any Labourers but the Soldiers, and so the Forces pass'd, and two Leagues from thence they came among many Farm Houses, and Corn Fields, from which last the *Indians* shot their Arrows, and the Horsemen kill'd them with their Spears. They found the Town of *Osachile* abandon'd, the Lord whereof would never appear. Some *Indians* were taken, who prov'd more tractable than the former, and because there was much Talk of the Province of *Apalache*, the Troops stay'd at *Osachile* but two Days, it being then Time to consider where they should Winter. They advanc'd
twelve

twelve Leagues over a Defert, and came to a Morafs
half a League over, where the *Indians* guarded the
Pafs ; and fome were kill'd and wounded on both Sides.
The next Day the Battle was more bloody, but at
length the *Spaniards* were Mafters of the Water, and
found it fordable, bating about forty Paces, over which
there was a Bridge of Trees made faft together. For
as much as beyond the Morafs, there was a very clofe
Wood, above a League and half through, which the
Forces could not penetrate in a Day, one hundred
Horfemen with Targets were order'd to lead the Van,
follow'd by one hundred Musketeers, and Crofsbow-
men, with Axes, to hew down, and make room for
the reft, to incamp, as they did, and when the others
came to the Place, they were difturb'd all the Night
by the Cries of the *Indians.* The next Day they were
in a more open Wood, where ftill the Natives were
troublefome, becaufe the Horfes could not do much
Service, and where there were any Plain fpots of
Ground, Trees were laid acrofs to hinder their paffing.
Two Leagues this troublefome Way held, and then
they came into a Champion, where marching two
Leagues farther, they kill'd and took all the *Indians*
that offer'd to make any Oppofition, which convinc'd
the reft that the *Spaniards* were not to be deftroy'd,
or expell'd the Country.

THE Adelantado thinking that enough had been
done that Day, order'd the Troops to incamp at the
Entrance of the till'd Lands, that belong'd to the *A-
palaches,* but the *Indians* continually pouring in their
Arrows, would not let them reft. The next Day
they march'd two Leagues through Corn Fields,
with Farm Houfes, where many Arrows were fhot at
them, and then came to a deep Brook, enclos'd with
Woods, and fortify'd with Palifades, to hinder the
Horfemen from paffing, but an hundred of them alighting, with their Swords and Targets, clear'd the Way, in
spight

ſpight of the *Indians,* who fought deſperately, many of them them being kill'd, and ſome Chriſtians. The next Day they march'd four Leagues, and the next to that, being inform'd that *Capaſi,* Lord of *Apalache,* lay two Leagues off with a great Number of brave *Indians,* the Horſe advanc'd, and *Capaſi* flying, they took ſome of his Men, and he eſcap'd. *Apalache* was a Town of two hundred and fifty Houſes, with others ſmaller about it, and abundance of Farm Houſes; the Climate is agreeable, the Soil fruitful, there is good Fiſh, and the Natives are warlike. After ſome Days reſt, Parties were commanded out to view the Country, and thoſe that went Northward ſaid, what they had ſeen was good, populous, clear from Woods, and Bogs, and that no Accident had befallen them. One who went to the Southward, reported he had met with uncooth and difficult Soil, which was the ſame where *Cabeza de Vaca* had been, for there is good and bad Land in this Province. The Adelantado being reſolv'd to winter at *Apalache,* becauſe it was then the Month of *October,* order'd Proviſions to be laid up, fortify'd a proper Place, and invited the Cazique *Capaſi,* the firſt they found who had any proper Name, but he would not conſent to any Peace. A Party was ſent back the ſame Way the Forces came, to the Sea Coaſt, being one hundred and fifty Leagues to bring away thoſe Horſemen, who had been left there; and in the mean Time, the Adelantado march'd eight Leagues to a Wood, where the Cazique had fortify'd himſelf, and being attack'd, maintain d a deſperate Fight, till at length they begg'd Quarter, which was granted, and the Cazique was brought to him on Men's Shoulders; becauſe being troubled with ſome Diſtempers, and very fat, he always was carry'd on a Bier, or crawl'd on all four. Thus the Adelantado return'd well pleas'd to his Quarters, commending his Men for their Bravery, ſuppoſing that the *Indians* would

would no more difturb him, but it prov'd quite o-
therwife, for that having no Head, they grew more
diforderly, and the Cazique's Commands to them to
be peaceable not availing, he faid, if they would fend
him fix Leagues from thence, whither the prime Men
were withdrawn, they might perhaps feeing him among
them obey his Orders. The Cazique being carry'd
to that Place, order'd all his People to appear before
him the next Day, becaufe he had fomething to im-
part that concern'd them. The *Spaniards* having pofted their Guards that Night, when the Day appear'd,
found neither the Cazique, nor any other, for he taking the Advantage of the Sentinels falling afleep,
had crept out upon all four, and the *Indians* carry'd
him to fome Place of more Safety than the former,
for he was never feen again. The *Spaniards* return'd
with much Shame to the Adelantado, faying, he had
been carry'd away through the Air, for there was no
other Way; and that Commander who was a difcreet
Man, not thinking fit to chaftize their Negligence,
with a fmiling Countenance admitted of their Excufe,
faying, it was likely enough, becaufe the *Indians* were
notable Sorcerers, his Aim being always to gain the
Affection of the Soldiers as far as was confiftent with
martial Difcipline, that they might be willing to endure all the Fatigues he expected to meet with in that
Enterprize. This Year 1539. expiring, we muft now
leave him here for a Time to return to the Affairs of
Peru.

C H A P.

CHAP. II.

The Towns of Arequipa, *and* Leon de Guanuco *founded*; Gonzalo Pizarro *discovers the Province of* Canela.

IT was now the Year 1540, when the Marquefs *Pizarro* had founded the City of *Arequipa*, reckned to be one hundred and thirty Leagues from *Lima*, feated in the Vale of *Quilca*, fourteen Leagues from the Sea, the Situation fo temperate, and agreeable, that it is look'd upon as the beft in *Peru*, the Soil producing very good Wheat. Within the Jurifdiction of this City are all the Towns, from the Vale of *Hacari* forward till beyond *Tarapaca*; the antient Cuftoms of the *Indians* in thofe Parts were the fame as has been mention'd of the other Parts of *Peru*. Being fo near the Sea, this City is plentifully fupply'd with all Neceffaries, and moft of the Treafure drawn out of the Province of *las Charcas* is fhipp'd off there. When *Pizarro* founded this City, he did not pitch upon fo good a Situation, and therefore it was remov'd to the Place where it now ftands, and near it is a burning Mountain, which has done much Harm. The Marquefs *Pizarro* being now fettled at *Lima*, thought the general Diftribution of the Lands in that Country ought not to be any longer delay'd, and refolv'd to proceed upon it, as the King had directed, in Conjunction with the Bifhop F. *Vincent de Valverde*, both of them taking an Oath, that they would act therein without Favour, or Prejudice, or any other View but doing Juftice to every Man anfwerable to the Service he had done. The Diftribution

tion was made, and whether it was through the Impoffibility of pleafing all People, or rather becaufe it was true, that he beftow'd all the beft Lands on his Relations and Servants, many of the Conquerors and Difcoverers were left very poor; whereupon he propos'd to build a City at *Guanuco,* tho' there was no occafion for it at that Time, and to that Effect pitch'd upon *Gomez de Alvarado,* Brother to *James de Alvarado,* to gain the good Will of that Gentleman, and by that means pacify the Men of *Chile,* againft whom he was fo often warn'd to be upon his Guard, becaufe by his having put him to Death, and ufurp'd his Government, where they expected to have been well provided for, they were difpers'd, poor, and flighted, and thus pufh'd on to Defpair; fo that tho' this Project of his was commended, it came too late, thofe Soldiers being then incens'd beyond Meafure. *Gomez de Alvarado,* who had hop'd that young *James de Almagro* would have been reftor'd to his Father's Government, having now fpent all he had upon the *Chile* Men, and being out of all Hopes, accepted of the Offer made him by the Marquefs, who tho' the Inhabitants of *Lima* complain'd that the building of this new City would be an Incroachment upon their Territory, would not defift from his Defign; but inftead of making it a City, declar'd it fhould be a Town fubject to the Jurifdiction of *Lima,* which difobhg d *Gomez de Alvarado,* who thereupon return'd to *Lima,* and that Place declin'd very much at that Time. The Situation is good and temperate, the Soil fruitful, producing all Things of the Growth of *Spain,* there are confiderable Breeds of Cattle, and great Numbers of all forts of Fowl, befides wild Beafts in the Woods, and there are Roads made by the *Ingas* to all Towns of Note; the Natives were in all Refpects like the reft of that Country. The *Conchucos,* the great Province of the *Guaycos, Tamaca, Bombon,* and other greater and smaller Places are subject to it ; the Houses are of Stone, but thatch'd, and in several Parts of its Territory there are rich Silver Mines.

THE Soldiers who had been in *Chile* were reduc'd to such Distress, that they went about the *Indian* Towns, almost naked, to get something to eat, complaining against the Governour for using them so ill ; and he to add to their Resentments, had turn'd young *Almagro* out of his House, and he was afterwards put out of another to flatter the Marquess. *John de Herrera* and *John Balsa*, who had been his Father's Friends, laying aside all Dissimulation, in Compassion to his Misfortunes, found out a Place for his Residence, and gave him part of what they had, which encourag'd others, who honour'd the Memory of his Father, to countenance him ; so that about thirty or forty attended him barefac'd, whilst others endur'd great Want, which the Marquess well knew, and yet he took no care to provide for them, as he might, and was his Duty to do, he being Governour, and they Soldiers that had serv'd the King. Such was the Distress those People were reduc'd to, that *Francis de Chaves*, *John de Saavedra*, *Christopher de Sotelo*, *Salzedo*, *Don Alonso de Montemayor*, *John de Guzman*, and other Commanders and Gentlemen of Note, suffer'd as much as the rest, and it hapned, that they had but one Cloak between twelve of them, so that when one went abroad, the other eleven were to stay at home, the Cloak was always in Use, and their Wants increas'd daily, finding no Charity among all the Inhabitants of *Lima*, either for fear of disobliging the Marquess, or for some other reason. All their Support was from *Dominick de la Presa*, who privately lov'd *Almagro*, and having a Town near *Lima*, by his *Indians* sent them Mayz, Wood, and other Things. At this Time, the Factor *Illan Suarez de Carvajal*, who was Deputy-Governour at *Cuzco*, writ a Letter in

Cyphers

Cyphers to the Marquefs, acquainting him that many of the *Chile* Soldiers reforted to *Lima,* and it was likely they might have fome ill Defign, for which reafon he defir'd him to look to himfelf, and beftow fomething on them, that Defpair might not put them upon fome mifchievous Attempt; but he took no Notice of it. *Alonfo de Alvarado* being now at *Lima,* hapned to have fome Words with *Francis de Chaves,* and *Gomez de Alvarado,* whereupon the latter challeng'd him, but the Marquefs prevented the Duel, and fhow'd much Favour to *Alonfo,* which difgufted *Gomez,* and all the *Chile* Men.

Gonzalo Pizarro was gone with Commiffion from the Marquefs his Brother, to govern the Northern Provinces, which was a falfe Conftruction he put upon the Power granted him by the King, to refign the whole Government of *Peru* to one of his Brothers, or whom he fhould think fit, but not to divide it. *Gonzalo Pizarro* being admitted into *Quito* without any Difficulty, all was thought to be fecure enough againft *Belalcazar,* tho' he fhould return from *Spain,* with the King's immediate Commiffion to govern thofe Provinces; for the Marquefs was refolv'd that no Man, whether he had the King's Commiffion, or not, fhould govern one Foot of Land in all that Part of the New World, as had already appear'd by his Behaviour towards *Almagro,* and *James de Alvarado* purfuant to his Refolution, *Gonzalo Pizarro* having being inform'd, that there was a very rich Vale call'd *Dorado,* and other Provinces, where the Men were arm'd with Plates of Gold, thought fit to undertake the Difcovery and Conqueft thereof himfelf, and having drawn together two hundred and twenty Horfe and Foot, befides others that afterwards join'd him, he crofs'd a fnowy Mountain, where above one hundred *Indians* perifh'd with Cold, and advanc'd to the Vale of *Zumaque,* thirty Leagues from *Quito,*

where

where he found Dwellings, and Provisions. Here it was agreed, that *Pizarro* should go before, with seventy Foot, because the Country was rocky, advancing Eastward, with Guides of the Country, and after some Days march, found those they call *Canelos*, that is, Cinnamon-Trees, being like large Olive-Trees, which produce gerat Buds, with Blossoms, and that is the Cinnamon, excellent good, and substantial, the like whereof had not been seen in any Part of the *West-Indies*, and that Cinnamon was carry'd about to all the adjacent Parts, by way of Trade. The Natives liv'd in little mean Houses, at a Distance from one another, and were very ignorant, had many Wives, and being ask'd, whether there were any of those Trees in other Countries about them? they answer'd, They knew not, nor what the Country was farther on, for that they were acquainted with nothing beyond their own Woods, but if they would proceed, perhaps some others might give a better Account. *Pizarro* being in a Passion because they did not answer to his Mind, ask'd again, and because they persisted in what they had said, he inhumanly caus'd several of those Wretches to be tormented to Death with Fire, and others to be torn in Pieces by the Dogs, the poor Creatures crying, that they dy'd innocent, and that neither they, nor their Parents had any way injur'd him. In this Fret, for finding no Way to proceed farther, nor any Information, he went and lay on the Bank of a River, where such an heavy Rain fell, that the River overflow'd, and had not the Sentinels given Notice, they had been all drowned. Retiring from thence to some Crags, they agreed to turn back, to find out some other Way. Accordingly, instead of going again to *Zumaque,* they proceeded to the Town of *Ampua,* four Leagues from the other, being carry'd over a River, they could not Ford, in Canoes, by the Lord of the Place, whom *Pizarro* made much of, giving

him

him Combs, Scissors, and other Baubles valu'd by those People. Inquiring then about the Way, that Cazique, who knew how the other *Indians* had been treated, told him, tho' it was false, that farther on there were great Towns, and very rich Lords. The *Spaniards* taking the Cazique with them, pass'd a River, where some *Indians* had pretended to oppose them, but fled upon firing a few Muskets, and so they proceeded into a large open Plain, from whence they saw the Woods, with small Towns, and little Provision. All the Forces being join'd here, *Don Antony de Ribera* was sent to discover farther, who having march'd twenty Leagues, passing through very thick Woods, came to a Town call'd *Varco*, in which was some Provision. As soon as *Pizarro* was inform'd of it, he march'd thither, with all the Troops, the Cazique was frighted at the Sight of the *Spaniards*, and their Horses, and would have fled, for which reason he was fetter'd, as were two others that came of their own Accord, and he that told them of the great Towns was also carry'd along, but not as a Prisoner.

THE *Indians* seeing their Caziques in Custody, came arm'd in many Canoes to rescue them, but to no purpose. The River they were now come to, being very large, and emptying itself into that which they call'd the fresh Sea, that falls into the North-Sea, and the *Indians* they had brought from *Quito* being either dead, or disabled, and no others to be had, it was thought requisite to build a Bark, to carry the Provisions, which was soon perform'd. Proceeding along down the River they met with some Towns, and a good Quantity of *Yuca*, Mayz, and Guayabas, which was a great Support, but the many Morasses were very troublesome, and deep Streams running out from those Bogs, the Horses were forc'd to swim, and sometimes were drowned with the Riders.

ders.

ders. The *Indians* they had to attend them fought out the Canoes that were hid, made Bridges of Trees, and thus they went down that River forty-three Day's Journey, every Day crossing one or two of those Rivulets, and now they began to be pinch'd with Hunger, having none left of the five thousand Swine they had brought from *Quito*. The Caziques that were Prisoners, for Fear of Death, said there was a populous Country farther on, and one Day finding an Opportunity, they threw themselves into the River, with their Fetters, and swam over. The *Indians* still affirming, that fifteen Day's Journey farther, there was a River much greater than that they were upon, on which were large Towns, and Plenty of Provisions, *Pizarro* order'd *Francis de Orellana* to go see it, with sixty Men, and return speedily with the Boat laden with Provisions, because they were in Distress, and he entrusted only him with the Boat, designing to follow as fast as he could. *Orellana* set out in the Boat, aboard which was some of *Pizarro*'s Baggage, and of others, who were willing to send it before. He sail'd some Days, without seeing any Habitations, but at last came to some, and would have return'd to the Place from whence they came, but thought it impossible, because they had run down three hundred Leagues, which *Orellana* confirm'd, and resolving to go on, fell into that great River of *Maranon*, or fresh Sea, as others call it, and what hapned to him in that Expedition shall be shown hereafter.

Gonzalo Pizarro, when *Orellana* was gone, held on his Way to the Eastward in much Distress through Want, the great Rains, Waters, Morasses, and other Difficulties, expecting the return of *Orellana*, and for Hunger eating their Dogs, and Horses, without wasting a drop of their Blood. *Pizarro* being in this Misery, sent Captain *Mercadillo* with some Canoes to seek for *Orellana*, who returning a Week after without

out any News of him, caus'd very much Affliction
among the Men, who had nothing then to eat but
wild Herbs and Fruit, and some Flesh of Horses and
Dogs, but so scantily, that it rather added to their
Hunger. *Gonzalo Diaz* being sent out again with
much Difficulty, came to a Place, where he found Yuca, and loading the Canoes return'd to *Pizarro,* with
a Supply. Being inform'd, that the Country whence
that Yuca had been brought was near at Hand, they
all cross'd the River in those Canoes. Hunger pressing so hard, a *Spaniard,* whose Name was *Villarejo,*
eat a white Root he found, and immediately ran mad.
Being come to the Place where the Yuca grew, they
halted. There they rested eight Days satisfying their
Hunger, and some eating too much dy'd, and others
swell'd so excessively, that they could not stand. *Pizarro* concluding that *Orellana* was dead, march'd up
the River in hopes to find some good Country, or a
Way to return from whence he came. The Sick
were set upon the Horses, and those that were able
clear'd the Ways. Having march'd forty Leagues
through those Fields of Yuca, they came to a little
Town, without any Interpreter, or Means to understand the Inhabitants. Those Barbarians being amaz'd
at the Sight of the *Spaniards,* talk'd from their Canoes, and barter'd for Provisions, casting them on the
Shore for Combs, Knives, Hawks-bells, and such Tri-
fles, which the *Spaniards* were wont to carry upon
their Discoveries. They continu'd eight Days longer
up the River, among such Habitations, but after that
could find no Dwellings, nor Roads, which the *Indians* told them by Signs, for they drove their Trade
along the River. *Gonzalo Diaz* was then sent up the
River, in two Canoes bound fast together. *Pizarro,*
with the Forces, following by Land, in a wretched
Condition, and so advanc'd fifty-six Leagues without
finding any thing to eat, but the Yuca they carry'd

R 4   with

with them, and some wild Fruit. *Gonzalo Diaz* having run up the River many Days, without finding any Thing he sought for, and thinking it impossible for the Forces to come thither, went ashore, and towards the Evening saw a Canoe coming down the River, and after it fourteen or fifteen more, each of them carrying eight arm'd Men. *Diaz* taking up the Musket, shot one dead, and his Companion *Bustamante* with a Cross-bow, wounded another in the Arm, who drew out the Shafts, and threw it at him. The *Indians* with mighty Cries, cast abundance of Darts, and the *Spaniards* charging again kill'd two more, and then were for falling on with their Swords and Targets, but the *Indians* making their Way down the River, they shot after them, killing some, whereupon they quitted their Canoes, and the *Spaniards* found some Provision in them, which was a great Relief, for they had fed some Days on Herbs and Roots. Those *Indians* came from a Town, that was at a Distance from the Shore, and one who was Fishing, spy'd *Gonzalo Diaz*'s Canoe, and went to give Notice of it, whereupon those People went out to seize him, and that hapned which has been related. *Diaz* and *Bustamante* cut Crosses on the Trees, that *Pizarro*, when he came, might know they had been there. The next Day being very bright, they discover'd high Mountains, which they suppos'd to be the *Cordillera*, or Mountain of *Quito*, or that near *Popayan*, or *Cali*, and found Stones in the Channel of the River, which they had not seen in three hundred Leagues. They went back down the River to find *Pizarro*, who was advancing in miserable Distress, having only two Dogs left of nine hundred he had carry'd out. They met about the End of this Year 1540, which therefore calls upon us to say what hapned before in other Parts.

AFTER the Battle of the Salt-pits near *Cuzco*, the Alcalde *James Nuñez de Mercado*, one of *Almagro*'s greateft Friends, made his Way from *Peru* into *Spain,* where he gave an Account at Court of all that had hapned at *Cuzco,* concluding that all had been thro' the Ambition of the *Pizarro's,* who would ingrofs all the Command, in Breach of the moft folemn Oaths and Contracts that could be made among Chriftians. This fame was confirm'd by Don *Alonfo Enriquez,* and foon after by *James Gutierres de los Rios,* and *James de Alvarado. Ferdinand Pizarro* arriving foon after, this Affair was prefs'd fo home, that the Council thought fit the King fhould fend over fome Perfon knowing in the Law, and of Authority to do Juftice in that Affair, and accordingly the Licentiate *Chriftopher Vaca de Caftro,* a Judge in the Court of *Valladolid,* was pitch'd upon. In the mean while *Ferdinand Pizarro* was not idle, but placing his Bribes into proper Hands, prevail'd to have this fame *Vaca de Caftro* chofen to go into *Peru,* as knowing him to be a fit Inftrument to ferve his Brother's turn, which was recommended to him by fome of the greateft Perfons; and *James de Alvarado* and others fent Word to young *Almagro,* and his Friends, that the Judge *Beltran,* and others of the Council, had been corrupted by *Pizarro,* whence they concluded that *Vaca de Caftro* would not do them Juftice. After much Contention between *Ferdinand Pizarro* and *James de Alvarado* before the Council, *Alvarado* offer'd *Pizarro* to decide that Quarrel by fingle Combat, and to prove his Breach of Oath, Difloyalty to the King, and his Cruelty and Ingratitude to *Almagro,* which was prevented by *Alvarado's* Death, hapning within five Days after, not without Sufpicion of Poifon. The Judges appointed to try this Caufe, in the firft Place order'd *Ferdinand Pizarro* to be fecur'd, and he continu'd Prifoner feveral Years; but there being none left to ftand up for the *Almagro's,* and the Son of the Adelantado acting afterwards as he did; befides feveral other Accidents, this

this Caufe was laid afide for Political Reafons, and *Ferdinand Pizarro* was at laft difmifs'd.

As to the Courfe to be taken for regulating the Affairs, there was great Variety of Opinions, fome for having a Council and Prefident eftablifh'd at *Lima,* to govern that whole Monarchy, others for a Viceroy, and others for erecting feveral Councils, or Courts. All thefe Forms being laid afide, the worft Method was pitch'd upon, which brought nothing to effect, and was the fending of *Vaca de Caftro,* as was pretended, to regulate the Execution of Juftice, and to affift and advife *Francis Pizarro* with Orders to examine into the Diforders that had hapned, and endeavour to prevent the like for the future. He was alfo charg'd to give all Encouragement towards the Converfion of the *Indians,* to take Care that they were no way opprefs'd, to enjoin all that had Lands given them to marry in a limited time, with much more to the fame Effect, as has been before-mention'd in the Inftructions given to others. All this Affair was manag'd with Political Views, in which is little regard to Juftice, the King being afraid quite to difoblige *Pizarro,* and at the fame time endeavouring to have a Check upon him, as knowing he had faid, That none but himfelf fhould govern between *Peru* and *Flanders ;* for which Reafon, in all Difpatches *Vaca de Caftro* and *Pizarro* were call'd *Our Governours,* and thus *Vaca de Caftro* was difmifs'd to go upon his Voyage.

CHAP.

CHAP. III.

Captain Orellana's *Voyage down the great River of the* Amazons, *to the Sea, and his Arrival at* Cubagua ; *with the best Account he could gather of those Countries.*

IT has been said before, that Captain *Orellana* being sent by *Gonzalo Pizarro* down the River, to seek for Provisions, having run above two hundred Leagues, and considering the great Difficulty of returning so far back against the rapid Stream, resolv'd to hold on his Course into the North-Sea. The next Day after he parted from *Pizarro*, he had like to have perish'd, because the Boat ran foul of a Piece of Timber, which broke a Plank, but being near the Shore the Men dragg'd the Boat to Land, and having repair'd it proceeded on their Voyage, running twenty or twenty-five Leagues a Day, by the Force of the Current, entring several Rivers on the South Side, and thus they went on three Days, without seeing any Dwellings. The Provisions they had brought being spent, and they so far from *Pizarro*, they thought it better to follow the Stream down, being reduc'd to such Want that they boil d and eat all the Leather they had, with some Herbs that could be gather'd, which was about the End of the Year 1540. On the 8th of *January* 1541, when they expected nothing but Death, the Captain heard *Indian* Drums, which rejoyc'd them all, believing they could not then perish with Hunger, and being upon their Guard, in the Morning, when they had run two Leagues, they discover'd four *Indian* Canoes, which immediately made away, and they saw a Town with a great Number of arm'd *Indians*.

The

The Captain commanded all his Men to Land, and keep their Order, without forsaking one another, and they were so encourag'd by the Sight of the Town, that falling on resolutely, the Inhabitants forsook it, leaving good Store of Provision behind them, which reliev'd their great Want, and about Two in the Afternoon the *Indians* return'd in their Canoes, to observe what strange People those were. *Orellana* spoke to them in the *Indian* Language, which though they did not perfectly understand, they could gather so much as to conceive, that he invited them, whereupon some drawing near, he gave them a few *Spanish* Toys, desiring them to call their Lord, who came in great State, and being courteously treated, and presented, was satisfy'd, promising to furnish what they wanted; and nothing being demanded of him but eatables, he immediately caus'd good Store of Turkeys, Partridges, Fish, and other Things to be brought. The next Day thirteen other Lords came, who were entertain'd after the same manner, they wearing great Plumes of Feathers, and Gold Plates on their Breasts, besides Jewels on other Parts. *Orellana* spoke to them very courteously, requiring them to submit to the King of *Spain*, which they agreed to, and he took Possession. Finding those *Indians* well dispos'd, and that they willingly brought him Provisions, having refresh'd his Men, and considering the Danger of running into the Sea in that Boat, and Canoes, he propos'd to Build a Brigantine; and here as F. *Gaspar de Carvajal,* who was present, relates, that one of those Caziques gave Intimation of the *Amazons,* and of the great Wealth there was farther down, as also of another rich and mighty Lord up the Country. The Work of the Brigantine was no farther carry'd on here than the making of about two thousand Nails, to which Effect it pleas'd God, that two Men did that which they had never been taught, and another undertook to make
Charcoal.

Charcoal. Bellows were made of Buskins, and so other Things, some hewing Fewel, others carrying, and the rest labouring other Ways, the Commander putting his Hands to every thing. When they had spent twenty Days in that Work, which Stay was prejudicial to them, as consuming the Provisions, that might have serv'd them afterwards, having run two hundred Leagues to that Place in nine Days, and lost seven of their Company that dy'd before for Hunger, they resolv'd, for fear of being troublesome to the *Indians*, to set out on *Candlemas* Day. Twenty Leagues from that Place, another smaller River fell into the great one, but so swollen, that the two Waters struggling, the Boat had like to have been cast away. This Danger being over, they found no other Town in another Run of two hundred Leagues, and endur'd many Hardships, till they came upon some Habitations, where the *Indians* were altogether undisturb'd, and to avoid alarming them, the Captain order'd twenty Men to go ashore, and civilly intreat them to find Provisions, of which they were in great Want. The *Indians* were glad to see the *Spaniards*, and gave them good Store of Tortoises, and Parrots. The Captain went to another Town on the opposite Side of the River, where no Resistance was made, but they also gave him Meat. Proceeding thus in Sight of good Towns, the next Day four Canoes came to the Boat, offering Tortoises, good Partridges, and abundance of Fish, *Orellana*, in Lieu thereof giving them such things as he had, with which and perceiving that he understood them, they were so highly pleas'd, that they invited him to see their Lord, whose Name was *Aparia*, and he was then coming with some Canoes. Both *Spaniards* and *Indians* landed, and as soon as *Aparia* came, *Orellana* discours'd him about the Law of God, and the Grandeur of the King of *Spain*, which those People listned to with much Attention. *Aparia* said,

that

that if they were going to fee the *Amazons,* whom in their Language they call *Coniapuyara,* fignifying Great Ladies, they were too few, and thofe Women very numerous. The Captain then defir'd they would fummon all the neighbouring Lords, who being come to the Number of twenty, he repeated what he had faid, concluding that they were all the Children of the Sun, and as fuch they ought to look upon them as Friends, which pleas'd them, and they all furnifh'd Provifions, being much delighted to talk with the Captain, who having taken Poffeffion, erected a Crofs on an Eminence to the great Satisfaction and Aftonifhment of thofe People.

Orellana being thus lovingly entertain'd, refolv'd to Build the Brigantine he had before intended, and it pleas'd God that there hapned to be a Carver among his Men, and though of fo different a Profeffion, he prov'd very ufeful. In thirty-five Days the Brigantine was launch'd, being caulk'd with Cotton, and daub'd with Pitch, furnifh'd by the *Indians.* At this time came to the Captain four *Indians* of a very large Stature, cloath'd, and with Jewels, their Hair reaching down to their Waftes, and laying much Meat before him, in very humble manner, faid, they were fent by a great Lord, to know, who thofe Strangers were, and whither they went. He gave them fome of his Toys, which they much valu'd, difcours'd them as he had done the others, and fo they went away. Here the *Spaniards* ftay'd all the *Lent,* two Religious Men they had with them performing the Divine Service, and exhorting them to be couragious under all the Difficulties they might meet, till they came to the end of them. The new Brigantine being furnifh'd, fit to Sail in the Sea, and the Boat repair'd, they fet out on the 24th of *April* from the Refidence of *Aparia,* and advanc'd eighty Leagues, without meeting any warlike *Indians,* after which they
came

came among Deferts, and the River ran furioufly;
finding no Place to reft, or Fifh, and thus feeding
on Herbs and fome toafted *Indian* Corn, on the 6th
of *May* they came to an high Ground, that feem'd
to have been inhabited, where they ftay'd to Fifh,
and it hapned, that the Carver, who had been fo ufeful in building the Brigantine, fhot with his Crofs-
bow at an *Yguana*, that was on a Tree near the River, and the Nut of the Bow flew off, and fell into
the River; after which a Soldier, whofe Name was
Contreras, threw an Hook into the Water, and drew
out a Fifh an Ell long, which being fo large, and
the Line fmall, he was forc'd to lift out with his Hand,
and opening the Belly found in it the Nut of the
Crofs-bow. On the 12th of *May* they came into
the Province of *Machiparo*, very populous, and bordering on another Lord's Territory, call'd *Aomagua*.
One Morning they fpy'd many Canoes, carrying
warlike *Indians*, who had large Bucklers of the Skins
of Alligators, Manaties, and Dantas, beating Drums,
Shouting, and threatning to eat the *Spaniards*, who
ftanding together, provided for the worft, tho' they
met with a great Misfortune, which was, that their
Powder had taken wet, fo that they could not ufe
their Muskets. The *Indians* drawing near, fhot their
Arrows, the Crofs-bows did them fome Harm, but
frefh Supplies ftill coming on, they made feveral bold
Attacks, and thus they ran down the River fighting,
till they came to a Town, on the Crags whereof ftood
many *Indians*, in fpight of whom, and thofe in the
Canoes, half the *Spaniards* landed, and drove thofe
People into the Town, which feeming to be large, and
the Inhabitants numerous, the Enfign return'd to acquaint the Captain, who was defending the Veffels
that were ftill attack'd by the Canoes. Underftanding
that there was Plenty of Provifions in the Town, the
Captain order'd a Soldier call'd *Chriftopher de Segovia*,
with

with twelve more, to go fetch some, who being loaded with it, above two thousand Indians charg'd him; he and his Men ingag'd them so furiously that they fled, and he proceeded with his Provender; but the *Indians* returning with Reinforcements from other Towns, wounded four of them, whereupon they were for retiring to their Vessels, had not *Segovia* told them they should not leave the Victory to the *Indians*, and accordingly they got the better of that Multitude, and went off safe. In the mean Time another great Parcel of *Indians* had attack'd the Brigantine and Bark two Ways, however after an obstinate Engagement of above two Hours, it pleas'd God to deliver them, some Persons from whom little had been expected having done Wonders. When the *Indians* were gone, they took care of the wounded, and had nothing to dress them with but blessing and praying, and yet they all recover'd, except one *Ampudia*, who dy'd eight Days after. In this Fight it appear'd, that the Commander's Example is a great Encouragement, for *Orellana* fought as well as commanded, and was no less conspicuous for his Conduct than his Valour; however, as fighting avail'd nothing, he resolv'd to proceed, and having put aboard the Provisions, and weigh'd Anchor, above ten thousand *Indians* appear'd on the Shore, who being able to do no other Harm, gave loud Cries, whilst Abundance of Canoes pursu'd the *Spaniards* all the Night, who in the Morning found themselves among many Dwellings, and being tir'd with the restless Night they had, went away to a desert Island, where they found no repose, because of the many *Indians* that landed, for which reason the Commander made away, one hundred and thirty Canoes still pursuing, and in them about eight thousand *Indians*, among whom were four or five Sorcerers, daub'd all over with Lime, casting Ashes out of their Mouths, and Water with Sprinklers, and it was dreadful to see

all

all thofe Savage People, and to hear the Noife of their Drums, Cornets, Horns, and Cries; fo that had it not been for fome Muskets they could ufe, and the Crofs-bows, they muft all have perifh'd, for the *Indians* refolutely boarding the Veffels with their Canoes, their Chief being foremoft, one *Cales*, a Musketeer fhot him dead, whereupon all the *Indians* flocking about him, the *Spaniards* had leifure to get out into the middle of the River, ftill purfu'd, without any Intermiffion two Days and two Nights, and thus they made away from the Dominions of that great Lord *Machiparo*. When the Canoes were gone, the *Spaniards* came to a Town, which the Inhabitants ftood ready to defend, and *Orellana* thinking it requifite to reft four Days, after the late Fatigue, order'd his Veffels to be brought into the Shore, and having difcharg'd the Muskets, and Crofs-bows, the *Indians* gave way, and the Town was enter'd.

THEY refted three Days in that Town, living at Difcretion, but feveral great Roads appearing to go from it, the Captain would not ftay any longer. From *Aparia* to this Place they reckned three hundred and forty Leagues, two hundred of them Defert, here they put aboard good Store of Bisket, the *Indians* had made of Mayz, and Yuca, befides much Fruit. They fet out on *Sunday* after *Afcenfion*, and having run two Leagues, found another great River fell into that they were on, having three Iflands at the Mouth of it, for which reafon they call'd it *Trinity* River; there were abundance of Towns, the Country feem'd to be good and fruitful, and ftill fuch Numbers of Canoes came out, that they were forc'd to keep in the Middle of the River. The next Day they came to a fmall but handfome Town, and tho' fome Oppofition was made, they enter'd it, and found much Provifion, and a Country-Houfe with fine Earthen-Ware, as Jars, Pitchers, and other Sorts of Veffels

glaz'd and painted with lively Colours, and good Figures drawn, all which Sorts of Things the *Indians*
faid were to be had up the Country, befides much
Gold and Silver; they alfo found Idols wove of Palm-
tree Leaves in a ftrange Manner, as big as Giants,
with Wheels in the Brawny Parts of their Arms and
Legs, like Guards for the Hand on Spears. They
alfo found fome Gold and Silver, but their Defign
being only to difcover, and fave their Lives, they
meddled with nothing. Two great Roads went from
this Town, along which the Captain walk'd about
half a League, and finding them grow wider, he return'd, and order'd the Men to imbark, and proceed
on their Voyage, becaufe it was not proper to ftay
all Night in fuch a populous Country. When they
had run above one hundred Leagues among thofe populous Nations, keeping the Middle of the River, to
avoid the *Indians*, they arriv'd in the Dominion of
another Lord, call'd *Paguana*, where the Natives were
peaceable, and gave what they had, and there were
Sheep like thofe of *Peru*, the Soil being fertil, and
producing excellent Fruit. On *Whit-Sunday* they had
Sight of a large Town divided into feveral Wards,
with each of them a cut to the River, and Abundance of People, who feeing the Veffels pafs by, went
into their Canoes, but feeling the Effect of Muskets, and Crofs-bows, drew off again. The next Day
they came to another Town, which was the laft of
Paguana's Dominion, where they took Provifion, and
enter'd upon the Territories of another Lord, whofe
Subjects were warlike, but they knew not his Name.
On *Trinity* Eve they landed at a Place where the *Indians* defended themfelves with large Bucklers, but
they enter'd the Town, and furnifh'd themfelves, and
prefently after, on the Left-hand, faw another River
falling into the great one, the Water whereof was as
black as Ink, and as fuch diftinguifhable from the
                                                    other

other Water for about twenty Leagues. They faw
many Towns, tho' fmall, into one of which they
went, and found much Fifh, having been firft oblig'd
to gain a Barrier of a wooden Wall, that enclos'd
the whole Place. Proceeding along they pafs'd between
very large Towns, and Provinces, taking in Provifion,
and the River was fo broad, that when they were near
the one Bank they could not fee the other. At one
Town they took an *Indian,* who faid, that the *A-*
mazons were Ladies of the Place, and there they found
an Houfe, in which there were Garments made of
Feathers of feveral Colours, which the *Indians* wore
on their Feftivals to dance in. They went on between many more Towns, the *Indians* crying out,
and calling to them on the Shore, and on the 7th
of *June* landed at a Town, without Oppofition, there
being none but Women, whence they carry'd aboard
much Fifh, ftaying there, at the Requeft of the Soldiers, becaufe it was the Eve of *Corpus-Chrifti.* At
Sun-fetting the *Indians* came in from the Fields, and
finding thofe Guefts, were for driving them out by
Force, but the *Spaniards* defended themfelves, and yet
Orellana would have his Men imbark, and held on his
Way, along populous Countries, till he came to fome
that were more peaceable. Beyond that again they faw
a great Town, and in it feven Poles, with each a Man's
Head fix'd on it, and therefore call'd it the Province
de las Picotas. From this Town there went great
Roads pav'd, with Rows of Trees along them ; and
the next Day coming to another Town like the former, they were oblig'd to enter it for Provifions, the
Indians hiding themfelves, to let them Land, and as
foon as afhore made up to attack them, with their
Lord, or Captain at their Head ; but a Crofs-bow-man
fhooting him, they all fled, and the *Spaniards* had Leifure to take Mayz, Tortoifes, Turkeys, and Parrots.

BEING

Being thus well furnish'd, they went to reft on an
Ifland, and were inform'd by an *Indian* Woman of
good Senfe they had taken, that there were many
Men like the *Spaniards* up the Country, and two white
Women, with a Lord that had carry'd them down
the River, and it was fuppos'd they might be fome
of thofe that belong'd to *James de Ordas*, or *Alonfo
de Heredia*. Paffing on, without touching at other
Towns, after feveral Days they came to another great
one, through which the *Indian* Woman faid was the
Way to the Place where the Chriftians were ; but their
Intention being otherwife, they pafs'd on. Four Days after they came to a Town, where the *Indians* made
no Oppofition, and they found *Indian* Wheat, and
Oats like ours in *Europe*, of which the *Indians* made
Liquor, like Ale, a Cellar whereof was found, fome
good Cotton Garments, and a Place of Worfhip,
with Weapons hanging in it, and two Miters, like
thofe of our Bifhops, of feveral Colours, and according to their Cuftom went to a Wood to lye, whither many *Indians* came to difturb them. The 22d
of *June* they defcry'd many Dwellings on the left
Hand of the River, but could not come at them by
reafon of the violent Current. *Wednefday* following
they found a Town, through the Middle whereof a
Rivulet ran, and there was a great Square, where they
got Provifions, and all along there were Villages of
Fifhermen, and having doubled a Point, faw very
many large Towns, where they had Notice of
the *Spaniards*, the Inhabitants coming out to them
by Water, with an ill Intention. Capt. *Orellana*
call'd to thofe *Indians*, offering them Toys, by
way of Barter, which they made a Jeft of, and farther on there were Multitudes of People in feveral Bodies. The Captain order'd the Veffels to fteer to the
Place where thofe People were, who fhot fuch Flights
of

of Arrows, that they wounded five Men, and among them F. *Carvajal,* whereupon *Orellana* made the more hafte to Land, where the *Indians* fought refolutely, and F. *Carvajal* fays they did fo, as being Tributaries to the *Amazons,* and that he and all the reft faw ten or twelve of them fighting, like Commanders, before the Men, fo defperately, that thofe *Indians* durft not turn their Backs, and if any one hapned to run away, they beat him to Death with Cudgels. Thofe Women appear'd to them very tall, ftrong limb'd, and fair, their Hair long, wound about their Heads in Treffes, ftark naked, only their Privities cover'd, carrying Bows and Arrows, feven or eight of whom the *Spaniards* kill'd, whereupon the *Indians* fled. I deliver this particular concerning the *Amazons,* as I found it in the Memorials of this Expedition. Abundance of *Indians* flocking together from all Parts, the *Spaniards* launch'd out into the deep, reckning they had till then run fourteen hundred Leagues, without knowing how far they had to the Sea; and here they took an *Indian* Trumpeter, about thirty Years of Age, who talk'd much of what was up the Country.

HAVING landed again, and feeing vaft Multitudes of *Indians, Orellana* thought fit not to expofe his Men at every foot. Here they obferv'd the Nature of the Country, which feem'd to be temperate, and fruitful; the Woods were of Oaks, bearing Acorns, and Cork-Trees, the Land high, with fpacious Plains, and Abundance of all Sorts of Grain. This they call'd the Province of St. *John,* extending above one hundred and fifty Leagues along the Coaft, well peopled, becaufe they enter'd upon it on *Midfummer* Day. They kept along the Middle of the River till they came to many Iflands, which they thought Defert, but there came from them above two hundred Piraguas, and in each of them thirty or forty gay *Indians,* with

S 3   all

all their forts of noify Mufick, who making an attack, were repuls'd by the Muskets and Crofs-bows. The Iflands appear'd high, fruitful, and very delicious, and they judg'd the largeft of them to be fifty Leagues in Length. Being pafs'd that Province of St. *John*, when the Piraguas left them, they went to reft them in a Wood of Oaks, where Capt. *Orellana*, having made an *Indian* Vocabulary, ask'd the Prifoner he had many Queftions, and was inform'd by him, that the Country was Subject to Women, who liv'd like *A-mazons*, and were extraordinary rich in Gold and Silver, and had five Temples of the Sun, plated with Gold, the Structures of Stone, their Cities wall'd, and fo many other Particulars, that I neither dare believe nor report them, becaufe the Relations of the *Indians* were little to be depended on, and Capt. *O-rellana* having before own'd that he did not underftand thofe *Indians*, it is not likely that in fo fhort a Time he could compofe fuch a copious Vocabulary, as to underftand all thofe Particulars, every Man may believe as he pleafes.

AFTER having refted in the Wood, they went on, expecting not to find any more Habitations, but they ftill faw many on the Left, yet did not draw near, to avoid provoking the *Indians*; however many of them came out to gaze at the Veffels, as in a Confternation, and the *Indian* aboard faid, that thofe Lands, being above one hundred Leagues in Length, belong d to the Lord *Cheripuna*, who had much Silver. There wanting Provifions, they landed, and the *Indians* kill'd a *Spaniard*, by which it appear'd, that thofe People poifon d their Weapons, and at this Place they firft difcern'd the Turn of the Tide. Farther on they refted in a Wood, and there were Fights made to the Veffels, againft the poifon'd Arrows. F. *Carvajal* affirms, that one Bird follow'd them above one thoufand Leagues, and that he heard it feveral Times cry'd, *Huy, Huy,* and other Time when
they

they came near Places inhabited, it said, *Huis,* signifying, Houses, other wonderful Things are related,
and that the Bird left them at this Place, so that they
never saw it again. After another Day's run, they
came to other inhabited Islands, and with much Satisfaction plainly perceiv'd the Tide, and a little farther saw an Arm of the River, not very large, from
which came two Squadrons of Piraguas, which attack'd
the Vessels, and the Fights prov'd of great Use;
but the *Indians* feeling the Effect of the Muskets,
and Cross-bows, made away, one *Spaniard* being kill'd
with a poison'd Arrow. This populous Country belong'd to a Lord call'd *Chipayo,* and the Piraguas again
returning, two *Indians* were kill'd with one Musket-
shot, many more falling into the Water, with the Fright
of the Report. A Soldier call'd *Perucho* shot a Prime
Indian, whereupon the Piraguas left the Vessels.

THE Country being so populous on the Right,
they pass'd over to the Left, where they rested three
Days, and the Captain sent some Men to go up the
Country about a League, who returning, said, that the
Country was good and fruitful, and that they had
seen many People, who seem'd to be hunting, and
here they began to find low Land, and many Islands
inhabited, among which they steer'd their Course to
get something to eat, but could never return again to
the Continent on either Side, till they were carry'd
into the Sea, judging they had run two hundred
Leagues among those Islands, all which Way they
drove down very rapidly. In this way, being in much
Want of Provisions, they saw a Town, and making
to it, the Brigantine took the Port, but the Boat
struck upon a Log of Wood, and breaking out a
Plank, sunk downright. They landed to seek Provisions, and were charg'd by such a Multitude of *Indians,* that they were forc'd to retire to their Vessels,
one of which was sunk, as has been said, and the o-

ther

ther on Ground, the Water being fallen off with the Ebb. In this Diftrefs, *Orellana* order'd the one half of the Men to fight, whilft the other half fet the Brigantine afloat, that they might repair the other. This was perform'd in three Hours, and then the *Indians* drawing off, they made away into the middle of the River, having got fome Provifions. The next Day they took up in a Wood, where they ftay'd eighteen Days to put their Veffels into a better Condition, being forc'd to make Nails, and in their great Diftrefs for Meat, it pleas'd God to relieve them with a *Danta,* as big as a Mule, that was driving down the River, having been drowned, on which they fed four or five Days.

WHEN come near the Sea, they made Rigging and Cordage of Weeds, and Sails of the Blankets they had to lie on, which took them up a Fortnight, having nothing to eat but what they found on the Shore; and thus poorly furnifh'd, they fet out from that place on the 8th of *Auguft* 1541, failing as the Tides would permit, ufing great Stones, inftead of Anchors, which very often dragg'd; but they had the good Fortune afhore to meet with *Indians,* who gave them *Indian* Wheat, and Roots, and treated them civilly. They put Water aboard in Pitchers, and Jars, every one taking what toafted Mayz he had, and Roots, and thus they made ready for Sea, to go as Fortune would guide them, without any Pilot, or Compafs, or other Help for Navigation, nor did they know what Courfe to fteer. The two Religious Men that perform'd this Voyage affirm'd, that all the Natives along the River were very underftanding, and ingenious, which appear'd by the Figures, Drawings, and Paintings in very lively Colours they made. They pafs'd out of the Mouth of the River into the Sea, between two Iflands, that were about four Leagues diftant from each other; and judg'd that the Mouth

of

of the River was fifty Leagues wide, its Water running out into the Sea twenty-five Leagues, and that it ebb'd and flow'd five or six Fathoms. They came into the Sea on the 26th of *August* 1541, the Weather proving so favourable, that they had no great Rains either in the River, or at Sea. They kept along in Sight of Land all the Day, bearing off at Night, seeing many Rivers that fell into the Sea. The Boat being one Night parted from the Brigantine, they never saw it again ; but after nine Days sail, they got into the Gulph of *Paria*, where they row'd seven Days, and could not get out, all their Food being a sort of Fruit like Plums, which they call'd *Hogos*, till at length they got through the *Dragon's Mouth*, or *Boca del Drago*, and two Days after, not knowing where they were, or whither to go, or what would become of them, they arriv'd at the Island of *Cubagua* on the 11th of *September*, the little Boat being come thither two Days before. They were very well receiv'd, and treated in *Cubagua*, whence Captain *Orellana* thought fit to come over into *Spain* to give the King an Account of his extraordinary Discovery on that River, which some call *Dorado*, others of the *Amazons*, and others from this Discoverer *Orellana*, and F. *Carvajal* says, they run one thousand eight hundred Leagues down it, reckning all the Windings.

C H A P.

CHAP. IV.

Some Ordinances of the King for the West-
Indies ; *Ships sent by the Marquess* del
Valle Cortes *to discover along the North-
West Coast of* America.

IT is not fit to forget the Family of the ever Re-
nowned *Christopher Columbus*, first Discoverer of
America, for which Reason we must observe, that in
the Year 1540, his Grandson Don *Lewis Columbus*,
being then Hereditary-Admiral of the *West-Indies*, after much Suit for his Right, was sent to the Island
Hispaniola with the Title of Captain-General. At the
same time many *Portugues* Caravels trading to that I-
sland, which at their Return did not carry their Car-
goes to the *India* House at *Sevil*, by which means the
King was defrauded of his Duties, it was order'd, that
none should be permitted for the future to take in any
Lading there without giving Security, that they would
enter their whole Cargoe faithfully at the said *India*
House. The Judge *Basco de Quiroga* of the Council
of *Mexico* having labour'd very zealously in advancing the Conversion of the *Indians* there, was now appointed to visit the Kingdom of *Mechoacan*, for regulating all Affairs in those Parts, and most particularly
to take Care that the *Indians* were well us'd ; all which
that Gentleman perform'd with much Honour and
Conscience, in return for which his Labour he was
constituted the first Bishop in that Kingdom. F. *John
de Zumarraga*, the first Bishop of *Mexico*, a most pious and virtuous Person, at his own Cost built an Ho-
spital in that City for the needy Sick, and to the end
that it might be the better supported, intreated the
King to accept of the Patronage thereof, which His
Majesty

Majesty readily agreed to, and gave bountiful Alms for the Improvement of it. In several Parts of this History it has been observ'd, that the King frequently sent Judges over to receive Informations against the Governours in all Parts, who misbehav'd themselves, many of whom were carry'd Prisoners into *Spain,* with their Processes, but they were generally clear'd there, tho' their Crimes were ever so heinous, which must be ascrib'd to the great Wealth they had amass'd, wherewith they corrupted those that should have punish'd them, making Friends of their Mammon, which could not be so well prevented in those Times of Confusion; but since that Government has been regulated, all Things proceed in an orderly manner. But of this enough at present, we will now proceed to farther Discoveries.

Ferdinand Cortes, now Marquess *del Valle,* perceiving that the Viceroy of *Mexico* Don *Antony de Mendoza,* would not desist from the Conquest of those large Provinces, which F. *Mark de Niza* had discover'd, as was said before, with Hopes of mighty Treasures to be found, and the Report of that vast City of *Cibola,* which was never after heard of; having several Ships in a Readiness, and depending on his Authority as Captain-General, and the Contract he had made with the King for carrying on Discoveries to the Westward, resolv'd to send out three of his Ships, under the Command of Captain *Francis de Ulloa,* and having so done, went away himself into *Spain.* The three Ships were call'd St. *Agatha,* St. *Thomas,* and the *Trinity,* under two hundred Tons Burden, which set sail on the 28th of *July* 1539, from the Port of *Acapulco,* the Ship St. *Agatha* being Admiral, which having spent her Mast, in a desperate Storm, they were oblig'd to put into the Port of *Colima,* where they stay'd twenty-seven Days to refit, and sail'd again on the 23d of *August.* On the 28th they had
another

another Tempeft, that carry'd them to *Guayaval,* on the Coaft of *Culiacan,* having loft the Ship St. *Thomas,* which they never faw again, they took into the Port of *Santa Cruz.* The two that remain'd fet out from thence on the 12th of *September,* holding along the Coaft from the River of St. *Peter* and St. *Paul,* they faw many other Rivers, and Lakes, with an agreeable Country, till they came into the Latitude of twentynine Degrees forty-five Minutes, where they call'd a Cape *Cabo Roxo,* whence ftanding ftill Northward, they enter'd a good Harbour, where they found Fifh-ing-Nets, and Fifhermen's Cottages, with much Fifh, and fome *Indians.* Proceeding on from thence they call'd another Cape *de las Llagas,* and beyond it the Sea look'd white as Lime, which was very furprizing; beyond which again it was ruddy and black like a Pool, and finding five Fathoms Water they drew near to the Land, where they anchor'd, and at Night heard the Sea fet in to the Shore in a violent manner, the Ebb returning in the fame fort, obferving it to be every fix Hours. Looking out from the Round Tops, they faw all the Country was fandy, and many Iflands. Advancing ftill with the Wind fcant, and fometimes quite calm, they faw high naked Mountains, and fome Fires. Beyond that again they perceiv'd a fpacious Harbour, with an Ifland out at Sea, about a Crofs-bow-fhot from it, feveral Rivers falling into that Harbour. The Captain fent out a Boat with twelve Men, who going afhore faw the Rivers running down from the Breaks in the Mountains, and that in the Ifland there was a Multitude of Sea-Calves, fome of which they kill'd to eat, and the Weather being fair, the Captain went afhore, and found twelve *Indians* fifhing on a Float, who fled, yet one of them was taken, naked, and could not be underftood, whom becaufe he wept bitterly the Captain let go, giving him a Cap, and fome Fifhing-Hooks. After fome Days farther

ther fail, fometimes finding the Land high, and fometimes low, and barren, having perceiv'd Fires in the
Night, the two Boats went afhore, and in fome Cottages found two *Indians* of a large Stature, who fled
fo fwiftly, that they could not be overtaken, then
coming to an Anchor clofe by, they call'd it Port St.
Andrew. From thence they fteer'd their Courfe between the Continent, and an Ifland, at about two
Leagues diftance from Land, which Ifland they judg'd
to be about one hundred and eighty Leagues in Compafs. Three Days the Wind prov'd fcanty, the
Continent appearing pleafant, and agreeable, with fome
Tokens of Fire, and here the Wind frefhned fo much,
that they were forc'd to take off the Bonet of the
Main Sail. *Sunday* the 12th of *October* they were
nearer Land, which was ftill more frefh and green
than that they were paft, faw fome Towns at Night,
and at Break of Day fpy'd a Canoe made of Reeds
rowing towards the Ship, but though the *Indians*
fpoke, they were not underftood, and fo it return'd.
Five other Canoes came out next, and being within a
Stone's throw of the Veffels, fpoke, but though Signs
were made to them to come nearer, they would not;
whereupon, as they return'd, the Commodore's Boat
row'd after them, and overtook one; the *Indian* leap'd
into the Water, and fome *Spaniards* after him, and
when they thought to lay hold on him he div'd, by
which means he got off.

WHEN they had held their Courfe fome Days
longer, the Country ftill appear'd more agreeable, with
fome Rivers falling into the Sea; the Captain landing
faw the Track of People, and abundance of Fruit-
Trees, and the 16th of *October* they were near a Point
of high Mountain Land, and the 18th enter'd the
Port of *Santa Cruz,* or the Holy Crofs, where they
ftay'd eight Days to reft, wood, and water. Twelve
Soldiers going afhore hid themfelves at *Grijalva*'s Well,
waiting

waiting to fee fome *Indian,* and at their return faw two that lay conceal'd in a Spot of Reeds, but could not take them. The 29th of the faid Month, as they were making out of the Port, the Ship *Trinity* ftuck a-ground, and was got off with much Difficulty, and could not make out to Sea in eight Days, by reafon of the contrary Winds, Rains, Lightning, and thick Weather, lying in much Danger becaufe of the Nearnefs of the Land. At this time the Sailors faw the Light over the Ship, which the *Spaniards* call'd *Santelmo,* and the *Romans* nam'd *Caftor* and *Pollux.* The 7th of *November* the Weather clear'd up, and they proceeded along the Coaft, a delightful Country, with fine Plains, and fome Woods, difcovering Smoaks at Night, fo that there feem'd to be People. The 10th of *November,* the fame beautiful Profpect continuing, they were within fifty-four Leagues of *California,* finding no Bottom at fifty-four Fathoms, the Ebb running off very far, as appear'd by the Sands. From the 11th of *November* till the 15th, they advanc'd but ten Leagues, by Reafon of the contrary Winds, and here the Ship *Trinity* was feparated for three Days, after which fhe again join'd the Commodore, faying, they had been feparated by a ftrong Current. Nothing remarkable hapned till the 2d of *December,* when they water'd, and about Two in the Afternoon two Parties of *Indians* came upon them, without having been perceiv'd by the Sentinels, fighting moft defperately with Arrows, Stones, and Spears. The Captain, and two others being wounded, the other *Spaniards* with their Dogs ran in upon them, and then they retir'd, and halted at a Diftance, making a Fire, becaufe of the fharp Cold. About Night the *Indians* went off, every one carrying a lighted Firebrand in his Hand, and the *Spaniards* return'd to their Ships. Ten Leagues from thence they found the Port of *San Abad,* which is very good, as is the Country, and fo proceeded till

the

the 9th of *December*, diſcovering very pleaſant Hills and Plains, and every Morning the Ships were cover'd with hoar Froſt. On the 10th there blew ſuch a violent Storm, that they loſt two Anchors, and ſplit their Sails, being forc'd to put into the Port of *San Abad*, where going to water, above two hundred *Indians* came upon them, adorn'd with great Plumes of Feathers, and obſtructed them. The next Morning early when their Veſſels were almoſt full, ſome *Indians* came, who by Signs barter'd for Beads, giving Plumes of Feathers and Sea-ſhells for them, which paſs'd the time, till they had water'd and went off, when the *Indians* deſiring ſtill to barter, and not being regarded, ſhouted and turn'd their Buttocks by Way of Contempt, throwing Stones at the Seamen that went to weigh the Anchors, for which Reaſon two Muskets were fir'd at them, which having kill'd one of them, the reſt fled, where it was obſerv'd that thoſe People did not underſtand the Interpreter the *Spaniards* had, who was a Native of *California*.

FROM that time till New Year's Day 1540, they ſail'd forty Leagues, and on the 5th of *January* they felt the Cold very ſharp, concluding that the Winter was there as it is in *Spain*, and found the Latitude to be thirty Degrees. The 13th they landed to water on a very ſtony Soil, and found the Track of Men; but the 18th they came to better Land, and ſaw many Canoes with *Indians* that ſtood to gaze at the Ships, as if they had been amaz'd. The 20th they had done Coaſting the Iſland of *Cedars*, when Landing again, the Natives threw Stones at them, yet the Captain would not ſuffer any to be kill'd, but ſet the Dogs at them, who ſeiz'd two, that were taken, and ſet at Liberty by the Captain, giving them Beads and Pendants. Here in a Cave an *Indian* was found ſo old, that his Chin almoſt touch'd his Knees, whom they
left

left there. The North Wind driving them back to the Island of *Cedars,* they stay'd there till the 8th of *February,* finding there good Water, Wood, and some Fish, which with the Shelter was a Comfort to them. The 22d of *February* they went a Hunting, and kill'd a Deer and some Rabbits, and then came on such stormy Weather that their Cables gave Way, and had not the Pilots been skilful they had all perish'd. Having recover'd their Anchors, and refitted, they sail'd again, but were drove back to the same Station, where they continu'd till the 24th of *March,* when being in Want of all Necessaries, and the Ships much shatter'd, it was thought fit to return to *New Spain;* but Captain *Francis de Ulloa* would not consent to it, whereupon it was concluded, that since the Ship St. *Agatha* was not fit to go any farther, the *Trinity* should be well refitted, for the Captain to proceed on his Discovery, and the other should return to *New Spain,* with such Persons as he appointed. Accordingly, having found a very proper Place for it, the Ship was patch'd up in five Days, and then they took Leave of one another with very heavy Hearts. The Ship St. *Agatha,* with the Long-Boat a-stern, came within three hundred Leagues of the Port of *Colima,* and thence with a fair Gale to near the Port of *Santa Cruz,* where they saw an infinite Number of Whales, in Conclusion, this Ship arriv'd safe in *New Spain;* but *Francis de Ulloa* went on, and was never after heard of.

CHAP.

CHAP. V.

Francis Vafquez de Cornado *difcovers the Provinces of* Cibola, *and* Quivira *by Land; by Sea* Ferdinand de Alarcon *makes Difcoveries to the Northward.*

DON *Antony de Mendoza,* Viceroy of *Mexico,* having employ'd F. *Mark de Niza* to make Difcoveries Northward, and heard the Account given by him of thofe Parts, as has been faid before, refolv'd that thofe Difcoveries fhould be carry'd on by *Francis Vafquez de Cornado* from *Culiacan.* Purfuant to his Orders that Gentleman fet out from *Culiacan* in *May* 1539, with one hundred and fifty Horfemen, many of whom had two Horfes, two hundred Foot well arm'd, with Store of Ammunition, fome fmall Field Pieces, and Abundance of Sheep, Swine, and other Provifions, and in four Days March came to the River of *Putatlan,* where the Natives were peaceable. In three Days more he advanc'd to the River of *Cinalo,* where he order'd ten Horfemen to proceed, making double Marches, as far as the Brook of *Cedars,* and there to turn into a Break the Mountains made on the Right, to difcover what was in thofe Parts, and he would expect them at the aforefaid Brook. Thofe ten Horfemen holding on their Way, found nothing remarkable, but only poor *Indians,* as far as the Brook *de los Coraçones,* or of Hearts, fo call'd by *Orantes,* and *Cabeza de Vaca,* on Account of a Prefent of the Hearts of Beafts there made them by the Na-

tives; and there those People had *Indian* Wheat, Kidney-Beans, and Pompions to feed on. Thence they
proceeded to the *Vale* of *Senora*, being the same Country, and Inhabitants. The *Indians* of this Vale at
first appear'd peaceable, but afterwards call'd in their
Neighbours, and kill'd some *Spaniards* with their poison'd Arrows. The ten Horsemen returning with an
Account of what they had seen, the Forces march'd
on some Days Journey, through Deserts, till they came
to a Brook call'd *Nexpa*, down which they proceeded
two Days longer, and leaving it then on the Right
Hand, at the Foot of a Ridge of Hills, in two Days
pass'd them, and came to another Brook, where there
was Water, and Grass for the Horses, and in three
Days more went on to the River of St. *John*, so
call'd, because they arriv'd at it on the Festival of that
Saint, or *Midsummer* Day. Two Days after they
came to the River of *Balsas*, or Floats, so call'd, because they were oblig'd to make them in order to pass
it. The next Day they were at a Brook call'd *del
Pinar*, or of the Pine-Tree Grove, in such Want of
Provisions, that Men were oblig'd to feed upon Herbs,
and three *Spaniards* dy'd of eating such as they knew
not. Two Days after they were at another Brook,
by them call'd *Bermejo*, or Red, always advancing
much about North-East, and where they saw two *Indians*, who, as it afterwards appear'd, belong'd to the
first Town of *Cibola*, where the *Spaniards* arriv'd a
few Days after, being the Place where *Estevanico*, the
Black was kill'd, as has been mention'd in its Place.
In this Province were five Towns, containing about
two hundred Houses each, built with Stone, and having flat Roofs; the Country cold, as appear'd by
their Houses, and the Stoves they had, but seem'd to
yield Plenty of Mayz, Kidney-Beans, and Pompions.
The said Towns are within the Compass of six Leagues,
the Soil somewhat sandy, and not well stor'd with Grass;
the

the Woods are Sabine; the Natives cloath'd in Deers-Skins very well dres'd, and some in Cows-Skins, after the manner of Rugs, and they have Cotton Mantles, which the Women wear over one Shoulder, like Gipsies, and girt lapping over. About five Days Journey North-East from *Cibola* is a Province call'd *Tucayan,* in which are seven Towns, all the Houses with flat Roofs, better than the others before mention'd, and the People cloath'd after the same Manner; and these, it is likely were the seven Cities F. *Mark de Niza* meant. All the Streams found in the Way to *Cibola* ran towards the South-Sea, and from thence forward to the North-Sea. The *Spaniards* march'd some Days about this Country, and in their way found a Town fortify'd with Earth, and upright Rocks, all the *Indians* every where receiving the *Spaniards* in friendly Manner, except only in the first Town of *Cibola.* At the River *Huex,* there are along it in the Distance of twenty Leagues fifteen Towns, of flat roof'd Houses built with Clay and Stone Walls, some of them on other Brooks that fall into it. There are other Towns worth observing, for that Counrty having Houses two Stories high, their Provisions and Cloathing as before, and they have very warm Mantles of Feathers twisted together, and wove, with very close Stoves under Ground, tho' not very neat, and the Country produces some Cotton. This River runs North-West, and South-East, which shows it falls into the North-Sea. In seven Days Journey still North-East they came to the River *Cicuyque,* and in five more enter'd upon the Plains, where the Cows graze, and in three Days more were amidst an infinite multitude of Cows, Bulls and Calves. Here the *Indians* made their Houses of long Poles ty'd together at the Top, and stretching out below, cover'd with Cows-Hides, those Creatures being their whole Support, affording them Meat, Cloathing, and Shoes,

besides

befides they have very large Dogs, whom they load with their Equipage, when they remove.

THE Forces march'd eight, or ten Days among thofe Waters, where the Cows are, and the Guide who had talk'd of great Wealth, either by his own malicious Contrivance, or fome others, led them into thofe Plains, out of their Way, in Hopes to deftroy them, and their Horfes. It pleas'd God, that another *Indian* of that fame Country, who was among the *Spaniards,* faid, they fhould cut off his Head, if that were the right Way. When they had held on the fame Courfe twenty Days, they came to another Parcel of *Indians,* who liv'd like the reft, and met with an old blind *Indian* with a Beard, who by Signs gave them to underftand, that he had before feen four Chriftians, fuppos'd to have been *Orantes* and his Companions. In this Perplexity *Francis Vafquez de Cornado* advis'd with his Officers, and it was refolv'd, that the Forces fhould return to the Place from whence they came, and thirty Horfemen fhould go feek out that rich Country, the *Indian* had fpoken of, which had occafion'd fo much Labour in vain. The *Indian* who gave them Notice that they were out of their Way, offer'd to be a good Guide to them, defiring no other Reward, than that they would leave him in his own Country, and that the other *Indian* fhould not go with him, becaufe he rail'd at, and always oppos'd him ; both thofe *Indians* had been found in *Cibola.* *Francis Vafquez* refolv'd to be one himfelf of the thirty Horfe, that were to proceed upon Difcovery, and accordingly they march'd thirty Days Northward, tho' their Journeys were not long, always finding Water, and numerous Herds of Cows, and on the Feaft of St. *Peter* and St. *Paul* they were upon the River they call'd by that Name, which the *Indian* knew, and faid, it was the fame he had look'd for. Having pafs'd it, they travell'd down the Stream, turning to

the

the North-Eaft, and three Days after met *Indians*
hunting Cows to carry to their Town, who began to
fly, carrying off fome Women they had; but the
Indian Guide talked to and appeas'd them, and having
got Quarters, treating the *Indians* civilly, feeing that
Country was very good, and hearing the Account
their Guide gave of the Government of a Province
farther on, call'd *Harae*, they guefs'd there muft certainly be fome *Spaniards* there of thofe that efcap'd upon *Panfilo de Narvaez*'s unfortunate Expedition. *Francis Vafquez* writ a Letter, which he fent by the faithful *Indian*, having always kept the other in the Rear,
that they might not fee one another. In that Letter
he gave an Account of the Place where he was, directing them to come to him, or fend Word how they
might be deliver'd, if detain'd. Then thofe thirty
Horfemen proceeded towards the populous Country,
where they found good Towns, near Brooks, falling
into a great River, which they crofs'd, and fpending five
or fix Days among thofe Towns, came to the fartheft
part of *Quivira*, where was a larger River, with more
Dwellings along it than the others. Enquiring what
was farther on, they were told, that there was nothing but *Arae*, juft like what they then faw. The
Lord of the Place being call'd, came, who was of a
large Stature, ftrong limb'd, and well fhap'd; and
with him two hundred Men almoft naked, or ill cover'd, with their Bows, and Arrows, and Plumes
on their Heads. Seeing little Encouragement to go
on, and Winter drawing near, for it was the latter
End of *Auguft*, it was refolv'd to go home, in order
to return again better provided at a proper Seafon. The
wicked *Indian* underftanding that the *Spaniards* were
for turning back, alarm'd the Country to kill them, whereupon the Commander caus'd him to be put to Death,
and thus they march'd back to join their other Forces.

ALL this Country of *Quivira* is more promifing
than the beft in *Europe*, for it is not very mountain-

ous, but has pleafant Hills, Plains, and Rivers, very proper to feed Cattle, as vifibly appeai'd. There were Plums, like thofe in *Spain*, between Red and Green, of a very agrecable Tafte. Among the Cows was found Flax, of the natural Product of the Soil, and very good, for the Cattle not eating it, the whole ftood, with its Buds and Bloffoms. Near fome Brooks there were well relifh'd Grapes, Mulberries, Walnuts, and other Sorts of Fruit. The Houfes here were of Straw, many of them round, the Straw reaching down to the Ground, and at the Top a Sort of Lanthorn, or Sentinel's Box, where they look'd out. Here the good *Indian* defir'd to be left behind, as had been promis'd him, which was accordingly perform'd, the General giving him a good Prefent, for his faithful Service, with which he was well pleas'd, and promis'd to ferve the *Spaniards* whenfoever there fhould be occafion. When thofe thirty Horfemen had join'd the other Forces they before left behind, *Francis Vafquez de Cornado* had a Fall from his Horfe, and hurt his Head, whereupon he refolv'd to return to *Culiacan,* and *New Galicia,* notwithftanding all the Remonftrances made by his Officers, and fome thought he did it only to fee his Wife. Many would willingly have ftay'd to fettle in that Country, but it was not permitted, only F. *John de Padilla,* of the Order of St. *Francis* remain'd, to endeavour to ferve God in the Converfion of thofe *Indians,* and with him a Lay-Brother of the famé Order, a little Slave belonging to a Captain, to learn the Language, fome Chriftian *Indians* of *Mechoacan,* and two Blacks, one of whom had a Wife and Children ; befides *Andrew de Campo,* a *Portuguefe,* and another Black, that took the Habit of a Frier. He had likewife Sheep, Hens, Mules, and one Horfe, with Veftments, and other fmall Matters ; but he was kill'd, whether it was to take what he had, or for any other Motive is not known. The
News

News of it was brought by the *Portuguese,* and a *Mexican Indian,* call'd *Sebastian,* who made their Escape, a shorter Way than that the Forces had march'd. The *Portuguese* made his Way to *Panuco,* and said, that after having once fled, he was taken again, and that carrying a Cross in his Hand, the People every where respected, and gave him Meat. The Forces at their going out march'd three hundred and thirty Leagues, and but two hundred in their return, having found a shorter Way. *Quivira* is in forty Degrees Latitude, where it was as dangerous travelling over the Plains as at Sea, because there is no Way, but where the Cows go, so that those who went out to hunt Cows were quite lost, when once out of Sight of the Forces. Two several Nations live among those Cows, and are Enemies to each other, well shap'd, and limb'd, and all painted. They worshipp'd the Sun, and no other Religion was discover'd; they exchang'd Cow-Hides, and Deer-skins well dress'd with their Neighbours for *Indian* Wheat. The Viceroy was much displeas'd at the quitting of those Countries; for though there was neither Gold, nor Silver, the Men would willingly have stay'd to build a Colony there.

AT the same time that *Francis Vasquez* went by Land to discover the Inland Northern Provinces, the Viceroy of *Mexico* sent *Ferdinand the Alarcon* to make Discoveries in that Part of the World by Sea. He sail'd from *Acapulco* on the 9th of *May* 1540, with two Ships, call'd St. *Peter* and St. *Catherine*, and met with such a Storm, that the St. *Catherine* threw overboard nine of her Guns, and other Necessaries, which oblig'd them to put into the Port of *Santiago* to refit, and coming at length to the Shoals where *Francis de Ulloa* had been, notwithstanding all their Care they were both a-ground, and must have perish'd had not the Flood brought them off. The 26th of *August*,

the

the Boat going up a River, the Men difcover'd a few
Cottages, out of which the *Indians* convey'd all they
had into the Woods, and then return'd threatning the
Spaniards, and bidding them be gone; however, no Injury being offer'd them, they drew nearer, and many
more began to appear, whereupon *Alarcon* made all
Tokens of Peace, laying down his Sword, and fhowing them Toys, and after much Confultation one of
them advanc'd, and gave the Commander fome Shells
at the end of a long Staff, who return'd fome Strings
of Beads, after which they all flock'd to him, he
gave them feveral Baubles; after fome other Precauti-
ons on both Sides, the Interpreter not underftanding
thofe People, *Alarcon* made Signs for fomething to eat,
they brought Mayz, and defir'd he would fire a Muf-
ket, which he did, and they all fled, except fome old
Men, who reprov'd the others for running away;
but they all took up their Arms, and *Alarcon* retiring
to his Boat, advanc'd farther up the River, the *Indians*
following along the Bank, and bidding him Land, and
he fhould have Meat, fome of them at the fame time
carrying it through the Water to the Boat, their
Number being increas'd to about one thoufand. Thefe
Indians were naked, fmutty, having on their Heads
Deer-skins made like Helmets with Plumes of Feathers;
their Weapons Bows and Macanas; of a large Stature,
and Limbs; their Wives and Boys with them; their
Nofes bor'd with fomething hanging; their Arms
wrought; their Hair before cut fhort, the reft hanging down to their Waftes. The Women were alfo naked, faving that to cover their private Parts, they had
abundance of Feathers before and behind, their Hair
like the Men. The next Day there was a great Noife
on both Banks, and many arm'd *Indians* appear'd, but
without Colours, and becaufe they did not underftand
the Interpreter, Signs were made to them to lay down
their Arms, which they did; *Alarcon* landed, and

went

went among them, giving them little Glaſs Beads of ſeveral Colours, and they return'd *Indian* Corn, and Skins well dreſs'd, by which means they grew very familiar. He perceiving that they worſhipp'd the Sun, ſignify'd to them that he came from thoſe Parts where he was, from which time they paid him much Reſpect, brought Preſents, came unarm'd, and were wonderful courteous, he giving them part of what he had, but it was impoſſible to have enough for them all; whereupon he caus'd Croſſes to be made of Paper and Wood, which they kiſs'd and hung about their Necks. Thoſe People being ſo affectionate, were eaſily prevail'd on to tow the Boat up the River, with a Rope from the Shore, becauſe the Current was too ſtrong to go up otherwiſe.

Alarcon order'd his Interpreter to ſpeak loud, to try whether any Body underſtood him, and at laſt one anſwer'd, whereupon ſtopping, that *Indian*, who underſtood, ask'd, What People thoſe were, whether bound, and whether they came out of the Earth, or Water, or had dropp'd from Heaven? The Interpreter anſwer'd, That they were Chriſtians, and ſent by the Sun. The other ask'd, How that could be, ſince the Sun was ſo high and always in Motion, and he had never ſeen any ſuch before? *Alarcon* reply'd, That he might ſee the Sun at his Riſing was near the Earth, and always came from the ſame Place, and that he was born in the Country from whence the Sun came, as were many others that went to ſeveral Parts, as he was ſent to view that River, to be their Friend, and to adviſe them not to make War. The *Indian* again ask'd, Why the Sun had not ſent him before? To which he ſaid, He came not ſooner becauſe he was then a Boy. In fine, they had much more ſuch diſcourſe, and the *Indians* underſtanding that *Alarcon* was the Child of the Sun, invited him to ſtay, and be their Lord; which he refus'd, ſaying, he would be their
Brother.

Brother. Then the *Indian* being perſuaded to come into the Boat, upon Enquiry ſaid, he had never ſeen any ſuch Men, nor knew any Thing of *Cibola*; but as to their Religion, they only worſhipp'd the Sun, becauſe he warm'd them, and produc'd all that they fed on, for which reaſon they threw ſome part of all they gather'd in up into the Air for him; but they had no Lord, only the eldeſt and braveſt commanded; that in War they did ſometimes tear out the Hearts of the ſlain, and then eat them, and burnt others, but were then for making no more War, as the *Spaniards* advis'd; though a Nation beyond the Mountain made War on them. The *Indian* being then weary went his Way, and the next Day, the Chief among thoſe People call'd *Naguachato* invited *Alarcon* aſhore to eat, where he had Cakes of Mayz, and Pompions given him, after a little had been toſs'd into the Air for the Sun. Abundance of People waited on the other Side of the River, calling *Alarcon*, to give him Proviſions; he went over to pleaſe them, where an old Man having given him what he had, turn'd to the People, and ſaid, This is our Lord, you know that our Forefathers ſaid, there were white bearded Men in the World, and we would not believe them; let us ſerve him, ſince he is for no War, and has Eyes, and Mouth, and talks as we do. Paſſing ſtill up the River, the principal *Indian* ſaid, There were People farther on that could underſtand the Interpreter, there being twenty-three ſeveral Languages along that River; that ſtill farther on there was a Nation that had Stone Houſes, clad in Skins, and came thither to Barter for Mayz; as to their Marriages, he ſaid, They were allow'd to have only one Wife, whom the Father conducted to ſome Place where many People were aſſembled, ſaying, he had a Mind to marry her off, and if any Man lik'd, he gave her, with ſome Preſent, and ſo the Wedding was celebrated with ſinging, dancing, and eating;

eating ; that Brothers did not marry their Sifters, or other near Relations ; that the Women did not converfe with Men till marry'd, but ftay'd at Home to Work, being look'd upon as fcandalous, if unchafte ; that Adulterers were put to Death ; that the Dead were burnt, and Widowers continu'd fix Months, or a Year unmarry'd ; and that they believ'd the Dead went into another World, where there was neither Blifs nor Punifhment ; that the greateft Diftemper among them was fpitting of Blood, for which there were Phyficians, who cur'd by blowing, and uttering fome Words. Their Food was Mayz, Pompions, and a fort of Seed like Millet. They had Grind-ftones, and Pots to boil in. Here the Interpreter not daring to go any farther, becaufe thofe Nations were his Enemies, went away.

ADVANCING ftill up the River, they found abundance of People, and another Interpreter, and *Alarcon* being afhore, an *Indian* came, and touching his Arm, fhow'd him two Parties of arm'd Men coming out of a Wood, whereupon he retir'd into the Boat, and was inform'd that thofe were Enemies to the other *Indians*. *Alarcon* ask'd this Interpreter, Whether he knew any Thing of *Cibola* ? Who anfwer'd, It was about a Month's Journey from thence, that the People there had Stone Houfes, and fuch Weapons as themfelves, were cloath'd, and had a Lord ; the Women white, and all cover'd, wearing abundance of blue Stones, which they took out of a Rock, and when bury'd, all they had was laid with them. Holding on his Courfe up the River, well receiv'd and entertain'd by all the People, he came into a Country, where they were fubject to one Lord, and the Interpreter feeing Difhes to eat on, faid, That the Lord of *Cibola* was ferv'd on fuch, but that they were green, and none had them but the Lord ; and feeing a Dog, *Alarcon* had faid, the Lord of *Cibola* had fuch another, which

he

he had taken from a Black Man, whom, he had been told, that Lord had put to Death ; and here the Interpreter took his Leave. Travelling one Day's Journey farther, he came to a Town that was abandon'd, where five hundred arm'd *Indians* appear'd, with the Lord *Naguachato,* bringing a Prefent of Rabbits, and Yuca Roots. Farther on ftill abundance of People came out of fome Cottages, with an old Man before them, who prefented him fuch as they had, in very refpectful manner, and the Interpreter underftood that they had Cotton, but did not weave it. At another Place higher *Alarcon* found many People fitting on the Ground, that waited for him, and gave Provifions. The Lord being call'd, came, on whom *Alarcon* put a Shirt, and gave him fome other Things, wherewith he was well pleas'd. The like hapned in feveral Towns he came to, where he alfo heard of *Cibola,* and faw fome Women walking more freely among the Men, which they told him were immodeft, and leud ; till at laft one *Indian* was brought, who faid, he had been at *Cibola,* and feen many Men that call'd themfelves Chriftians, having Beards, certain large Beafts, and others fmaller, Black, and Fire-arms, like thofe there fhow'd them ; and that they had punifh'd the Lord of *Cibola* for having kill'd a Black Man ; by all which it appear'd, that the Forces under *James Vafquez de Cornado* were meant.

TURNING back from this Place, *Alarcon* ran as far in two Days, as he had been fifteen running up, feeing many People on the Banks, who cry'd out, asking, Why he would go and forfake them, fince he was their Lord, and they hop'd to live in Peace under him ? That if any Man had offended him, he fhould declare it, and they would revenge his Quarrel. Being come to the Ships, he made ready all the Boats to go up the River again to join *James Vafquez de Cornado,* calling that River *de Buena Guya,* or of the good Guide.

Guide. He began to go up on the 14th of *September,* and as he pass'd on gave the *Indians* some Seeds to sow, and Hens to breed, recommending it to them to live peaceably among themselves, to wrong no Man, and to be kind to Strangers. In his Passage he desir'd an old Man to give him a Draught of the several Countries and Towns along the River, which he did upon *Alarcon*'s promising to give him another of his Country. Being come to some Mountains, where the River was very narrow, they told him that a Sorcerer had set some Reeds a-cross it, to obstruct his Passage, yet he went on much farther; but having gone up eighty-five Leagues, without hearing any thing of what he look'd after, he turn'd back to the great Grief of the *Indians,* because he would leave them. Just as they were upon parting, they heard the Cries of a Woman, who cast her self into the Water; and being taken into a Boat, crept under a Bench, or Thowl, whence they could not remove her, saying, She would positively go with the Christians, because her Husband had forsaken her, and liv'd with another Woman, by whom he had Children. *Alarcon* consented that she should stay with him, as did an *Indian* Man, who would not remain in his own Country; but was always very pleasant and merry, and prov'd a good Christian. After this the Ships held on their Voyage, coasting along, and landing at several Places, making the best Observations they could of the Country, and enquiring after *Francis Vasquez de Cornado*; but hearing nothing of him, though all possible Endeavours were us'd, sending several *Spaniards* and *Indians* many Leagues up the Country, when they had pass'd four Degrees farther than the Ships of the Marquess *del Valle,* before spoken of had done, they return'd to *New Spain.*

The End of the Sixth Book.

THE

THE
General HISTORY

Of the vaſt CONTINENT and ISLANDS of

A M E R I C A, &c.

C H A P. I.

The Licentiate Chriſtopher Vaca de Caſtro *ſent by the King to examine into the Affairs of* Peru ; *his Behaviour there, and other Tranſactions during the Year* 1541.

HE Licentiate *Chriſtopher Vaca de Caſtro* having been a ppointed by the King, as has been ſaid before, to go over into *Peru* to enquire into the Miſmanagements of the Marqueſs *Pizarro,* and do Juſtice to ſuch as were wrong'd, among his other Inſtructions, was directed to ſee that the Lands ſhould be divided according to the Merit of every Perſon, and their Service, that

none might go unrewarded, nor *Pizarro*'s Friends and
Relations be unreasonably promoted, to the Prejudice
of others; that for the future the *Spaniards* should
keep no fierce Dogs to terrify the *Indians*, since there
was no longer need of them; that the *Indians* should
not be permitted to work on *Sundays* and Holy-Days,
though they were not Christians; that towards Sup-
pressing of Idolatry, all their Places of Worship should
be destroy'd; that *Spaniards* who went about marauding should be punish'd, and the *Indians* not oblig'd to work more than they were wont before; that
Religious Men, who were not very regular should be
banish'd; that all *Spaniards* who had Lands should
keep Arms, and Horses; that special regard should be
had to the honourable Entertainment of the *Inga Paul*,
and an Account taken of the Children of *Guaynacava*
and *Atabualpa*, in order to make Provision for them;
that no Person should under any Colour or Pretence
whatsoever carry any *Indian* into *Spain*; that the Caziques should not make Slaves of any of their Subjects
for Offences committed, *&c. Vaca de Castro* having
dispatch'd all his Affairs, imbark'd at *Sevil,* and having
touch'd at *Hispaniola,* proceeded to *Nombre de Dios*, and
Panama, where he arriv'd about the Middle of *January* 1541, whence, with all speed he sail'd for *Peru.*
Advice being brought into that Country of *Vaca de
Castro*'s coming, the *Chile* Men began to conceive Hopes
that they should have Justice done them; though in
the mean time they were miserably poor, and some of
them liv'd in a Farm *Dominick de la Presa* had either
given or sold them, which, he dying, *Pizarro* took
from them, so that their Distress became greater;
after which he sent Word to the Captains *John
de Saavedra, Christopher de Sotelo,* and *Francis de Chaves,*
that he would assign them Lands for their Mainte-
nance; but they being thoroughly inrag'd, answer'd,
that they would rather perish than receive any thing
at

at his Hands, and agreed, that *Alonſo Puerto Carrero,* and *John Balſa* ſhould go in Mourning to meet *Vaca de Caſtro* at *Piura,* to acquaint him with the Cruelty of the *Pizarro*'s towards them, and the late Adelantado *Almagro,* and to demand Juſtice.

T H E Marqueſs *Pizarro* was in a Conſternation a-bout *Vaca de Caſtro*'s coming, yet endeavour'd to con-ceal it, and ſent *Alonſo de Cabrera,* his Chamberlain to compliment him. At this time the *Spaniards* began to live at their Eaſe, and very orderly in their ſeveral Co-lonies, the *Indians* being peaceable, and all Things that had been brought out of *Spain* thriving and encreaſing, which Tranquility in all Likelihood might have con-tinu'd, had it not been for the Inſolence of *Antony Prado,* the Marqueſs's Secretary, who continually in-cens'd him againſt the Men of *Chile,* perſecuting and inſulting them ; which gave thoſe People occaſion to ſuſpect that, after all their Sufferings, they ſhould be Maſſacred, and put them upon providing of Arms for their Defence, whereupon the Marqueſs's Friends advis'd him to keep Guards. In the mean time *Vaca de Caſtro* was ſailing for *Peru,* but met with ſuch Storms, that he had lik'd to have periſh'd, and with much Difficulty got into the Port call'd *Buenaventura* ; but the other Veſſels that were with him being lighter, made their Way, and came ſafe to *Lima,* where upon this Advice that *Vaca de Caſtro* was coming, *Pizarro*'s Party ſeem'd to rejoyce, but the *Chile* Men looking upon this as a longer Delay to their Deliverance from all their Sufferings, came to a Reſolution to kill *Pizar-ro* on *Midſummer* Day, alledging, that it was intolera-ble that they who had ſerv'd ſo well ſhould be ſtarv'd to Death in the *Weſt Indies* ; however the Execution was put off by the Advice of *Chriſtopher de Sotelo,* who was one of the twelve Gentlemen mention'd be-fore to have had but one Cloak among them, think-ing it better to wait the coming of *Vaca de Caſtro,* and

in

in cafe he favour'd *Pizarro,* as they were inform'd he would, then to kill them both. *Pizarro* had feveral Intimations given him of the Defign againft his Perfon, whereupon he gave Orders for fecuring the Heads of the *Chile* Men. This was on a *Sunday* Morning, when one *Peter de San Millan* went with hafte to *John de Rada,* a Chief Leader of thofe difcontented People, and told him, that they were all to be hang'd and quarter'd within two Hours. *Rada* then arming himfelf with all fpeed, and joyn'd by feventeen others, all able, and daring Men, they refolv'd to kill the Marquefs immediately, and acquainting twelve others no way inferior to themfelves with the Defign, they alfo agreed to carry it on. Thefe bold Men being all together, *John de Rada,* with much Refolution told them, That if they had Courage, and kill'd the Marquefs, they fhould revenge the Death of their Friend *Almagro,* and obtain the Reward due to their Services; but if they fail'd, their Heads would be foon fet upon Poles in the Market-Place, and therefore it behov'd them to mind their Hits. Being all defperate Perfons, they anfwer'd to his mind, and accordingly that being *Sunday* the 26th of *June,* this Year 1541, they all fet out arm'd from *Almagro's* Houfe, he neither commanding, nor contradicting, and marching in a Body towards the Marquefs's Houfe, publickly faid, May the King live, and Tyrants die; fometimes naming *Almagro.* Upon a Signal given with a white Cloth, from a Window in *Almagro's* Houfe, feveral others fally'd out from the Houfes where they had lurk'd, waiting for the Time. Some ftay'd to fecure the Streets that none of the other Party might go in to defend *Pizarro,* fo that thofe who made to his Houfe were on y Nineteen; and it was very unaccountable that fo fmall a Number fhould pafs through the Streets, and the Market-Place, where above a thoufand

Men were, and yet no Creature offer'd to oppose them, but said, They are either going to kill the Marquess, or *Picado.* The Conspirators came to the Marquess's House, which was strong, and had two Courts, with a Gate, which, if bolted, could not have been forc'd by two hundred Men, besides the Door where the Marquess was, if it had been defended, would have disappointed the Conspirators, but nothing was regarded. In the Court, they found three of his Servants, and in the Room with him were the elect Bishop of *Quito,* twenty Gentlemen, and some Servants, with a Page, who having seen the Conspirators march through the Market, came in running, and crying, To Arms, for all the *Chile* Men are coming to kill my Lord the Marquess. Upon this Cry, the Marquess, and all the rest started, and went down as far as the half Pace of the Stairs, to see what was the matter, at the very Time when the Conspirators enter'd the second Court, crying, *Long live the King, and let Tyrants die.* Those who came down the Stairs, return'd into the Chamber, some scampering one Way, and some another, and two leaping out of the Windows into the Garden. The Marquess, and four others went into the with-drawing Room to arm themselves, five others stood astonish'd in the Room. The Conspirators came up the Stairs, *John de Rada* saying, *Happy Day, when it will be known that* Almagro *had such Friends as durst revenge his Death.* They found the Door of the Room latch'd, but Capt. *Francis de Chaves* order'd it to be open'd, tho' he was told, it were better to keep it shut, till some Relief came. The Door being open'd, *John de Rada* was the first that went in, and *Francis de Chaves* said, *What is the meaning of this, Gentlemen? Let not me share in your Prejudice to the Marquess, for I was always a Friend; take heed, for you are ruining yourselves.* The foremost of them took no

Notice

Notice of him, but they paffing on, *Arbolancha* ran
him through, and he fell down dead, they alfo kill'd
Francis Mendo, and *Peter,* Servants to *Francis de Chaves.*
When come into the Room, they faid, *W re is the
Tyrant ? Martin de Bilbao* coming to the Marquefs's
Bed-chamber, was wounded by *John Ortiz de Za-
rate,* who was with the Marquefs. *Francis Martinez
de Alcantara,* with his Sword and Cloak made good
the Door of the Anti-chamber, but feeing the fecond
Door loft, retir'd to the Bed-chamber. The Confpirators cry'd aloud, *Kill the Tyrant for we lofe Time.*
The Marquefs faid, *What Infolence is this ? Why will
you kill me ?* They prefs'd on, calling him Traytor ;
whilft he guarded the Door, with his two Pages, fo
that they could not get in, till thrufting on *Narvaez*
upon him, they all rufh'd in, and fell upon the
Marquefs, wounding him till he fell, calling upon
JESUS CHRIST, and then *John Rodriguez Borregan*
gave him fuch a Blow in the Face with a Glafs-Bot-
tle full of Water, that he prefently expir'd, being
then fixty-three Years of Age. This great Man who
rul'd over Countries extending nine hundred Leagues
in Length, from the City *de la Plata* to that of *Cartago,* was born in the City of *Truxillo,* and had by
feveral Noble *Indian* Women three Sons and one
Daughter. With him dy'd, as has been faid, *Francis Martinez de Alcantara,* and the two Pages *Efcan-
don* and *Vargas;* befides whom *Don Gomez de Luna,
Gonzalo Hernandez de la Torre, Francis de Vergara,*
and *Hurtado* were much wounded, and tho' the Confpirators might have kill'd them, they would not.

The Confpirators leaving *Pizarro* dead, went out
into the Streets, crying, *Long live the King, the Tyrant is dead; let Juftice be adminifter'd in the Country.*
Then all the *Chile* Men being their own Paray, who were
in the City, amounting to above two hundred Soldiers
joyn'd them, and Proclamation was made that all the

Inhabitants

Inhabitants fhould retire into their Houfes, and none to ftir out upon Pain of Death. As foon as *Antony Picado* heard what had hapned, he went away to hide himfelf in the Houfe of the Controler *Alonfo Riquelme*, and the Licentiate *John Velafquez* retir'd to the Monaftery of St. *Dominick*. Don *James de Almagro* attended by all the Prime Men of his Faction, took up his Quarters in the Marquefs's Houfe, his Friends, with much Joy, declaring, that he fhould be Governour, and the King would approve of it. Order was taken to fecure all the Arms, and Horfes in the City, and fome Infolencies were committed, as is ufual upon fuch Confufions. The Houfes of the Marquefs *Pizarro, Francis Martinez de Alcantara,* and *Picado* were plunder'd, what was taken belonging to the Marquefs, being valu'd at above ten hundred thoufand Pieces of Eight; his Brother's at fifteen thoufand, and *Picado*'s at fixty thoufand, and above the value of fourteen thoufand in Gold was taken from *James Gavilan,* the Conqueror. The *Mercenarian* Friers, to prevent more Mifchief, brought forth the Blefied Sacrament, and the Confpirators having fecur'd whom they thought fit, propos'd to have *Don James de Almagro* own'd as Governour, till fuch Time as the King fhould confirm him; which after fome Controverfy was perform'd, and new Magiftrates appointed. Advice was fent of the Marquefs's Death to all Parts, and many fubmitted to *Almagro*; but *Alonfo de Alvarado,* who was among the *Chiachiapoyas,* went away to St. *John de la Frontera,* where he caus'd himfelf to be proclaim'd Governour, and Captain-General, againft all Perfons whatfoever, that fhould prefume to ufurp thofe Provinces againft the King's Will, declaring himfelf an Enemy to the *Chile* Men, and fending away a Meffenger to the Licentiate *Vaca de Caftro,* to acquaint him, that he had two hundred Men well arm'd, many

ny of them with Silver Armour, and their Spears headed with the fame Metal, for want of other Arms. Ambition began to ftir up fome Emulation among the Men of *Chile* at *Lima.* The Bifhop, his Brother, and fixteen more *Spaniards* attempting to go away by Day, to the Licentiate *Vaca de Caftro,* and putting into the Ifland *Puna,* were there kill'd by the Natives. Twenty *Spanifh* Traders travelling for *Quito* with abundance of Goods, were all Slain by the Cazique *Chaparra,* in the Province of *Carrochanba,* and all they had carry'd away. Several *Spaniards* were alfo beheaded by the then prevailing Party, as Mutineers, for encouraging others to rife in Arms, againft thofe in Power.

At *Cuzco,* after fome Struggle, *Almagro* was own'd Governour-General, and *Gabriel de Rojas* his Lieutenant in that City; but thofe that were of the *Pizarro* Faction withdrew themfelves, and fent to *Peralvarez Holguin,* who was then on his March to fubdue the *Chuncos,* offering, in cafe he would return and efpoufe their Quarrel, to declare him Captain-General. *Peralvarez* proud of that Title, return'd immediately, joyn'd all that had invited him, and marching to *Cuzco,* compell'd them to receive him as fuch, difpatching Meffengers to feveral Towns to perfuade them to efpoufe his Party. The Licentiate *Vaca de Caftro* being on his way from Port *Buenaventura* to *Popayan,* receiv'd Advice of the Death of the Marquefs *Pizarro,* but faid he would not give Credit to it till he had a Confirmation. At *Lima, Almagro* and *John de Rada,* having often prefs'd *Antony Picado* to difcover where *Pizarro's* Treafure was hid, upon his Refufal, put him to the Rack, where he bid them ask *Hurtado,* the Marquefs's Servant, who faid, his Mafter had nothing but what they found, and if there were he would declare it, whereupon he was difmifs'd; but *Picado* had his Head ftruck off the

next

next Day, being the 29th of *September* 1541. In the mean Time, the Cities of *la Plata*, and *Arequipa* declar'd against *Almagro*, putting themselves under the Conduct of *Peralvarez Holguin*; and *Alonso de Alvarado* mov'd from St. *John de la Frontera* as far as *Cotabamba*, looking upon it as a Place of Strength, and sent to acquaint *Vaca de Castro*, that he expected his Orders there; the said *Vaca de Castro* then receiving the Confirmation of the Death of *Pizarro*, with other Particulars that ensu'd upon it. Hereupon he resolv'd to assemble what Forces he could, and being himself no Soldier, summon'd all the Commanders in those Parts, and particularly the Adelantado *Belalcazar*, desiring him to bring all the Troops he could gather, since it was the greatest Service he could do the King. *Belalcazar* readily comply'd, and being come to *Popayan*, *Vaca de Castro* produc'd the King's Commission he had for governing the Dominions of *Peru*, in case the Marquess *Pizarro* were dead, which all there obey'd, and began to consult what was fit to be done. Some advis'd him to return to *Panama* to gather Forces, and come with great Power, others were against admitting of that Delay, which would give Time to *Almagro* to grow stronger, whereas, if he advanc'd, Men enough would come in to him to serve the King, and thus he march'd to *Quito*, where he was admitted as Governour, and receiv'd the Message sent him by *Alonso de Alvarado*, to whom he return'd Thanks for his good Will, and was well pleas'd to find so agreeable a Reception. *Vaca de Castro* sent Word to all the *Spanish* Towns in *Peru*, of his being Governour, many of which submitted to him; and the more to strengthen himself, he also sent to invite *Gonzalo Pizarro*, who was then upon the Discovery that has been before spoken of, in the Vale of *Canela*, as concluding that he would readily come in to revenge his Brother's Death.

AT

AT *Cuzco, Peralvarez Holguin* having drawn together three hundred Horse and Foot, march'd out to meet *Vaca de Castro,* and to fight *Almagro,* if he met him. On the other hand, *Almagro's* Party had Intelligence of all that was done, but were not very unanimous among themselves, *Gomez de Alvarado* and *John de Saavedra* being disgusted that *John de Rada* should be General, because he had been a private Soldier, tho' he wanted neither Valour nor Conduct. They likewise differ'd in Opinion, some being for marching directly to secure *Vaca de Castro,* others rejecting that Design, as too bare-fac'd against the King's Authority, after which they should be able to make their own Terms. In Conclusion, they march'd out from *Lima* to the Number of five hundred and seventeen *Spaniards* well equipp'd and arm'd, of which one hundred and eighty were Horse, the rest Foot, arm'd with Pikes and Muskets, carrying five Pieces of Artillery. The General *John de Rada,* being in Years, and much broken with what he had endur'd, fell sick, and being unfit to Command, which prov'd the Ruin of *Almagro,* desir'd that *Christopher de Sotelo* and *Garcia de Alvarado* might take the Command in his Stead, which was pernicious Advice. On their march towards *Xauxa* some deserted from, and others to them. Before the Forces came thither, twelve Soldiers who had been sent before to get Intelligence had been surpriz'd there by *Peralvarez Holguin,* who hang'd two of them, and dismiss'd the rest, bidding them go tell *Almagro,* not to proceed in his Courses lest he should be punish'd; and that he was going to *Caxamalca,* to avoid fighting, not for Fear, but to give him time to see his Error, and beg Pardon of the King. Upon the Advice brought by those Soldiers, *Christopher de Sotelo* would have march'd the shortest Way to fight *Peralvarez Holguin,* but *John de Rada* oppos'd it, whereupon *Sotelo* quitted his Command. This was very agreeable

U 4

to *Peralvarez*, who thereupon advanc'd in good Order, and the *Chile* Men coming to *Xauxa*, and being fenfible of the Opportunity they had loſt, thought to have retriev'd it by ſpeedy Marches, but the Floods in the River, and want of Proviſions obſtructed them. Not being able to overtake *Peralvarez*, though they did ſome Harm among his Baggage, the *Chile* Men reſolv'd to proceed to *Guamanga*, and thence to *Cuzco*, to reinforce their Army, get ſome Artillery, and wait to ſee how *Vaca de Caſtro* would behave himſelf. *John de Rada* dy'd at *Xauxa*, to the great Grief of all that Party, for his great Prudence, and becauſe he was a faithful Friend to both the *Almagro's*, Father and Son. At the ſame time *Peralvarez* march'd on with the utmoſt Precipitation, over Rivers and Mountains, the *Indians* telling him, that the *Chile* Men were at his Heels, till he came to *Tambo*, a ſtrong Houſe of the *Ingas*, half way between *Xauxa* and *Caxamalca*, where he made an halt, to reſt the Men and Horſes, both being much fatigu'd ; and from thence he ſent to *Vaca de Caſtro*, for Orders, and to *Alonſo de Alvarado* to join him, but he would not, becauſe every one aim'd to Command in Chief. However *Alvarado*, upon ſecond Thoughts, proceeded to *Guaylas*, and halted one Day's March from *Peralvarez*, and thus both Parties lay waiting for *Vaca de Caſtro*.

HE being at *Quito* with one hundred and twenty good Soldiers, and the Adelantado *Belalcazar*, upon the Advice, that Captain *Peter de Vergara*, who was then among the *Bracamoros*, would join him with his Men, and that *Alvarado* and *Peralvarez* expected him with their Forces, reſolv'd to move forward from that City, having firſt ſent the Adelantado *Belalcazar* to diſcover, becauſe he was known to and reſpected by the *Indians*, as having conquer'd that Country. *Belalcazar* ſoon after met Captain *Francis Nuñez de Pedroſo*, who had been concern'd in the Death of the
Marqueſs

Marquefs *Pizarro*, and was going to *Quito* to fue for his Pardon, but he advis'd him rather to make the beft of his Way to his Government of *Popayan*, where he fhould be fafe. This could not be done fo privately, but that *Vaca de Caftro* was inform'd of it, and *Laurence de Aldana*, who was an Enemy to *Belalcazar* made the moft of it, adding, that the faid Gentleman had declar'd, that young *Almagro* could do no lefs than revenge his Father's Death. Upon thefe Whifpers, *Vaca de Caftro* growing daily ftronger, fent Orders to *Belalcazar* to return to his own Government; and though he urg'd, that it would be a difhonour to him, yet the other perfifting, he went himfelf to *Vaca de Caftro*, to whom he reprefented, how great a difcredit it would be to him to be fent away at that time, when he might ferve the King, as if he were not to be trufted. *Vaca de Caftro* alledg'd againft him, what has been faid, of his having affifted Captain *Francis Nunez de Pedrofo* in making his Efcape, and faying that *Almagro* did well in revenging the Murder of his Father. *Belalcazar* with much good Breeding, told him, he fpoke like a Lawyer, there being nothing more frequent among Soldiers than to fuffer one another to efcape upon fuch like Occafions; and that for himfelf he came not from his Government to revenge the Marquefs's Death, but to ferve the King, againft all that fhould be Difloyal to him, the Difference being very great between *Almagro*'s revenging his Father's Death, and his Majefty's Service, fince all the World muft approve of the Son's revenging the Murder of his Father. All he could fay not availing, he defir'd that the fending of him away might not be mifreprefented to his Prejudice, and *Vaca de Caftro* promis'd to give the moft favourable Account of him, yet he did the very reverfe. This Behaviour of *Vaca de Caftro* was much condemn'd, as being an Affront put upon fo loyal and worthy a Perfon as *Belalcazar*, befides that

it

it difcover'd his Partiality, as if he were come rather to punifh thofe who had kill d *Pizarro*, than to reftore Peace to the Country ; and this his Management drove *Almagro* to defpair of any Accommodation, and was the Occafion of the Civil War.

Vaca de Caftro being advanc'd to the Vale of *Xayanque*, was there met by *Don Alonfo de Montemayor* and *Vafco de Guevara*, as alfo *Peter de Vergara* with his Troops from the Province of the *Bracamoros.* Here fome advis'd him, rather to endeavour to adjuft Affairs in a peaceable manner, than to decide the Quarrel by Force of Arms. He having refolv'd upon the contrary, and knowing that *Peralvarez Holguin* and *Alonfo de Alvarado* both afpir'd to the Poft of Captain-General, declar'd he would take that Command upon himfelf, promifing to reward the Pretenders to it otherwife, and accordingly he was receiv'd and own'd as fuch by the Forces under both thofe Commanders. In this he was judg'd to have proceeded difcreetly for preventing of all Animofities. Thefe Things hapning about the beginning of the Year 1542, it will be convenient to leave him with thofe Forces for a while, to fee what hapned in other Parts during the Year 1541.

C H A P. II.

Actions of Peter de Valdivia *in the Kingdom of* Chile *in the Year* 1541, *and the Defcription thereof.*

THAT the Affairs of *Chile* may not be forgotten, we muft turn back to fpeak of the fecond Enterprize undertaken into that Kingdom by the *Spaniards*, the firft having been that which has been before fpoken of under the unfortunate *Almagro*, who defifted from it to his own Deftruction. When that

Gentleman

Gentleman had been put to Death, the carrying on of that new Conquest had been laid afide, for fome time, till at length *Peter de Valdivia*, who was settled at *los Charcas*, having ferv'd *Pizarro* at the Battle of the Salt-pits, begg'd of him a Commiffion for that undertaking, which was eafily granted, and he fet out with about one hundred and fifty *Spaniards*. Being come into the first Part of that Kingdom, that is, the Vale of *Copayapo*, which fignifies Seed Plot of Turkey-Stones, becaufe there are many of them on an Hill, though little valu'd on Account of their Plenty, he would not build a Town there, notwithftanding it is the moft fruitful Part of the whole Kingdom, for the Reeds of the Mayz, or *Indian* Wheat are as long as an Horfeman's Sphear, and the greateft Ears a out half a Yard in Length, the fhorteft a full Quarter, for which reafon they gather no more of it than they have occafion for, leaving the reft upon the Reed, only twifting the Knot of the Ear, that it may not fhoot out again. A Bufhel yields above three hundred, and all other Things fown in this Vale, whether of the Growth of the Country, or brought from *Spain*, increafe wonderfully, and are very good. A mall River falling from the Mountain, and running abou twenty Leagues a-crofs the Vale, waters it, and falls into the Sea at a Bay, which ferves for an Harbour, where Ships may anchor, being in twenty-fix Degrees of South Latitude. From this Vale to the Port and Vale of *Guafco* there are thirty-five Leagues, the Coaft bearing South and by Weft, the Port of *Guafco* in twenty-nine Degrees, being a Bay into which a fmall River empties it felf, coming down from the fnowy Mountain to the Eaftward, ferving to water the Lands, and this Vale is almoft as fruitful as that of *Copayapo*. In this and the other Vales there are abundance of Partridges, with Sheep, and Afh-colour Squirrels, whofe Firs are very fine. The reafon why *Peter de Valdivia* would not

fettle

settle a Colony in the first Vale, but go on to the second, was suppos'd to be, because if it were left in peaceable Disposition, there would be a ready open way for his Men to go back, being sensible of the great Difficulties People are to struggle with upon the first building of a Town, and therefore he proceeded to the Vale of *Guasco,* to the Place the Natives call'd *Mapocho,* where, on the 24th of *February* 1541, he founded the City of *Santiago de la Nueva Estremadura,* fourteen Leagues from the Sea, where is a small Harbour. At the same Time, he rais'd a Fort, for the Defence of the Inhabitants, as knowing that the Natives were Men of Valour, tho' he from the first endeavour'd to reduce them by Art, and fair Means, and accordingly they submitted to him. When the *Indians* had kept the Peace some Months, they began to hold private Cabals, without any Provocation given them, and resolv'd to kill all the *Spaniards Valdivia* had with him, and in regard that the Ground was plain, and proper for the Horses, and that they might find the *Spaniards* divided, they agreed to make the Onset, when *Valdivia* went out with the Horse, as he was wont to do.

Valdivia had learnt Experience in the Wars of *Europe,* and was very vigilant, so that by his Industry, he got Intelligence of the Conspiracy, seiz'd some of the Lords, put them into the Fort, and nevertheless went out with sixty Horse, to scour along the River *Cachapoal,* which is fourteen Leagues from *Santiago.* The *Indians* laying hold of that Opportunity, without any Regard to the Prisoners, attack'd the Fort, which was defended by Capt. *Alonso de Monroy,* Lieutenant to *Valdivia,* who having Notice, that he should be attack'd, sent after *Valdivia,* who was overtaken eight Leagues off, and answer'd, that might be *Indian* News, and therefore he would not hinder his March; but in case it should prove true, they must
stand

ſtand to it, and he would do the ſame. The *Indians*, without loſing Time, attack'd the Fort, and fought from Break of Day till Night. Whilſt the Men were ingag'd, the Lady *Agnes Suarez*, to prevent the *Indians* releaſing the Caziques, without any Orders for it, kill'd them all with an Axe, a wonderful Bold-neſs, and no leſs Cruelty, which Women have at o-ther Times been known to be guilty of. The moſt prejudicial Thing to the *Spaniards* in this Attack, were the Encloſures, or Yards they had made of Timber, and Boughs to their Houſes, where the *In-dians* fortify'd themſelves, becauſe the Horſe could not come at them; which was a Reflection upon *Val-divia*, becauſe, being a Soldier, he had not made an Eſplanade to the Fort. The *Spaniards* all abandon'd the Fort, and in a Body march'd to a plain gravelly Ground near the River that runs by the City, the Lady *Agnes*, and all the Children and *Indian* Servants being in the Center. The *Indians* thereupon drew out into the Plain, ſetting Fire to the Baracks, and then the Horſe charg'd and routed them, killing very many, to the great Satisfaction of the *Spaniards*, for when Things ſucceed no Fatigue is troubleſome. *Valdivia* returning, found all his Houſes burnt, but was moſt concern'd for the Deſtruction of his Pro-viſions; however being reſolv'd rather to dye than to abandon that Kingdom, he fell to build again, and ſeek out for Proviſions, wherein his Men ſuffer'd ſo much through Want, and continual Toil, that they began to think of returning to *Peru*, and in order to it, reſolv'd to murder their Commander. He being inform'd of it, puniſh'd the Ring-leaders, which quell'd the Commotion, and he took the Title of Go-vernour, and behav'd himſelf with ſuch Bravery and Conduct, that at length the *Indians* of the Vale of *Chile*, being the Chief of all the reſt, ſubmitted to him, and were content to be directed by him, and then

then he began to work the Mines of *Quillota,* which prov'd fo rich, that he built a Fort for the Security of the Men employ'd at them, put a Garrifon into it, order'd a Frigate to be built on the River, to trade to *Peru* by Sea, and that there might be a Communication by Land, he fent thirty Horfemen to the Vale of *Guafco,* ordering Capt. *Monroy,* with fix others to the Vale of *Copiapo,* and thence into *Peru,* which was a Matter of much Difficulty, and Danger. And in order to made a Show of the Wealth of the Country, he order'd fix pair of Stirrops, the Buckles of the Girts, Breaft-plates, and Hawks-bells to them all, and the Pommels of the Saddles to be made of pure Gold, to draw People to him, but the *Indians* of the Vale of *Copiapo* falling upon Capt. *Monroy* by furprize, as he was preparing to pafs the Defert of *Atacama,* kill'd five of his Men, whilft he and *Peter de Miranda* leap'd upon their bare Horfes, and fled over the Vale to fome fandy Hills, wounded in feveral Places with Arrows, and purfu d by a Commander call'd *Cotco,* with one hundred Archers; and they being wounded, and their Horfes tir'd, he overtook, and carry'd them back, with their Hands ty'd behind them to a prime Cazique of the Vale, whofe Wife was Heirefs of the whole Vale, for there the Inheritance comes by the Mothers, and when they are marry'd, the Hufband rules.

THE two *Spaniards* being bound in order to be kill'd, it pleas'd God to touch the Heart of that Lady, who commiferating their Condition, ftarted up, and unbound them with her own Hands, caus'd Water to be brought to wafh off the Gore from their Wounds, gave them fome of her Liquor to drink, taking the Effay of it as is their Cuftom, bidding them not to fear, for they fhould not dye; for which *Peter de Miranda,* who underftood the Language, return'd her Thanks. Then came the

Indian

Indian Commander, who had taken them, saying, they might be easy, since the Lady that commanded them all, had given Orders that they should not dye. Those two *Spaniards* continu'd six Months in that Vale, and Capt. *Monroy* advising the Lord of it to learn to ride, he was pleas'd with it, and rode about with some others, on the Horses they had taken, the Cazique having a Spear, and a naked Sword carry'd before him, with his Guard of Archers. *Monroy* and *Miranda* were also mounted, as was another *Spaniard*, call'd *Casco*, who had been among the *Indians* ever since the Time when *Almagro* was there. Capt. *Monroy* resolving to make his Escape from among those People, seriously consider'd how he might recover his Liberty, and when he found a proper Opportunity, as he was riding with the Cazique, clos'd with, and wounded him in several Places with a little Knife he had, so that he fell, but dy'd not in four Months after. *Miranda* ran at the *Indian* that carry'd the Spear, and snatch'd it from him, as he did the Sword from the other. The rest of the *Indians* being in a mighty Consternation, fled; then *Monroy* and *Miranda* turning to *Casco*, commanded him to go on, or they would kill him, and thus driving him before, they took the Way to the Desert. As they were going out of the Vale, they met an *Indian* Woman going from one Town to another, driving a Sheep loaded with some Sacks of toasted *Indian* Corn, which they took up behind them, and by that Support pass'd the Desert, which is ninety, or one hundred Leagues over. Being come to the Vales of *Atacama*, which were then in Arms, they turn'd away towards the snowy Mountain, and with much Difficulty arriv'd safe at the Mines of *Porco*, where they rested, furnish'd themselves with Necessaries, and proceeded to meet the new Governour *Vaca de Castro*; who considering the great Importance
of

of the Kingdom of *Chile*, fupply'd *Monroy* with what was requifite for raifing Men; and he accordingly return'd to *Chile* with fixty, being the firft Reinforcement the Governour *Valdivia* receiv'd, without which he could not have ftood his Ground. Upon the Report fpread abroad of the great Wealth of the Country, Capt. *John Baptift de Paftena* went thither with a Ship carrying Cloaths, and other Neceffaries, much wanted at that Time, and then the Governour fent him to difcover all the Northern Coaft, of which he gave a good Account at his Return.

BY means of the Fort *Valdivia* had rais'd at the Mines of *Quillota*, great Advantage was made, and he had pofted *Gonzalo de los Rios* there, to gather the Gold; but the *Indians* flily carry'd him a Pot full of Grains of Gold, as a Sample, faying, they would give much more of the fame. The *Spaniards* going to fee it, fell in among a Number of *Indian* Archers, who kill'd all the Soldiers, none but *Gonzalo de los Rios*, and a free Black, call'd *John Valiente*, efcaping on the bare Horfes. The Governour being inform'd of it, and that the *Indians* had burnt his Frigat, which was almoft finifh'd, took fifty Soldiers with him, and built a ftrong Houfe in the Vale of *Quillota*, which is that of *Chile*, where he plac'd a Garrifon, and having made fome Examples, Peace was reftor'd, and the Work of the Mines carry'd on again. This being as much as hapned in the Year 1541, before we proceed to other Parts, it will be convenient to give fome Defcription of this Kingdom.

IT is generally call'd *Chile*, tho' more properly *Chille*, the Name of a River running through the Vale of the Denomination, from whence the *Ingas* carry'd away much Gold, lying aloug the South-Sea, which extends from thence to *China* two thoufand one hundred Leagues. The firft inhabited Part of this Kingdum

dom of *Chile* is the Vale of *Copiapo,* whence the Coaft
extends to the Streights of *Magellan* Southward four
hundred feventy-two *Spanifh* Leagues, in he midft of
which Length, being the Province of *Guadalauquen,*
was founded the City of *Valdivia,* two Leagues from
the Sea, up a River, in bare forty Degrees of S. Lat.
Here the Spring begins in *September,* the Summer in
December, Autumn in *March,* and Winter in *June,*
being the oppofite of our Summer, and Winter, becaufe beyond the Line, and accordingly their Seafons
for reaping, fowing, and planting are directly the reverfe of ours; the longeft Day there being St. *Lucy's,*
and St. *Barnabe's* the fhorteft. There is never any
Thunder, or Lightning, but fo great a Dew falls in
fome Vales at certain Seafons, that it congeals, and is
gather'd like Loaf-Sugar, and is fo wholfome, that
they give it the Name of *Manna.* There is fo much
Moifture, that the Grafs is green all the Year about,
and the Trees are never without Leaves, fo that the
Horfes graze continually. The Paftures, Woods, and
Fifheries are common to all by the King's Order.
Travellers from one End to the other of the inhabited Country pay nothing for their Diet. The Foreheads of the Natives are downy, and they have throve
under the *Spaniards,* for they went naked, and now
they have much Cattle, are cloath'd with their Wooll,
and eat the Flefh, they are good Pay-mafters, and
given to gaming; play at the Sport call'd *Chueca,* like
our Bandy, one Party againft another, and do not regard the Inequality of Numbers, but the Women ufe
it as well as the Men. There were no Caziques in
Chile, and tho' the Name is fometimes made ufe of
in this Hiftory, it is only to denote the Heads of
the Kindred, or Clan, who were richeft, and moft
powerful, and as fuch refpected, yet they paid no Tribute to them, but only Obedience in War, and fuch
like Occafions, which did not give them any Sove-

VOL. V. X reignty.

reignty. As far as thirty-four Degrees Lat. they water their Lands with Trenches, and from thence Southward, they have Rain. As far as twenty-three Degrees South, the Wind is always at S. and from that Lat. forward towards the Streight of *Magellan*, there are three different Winds; South in Summer; the North when the Weather is fair in Winter, and some rainy Days, and the West when the North ceases, sometimes with heavy Rains, being a-thwart the Coast, and so fierce, that it bows the Trees and carries off the Leaves and Branches. The Dew begins to fall in the Evening, whereas in *Spain* it is after Mid-night. This may suffice at present as to *Chile*.

AFTER several Attempts made for carrying on a Trade from *Spain* to *Peru* and *Chile*, through the Streights of *Magellan*, to save the Trouble of the Land Carriage between *Nombre de Dios*, and *Panama*, *Don Gutierre de Vargas*, Bishop of *Plasencia* fitted out three Ships which sail'd from *Sevil* in *August* 1539, and enter'd those Streights in *January* 1540, where one of them perish'd, another pass'd through, and arriv'd at the Port of *Arequipa* in *Peru*, of which more shall be said hereafter, and the third having been oblig'd to winter in the Streight, after many Difficulties and Hardships, return'd into *Spain*, which being all that is worth mentioning as to those Ships, we will also return to see what was doing in *Florida*.

CHAP.

C H A P. III.

The Continuation of the Actions *of the* Adelantado *Ferdinand de Soto, in the Province of* Florida, *during the Years* 1540, *and* 1541.

WE left *Ferdinand de Soto* wintering, with his Forces at *Apalache,* in the Province of *Florida,* having sent *John de Anasco,* with thirty Horse, back again to *Herriagua,* towards the Sea, to bring away Capt. *Calderon,* and the Men that had been left in those Parts to joyn him. *John de Anasco* being come to the River *Ocali,* was oblig'd to make a Float, in order to pass it, because there was a great Flood, and tho' they us'd the utmost Diligence, the *Indians* on both Sides of the River were ready in Arms to oppose them, so that the *Spaniards* were oblig'd to fight on both Sides, whilst their Baggage, and themselves were wafted over, which being done, they resolv'd to go to the Town, because one of them was quite benumm'd in passing the River, and the *Indians* believing their Number had been greater than it was, defended themselves till their Wives and Children were convey'd into Safety, and then abandon'd the Place. The *Spaniards* made four Fires in the Market, endeavour'd to cherish the Person before-said to be benumm'd, gave him the only clean Shirt they had among them, and dry'd their Cloaths, and Saddles, furnishing their Wallets with Provisions, ten Horses feeding, whilst the rest stood Bridled. About Midnight one of those that stood Sentinel, heard a great Number of *Indians,* they all mounted,

and

and made the Man that had been benumm'd and was then somewhat recover'd, faſt on his Horſe, led by another, and then march'd ſo faſt, that by Break of Day they had gone above five Leagues, trotting on where the Country was inhabited, and walking over the Deſert. The ſeventh Day after they parted from the other Forces, *Peter de Atienza* was taken ill, and within a few Hours dy'd on his Horſe. Having that Day travell'd near twenty Leagues, they came to the great Marſh, which was then overflow'd, and lay on the Edge of it that Night, making good Fires. The next Day they would have begun to paſs, but the Horſes would not, becauſe of the violent Cold, till towards Noon, the Sun yielding ſome Warmth, they went over. The third Day, advancing with the ſame Speed, they ſaw the Track of Horſes, and ſome Tokens of Lye and Waſhing in a Pool, which much rejoyc'd them, and the Horſes took Heart, ſmelling the Track of the others, which was a great Satisfaction, becauſe they fear'd that Capt. *Calderon,* who had been left behind with the forty Horſe and eighty Foot, might have been gone away to *Cuba,* or ſlain by the *Indians.* They came in Sight of *Hirrihiagua* about Sun-ſetting, when the Horſe Patroulle was going out of the Town, then the new Comers giving a Shout for Joy, Capt. *Calderon* came out, and they met with mutual Satisfaction. The Cazique *Mucozo,* being told, that *John de Anaſco* was come, went to viſit him, and brought the Horſe belonging to the Man that dy'd by the Way, which being tir'd, had been left in a Meadow, with the Saddle hanging on a Tree, and brought by the *Indians* on their own Backs, becauſe they knew not how to girt it on. *Mucozo* enquir'd after the Adelantado, and ſaid, he was ſorry that all the Caziques were not of his mind. They preſently began to conſult about going back, and there being
good

good Store of Provifions, Shoes, and Cloaths, which
the Adelantado as a rich Man had plentifully
provided, they refolv'd all fhould be carry'd to
Mucozo's Houfe, to be fecur'd, and order'd two
Brigantines to Coaft along, as far as the Bay of *Aute,*
which *John de Anafco* had difcover'd, and march'd
down, when fent by the Adelantado to difcover
Southward.

Seven Days after, all things being in Readinefs,
Anafco fet out with the Brigantines for the Bay of
Aute, and Capt. *Calderon* by Land for *Apalache,*
with feventy Horfe, and fifty Foot, the reft going
by Sea. The fecond Day, *Calderon* came to *Mucozo,* where he was well entertain'd by that friendly
Cazique. Nothing remarkable hapned till they came
to the great Morafs, befides one Horfe being kill'd
with an Arrow, which penetrated through his Breaft
to his Bowels, thofe *Indians* being fuch Archers that
they have been known to fhoot through four Folds
of Mail, for which reafon the *Spaniards* laid afide
their fine *Spanifh* Armour, and us'd Efcaupiles, ftuff'd
with Cotton, for themfelves and their Horfes. In
fhort, they travell'd one hundred and thirty-five Leagues
without any Oppofition to the Morafs of *Apalache,*
where the *Indians* attack'd them, kill'd one Horfe,
and fought defperately. The next Day they were
again attack'd, and difturb'd all the Night, the *Indians* calling them Robbers and Vagabonds, and
threatning to quarter them. The Day after that
again, they reach'd *Apalache,* where ten or twelve
Men dy'd of their Wounds. The Brigantines arriv'd at the Bay of *Aute,* and *Anafco* came that
Way fafe to *Apalache. Ferdinand de Soto* having got
all his Men together, fent *James Maldonado* to coaft
with the Brigantines Weftward, ordering him to return in two Months, with a Particular of all the
Ports, Creeks, and Points he faw, which he did, and

faid,

said, there was a very fine Harbour call'd *Achufi*, fixty Leagues from *Aute*, and brought two *Indians* he had taken there. He then commanded him to go over to *Havana*, with the Brigantines, to visit his Wife, and to give out in *Cuba* his finding of that good Harbour, and that the Country was good, to the End, that the People there might incline to come and settle at it, which was all punctually perform'd by *Maldonado*, as being a very industrious Man. Seven Horsemen going out of *Apalache* a Horseback, saw an *Indian* Man and a Woman, gathering old Kidney-Beans; the Man seeing the Horses, took up the Woman in his Arms, and carry'd her into the Wood, after which he return'd for his Bow and Arrows, attack'd the Horsemen, who would have sav'd his Life for his Bravery, calling to him to yield, but he was so desperate, that he wounded them all, and when his Arrows were spent, gave one such a Stroke with the Bow, on the Head-piece, that it stunn'd him, upon which Provocation he kill'd the *Indian* with his Spear. Whilst the Adelantado lay at *Apalache*, he made it his Business to get Intelligence about the Country to the Westward, in order to proceed on his Discovery, and among other *Indians* taken there hapned to be one seventeen Years of Age, Servant to Merchants that travell'd up the Country. This Man said, and another confirm'd it, that about thirteen or fourteen Days Journey farther on was a Province call'd *Cofachiqui*, where there was Gold, Silver, and Pearls, which was pleasing to the Forces, and made them wish for the Season to march. When any Parties of *Spaniards* went out, the *Indians* seldom fail'd of killing some of them, or their Horses, with their Arrows, at a Distance, tho' they would not encounter them in open Field, but always kept within the Woods.

THE

THE Seafon being come for taking the Field, the Forces march'd Northward, and the third Day lay on a Peninfula form'd by a Marfh, with wooden Bridges to it, and being high, feveral Towns could be feen from it, ftill in the Province of *Apalache,* where they refted two Days, and feven Men going out of that Place, without Orders, before they had gone two hundred Paces, fix of them were kill'd by the *Indians,* the feventh efcaping with two Wounds. Leaving the Province of *Apalache,* they enter'd upon that of *Atalpaha,* the firft Town whereof was abandon'd, however fix *Indians* were taken, who had ftay'd to fee all the People out, becaufe they were Commanders, who very boldly ask'd, *What are you for, Peace, or War?* The Adelantado by his Interpreter anfwer'd, He was not for War, as only intending to pafs through, and fhould do no other Harm, but defire Provifions. They reply'd, There was no Occafion to make them Prifoners, if that were all their Bufinefs, for they would treat them better than the others had done at *Apalache;* and accordingly they fent fome Servants to order the People to come in and ferve the *Spaniards,* whom they conducted to a better Town, whither the Cazique came to ratify the Peace, which was punctually obferv'd, during three Days they ftay'd there. From thence they advanc'd ten Days Northward, along the Banks of a River, the Country fruitful, and the Natives peaceable, who behav'd themfelves friendly. They came into the Province of *Achalaqui,* which is poor, barren, and thinly inhabited, having few young *Indians,* the old ones fhort fighted, and many quite blind. Proceeding thence in hafte to get out of that Country, the next they came to was *Cofachi,* the Adelantado among other Things giving the Cazique Boars, and Sows to breed, for he brought above three hundred of them into *Florida,* which increas'd

X 4 very

very much, none being kill'd, becaufe they found
Plenty of Provifions. It was the *Adelantado's* Cuftom,
before he enter'd any Province, to fend Word to
the Lord of it, and offer Peace, that they might
not be frighted at the Sight of fuch ftrange People,
befides that it was always his Intention rather to
make ufe of fair than foul means. Having accordingly fent a Meffage to the Lord of *Cofa*, he comply'd,
and came out to meet the *Spaniards*, appointing them
all their Quarters himfelf, where they refted five
Days, the Lord requiring it, and they had Plenty of
all Things, the Land being fruitful, and the Natives
peaceable. The next Province belong'd to a Brother
of *Cofa*, whofe Name was *Cofaqui*, who came out to
meet the Forces, with many of his People, all finely
drefs'd with Plumes of Feathers, and rich Mantles of
Sables, and other valuable Furs, where when the *Spaniards* were quarte'd, the Cazique went away to a-
nother Town, to leave that entirely to them. The
next Day the Cazique *Cofaqui* return'd, offering
arm'd *Indians*, and Provifions, to pafs a Defert of
feven Days Journey to *Cofachiqui*, and immediately
came four thoufand *Indians* to carry Burdens, and
the like Number arm'd. There was much Store of
Mayz, which in thofe Parts is us'd as Wheat is a-
mong us, as alfo much dry Fruit, but no Flefh, for
they had none but what they hunted. The Adelantado feeing fo great a Number of Men, was upon
his Guard, like a good Soldier, and difcreet Man.
The Cazique told a Commander, who was to lead
his Forces, that fince he knew the antient Enmity
there was between him, and the People of *Cofachiqui*,
he fhould not let flip that Opportunity, when he
was fupported by thofe brave Strangers, but execute
his utmoft Revenge on them. That *Indian*, taking
off a Mantle of Furs he had on, flourifh'd a two-
handed-wooden Sword he wore as Captain-General,
telling

telling the Lord, what he intended to do in his
Service; and the Cazique took off a rich Mantle of
Sables, thought to be worth in *Spain* one thousand
Ducats, which he put upon his General; which
giving of the Mantle and Plume of Feathers was the
greatest Favour those Lords could bestow. The
Night before they set out, two *Indians*, the one
call'd *Mark*, and the other *Peter*, tho' they were
not Baptiz'd, being as familiar as if they had been
Spaniards, cry'd out, that *Peter* was in Danger to be
kill'd. All the Forces were immediately at Arms,
and found *Peter* quaking, who said, That the Devil,
attended by many of his Companions, had threatned
to kill him, in case he conducted the *Spaniards* as he
had promis'd; that he had dragg'd and beaten him,
so unmercifully, that had they not come in to his
Assistance, he would have kill'd him, and since the
great Devil had fled from two Christians, he desir'd
they would Baptize him, that he might be a Christian as well as they. This appear'd to be no Fiction
by the Bruises, and Swellings, whereupon the Adelantado deliver'd him to the Priests, who stay'd with
him all Night, Baptiz'd him, and the next Day he
was mounted a Horseback, because of his Hurts.

THE two Armies march'd a-part, the *Indian* with
a Van, and Rear Guard, and those that carry'd Burdens in the Center, in excellent Order, and at Night
they lay asunder, keeping Guards. The third Days
Journey from *Cofaqui*, they enter'd upon the Desert,
travell'd six more thro' it, the Country agreeable, and
forded two rapid Rivers, making as it were a Wall
with the Horses, from the one Side to the other,
and by their Help they all pass'd safe. The seventh
Day, both *Spaniards* and *Indians* were in much Confusion, for the great Road they had follow'd was at
an End, so that they knew not which way to take
in that Wilderness. *Ferdinand de Soto* ask'd the *In-*

dians

dian General, How it could be poffible that among
eight thoufand Men he had there, no one fhould
be able to lead them out of that Diftrefs, and that
having been always at War with thofe Nations they
were then going to, they fhould all be unacquainted
with the Place they were in? He anfwer'd, That
no Man among them had ever been there, and that
their Wars had never been manag'd with compleat
Armies, but that they kill'd and made one another
Prifoners whenfoever they hapned to meet at the
Fifheries on the Rivers, or in Hunting, wherein thofe
of *Cofachiqui* having prov'd moft fuccefsful, his Countrymen did not go fo far, which was the reafon of
their being unacquainted with the Country; and if
he fufpected any Fraud, he might reft fatisfy'd, that
neither his Lord, nor himfelf, being both Men of
Probity, could ever be guilty of fuch a Thought;
for farther Security whereof he might take what
Hoftages he thought fit, and if that were not fufficient, he would be content that he fhould cut off
his Head, and thofe of all his Men, whenfoever he
found them faulty. The Adelantado was fatisfy'd
with this Anfwer, and then call'd *Peter*, the *Indian*,
who was alfo at a Lofs, becaufe he had not been
there in five Years. They march'd on the remaining
Part of the Day, as they found the Woods moft
paffable, without knowing any thing of the Way,
and came to a great River, that could not be forded,
which was an Addition to their Sorrow, for that
having only feven Days Provifion, it would not
hold out till they could make Floats to pafs over
the River. The next Day the Adelantado fent out
four Parties, two of them up and down the River,
and the other two up the Country, ordering them to
return within five Days, with an Account of what
they found. With each of thofe Parties of *Spaniards*
went one thoufand *Indians*, to endeavour to find out
some

some Way. The *Indians* that carry'd Burdens went out in the Morning with their Arms, and return'd at Night with Herbs, Roots, Birds, some small Land Animals, and a little Fish, of which they gave the *Spaniards* part, but all this was inconsiderable, whereupon having held out with hungry Bellies, the Adelantado order'd some Swine to be kill'd, and eight Ounces to be distributed to every Man, including the *Indians*, which was only protracting their Misery, and yet all show'd wonderful Patience, because the Commander in Chief gave them a good Example. The Companies sent out to discover march'd six Days, and three of them found nothing ; but *John de A-nasco*, who commanded the fourth, and went up the River met with a Town seated on the same Side of it as he was, which tho' small, had good Store of Provisions, and higher still saw several Towns, and Land sow'd. He sent back four Horsemen to carry this good News to the Forces, and by them many Ears of *Zara*, and some Cows Horns, without knowing whence they came, for till then they had seen no Cows. The *Indian* General *Patofa*, and his Men, the first Night they lay in that Town, kill'd all the Natives they could lay Hands on, took off their Skulls, and plunder'd the Temple, which was the Place of Burial, where they had the best of their Effects, this Town being in the Province of *Cofachiqui*, where much Mischief was done by the other *Indians*, whereupon the Adelantado dismiss'd those People, to prevent any farther Injury being done under his Protection ; and having given their General and other Commanders some Presents, with Provisions for their Journey, they went away well pleas'd.

Soto advanc'd through a pleasant, and plentiful Country, but abandon'd by the Natives, on Account of the Slaughters committed by his *Indian* Friends. Three Days after, to avoid going on at random,

he

he fent *John Anafco,* with thirty Horfe, to make fome
Difcovery in the Country. He fet out a little before
Night, and having advanc'd fomewhat above 2 Leagues,
heard Dogs bark, and Children cry, and faw Lights,
when preparing to feize fome *Indian,* they perceiv'd
that the Town was on the other Side of the River,
they halted at a Place where Canoes us'd to come a-
fhore, and when they had fed and refted their Horfes, return'd to give the Adelantado an Account of
what they had found, and then he went with one
hundred Horfe, and as many Foot to view the Town,
the two Chriftian *Indians,* *Peter,* and *Mark,* calling
to fome *Indians* that fled at the Sight of the *Spaniards.*
At the Call of thofe *Indians* fix came over in a Canoe,
the Adelantado being feated on a Chair, that was always carry'd for him to receive Compliments with
State, as the Cuftom of thofe People requir'd. Thofe
fix *Indians* approaching made their Obeyfance, firft
to the Sun, then to the Moon, and next to the A-
delantado, and then faid, Sir, Are you for Peace, or
War? He bid the Interpreter tell them, he was for
Peace, and requir'd nothing but Provifions, defiring
they would excufe him for giving them that trouble.
They reply'd, they accepted of Peace, but were concern'd about Provifions, for they had but little, by
reafon of a Plague; that they were Subjects to a Mai-
den Lady, whom they would acquaint with it. As
foon as ever they had deliver'd their Meffage to her,
two great Canoes were fet out with Awnings, feven
or eight Women went into one of them, and the
former fix Men in the other. Among the Women
was the Lady, and being come to the Place where the
Adelantado was, fhe fate down on a Stool they had
carry'd for her, and after fome Compliments, faid,
She was forry for the Scarcity of Provifions there
was in the Country, but that fhe had two Store-Houfes for the Relief of the Needy, one of which fhe gave
them,

them, and defir'd they would leave her the other; for fhe had two thoufand Bufhels of Mayz in another Town, which fhe would alfo give him, and would quit her own Houfe, and half the Town to quarter his Men, and if he requir'd it, it fhould be all clear'd. The Adelantado anfwer'd in moft courteous manner, returning Thanks, and telling her he would be fatisfy'd with what fhe pleas'd to give him. Whilft he was fpeaking, fhe took off a String of Beads fhe had round her Neck, and deliver'd it to the Interpreter *John Ortis,* to give to the Adelantado, faying, She did not give it with her own Hand to avoid tranfgreffing againft Modefty. The Adelantado ftood up, receiv'd it with much Refpect, and prefented her with a Ruby he had on his Finger. Thus the Peace was ratify'd, the Lady went away, all the *Spaniards* admiring her Beauty, and good Behaviour. The Forces were carry'd over on Floats, and in Canoes, four Horfes were drowned in the Paffage; the Forces were all quarter'd in the Middle of the Town, and the Adelantado enquiring into the Affairs of the Country, found it was extraordinary fruitful, and that the Lady's Mother liv'd retir'd like a Widow twelve Leagues from thence. Tho' her Daughter fent for her to fee thofe ftrange People, fhe was fo far from complying, that fhe reprov'd her for being fo eafy in admitting thofe fhe knew nothing of. The Adelantado fent *John de Anafco,* with thirty Horfe, and an *Indian* of Quality to defire her to come. When they had travell'd fome Leagues, they fate down under a Tree to eat, and the *Indian* Gentleman being very penfive, put off the Sable Mantle he had on, and one by one drew out of his Quiver the Arrows, which were of Reeds, moft curioufly wrought, headed with Deers-Bones that had three Points, and Fifh-Bones, feather'd Triangularwif., and the Bow was dy'd with colour'd Bituminous Matter, which look'd like Enamel.

mel. The laſt Arrow the *Indian* drew out was headed with Flint, ſhap'd like the Point and Edge of a Dagger. He obſerving, that the *Spaniards* were intent upon obſerving thoſe curious Arrows, cut his own Throat
with that which had the Flint Head, and fell down
dead, which the *Indians* ſaid, they thought he had
done, believing he was going on a Meſſage that was
diſagreeable to the Widow. As they were going on,
one of the *Spaniards* ſaid to *John de Añaſco*, that they
went on blindly to ſeek for a Woman, who they had
heard was remov'd to another Place, to hide herſelf
from them ; that ſince the Adelantado had the Daughter in his Power, he had no Occaſion for the Mother, and that ſince, their Number being ſo ſmall,
they were expos'd to much Danger, it was better to
return to the reſt of the Forces. This Advice being
well lik'd, they turn'd back. Three Days after, the
Adelantado ſent twenty *Spaniards* up the River in two
Canoes, by the Advice of the Daughter, to ſeek for
the Mother, an *Indian* offering to conduct them to
the Place where ſhe was. Thoſe Men remembring
that the two Chriſtian Youths had ſaid, there was
much Gold and Silver in that Province, upon ſearch
found much Copper of a Golden Colour, and great Plates
of Oar, which were very light, and moulder'd like
Earth, was perhaps what deceiv'd the young Men.
A wonderful Quantity of Pearls was found, and the
Lady gave them leave to go to an Houſe they held
as ſacred, being the burial Place of the Nobility, and
to take what Pearls were there, and thoſe in another
Temple near the Town, being the burial Place
of her Forefathers, where they foundgreat Plenty.

WHEN *John de Añaſco* return'd, they found wood-
en Cheſts laid by in the Temple, in which were
the Bodies of the Dead ; for no other uſe being made
of thoſe Temples, or Houſes, they regarded not
the

the ill Scent. In Baskets made of Reeds there were abundance of large and feed Pearls, as alfo Garments for Men and Women, of Furs, and Skins; the King's Officers foon weigh'd five hundred Weight of Pearls. The Adelantado order'd, that the Forces fhould not be encumber'd with Loads, fince half an hundred Weight would be fufficient to fend to the *Havana,* to know their Finenefs and Value; however the Officers defir'd, that fince they were weigh'd, he would permit them to be carry'd, to which he confented, and gave the Captains two Handfuls of them, to make Beads, for they were as large as Peas. Going on to another Town, call'd *Tolomeco,* on the upper Part, oppofite to the Palace, was an Houfe, or Temple, where they found very large Strings of Beads hanging, and others in Chefts, with many very fine Garments, like thofe before-mention'd, and in Rooms about the Charnel, which is the proper Name, there were great Numbers of Pikes, with Copper Heads, that look'd like Gold, Clubs, Staves, and Axes of the fame Metal, Bows, Arrows, Targets, and Breaft-plates. The Adelantado would take none, refolving to march on, and accordingly took his Leave of the Lady of *Cofachiqui,* dividing the Forces into two Parts, for the Conveniency of Provifions, the one under the Adelantado, and the other under *Baltafar de Gallegos.* Thus they mov'd towards the Province of *Chalaque,* and the next Day there was fuch a Storm of Wind, Lightning, and Hail, as big as Pigeon's Eggs, that had not they taken Shelter under the Trees, many of them had perifh'd. The fixth Day they came into the Vale of *Xaula,* a pleafant Country to the North-North-Eaft, and talking of the River at *Cofachiqui,* the Sailors faid, They believ'd it to be the fame that on the Coaft of the North-Sea is call'd St. *Ellen's,* and according to the Computation of four Leagues a Day's March, it appear'd that the

Forces

Forces had advanc'd from *Apalache* to *Xaula* two hundred Leagues, which with a hundred and fifty from the Bay of the Holy Ghost to *Apalache*, made four hundred and ten Leagues. In the Province of *Cofachiqui* there were many foreign *Indian* Slaves, taken in War, whom they put to tilling the Ground, and other Sorts of Labour, and that they might not run away, they us'd to cut their Heels, or some Sinews in their Legs, so that they were all Lame.

C H A P. IV.

Continuation of the Progress of Ferdinand de Soto, *in the Province of* Florida.

THE Forces rested a Fortnight in the Vale of *Xaula*, subject to the Lady of *Cofachiqui*, tho' a seperate Province, there being plenty of all Things, and in order to recruit the Horses; after which they march'd one Day, through an agreeable Country, and five over a desert Mountain, tho' not disagreeable, having many Groves, Waters, and Pasture Grounds, the way over it being about twenty Leagues. Four *Indian* Gentlemen went with them by Order of the Lady of *Cofachiqui*, sent to tell the Lord of *Guanale*, that he should be kind to the *Spaniards*, and in case of Refusal to declare War. On their March, *John Terron*, a Foot Soldier pull'd out of a Wallet, a little Bag full of large Pearls, not bor'd, and well colour'd, which he offer'd to an Horseman, who refus'd them, bidding him keep them, for that their
General

General defign'd to fend to *Havana,* where he might
have an Horfe bought for them, to eafe him from
marching a-foot. Hereupon the Owner threw them
out on the Ground, becaufe they were a Trouble
to him, and others pick'd them up, which he afterwards repented, for it was judg'd, that they would
have been worth fix thoufand Ducats in *Spain.* The
Army ftay'd four Days at *Guaxale,* and in
five more reach'd *Tchiaha,* a Town feated in an
Ifland on a River, above five Leagues in Length,
where the General ftill inquiring about the Country,
as was his Cuftom, *Tchiaha* told him, That thirty
Leagues farther there were Mines of yellow Metal,
whereupon two *Spaniards* were fent to view them, and
the Cazique prefented the Adelantado with a long
String of large Pearls, which, if they had not been
bor'd, would have been of extraordinary Value, and the
Adelantado feeming to value them, that Lord told him,
there were very many at the Burial-Place of his Anceftors, which if he pleas'd he might freely take. In
return the Adelantado gave him fome Pieces of Sat-
tin and Velvet, which much oblig'd the Cazique.
The next Day Men were fent out to fifh for Oyfters
in the River, and foon brought a great Quantity,
which they laid on the Fire, where they open'd, and
the Pearls were taken out fomewhat damag'd by
the Heat. A Soldier boiling fome of the Oyfters,
faid, That as he was eating them, he had almoft
broke his Teeth with a Pearl as big as an Hazle-Nut,
which he prefented to the Adelantado for his Lady,
becaufe it was bright, and well fhap'd; he refus'd
it, bidding him keep it to buy Horfes, and in return for his good Will, paid the King's Fifth out of
his own Money, which was valu'd at four hundred
Ducats. *Soto* was generous, and knew how to oblige
the Soldiers, making no Diftinction between himfelf
and them, in eating, cloathing, and enduring Hard-

fhips. Thofe that went to the Mines returning, reported that they were of Copper, the Soil fruitful, and that they had been well entertain'd.

The *Spaniards* departing from *Tchiaha*, advanc'd to *Acofte*, where the Lord receiv'd them with ill Looks, and the *Indians* proving refractory, there had like to have enfu'd an open Breach; but the Adelantado prevented it, to continue the Peace he had preferv'd fince his coming from *Apalache.* The next Day the *Indians* became better humour'd, and having contented them, the Adelantado crofs'd the River, where he enter'd into the large Province of *Coza*, very populous and fruitful, the *Spaniards* were receiv'd in a peaceable manner, and march'd one hundred Leagues through it, all the way well treated, and quarter'd. At *Coza*, the Cazique came out to meet the Adelantado, attended by one thoufand *Indians*, wearing Plumes of Feathers, and rich Mantles of Furs. The Town confifted of about five hundred Houfes along the River Side, where they were very much made of, and the Cazique dining one Day with *Ferdinand de Soto*, pray'd him to winter in his Country, which was better Land than that he had pafs'd through, and to eftablifh a Colony in it He return'd many Thanks, and faid, It was requifite for him to know what there was up the Country, for carrying on Trade, and bringing over Seeds and other Neceffaries, for which reafon, he would firft take a View of thofe Provinces, and afterwards accept of his Favour. Having ftay'd there twelve Days, rather to oblige the Lord, than on any other Account, he fet out making towards the Sea, which he had defign'd long before, marching about in a Semi-circle, to come to the Port of *Anchufi.* In five Days he came to *Taliffe*, a Town fortify'd with Intrenchments made of Timber and Earth, on the Frontiers of the Lord of *Tafcaluza*, an Enemy to *Coza*, who, to terrify him, went fo

far

far with the *Spaniards.* Thither came a Son of *Tascaluza*, eighteen Years of Age, and so tall, that no *Spaniard's* Head reach'd above his Breast, who offer'd his Father's Friendship. *Tascaluza* receiv'd the *Spaniards*, sitting on a Chair, after their Manner, with abundance of Men standing about him, and tho' the Commanders came up to pay him Obeysance, no Man stirr'd, till the Adelantado came, when the Cazique stood up, and advanc'd twenty Paces, to meet him. He was taller than his Son, like a Giant, well shap'd, and of a good Aspect. The Forces were well quarter'd and treated, and set out again the third Day, when *Tascaluza* would go with them, and one of the Adelantado's Baggage Horses was pick'd out to carry him, and when mounted, his Feet were not a Span above the Ground, not that he was fat, his Waste being under a Yard, nor old, for he was not above forty.

THEY came to a fortify'd Town, cross'd the River with some Difficulty by reason they were ill furnish'd with Floats, took up their Quarters, and missing two *Spaniards*, suspected they were kill'd, because enquiring of the *Indians* for them, they ask'd in an haughty Manner, whether they had been given to them in keeping. Upon this Jealousy, the Adelantado sent three notable *Spaniards* to take a view of *Mavila*, a League and half from thence, where, it was said the Cazique had assembled a great Number of Men, on Pretence of serving the *Spaniards* the better. Those Discoverers returning, reported, that they had seen no Body by the Way, but that *Mavila* was a fortify'd Town, and they had not seen such another in those Parts. The Adelantado led the Van with one hundred Horse, and one hundred and fifty Foot, *Tascaluza* bearing him Company, he made haste, and came to the Place at Eight in the Morning, the rest of the Troops marching more slowly, by reason of the Peace.

The

The Town confifted of eighty Houfes, but each of them could contain one thoufand Men, feated in a Plain, enclos'd with Piles drove down, and Timbers athwart, ramm'd with long Straw and Earth between the hollow Spaces, fo that it look'd like a Wall fmooth'd with a Mafon's Truel, and at every eighty Paces diftance was a Tower where eight Men could fight, with many Loop-holes, and two Gates, and in the Midft of the Town was a large Square, into which the Lord of *Tafcaluza,* and the Adelantado being come, as foon as alighted, the former faid to the Interpreter, The General fhall take up his Quarters in that Houfe, with as many as he pleafes, and may have his Kitchen in that other; there are Huts and Baracks provided without the Town for the reft. The Adelantado anfwer'd, that as foon as his Major-General came, he would diftribute the Quarters, and then *Tafcaluza* went into an Houfe, where he had commanded his Officers to affemble, in order to kill all the *Spaniards,* as he had intended long before. It was propos'd among thofe People to cut them off as they were divided, before the reft could join thofe in the Town; but their Opinion prevail'd, who advis'd to take them all together, for which Purpofe they had a great Number of Men in the Houfes. When the Meat was drefs'd, *John Ortis,* the Interpreter went to call *Tafcaluza,* but they would not let him in, to deliver his Meffage, whereupon he preffing to have him go fpeedily, out came an *Indian,* in an outragious manner, crying, *What would thefe unmannerly People have with my Lord? Down with thefe Villains, there is no enduring of them.* No fooner had he fpoke thefe Words, but a Bow was put into his Hand, and he cafting his Mantle over his Shoulder, level'd at fome *Spaniards* that were in the Street, but *Baltafar de Gallegos,* who hapned to be by the Door, gave him a cut

on

on the left Shoulder, that clove him down to the Waſte.

THE Moment that the *Indian* was kill'd, the Alarm was given, and above ſeven thouſand of thoſe People ſallying out of the Houſes drove the few *Spaniards* that were in the great Street, out of the Town. As ſoon as *Baltaſar de Gallegos* had given the aforeſaid Cut, an *Indian* Youth, in a Moment let fly ſix or ſeven Arrows at him, which did him no Hurt, becauſe he was in Armour ; after which the young Fellow gave him three or four Strokes on the Helmet, with his Bow, which broke his Head, but he kill'd him with two Thruſts of his Sword. The *Spaniards* that manag'd beſt, ran to mount their Horſes, that wery ty'd, without the Town, others cut their Halters, or Reins, that the *Indians* might not ſhoot them ; thoſe that could not get out, left them ty'd, and they were kill'd by the *Indians*, who plunder'd the Baggage that was come up, and lay about the Plain, waiting for Quarters. The *Spaniards* that could mount, with ſome others that were juſt come, charg'd the *Indians* that were ingag'd with their Infantry, making Room for them to draw up, and then a Troop of Horſe, and a Company of Foot, fell ſo furiouſly upon the *Indians*, that they drove them into the Town, and then attempting to get in at the Gate, there came ſuch a Volley of Arrows and Stones, that they were oblig'd to retire, when the *Indians* ſally'd with ſuch Fury, that they made the *Spaniards* retire two hundred Paces, but without turning their Backs, for therein conſiſted their Safety. They then again gave a freſh Charge, and drove the *Indians* to the Town, not daring to come too near the Wall, and thus the Fight continu'd, gaining and loſing Ground, ſeveral being kill'd and wounded. The *Indians* finding that they had the worſt of it in the open Field, kept in the

Town,

Town, and defended their Walls. The Adelantado alighted, ordering fome Horfemen to do fo, and attack the Place with Targets, when two hundred Men, with their Axes hew'd down the Gate, and rufh'd in, tho' not without much Hazard and Lofs. Others battering the Timber, the Earth that was between them fell out, and thus the hollow Parts, and Ligaments being laid open, they mounted that Way, helping one another, and hafting to fuccour thofe that had gain d the Gate. The *Indians* feeing the *Spaniards* in the Town, which they had look'd upon as impregnable, fought defperately and did harm from the Tops of the Houfes, and Galeries, for which reafon they were fir'd.

Ferdinand de Soto having thus enter'd the Town, like a brave and experienc'd Commander, mounted his Horfe again, and charg'd a Body of the Enemy in the Market-place, killing many with his Spear, but as he rais'd himfelf on his Stirrops to ftrike, an Arrow pierc'd through his Armour, and penetrated into his Buttock, yet he to avoid difcouraging the Men, fought as long as the Action lafted, ftanding all the while upon his Stirrops. Another Arrow pierc'd quite through *Nuño de Tovar*'s Spear, near his Hand, and yet the Staff did not break, but the Arrow being cut off, ferv'd again. The Fire grew fierce in the Houfes, where great Numbers of *Indians* perifh'd. The Fight lafted till Four in the Afternoon, when the *Indians* being fenfible of their own weaknefs, turn'd out the Women, who had fought with the Spears, Swords, and Partefans the *Spaniards* had loft, and fome with Bows and Arrows, as dexteroufly as their Hufbands, and fome with Stones, boldly expofing themfelves to Death. The foremoft of the other *Spanifh* Forces, who were on their March, little thinking what had hapned, hearing the Noife of the Trumpets, Drums, and Shouts, gave the Alarm, for the reft to hafte forward.

ward, and came up towards the latter End of the Engagement. Many *Indians* got over the Wall into the Field, attempting to make Head, but were kill'd. When the Forces were come up, about twelve Horsemen charg'd a Body of Men and Women, that were still fighting in the Market-place, and soon routed them, and thus the fight ended about Sun-setting, when it had lasted nine Hours, being on St. *Luke*'s Day, this Year 1541. The Adelantado order'd the Dead to be bury'd, and the best Care that could be to be taken of the wounded, some of whom dy'd, for want of proper Necessaries, there being no Rowlers, nor Lint, nor Medicines, nor Oyl, for all these Things being among the Baggage, with the spare Cloaths for Winter, had been plunder'd by the *Indians*, and carry'd into the Town, where all was burnt. Forty-eight *Spaniards* were kill'd in the Fight, thirteen more dy'd of their Wounds presently, and twenty-two some time after, so that the whole loss amounted to eighty-three Men, and forty-five Horses, which last were sufficiently lamented, as being their main Strength. Of the *Indians* it was reckned that eleven thousand perish'd, for near four thousand were found without the Town, and among them young *Tascaluza.* The Streets of the Town were so full of dead Bodies, that they were computed to be above three thousand, and it was taken for certain that upwards of four thousand were consum'd by the Fire in the Houses, for above one thousand perish'd in one House, the Fire beginning at the Door, so that they were all stifled. The *Spaniards* riding out to scour the Country, found many that had dy'd of their Wounds four Leagues about the Place. *Tascaluza*'s Body could not be found, whence it was concluded that he perish'd in the Flames, he having premeditated what he did, from the very first Advice he receiv'd of the *Spaniards.* The Women that escap'd,

Y 4   said,

said, that the *Indians* of *Taliffe* complaining becaufe their Lord commanded them to carry the Burdens of the *Spaniards, Tafcaluza* bid them not to be concern'd, for he would foon deliver them up to be their Slaves. This they affirm'd, and added, that they were Strangers, and came thither with their Husbands who had been fummon'd by *Tafcaluza,* promifing to give them Scarlet and Silk Cloaths, Jewels to adorn them at their Dances, and the Horfes, as well as the *Spaniards* themfelves; that all the Women, marry'd and fingle went, being affur'd, that after the Deftruction of the *Spaniards,* there fhould be an extraordinary Feftival celebrated, in Honour of the Sun, who was to affift them. The *Spaniards* fuftain'd another Lofs, which they much lamented, being the burning of three Bufhels of *Spanifh* Wheat, a little Wine, their Chalices, and Veftments for faying Mafs, fo that afterwards they were oblig'd only to read Prayers, and Preach, without any Confecration, and fo they continu'd till they return'd among Chriftians.

DURING a Fortnight they ftay'd at *Mavila,* which was the Name of that Town, making Excurfions into the Country, they found plenty of Provifions, and were inform'd by twenty *Indians* taken Prifoners, that there were none left to take up Arms, becaufe all the braveft Men had been kill'd in the Battle. Here they receiv'd Advice, that *Maldonado,* and *Gomez Arias,* were upon Difcovery along the Coaft, and the Adelantado had Thoughts of Planting a Colony at *Achiufi,* to carry on a Trade with another he intended to found twenty Leagues up the Country, which was obftructed by others, who thought the *Spaniards* too few, confidering the Fiercenefs of the *Florida Indians,* by the Experience of the Battle of *Mavila,* to fubdue fuch warlike People; befides that there was no reafon to run fuch Hazards, without Hopes of any Reward, fince there were no Mines in all the vaft Tract

of

of Land they had travell'd over. This was very per-
plexing to *Ferdinand de Soto*, becaufe he had fpent all
his Subftance, and was afraid that his Men would
forfake him, if he came near the Coaft, when he was
not in a Condition to raife new Forces, whereupon
he refolv'd to penetrate up the Country, and being
difgufted to fee all his Projects difappointed, from that
Time forward never fucceeded in any thing he undertook. When the fick and wounded were in a
Condition to travel, he fet out from *Mavila*, march'd
three Days through a good Country, and enter'd the
Province of *Chioza*, where they would not receive
him in peaceable manner, for the Natives having a-
bandon'd their Town, had taken Poft to defend the
Pafs of a very deep River, that had many craggy Places in it, and foon after above eight thoufand of them
appear'd, feveral Parties of whom came over in Canoes,
and gave Onfets ; but the Adelantado caus'd Trenches
to be made, where the Crofs-bow-men, Musketeers,
and Targeteers lay conceal'd, and when the *Indians*
came over fell in upon their Rear, which having been
done twice, they forbore thofe Attempts. There being no Way to make any Advantage of the *Indians*,
two very large Piraguas were privately built in twelve
Days, and then drawn out of the Wood, by Horfes,
Mules, and the *Spaniards* themfelves, and having laid
Roulers under them, they were launch'd one Morning, before the *Indians* perceiv'd any thing of
it. The Horfes, and forty Musketeers, and Crofs-
bow-men being put aboard each of them, tho' they
us'd the utmoft Diligence in croffing the River, they
were defcry'd by five hundred *Indians*, that were fcou-
ring the Country, who with loud Cries gave the A-
larm to the reft, and they immediately came up to
make good the Pafs. The *Spaniards*, tho' moft of
them wounded, the *Indians* fhooting at a fure Mark,
reach'd the Shore, one of their Piraguas at the Landing-
Place,

Place, but the other having been drove below it, was oblig'd to tug up again. Two Horsemen landing, drove the *Indians* above two hundred Paces from the Landing-Place, and charg'd them four several Times before any Relief came to them, the others being in Confusion without knowing how to Land; till at length, four more Horsemen recover'd the Shore, which made six, and after several Onsets, the Foot Soldiers being all wounded took into a Town there was. The Adelantado pass'd over at the second Time, with sixty Men, when the *Indians* seeing the Number of the *Spaniards* increase, retir'd to a Fort they had, whence they sally'd to skirmish; but the Horsemen killing them with their Spears, the rest at Night quitted that Post.

The *Spaniards* then broke up the Piraguas, keeping the Iron-work, and advanc'd farther, after four Days march arriving at *Chicoza,* a Town well seated between Brooks, with Abundance of Fruit-Trees. There they resolv'd to stay the remaining Part of the Winter, having gather'd all the Provisions they could, made Huts, and fortify'd the Place. Here they continu'd almost two Months in Peace, the Horsemen scouring abroad for Provisions, the *Indians* that hapned to be taken being presently set at Liberty, with some Baubles given them, and Presents sent to their Lords, desiring them to repair to the Town. They return'd Presents of Fruit, intimating that they would go see the Governour, soon after which, the *Indians* began every Night to alarm the *Spaniards,* and when they thought they had kept them long enough watching, three Bodies of them advanc'd about Midnight in very silent manner, till being within one hundred Paces from the Quarters, they discover'd themselves with mighty Shouts, and Noise of their warlike Instruments, and Lights of a certain Plant, which, when shaken, burns like Straw,

then

then fixing Wreaths of it to their Arrows, they fir'd
the Town, the Houfes being all Thatch'd. The
Spaniards not being difmay'd at this Accident, repair'd
regularly to their refpective Pofts, and the Adelantado
was the firft that appear'd with his Head-piece, and
the Cotton Armour call'd an *Efcaupil,* for he always
lay in his Cloaths, and being mounted, and follow'd
by others, they could not come at the Enemy for
the Fire, yet he was the firft that kill'd an *Indian,* for
wherefoever there was any Action he gave a wonderful Example. Some fick *Spaniards* were burnt,
and fome Horfes, but Capt. *Andrew de Vafconcelos,*
with four Horfemen falling in furioufly, made the
Enemy retire, where the Engagement had been
hotteft. The Adelantado being eager to wound an
Indian that particularly fignaliz'd himfelf, lean'd forward fo much to reach him, that he fell from his
Horfe, together with the Saddle, but being bravely
refcu'd, and mounted again, he return'd to the Fight.
At length the *Indians* dreading the *Spanifh* Swords, and
Spears, fled, being purfu'd as far as the Light of the
Fire could extend, and then the Adelantado founded
a Retreat, after having been two Hours in the Action. Forty *Spaniards* were loft, and fifty Horfes,
twenty of them burnt; all the Swine perifh'd alfo in
the Flames, except fome few that broke through the
Enclofure of a Yard, where they were fhut up. Prodigious Shots of Arrows were obferv'd, efpecially one,
that pierc'd both the Blade-Bones of an Horfe, and came
out four Fingers on the farther Side, which was
aftonifhing, tho' many very extraordinary had been
feen before. The Adelantado thought fit to remove
his Quarters to *Chicacolla,* as being a better Place for
the Horfes, but one League diftant, where when
they had fortify'd themfelves, they made Saddles,
Spears, Targets, and Cloaths for themfelves of Goats-
Skins, becaufe all they had was burnt, and there they
                                                                spent

spent the reft of the Winter, enduring much Hard-
fhip, for want of Cloathing, the Weather being very
cold.

C H A P. V.

*A farther Continuation of the Adelanta-
do* Ferdinand de Soto's *Progrefs in*
Florida *in the Year* 1542.

THE *Indians* being fenfible that they had done
the *Spaniards* much Harm, return'd a ain a few
Days after; but the great Rain that fell having
wetted their Bow-Strings, they went off again, as
was own'd by an *Indian* that hapned to be taken;
however they came every Night to give the Alarm,
and always wounded fome Body, notwithftanding that
the Horfemen fcour'd the Country four Leagues
round, who could meet no Natives, and it was
wonderful how thofe People could come from fo far
to make a Difturbance. In that poor Condition,
as has been faid, the *Spaniards* fhifted till about the
latter End of *March* 1542, when they mov'd from
thence, and having march'd four Leagues, the Fore-
runners return'd, faying, They had feen a Fort, in
which there might be about four thoufand Men.
The Adelantado having view'd it, told the Soldiers,
It was requifite to diflodge thofe People, who would
otherwife pefter them with Parties in the Night;
befides, that they were oblig'd to do it to preferve
the Reputation they had gain'd in fo many Provinces.
The Fort was call'd *Alibamo,* being Square, the
Length

Length of each Side four hundred Paces, and the Gates so low, that Horsemen could not ride in, the manner of it like that before describ'd at *Mavila.* The Adelantado commanded three Captains with their Companies, to attack the Gates, those that were best arm'd leading the Van, and as they were just ready to give the Assault, one thousand Men sally'd, adorn'd with Plumes of Feathers, and their Bodies and Faces painted of several Colours, who at the first flight shot five *Spaniards,* three of which Number dy'd of their Wounds. The *Spaniards* to prevent the *Indians* spending more Arrows, clos'd with, drove them to the Gates, and enter'd Pelmel, making a most dreadful Havock with their Swords, as may be imagin'd on naked Men, who in that Distress, threw themselves down from the Walls, and there fell into the Hands of the Horsemen, who stuck them with their Spears. Others endeavour'd to make their Escape by swimming a River that was behind the Fort; and one *Indian* that stay'd without the Wall, call'd to and challeng'd *John de Salinas,* who, tho' his Comrade offer'd to cover him with his Target, refus'd it, thinking it a Shame for two to ingage one. The *Spaniard* shot his Shaft through the *Indian's* Breast, so that he fell, and the *Indian's* Arrow went through *Salinas's* Neck. A Squadron of Horse pass'd the River, and kill'd many, so that the whole Number of the slain was thought to amount to two thousand.

The *Spaniards* now wanted Salt, which was very Prejudicial, for they fell into lingring Fevers, of which some dy'd, and their Bodies stunk so violently, that there was no coming near them. The *Indians* taught them a Remedy against this Evil, which was burning a Sort of Herb, of the Ashes whereof they made a Sort of Lye, dipping what they had to eat in it, like Sauce, and found it preserv'd them. There

was

was much Trouble about Interpreters, becaufe they were forc'd to ufe thirteen or fourteen befides *John Ortiz,* by reafon of the great Diverfity of Languages, in the feveral Provinces; but the Women of the Country when they had been two Months with the *Spaniards* underftood them. Having march'd three Days from *Alibamo,* they came to *Chifca,* upon a River, which they call'd *el Grande,* or the Great, becaufe it was the largeft they had yet feen. Moft of the Inhabitants of this Town were taken, as having been furpriz'd; fome made their Efcape to the Lord's Houfe, which ftood on a Ridge, to which there was no Way up but by Stairs. He was old, and fick, yet got up, and was coming down the Stairs, threatning the *Spaniards* with Death; but his Women, and Servants ftopp'd him. The Place not being proper for the Horfemen, becaufe they had not room to wheel, befides that *Ferdinand de Soto* was always inclin'd to carry on his Defigns by fair means, he very courteoufly offer'd Peace. Above four thoufand *Indians* were drawn together in lefs than three Hours, among whom there was difference in Opinions, fome according to their natural Fiercenefs being for War, to recover their Wives and Children; but the wifer fort, faid it was better to make Peace, by which they might retrieve their Loffes without Blood-fhed, and fave the Deftruction of their Corn, which was then ripe. This Advice prevail'd, and Peace was concluded, upon Condition, that the *Spaniards* fhould not go up to the Lord's Houfe. The Prifoners were fet at Liberty, the Plunder reftor'd, and the *Spaniards* were furnifh'd with Provifions. When they had refted fixteen Days in that Town, for the fake of the fick, and gain'd the Friendfhip of the Cazique, the Forces march'd four Days to find a Place to pafs the River, becaufe all the Banks were clofe wooded, and upright, and tho'

above

above fix thoufand *Indians,* with Abundance of Canoes, appear'd on the other Side to defend that
Bank, it was thought neceffary to go over. The
next Day four *Indians* came, who after paying Ado-
ration to the Sun, and Moon, and their Refpect to
the Adelantado, faid, They came from the Lord of
the Province he was in, to bid him welcome, and
offer his Friendfhip. *Soto* return'd a courteous Anfwer,
and was well fupply'd as long as he ftay'd there;
but the Lord could never be feen, ftill excufing himfelf with want of Health, and it was found, that
this Peace was concluded to fave the Harveft,
which was then ready to be carry'd home. In fifteen Days two large Piraguas were finifh'd to crofs
the River, fome Damage having been receiv'd in
the mean Time by the Canoes plying up and down,
but they return'd it by means of their Men lying
conceal'd behind Trenches. The Piraguas held one
hundred and fifty Foot, and thirty Horfe, who
went aboard them in Sight of the *Indians,* and ply'd
up and down with Oars and Sails, fo that thofe
People being aftonifh'd at thofe great Machines,
abandon'd their Poft. Having pafs'd the River,
they difcover'd a Town of about four hundred
Houfes, feated on high Ridges, near another River,
and about fpacious Fields of *Indian* Wheat, and feveral Sorts of Fruit, where the *Spaniards* were well receiv'd, and the Lord, whofe Name was *Cafquin,* fent
to compliment them. Here they refted fix Days,
and then proceeded up along the Bank of the River,
through a plentiful and populous Country, till they
came to the Lord's Town, who entertain'd the Forces
very willingly.

WHEN the Forces had been three Days at *Cafquin,*
the Lord went to the Adelantado, and after having
made Obeyfance to the Sun, and to him, faid, He
knew the *Spaniards* had a better God than the *Indians,*

dians, since he gave so small a Number Victory over many, for which reason he begg'd, he would pray to him that it might Rain, because they were in want of Water. The Adelantado answer'd, That, tho' all those *Spaniards* were Sinners, they would pray to God to shew his usual Mercy; and then order'd a Cross to be erected on an Hill, whither all the Forces, except only a Party left to guard the Quarters, went in Procession, as did the Cazique, with some *Indians,* the Priests singing the Litanies, and the Soldiers answering; being come to the Cross many Prayers were said, on their Knees, and then they return'd to their Quarters, singing Psalms; above twenty thousand Souls gazing at what the *Spaniards* did from the other Side of the River, now and then giving great Shouts, as it were begging of God to hear them. It pleas'd God to hear their humble Prayers, for at Midnight, such a Rain fell, that the *Indians* were very well satisfy'd, and the Christians return'd Thanks for that Mercy. Nine Days after, they set out from thence, in Company with the Lord, and a great Number of *Indians* carrying Water, and other Necessaries. He had also with him five thousand arm'd *Indians,* because he was at War with the next Cazique, and thought to make use of the Opportunity of the *Spaniards* assisting him. They spent three Days in passing a Morass, and then came in Sight of *Capaha,* which being the Frontier Town to *Casquin,* was fortify'd with a Ditch forty Fathoms wide, and ten in Depth, full of Water, convey'd to it through a Canal from the great River, being the Distance of three Leagues. The Ditch enclos'd three Parts of the Town, the fourth being secur'd with high and thick Palisades. When the Lord of *Capaha* spy'd his Enemies, being unprovided at that Time, he went away in a Canoe along the Canal to an Island he had fortify'd in the great River. Many follow'd him, and the rest perish'd

by

by the Hands of the *Casquines,* who took the Skulls
of thofe they kill'd, to carry them home as Trophies.
They plunder'd the Town, took many Prifoners,
and particularly two beautiful Wives of *Capaha*;
went to the Burial-Place of his Anceftors, tore it
in Pieces, trampled on the Bones of the dead, and
recover'd the Skulls of their own Countrymen, which
were hung up there in Token of Victory. All this
was done before the Adelantado came up, *Cafquin*
having never told him any thing of that Enmity,
who would have burnt the Town and the Burial-
Place, had he not thought it would offend that
Commander, who being told of *Capaha*'s Flight, fent
to offer him Peace by the Prifoners, which he would
not admit, refolving to be reveng'd on his Enemies.
Cafquin being inform'd that the Adelantado was making Preparations againft *Capaha,* defir'd him to ftay
till fixty Canoes arriv'd, that were coming up the
River from his Country, and would be of ufe to
carry on the War againft the Ifland. The Army
march'd with the Front extending a Mile in Length,
the *Cafquines* wafting the Country, and by the Way
found fome of their Countrymen, who were there
in Captivity, and tho' Lame, for, as has been faid,
they did cut their Sinews, that they might not run
away, yet they recover'd their Liberty. Being come
to the Ifland, they found it fortify'd with ftrong
Palifades, and on another Side the Thicknefs of the
Briers and Brambles obftructed their entering. The
Adelantado order'd two hundred of his own Men,
and the *Cafquines* to endeavour to Land. One
Spaniard was there drowned, endeavouring to be
the firft that landed, but the reft behav'd themfelves
fo well, that they gain'd the firft Palifades, which
put the Women and Children into fuch a Confternation that they gave a mighty Skreek. Much Oppofition was made at the fecond Work, wherein con-

VOL. V.   Z   fifted

fifted the Safety of all the Defendants, the *Capaha's* calling the *Cafquin's* Scoundrels, asking them, when they had the Courage before to come to that Place? And threatning, that the Strangers would be gone, and then they fhould pay for all. This ftruck fuch a Terror into the *Cafquins,* that notwithftanding all their Lord's Threats, they fled in the forty Canoes, and would have carry'd off the other twenty, had not two *Spaniards* that were left in each defended them with their Swords.

THE *Spaniards* thus forfaken by the *Indians,* and having no Horfes, began to retire, and when the Enemies would have purfu'd them, *Capaha* would not permit it, thinking that a proper Opportunity to imbrace the Peace he had before rejected. The next Day, without taking any Notice of *Cafquin,* he fent four *Indians* to the Adelantado, to fue for Peace, and Leave for *Capaha* to fee him ; which he was well pleas'd with, excufing himfelf with their Mafters having before refus'd the Peace, and then they all went to the Town. The next Morning *Capaha* came with one hundred *Indians* finely adorn'd after their manner, and before he faw the Adelantado, went to the Burial-Place of his Anceftors, took up their Bones with his own Hands, kifs'd and laid them in the Chefts or Coffins. Being come to the Adelantado they complimented one another, and talk'd long about the Affairs of the Country, of which *Capaha* gave a good Account, tho he was but twenty-fix Years of Age, and then turning to *Cafquin,* faid, *I fuppofe you are now well pleas'd, having feen what you never imagin d ; thank the Power of thefe Chriftians ; but they will be gone, and we fhall underftand one another, I beg of the Sun and Moon to give us good Seafons.* The Adelantado being inform'd of what *Capaha* had fpoken, without giving *Cafquin* Time to anfwer, faid, *He came not into their Countries to add to their Enmity, but to reconcile them.* Having spoken more to that Effect, *Capaha* confented to be Friends, they both din'd with him, after which the two Women that had been taken were reftor'd, with which *Capaha* was pleas'd, and prefented them to the Adelantado, who refufing to accept of them, he bid him give them to whom he pleas'd, for they fhould not ftay with him, whereupon they were admitted. It was thought *Capaha* did it, as not valuing them, becaufe they had been in the Cuftody of others.

THERE was exceffive want of Salt among the Forces, when eight *Indians* that kept among them, faid, There was Plenty of it, and of the Metal they call'd Gold, four Leagues from thence. The Adelantado fent *Ferdinand de Silvera,* and *Peter Moreno* with thofe *Indians,* ordering them to obferve diligently all Particulars of the Country they pafs'd through. Eleven Days after they return'd with fix Loads of Rock-Salt, as clear as Chryftal, which grew naturally, and one Load of fine Copper, faying, the Country they had pafs'd through was barren, and not well inhabited. The Adelantado refolv'd to return to *Cafquin,* in Order to proceed to the Weftward, for he had march'd Northward all the Way from *Mavila,* to remove from the Sea. Having refted five Days at *Cafquin,* they march'd five Days down the River, to the Province of *Quiguate,* where at a Town that was two Days Journey within, the Inhabitants fled, without any Provocation; but they return'd two Days after, and their Lord begg'd Pardon. During their Abfence thofe *Indians* wounded two *Spaniards;* which the Adelantado conniv'd at, being very difcreet in all his Actions. The feventh Day they departed *Quiguate,* and the fifth Day after arriv'd at the Province of *Colima,* ftill down the River, where they were friendly receiv'd, and found another River, the

Z 2   Sand

Sand whereof being Blue, they tasted, and it was salt. They cast some into Water, rubb'd, and then strein'd it, which they boil'd made good Salt, for Joy whereof some eat so much of it, that ten of them dy'd. Departing this Province, which they call'd of Salt, in four Days they came to *Tula*, through Deserts, and upon their approaching a Town, both Men and Women came out to fight, but were repuls'd, and the Soldiers rush'd in with them, and kill'd all, because no one would yield. *Reynoso Cabeza de Vaca* going into an House, five Women that were skulking in a Corner, rush'd out, and would have stifled him, had not two Soldiers accidentally come in, who were oblig'd to kill those Women to rescue him out of their Hands.

THE Adelantado sent Parties of Horse to view the Country, and the *Indians* they took laid themselves on the Ground, saying, *Either kill me, or leave me* ; refusing to give the least Account of any thing. Cows-Hides well dress'd were found, tho' they could never hear from whence they came. There were also other good Skins. Four Days after, the *Indians* before Day, attack'd the *Spaniards* by Surprize, three several Ways, all crying *Tula*, that they might know one another, whilst the *Spaniards* invok'd the Blessed Virgin, and their Patron the Apostle St. *James*, for they had never been in greater Peril. The *Indians* fought outrageously with great Clubs, which had never before been seen in *Florida*. This bloody Battle held till the Sun was up, with such Obstinacy on the Part of the *Indians*, that the *Spaniards* were forc'd to lay aside all Punctilio's of Honour, often submitting to their Inferiors when it was necessary. At length the *Indians* retir'd, and the *Spaniards* did not pursue them, some being wounded, and four kill'd. Whilst the *Spaniards*, according to Custom, were looking upon the Dead, and observing the dreadful Wounds made by their Swords,

Swords, and Spears, an *Indian* ſtarted up from among the dead, and *John de Carranza* running to him, the *Indian* gave him ſuch a Stroke with a Battle-Axe he had got from the Chriſtians, that it clove his Target, and wounded him in the Arm ; *James de Godoy,* came up as to a Man unarm'd, but was himſelf diſabled ; *Francis de Salazar* came on next, and having made ſeveral Paſſes at the *Indian,* who skulk'd behind a Tree, at length receiv'd ſuch a Blow on his Neck, that he dropp'd from his Horſe. The fourth *Spaniard* that came on was *Gonzalo Silveſtre,* who proceeding more cautiouſly, avoided a Blow of the *Indian,* and at the ſame Time with his Sword gave him a back-ſtroke cut on the Forehead, whence ſliding down his Breaſt, cut off his left Hand at the Wriſt ; the Barbarian ruſh'd on to aim at the *Spaniard's* Face, but he warding the Blow with his Target, underneath it with another back-ſtroke cut him almoſt in two at the Waſte. The Adelantado, and many more went to look upon the dead *Indian,* for his Valour, and on Account of the wonderful Cut given him by *Gonzalo Silveſtre,* who in the Year 1570, was at the Court of *Madrid,* and well known for his Valour and Dexterity. After twenty Days the *Spaniards* departed from *Tula,* with only one *Indian* Woman, that would go along with *John Serrano de Leon,* and one Boy with *Chriſtopher de Moſquera.* In two Days the Army came to another Province call'd *Vitangue,* where the Town was abandon'd, and the *Indians* continually were troubleſome ; but becauſe the Situation was good, the Place incloſ'd, there was Proviſion for Men and Horſes, and the Winter advanc'd very ſharp, the Adelantado reſolv'd to ſtay there ; where we muſt leave him till the next Year, to ſpeak of what was doing in other Places, whilſt the Things above-mention'd hapned in *Florida.*

Z 3   C H A P.

C H A P. VI.

Alvar Nuñez Cabeza de Vaca *made Go-*
vernour of the River of Plate ; *his Voy-*
age and Proceedings there.

THE King being inform'd, that *Don Peter de*
Mendoza had dy'd in his Return from the *Ri-*
ver of Plate, and that there was no News of *John de*
Ayolas, whom he hada ppointed his Succeſſor, conſtitute-d
Alvar Nunez Cabeza de Vaca, who was return'd into
Spain, after his Captivity in *Florida*, which has been
before ſpoken of, Governour of the Provinces about
the ſaid River, with the Title of Adelantado, or Lord
Lieutenant. Among his other Inſtructions, it was
ordain'd, That there ſhould be no Lawyers, Experience having ſhown, that they ſow'd Diſcord in thoſe
Countries ; that thoſe who had held Lands five Years,
ſhould be entitled to them for ever ; that the *Spani-*
ards might trade with the *Indians* ; that ſuch as would
might come over into *Span*; that none ſhould be
hindred from writing, or ſending to the King ; that
the Rivers ſhould be in common ; with ſeveral other
Particulars much as in other Places. *Alvar Nuñez* having diſpatch'd his Affairs at Court, went away to *Se-*
vil, where having bought two Ships, and a Caravel,
he put aboard them four hundred Soldiers well equipp'd,
beſides the Sailors, with all proper Stores, and ſail'd
from the Bay of *Cadiz*, on the 2d of *November*, in
the Year 1540. On the 29th of *March* 1541, he
arriv'd at the Iſland of St. *Catherine*, which in is the
Lat. of twenty-ſeven Deg. bare, where he landed
twenty-ſix Horſes he had left of forty he put aboard,
that

that they might recover after the Voyage. Thither repair'd to him F. *Bernard de Armenta*, and F. *Alonſo Lebron, Franciſcan* Friers, who had been preaching to the *Indians* on the Continent. The Caravel was ſent to the *River of Plate*, which return'd without having been able to get in, by reaſon of the bad Weather, but took in nine Soldiers that were fled from *Buenos Ayres*, on Account of the ill Uſage of the Commanders, and gave an Account that *John de Ayolas* returning from his Excurſion to the Port *de la Candelaria*, or of *Candlemas*, where he had left his Ships, on the River *Paraguay*, was ſlain by the *Indians*, and that the City of the *Aſſumption* was founded one hundred and twenty Leagues below the aforeſaid Port, on the Bank of the ſaid River, where were moſt of the *Spaniards*, being about three hundred and fifty Leagues above *Buenos Ayres*; that *Dominick de Irala* was Governour, and that the King's Officers, and the Commanders much miſus'd the *Indians*, and Chriſtians, for which reaſon they had ſtolen that Boat, and were going to give the King an Account of the State of thoſe Provinces. *Alvar Nuñez* conſidering his Voyage by Sea would be tedious, ſent *Peter de Orantes*, with ſome *Spaniards* and *Indians*, to find out the Way to go by Land, who after three Months return'd to him, ſaying, he had croſs'd vaſt Mountains, and a deſert Country, and at length came to the Plain, where the Land begins to be inhabited. On Account of theſe Difficulties, and by the Advice of the Natives, he ſent to diſcover the River *Itabuca*, twenty Leagues from St. *Catherine*'s Iſland, up which he was told, he might come into the inhabited Country.

HAVING found the aforeſaid River, he ſet out to diſcover that Country, on the 8th of *October* 1541, with the beſt Men he had, the twenty-ſix Horſes, and the Mares, taking the two *Franciſcan* Friers; deſigning to make all ſpeed to *Buenos Ayres*, and leaving

Peter

Peter Eſtopinan, to follow him to that Place, with the Ships. The Governour *Alvar Nuñez* travelling along the River *Itabucu,* with two hundred and fifty Muſketeers, and Croſs-bow-Men, endur'd many Hardſhips for the Space of nineteen Days, croſſing many Mountains, and cutting down Woods to make a Paſſage, and having ſpent all their Proviſions in thoſe nineteen Days, thoſe Men were ſo fortunate as to diſcover the firſt Habitations, call'd *del Campo,* or of the Field, or open Country, being the Lordſhip of *Aniriri,* and a Days Journey from thence the Dominion of *Cipoyay,* and next that of *Tocanguazu,* who all gave the Forces a good Reception, furniſhing Proviſions, for which the Governour gave them Shirts, and other *Spaniſh* Goods, wherewith they were well pleas'd. Thoſe People are call'd *Guaranies,* who ſow, and reap *Indian* Wheat twice a Year, have Cazabi always, breed *Spaniſh* Hens and Geeſe, had many Parrots in their Houſes, did eat Human Fleſh, were warlike, and revengeful, and this Country *Alvar Nuñez* call'd the Province of *Vera.* The 2d of *December* he came to the River *Yguazu,* ſignifying Great Water. The next Day, with much Difficulty they paſs'd the River *Tibagi,* which having broad flat Stones at the Bottom, occaſion'd the Horſes to ſlip, and by reaſon of the ſtrong Current, the Men held Hand in Hand to paſs over. They every where found peaceable *Indians,* who ſupply'd them with Proviſions, on Account of *Alvar Nuñez's* courteous Behaviour, and the Preſents he made them, the Fame whereof ſpread through all the Country, and the Natives laid aſide all Fear. The next Day came a Chriſtian *Indian* of *Braſil,* call'd *Michael,* who was going from the City of the *Aſſumption* into his own Country, and gave a good Account of the *Spaniards* of that City, after which, of his own accord, he undertook to guide the Governour to the City of the *Aſſumption ;* whereupon he diſcharg'd the

Indians

Indians of the Ifland of St. *Catherine,* that they might return Home, with Gifts of Shirts, and feveral Toys, that pleas'd them. The *Spanifh* Soldiers being raw, and not us'd to thofe Parts, and the *Indians* very apt to take Offence at fmall Matters, which might prove of ill Confequence ; Orders were given that none fhould trade with them, nor go to their Houfes, or Villages, but only fuch as were in Company with thofe that underftood the Language, and they alone fhould trade. No Horfes having been feen till then in that Country, the *Indians* admiring fuch Beafts, brought them Fowls, Honey, and other Provifions, that they might not be angry. *Alvar Nuñez* acting fo difcreetly, and taking up his Quarters without the Towns, the *Indians* fecurely reforted to him, with their Wives and Children, bringing Provifions from very far, only to fee fuch ftrange Things as the *Spaniards,* and their Horfes.

ONE of the Lords of *Guaranies* came out from his Town very joyfully, with all the Inhabitants to meet the *Spaniards,* bringing Honey, Fowls, Geefe, Meal, and *Indian* Wheat, and they were highly pleas'd with the Knives, Sciffors, and other Toys given them. The 7th of *December* they came to the River *Taguari,* on the Bank whereof ftands the Town *Abangobi,* where they were well entertain'd, and *Alvar Nuñez* always endeavouring to leave the *Indians* well fatisfy'd, the Fame of it fpread abroad, and he was every where kindly receiv'd. Being come to another Town, call'd *Tocanguzir,* he refted a Day, becaufe the Men were fatigu'd, and there the Pilots took an Obfervation, and found the Latitude to be twenty-four Degrees and an half; all this Country very agreeable, and fruitful, with large Plains, Rivers, and Woods. They advanc'd five Days without finding any Inhabitants, enduring very much, by reafon of the large Rivers, and bad Ways, being oblig'd to make many Bridges, and paffing high craggy Mountains, very often cover'd with prodigious thick Reeds, and

Variety

Variety of Trees, so that twenty Men always went before to clear the Way, the Sky being quite hid from them. Having cros'd that Desert, they came to a Town, still of the Race of the *Guaranies,* where they were very affectionately entertain'd, and furnish'd with the above-mention'd Provisions, as also *Batatas,* Flower of Pine-Apple-Kernels, and Fruit, there being abundance of Pine-Trees, so thick, that four Men Hand in Hand cannot grasp them, and they are very tall and strait, the Kernels as big as Acorns, their Shell like that of a Chest-nut, differing in Taste from those of *Spain.* The *Indians* gather, and make Meal of them for their Sustenance. There are Abundance of Swine, and Monkeys, and sometimes the Monkeys as they are feeding throw down the Pine-Apples, the Swine run to eat them, and the Monkeys give horrid Cries on the Trees. In this last Town *Alvar Nunez* resolv'd to rest some Days, being encourag'd to it by the good Usage he found, tho' it prov'd Prejudicial to the Soldiers, who lying still, and feeding plentifully, fell into Fevers, which was not so when they travell'd, and it often hapned, that the sick Men marching two Days recover'd with the Exercise; thus Experience taught them, that the Governour had reason not to be pleas'd that they should rest. The same Day they departed that Town, they came to a very great River, the Current whereof was very rapid, and on its Banks were Groves of Cedar, Cypress, and other Trees. Three Days after passing that River, they proceeded among Towns of those *Guaranies,* by whom they were well us'd, and supply'd. At the End of this good Country they came to thick Woods, and Grounds full of Reeds, in the Hollows of which Reeds, they found white Worms, as long and thick as a Man's Finger, which they did eat fry'd, much fat coming from them, and in the same Reeds there was Water so agreeable, that the Men delighted in it; thus they made amends for the Want they had endur'd in the Desert, where they cros'd two

great

great Rivers, which ran to the Northward. The next
Day having seen no Habitations, they took up at Night
on the Bank of another great River, and the Day
after travell'd through a good Country, having good
Water, and abundance of wild Swine, and Deer,
which the Men kill'd with much Delight. Four
Days more they march'd among Habitations of the
same *Guaranies*, well supply'd with Provisions. The
Francisan Friers going before, and taking the Provisions
the *Indians* gave, to distribute among useless People
that follow'd them, and not desisting, tho' they had
been forbid, the Soldiers were upon the Point of
Mutinying, because of the Loss they sustain'd by it,
for which reason the Governour would have them
part Company, whereat they were so much offended
as to take another Way, but some Days after *Alvar
Nunez* caus'd them to be brought back from an *Indian* Town, to save them from the Danger they were
in. Four Days more were spent in passing several
Rivers, Brooks, and difficult Mountains, every one
of them having a fruitful Vale, a River, and several
Springs, and Groves. These Days they had mov'd
Westward. Still they continu'd among the *Guaranies*, who went stark naked, were generous in furnishing Provisions, stood in much Fear of the Horses, and quak'd when they came near them. They
came to a great River Westward, in twenty-five Deg.
Lat. on the Bank whereof stood a good Town, and
they were inform'd, that all the Length of the River was well inhabited, the Lands well sow'd, with
numerous Breeds of Hens, Geese, and other Birds,
besides Abundance of Swine, Deer, and Dantas;
much Honey, variety of Fruit, and Plenty of Fish
in the River. From this River, call'd *Piqueri*, the
Governour sent two *Indians*, to the City of the
Assumption, to give Notice of his coming, and left
behind him fourteen *Spaniards*, that were sick with
the

the Fatigue of the Journey, recommending them to the *Indians*, that they might be fent to him as foon as recover'd. They advanc'd eight Days through a Defert, till they came to the River *Iguazu*, being the fame they had crofs'd at their firft fetting out from the Coaft of *Brafil*, running Eaft and Weft, and no Habitation on it. Here they were inform'd that this River falls into the *Parana*, call'd the River of *Plate*, and that there the *Indians* had kill'd the *Portuguefes*, fent by *Martin Alonfo de Soufa* to difcover that Country ; whereupon *Alvar Nunez*, imbark'd on fome Canoes he bought of the *Indians*, with eighty Men, and went down the River, ordering the reft of the Men and the Horfes to march by Land till they came to the *Parana*. Being come to a Fall the River makes down vaft high Rocks, the Water making fuch a Noife, that it is heard at a great Diftance, and foaming prodigioufly, they were oblig'd to go afhore and carry their Canoes half a League by Land, beyond the Fall, which was an incredible Labour. Imbarking again, they came to the River *Parana*, and met thofe that went by Land, and at the fame Time a great Number of *Indians*, ftill of the fame Race, with Plumes of Feathers, daub'd and painted after feveral Manners, with their Bows and Arrows, drawn up in a Body, but in much Fright and Confufion. *Alvar Nunez* being acquainted with the Nature of thofe Barbarians, fending Meffengers with Prefents, pacify'd, and brought them to his Friendfhip, fo that they were very affifting to him in paffing the River *Parana*, which was eafily perform'd, joyning together two or three Canoes, for the more Security. This River, where they crofs'd it, was above a Crofs-bow-fhot over, very deep, the Current rapid, for which reafon it has many Whirl-pools. Only one *Spaniard* was drowned, ed, a Canoe finking, and the Stream carry'd him away, fo that he was never feen again. This is what hapned there till the End of the Year 1541; we muft now fee what was doing in other Parts.

The End of the Seventh Book.

THE

THE
General HISTORY
Of the vaſt CONTINENT and ISLANDS of
A M E R I C A, &c.

DECAD IV. BOOK VIII.

C H A P. I.

The Great Marqueſs Cortes *goes over into*
Spain ; *the famous* Don Pedro de Alvarado *kill'd in* New Galicia ; *the Vice-*
roy of Mexico *goes to ſuppreſs the re-*
volted Indians; *City of* Guatemala *de-*
ſtroy'd, and other Miſchiefs done by a
dreadful Tempeſt.

HE Viceroy of *New Spain* refuſing to de-
ſiſt from his Enterprizes in the new Northern Diſcoveries, the Marqueſs *Cortes,* who
thought that his Right, as Captain-Gene-
ral, went away into *Spain,* to ſettle that Affair with
the King, never conſidering that Monarchs ſeldom
care

care to raife any Man fo high as to have caufe to be
jealous of him. Being at Court he profecuted *Nuño de Guzman,* for the many Wrongs he had done
him, and obtain'd Judgment for feveral thoufands of
Pieces of Eight.

AT this fame Time *Don Pedro de Alvarado,* fo famous in this Hiftory, under *Cortes,* having obtain'd
of the King a Commiffion for making Difcoveries
on the South Sea, to the Weftward, fitted out
twelve large Ships, and two Veffels to row, the one
of twenty, and the other of thirteen Benches,
which he plentifully furnifh'd with all Sorts of
Stores, eight hundred Soldiers, and one hundred and
fifty Horfes, befides a great Number of *Indian* Servants, notwithftanding the Oppofition made by the
Bifhop againft his taking them out of their native
Country. This Fleet he order'd to fail to fome Port
of *New Galicia,* whilft he travell'd by Land to *Mexico,* to concert Meafures with the Viceroy. At the
fame Time it hapned in the Kingdom of *New Galicia,* that the Towns of *Suchipilan, Apozol, Xalpa,*
and others, in the Diftrict of the *Spanifh* Town of
Guadalajara, the Inhabitants whereof were *Chichimecas,* a barbarous, fierce, and implacable Generation,
to avoid paying their Tributes to their Lords, tho'
very moderately tax'd, revolted, and quitting their
Habitations, and Lands, withdrew to the Tops
of the Mountains call'd *Peñoles.* The firft they
fortify'd themfelves on, was that of *Mixtan,* the fecond *Nuchiztlan,* the third *Acatique,*
and the fourth *Cuina.* Hereupon Captain *Chriftopher de Onate,* who was Deputy-Governour to
Francis Vafquez de Cornado, gather'd about forty
Horfe, and as many Foot, with fome friendly *Indians,* and march'd from *Guadalajara,* to the *Peñol,* or
Rock of *Mixtan,* where he us'd all fair Means to
reduce thofe People, who being perfect Savages,

murder'd

murder'd a *Francifcan* Frier that went to offer them
Peace, and Pardon, and afterwards, having engag'd
their Faith that they would comply, when they
thought the *Spaniards* in profound Security, came
down one Morning, before Break of Day, to the
Number of fifteen thoufand, fell furioufly upon
the *Spaniards*, and tho' they were upon their Guard,
prefs'd fo hard, that they made them turn their
Backs, leaving many dead, befides friendly *Indians*,
and all the Blacks. Thofe that efcap'd making their
Way to *Guadalajara*, fent Advice to *Mechoacan*, *Colima*, *Zacatula*, *the Purification*, *Compoftela*, and other
Spanifh Towns, whence about fifty Horfe came to
their Affiftance, who having been there about a Fortnight, were inform'd by fome *Indian* Friends, that
Tenamaftle, and *Don Francis*, Lords of *Muchiftlan*,
and feveral others were joyn'd, in Order to attack
Guadalajara. They that were in the Place, thinking
themfelves too weak to withftand fuch a Number
of *Indians*, and underftanding that *Don Pedro de Alvarado* was then on the Coaft at the Towns of
Avalos, twenty Leagues from them, fent him Advice
of what had hapned. He, being a Man of much
Honour and Worth, and inclin'd to give his Affiftance, where any Danger threatned, fet out immediately with a confiderable Part of his Horfe and
Foot, and in one Night and a Day crofs'd all
the uncooth Defart of *Tonala*, generally reckoned
three Days March, by Reafon of the Badnefs of
the Way, and of the River, the Banks whereof
are inhabited by the *Indians* call'd *Zacatecas*. Being
come to *Guadalajara*, upon Confultation among the
Commanders, it was not thought proper to expect
the *Indians* in that Place, but to meet them, and accordingly coming to the Town of *Muchiztlan*, he
found that the *Indians* were withdrawn to the Mountain. Having taken Quarters in that Town, feveral
Meffengers

Meffengers were fent to offer Peace and Pardon ; but
they perfifting in their Rebellion, it was refolv'd to
attack them on their Rock or Mount, notwithftanding it was high, fteep, and of difficult Accefs, and
the Defendants very numerous, obftinate, ftrong of
Body, able Archers, and very dextrous at cafting
Darts, or long Rods, hardned in the Fire at the Ends,
thofe Men being every where much dreaded, as being cruel beaftly *Chichimecas,* who facrific'd Children,
ripping up their Breafts with Knives made of Flint,
tearing out their Hearts, and eating their Bodies.

THOSE *Indians* pofitively refufing to fubmit, *Alvarado* and the other Officers confidering, that it
would be an Encouragement to them, if they were
left there, order'd Captain *Falcon* to attack the Rock,
with five thoufand *Indians* of *Mechoacan,* commanded by a noble *Indian,* call'd *Don Pedro,* and one hundred *Spanifh* Foot, but not to do it till fupported
by the Horfe ; however Captain *Falcon* being too daring, climb'd the Hill, without ftaying for the Cavalry, and when at the Top, tho' warn'd of his Danger, and charg'd to ftay for them, he rafhly went
on, when he might have been fatisfy'd with the
gaining of that Poft, and the *Indians* being very
numerous, and feeing no Horfemen, waited till the
others were quite up, when marching forward in good
Order to cut off the *Spaniards* and *Mechoacans,* two
feveral Ways, prefs'd fo hard upon them, that the
Cavalry not being able to come in to their Relief,
they were oblig'd to retire, Captain *Falcon* being the
firft Man kill'd, with feven or eight *Spaniards,* and
feveral *Indians,* and the Slaughter would have been
greater, had not the Retreat been regular. The
Rebels not fo fatisfy'd, went down to the Plain,
where, had not the wet Seafon made the Ground
boggy, they would have been fufficiently chaftiz'd ;

but the *Spaniards* did not think fit for that Reafon to engage them, and therefore retir'd to a Country-Houfe call'd *Ayualica*, in the Territory of *Guadalajara*; the *Indians* ftill purfuing to a River, on the other Side whereof is fuch a fteep Afcent, that there is no riding up it, but the Horfes muft be led. *Alvarado* ftaying to bring up the Rear, an Horfe that went before fell, and lighted upon him, who being in Armour, and then grown an heavy Man, could not get out of the Horfe's Way, but was fo bruis'd on the Breaft, that he dy'd within three Days. The *Indians* did not pafs, thinking they had done enough in obliging their Enemies to retire, but return'd to their Mountain. The unfortunate Death of *Alvarado* difappointed any farther Proceedings of his Fleet, Part whereof return'd to *Guatemala*, many of the Men ftaying in *New-Galicia*. The Viceroy of *Mexico* hearing of this Misfortune, and being fenfible that the *Indians* would grow haughty upon it, fent away Captain *Anuncibay*, with fixty Horfe, who arriv'd fafe at *Guadalajara*. The Natives, on the other Part, affembled to the Number of fifteen or fixteen thoufand, under the Command of *Tenamaftle*, who coming near to the Town, drew up in good Order, forming Batallions, with their Files feven Men deep, a Thing never before feen in *New Spain*. They were all ftark naked, according to their Cuftom, having Bows and Arrows, and every Batallion Plumes of feveral Colours. The Archers led the Van, follow'd by thofe that threw Darts, with Clubs, and fharp Swords of Flint. They firft attack'd a ftrong Houfe, where the *Spaniards* were, and after two Hours Fight began to flag, for want of knowing how to carry on the Affault. Upon their falling off, Captain *Anuncibay* fally'd with fifty Horfe, and after an Hour's Difpute, put them to the Rout, fo that they fled into

to the Woods and Corn-Fields, for which Reason they could not be pursu'd far, and yet above one thousand were kill'd, and several taken, who gave an Account, that all the Country was in Arms, and they doubted not but that they would make another Attempt upon the Fort.

THE Viceroy of *Mexico* had resolv'd to go in Person to quell this Rebellion, fearing that those *Chichimecas,* being a bold and barbarous People, and encourag'd with Success, might occasion greater Troubles than had been imagin'd. But his Enterprize hapning another Year shall be referr'd till then, and before we proceed to other Affairs, it will be proper to say something of those People. This Name of *Chichimecas* is *Mexican,* compos'd of *Chichi,* which is a Dog, and *Mecatl,* a String, Cord, or Leash, as if they meant a Dog in a String, or in a Leash ; tho' they are not all call'd by this Name, for there are among them several Nations, Languages, and Appellations ; however they were all of the same Sort, savage and beastly, going naked, only covering their Privities, the Women wearing Deer-Skins hanging down from their Navels to their Knees. They did not live in Towns, or till Land, tho' what they had was very good, but fed upon Deer, Rabbits, Hares, Vermin, and wild Fruit, as Tunas and Mezquit was also Honey, stealing Cows from the *Spaniards,* when they could. They were cruel Thieves and Robbers, their Weapons Bows and Arrows, at which they were very dextrous, but us'd no Poison. These joyn'd with the revolted Troops of *Xalisco,* and being mighty Robbers, as has been said, at first made War in a very cowardly Manner, many of them joyning against one *Spaniard* ; but by Degrees they grew bolder, and lay in wait in Places where the Horses could do little Service, and when they met with any Success,

which

which was generally through the Negligence of the
Spaniards, were wonderful quick in plundering, scarce
ever sparing the Lives of any that fell into their Hands,
fleaing their Heads and Faces alive, and killing the
Women after ravishing them. When they bolted
out of an Ambush, it was done with such Fury
and Noise, as frighted both Men and Horses, which
Consternation is increas'd by knowing, that if they
are vanquish'd, no Man is to expect his Life.

LET us see the Disaster that hapned this same
Year 1541, in the City of *Santiago de Guatemala.*
On the 8th and 9th of *September,* much Rain fell
in that Place, the Season having been very wet long
before, and on *Saturday* the 10th, two Hours after
Night, such a dreadful Storm came down from the
Top of a burning Mountain, which was near by,
with so great an Inundation of Water, driving vast
Stones, Pieces of Timber and Trees before it, that
entring the City it bore down the Walls of the
Houses, and among the rest overturn'd an Oratory,
in the House of the Governour *Don Pedro de Alvarado* abovesaid, to have been unfortunately kill'd in
New Galicia, which kill'd his Lady, and several Servants, and other Persons. Two Thirds of the City
were entirely destroy'd, six hundred *Indians* perish'd,
and a great Number of *Spaniards,* among whom were several of Note, and many were sav'd after a miraculous
Manner, after having been carry'd quite out of the
Place by the Violence of the Current, among whom
some had their Arms or Legs broke, of which they
afterwards dy'd. *Don Francis de la Cueva,* who was
Deputy-Governour, hearing the Noise, as he was
going to Bed, went out, thinking it had been some
Quarrel, but coming into his Court found it full of
Water, then thinking to go to the Assistance of the
Governour *Alvarado*'s Lady, saw the Water so high,
that he concluded the House would be full, whereupon

upon he ran out into the back Yard, where he
was up to the Middle in Mire, not knowing how
to get forward or backward, but at laſt ſaw ſome
bulky Thing, which he found to be a drowned
Horſe, on which he mounted, and ſtay'd there till
Morning. The City was quite ruin'd, and the
Inhabitants who had eſcap'd in ſuch a Fright, that
they were for leaving it, fearing that the Houſes
which were then left ſtanding, would fall at the firſt
Shake; beſides, that the Stones, ſo large that four
Yoak of Oxen could not move ſome of them, carry'd away by the Water, as if they had been Cork,
with the Mire, Timber, and Trees, had ſo fill'd
up all Places, that it ſeem'd impoſſible to cleanſe them.
Of all the Governour's Houſe nothing was left
ſtanding but only his Lady's Bed-chamber; ſo that
had ſhe ſtay'd there ſhe had been ſafe, but ſhe ran
to her Chapel to pray to God. A Cow was ſeen
in the City that hinder'd many from paſſing, abundance of Cattle having fled thither out of the Fields
in the Fright. The ſame Night, to the Eaſtward
of the City, not above three Croſs-bow-ſhot from
it, there was another Eruption of the ſame burning
Mountain, conſiſting of Stones and Trees, which
overthrew all that ſtood in the Way, and kill'd abundance of *Indians,* and Cattle, and had both thoſe E-
ruptions fallen together, not one Man had been left
alive in the City. The next Day, the Biſhop
aſſembled the Inhabitants in the Cathedral, where
after having offer'd up their Prayers to God, he
made a ſhort Sermon, comforting and encouraging
them, ſaying, among other Things, That God had
taken the beſt to himſelf, and given the reſt ſuch
Warning, that they might for the future live ſo,
as never to be afraid to dye. He advis'd them to
faſt *Wedneſday, Friday,* and *Saturday,* to be earneſt in
Prayer, and the Service of God; and in regard that

the

the Inhabitants were then in Mourning for the Death of their Governour, above-mention'd, there being now fo many more to lament, he told them, It was no Time to bewail the Dead, but to endeavour to move God to Mercy. He caus'd the Mourning to be laid afide, and the People to chear up, fince all their Sorrow could not equal fo great a Lofs. This he partly did in Confideration, that too much Dejection and Grief might raife fome pernicious Thoughts among the Natives, to the difturbing of the publick Peace, for which Reafon ftrict Guard was kept; notwithftanding that all the *Indian* Lords, and Caziques in the Country about, came to offer their Affiftance, wherefoever it fhould be neceffary, and to exprefs their Concern and Affliction for fo great a Calamity. Next the *Spaniards* apply'd themfelves to build Huts, or Baracks in the Field, to live in till the Town could be repair'd; where much Wealth was loft, and the King favour'd the City, that it might be the fooner rebuilt, exempting it from all Duties, allowing Sums of Money, and granting other Immunities, with which the Inhabitants were well pleas'd.

C H A P.

C H A P. II.

Vaca de Caſtro *admitted as Governour and Captain-General of* Peru; *marches to* Guamanga, *where he fights, and defeats* Almagro; *ſome Account of the City of* Guamanga.

IT is Time to return to *Peru*, where we left *Vaca de Caſtro*, about the Beginning of the Year 1542, after he had joyn'd the Forces of the Commanders *Alonſo de Alvarado* and *Holguin*, which laſt had conſented to reſign the Poſt of Captain-General, tho' with ſome Reluctancy, as having expected that *Vaca de Caſtro* would have made him his Lieutenant, for the Management of martial Affairs. *Vaca de Caſtro* having aſſembled all the Commanders, and Men of Note, in a ſhort Harangue commended them for having loyally come into the Service of the King, in Oppoſition to thoſe that were diſobedient to his Commands, promis'd they ſhould be rewarded by his Majeſty, and by himſelf, as far as his Power extended. After which, tho' they had ſeen Copies of his Commiſſion, he produc'd the Original for their Satisfaction, whereupon they all cry'd, *Long live the King*, and receiv'd him for their Governour, and Captain-General. At the ſame Time *Don James de Almagro*, having appointed *Chriſtopher de Sotelo* his Major-General, went away to *Cuzco*, where all the Gold and Silver from the Mines of *Porco* was brought him, and all Preparations for War were carry'd on. Upon Advice that *Alonſo*

de

de Alvarado and *Peralvarez Holguin* had joyn'd *Vaca de Caftro*, *Almagro* fent to require him not to take up Arms againft him, but to act as Governour, till the King fhould order otherwife. Then calling together all his Officers, and other Perfons of Diftinction, He put then in mind of his Father's Services to the Crown, the unjuft Death he had been put to, the many Sufferings of themfelves, through the Cruelty of *Pizarro*, which had oblig'd them to kill him in their own Defence, and declar'd, that he had no Intention to faulter in his Duty to his Sovereign, but only to vindicate his own Right, as his Majefty's Governour of the new Kingdom of *Toledo*, which *Vaca de Caftro* had no Authority to take from him, and therefore pray'd that they would ftand by him. His Commiffion being then read, and all concluding that they went upon a juft Caufe, they refolv'd to fupport that Youth, in whom they thought his Father s Virtues were reviv'd, and in order to it they took a folemn Oath, both Commanders and Soldiers, acknowledging him for their Governour, and he promis'd to requite them. It hapned that foon after, *Sotelo*, who, as has been faid, was Major-General to *Almagro*, hang'd a Soldier, for a Murder and Robbery he had committed, whereupon *Garcia de Alvarado*, who was before at Variance with *Sotelo*, took Occafion to pick a Quarrel with, and murder'd him bafely. *Almagro* refenting the Lofs of fo able a Commander as *Sotelo*, would have put *Alvarado* to Death, but perceiving he had too many Friends, and that there was no Poffibility of doing Juftice at that Time, by the Advice of thofe he moft confided in, he confented to make him his Captain-General, and acccordingly fent him his Commiffion, which was proclaim'd by Sound of Trumpets. All this was nothing but Falfhood on both Sides, *Alvarado* refolving to murder *Almagro*, and he to deftroy ſtroy *Alvarado,* as he did a few Days after, in his own Houſe, whereupon all was huſht again.

Vaca de Caſtro having taken upon him the Title of Captain-General, as well as Governour, appointed *Paralvarez Holguin* his Major-General, ordering him to march his Army to *Xauxa,* going away himſelf to *Lima,* to ſecure that Place, and raiſe Men and Money; where having given the neceſſary Orders for thoſe Ends, he departed, and join'd the Forces at *Xauxa.* This Vale of *Xauxa* was ſo call'd by the *Spaniards,* becauſe they had their firſt Eſtabliſhment in the *Tambo* of *Atunxauxa,* the Inhabitants of the Vale being call'd *Guamas,* and they are thirty-ſix Leagues from *Lima.* It was ſubdu'd by the Marqueſs *Pizarro* ; the Country is rather Cold than Hot, and has Summer and Winter ; the Plain extends nine Leagues, one over or under ; through it runs a conſiderable River, iſſuing from the Lake of *Chinchacocha,* which neither waters the Land, nor affords Fiſh ; the Paſture is on the upper Grounds ; Mayz, Wheat, Papas, and other Grain thrive plentifully ; there are Breeds of Hens, Sheep, Cows, and Swine ; their wild Game Creatures are Deer, Vicuñas, Guanacos, Foxes, ſmall Lions, Partridges, and Viſachas, which are like Rabbits. The Natives are ingenious, and given to Husbandry. Before they were ſubdu'd by the *Ingas,* the Inhabitants of the two Sides of the River had Wars together, for Lands, and Dominion ; afterwards they learnt the Religion, and Policy of thoſe Monarchs. Their Habit is like the others elſewhere mention'd, only wearing the Mark of Diſtinction on their Heads, to be known from other Nations. There are Silver, Copper, and Lead Mines among them.

Almagro having made the neceſſary Diſpoſitions, mov'd from *Cuzco* to *Xaquixaguana,* where all his Forces rendevouz'd, being very unanimous, and advanc'd in Order, making ſhort Marches, and always upon
their

their Guard ; not eating in their Tents, but in publick, their Provisions being in common, and all Things
very regular ; the Commanders did their Duty, and
exercis'd the Men, for tho' they were good Soldiers,
they thought them too few for what they heard *Vaca de Caſtro* had. It was therefore at firſt concluded
to paſs the Bridge of *Apurima*, and then to turn off
a little, to gain ſome Advantage ; but a Prieſt telling
them, that *Vaca de Caſtro* had not ſo many Men as
was reported, and that they were ill arm'd, the Reſolution was taken to march to *Guamanga*, and fight,
the Men, being all very willing. Accordingly they advanc'd towards *Andaguaylas*, and ſent the Licentiate
Gama, and others, to propoſe an Accommodation, to
which *Vaca de Vaſtro* anſwer'd, That they ſhould ſend
John Balſa, and ſome other prime Perſon to adjuſt
Affairs. From *Bilcas*, *Almagro* ſent *Lope de Ydiaquez*
and *James Nuñez* to treat, with a Letter from himſelf, repreſenting, how much his Father had ſerv'd
the King, how unjuſtly the *Pizarros* had dealt with
him, only to uſurp the Government given him by
the King ; admiring that *Vaca de Caſtro* ſhould eſpouſe
that Party which had acted ſo diſloyally, and proteſt-
ing his full Reſolution never to depart from his Duty to his Sovereign. The Commanders alſo writ a
Letter, complaining of his Partiality, in rejecting them
as if they had oppos'd their Sovereign, declaring themſelves Loyal Subjects, and praying that all Things
might be amicably adjuſted, to prevent the Miſchiefs
that muſt otherwiſe enſue, all which would be chargeable upon *Vaca de Caſtro*. Theſe Letters were dated
at *Bilcas*, the 4th of *September* 1542.

Vaca de Caſtro being inform'd that *Almagro* was at
Bilcas, march'd with all poſſible Expedition, and pof-
feſs'd himſelf of *Guamanga*, but incamp'd in the Fields
next to *Bilcas*, whither came to him the two aforeſaid
Meſſengers *Lope de Ydiaquez*, and *James Nuñez* from
Almagro,

Almagro, with the Letters above-mention'd, *Almagro* propoſing that both Parties ſhould disband their Forces, and *Vaca de Caſtro* retire to *Lima*, as Governour of *New Caſtile*, and *Almagro* to *Cuzco*, as Governour of the Kingdom of *New Toledo*, till the King ſhould order otherwiſe. After adviſing with the Commanders, *Vaca de Caſtro* reſolv'd to return a mild Anſwer, only inſiſting that *John Balſa* ſhould be ſent to treat, and he would deliver *Alonſo de Alvarado* a Hoſtage for him. The Meſſengers returning to their Camp, *Vaca de Caſtro* ſent a *Spaniard* thither as a Spy, diſguis'd like an *Indian*, who was taken and hang'd; he alſo ſent a real *Indian* with Letters to *Peter de Candia* to perſwade him to play Booty with the Artillery, which he diſcovering, the two Meſſengers *Ydiaquez* and *Nunez* had like to have loſt their Lives, being ſuſpected of double dealing, becauſe ſuch treacherous Practices were carrying on at the ſame Time that they were treating; but at laſt they were diſmiſs'd with Directions to tell *Vaca de Caſtro*, that ſince he acted ſo baſely, they would decide the Quarrel by Dint of Sword. Then *Almagro* made a ſhort Speech to his Men, putting them in Mind of his Father's Generoſity, and the Affection he had born them all; of the Ingratitude and Villainy of the *Pizarros* towards his ſaid Father, who had been the raiſing of them; encouraging them to dye bravely rather than give Way, and promiſing every Soldier to give him the Eſtate of any Man whoſe Head he ſhould bring, and his Wife, if ſuch Perſon were marry'd. No ſooner had he ceas'd ſpeaking, than the Soldiers holding up their Right Hands, call'd out to be led on to Battle, declaring they would willingly dye for him. Whereupon decamping, they advanc'd to *Pomacacha*, a ſtrong Place. *Vaca de Caſtro*, on the other Hand, fearing leſt the Enemy might make their Way to *Lima*, through *Guaytara*, remov'd his Camp

to the Plain of *Chupas*, where that Night they had
such a Storm of Rain, Thunder, and Snow, that
they thought they should have all perish'd. *Ydiaquez*
and *Nunez* the afore-mention'd Messengers returning
to this Place, with the Resolution of *Almagro*'s Men.
Hereupon *Vaca de Caftro* by Beat of Drum and Sound
of Trumpet declar'd all *Almagro*'s Party Traitors, unless they submitted within six Days, granting all that
belong'd to them to his Soldiers as lawful Booty; tho'
it was reported, that he had no Power from the King
to act in this manner.

Almagro's Council had resolv'd to march along the
rising Ground, and so turning off on the Right to
get into *Guamanga*; but *Vaca de Caftro* having sent
to observe their Motions, order'd Capt. *Nuño de Caftro*
with one hundred Musketeers to secure that Eminence,
being supported by a Troop of Horse, following himself with all the Forces, and it being then past Noon,
a Resolution was taken to fight the next Day. The
same was agreed on by the Adverse Party, and accordingly both Sides prepar'd for the Action. It was a
notable Sight to behold all the adjacent Hills cover'd
with *Indians* of both Sexes, that follow'd the two
Camps, some shrieking, and weeping at the Thoughts
of seeing their Masters in that frightful Conflict, and
others rejoycing, as taking it for some Revenge of the
Wrongs done them, and the Loss of their Liberty.
The next Day, being *Saturday* the 16th of *September*
1542, in the Afternoon, *Almagro*'s Men planted their
Artillery, being sixteen small Pieces of Cannon, as
was thought most Advantageous; their Cavalry form'd
two Wings, the Infantry was drawn up behind the
Artillery, and the Musketeers made a separate Body
by themselves. Their whole Number was about five
hundred and fifty Men, all of invincible Courage;
and among them many Gentlemen of much Experience
in War. *Vaca de Caftro* being inform'd by his Scouts
of

of the Enemy's Posture, order'd his Men to march more to the Right, the Horse on the Wings; being in all above seven hundred Men, and among them one hundred and seventy Musketeers. *Vaca de Castro* would have march'd at the Head of the Horse, but the Commanders would not consent to it, whereupon he form'd a Troop of forty good Horsemen, to remain with himself, as a Reserve, to charge wheresoever there should be occasion. Both Parties drawing near each other, their Musketeers gave Fire, the *Chile* Men crying, *Long live the King, Almagro*; and the others, *Long live the King, Vaca de Castro*; all calling upon St. *James* the Apostle. *Peralvarez Holguin* spurring on to charge the Enemy drop'd down dead, with two Musket-Balls in him, as did Capt. *Ximenez*, and *Gomez de Tordoya* was dangerously wounded. The Battle then beginning, *Almagro*'s Artillery was unadvisedly remov'd, which prov'd their Ruin, for only one Gun did any Harm among the Governour's Men, the rest of their Shot flying over. Then the Horse charg'd with much Resolution, and *Almagro* being told that there was Treachery among the Artillery, ran to *Peter de Candia*, who commanded it, and kill'd him, appearing in all Parts, to encourage his Men, with wonderful Resolution. The Infantry fought desperately at push of Pike, and it is reported, that being quite tir'd, they ceas'd to breathe. Night drew on, and *Alvarado*'s Horse began to flag, which made *Almagro* cry, *Victory, take, and do not kill*; but *Vaca de Castro* perceiving the Distress *Alvarado* was in, charg'd with his Troop, which prov'd the gaining of the Victory, for Numbers began to prevail above Valour. The Sun was then set, and tho' *Almagro* and his Commanders did all that was in the Power of Men, Fortune declar'd for *Vaca de Castro*. When the Action was over, the *Indians* and Blacks kill'd all that they found alive, and Cruelty prevail'd, for the

Prisoners

Prifoners were hack'd, revil'd and abus'd by the Conquerors, which was barbarous Behaviour. *Almagro*
and *James Mendez* fled towards *Cuzco,* the Victors
plunder'd their Camp, and the Faction of *Chile* became
extinct for ever. *Vaca de Caftro* rejoycing for his
Victory, order'd the Religious Men to go affift the
wounded, gave Directions for burying the Dead, and
that Search fhould be made for the Murderers of the
Marquefs *Pizarro*; yet Night coming on, there was
no regard to any thing but plundering. Two hundred and fifty *Spaniards* were kill'd in this Battle, on
both Sides, tho' fome fay more; befides whom about
thirty were afterwards executed, moft of them Commanders and Officers; others were banifh'd to *New
Spain,* but they poffeffing themfelves of the Ship that
carry'd them, put into *Panama,* where they appear'd
before the Royal Court, pleading, that they had never
intended to rebel againft the King, but only to defend themfelves from the Tyranny of *Vaca de
Caftro,* and accordingly were all acquitted by that
Court, which fent the King an Account of the Victory
obtain'd.

PEACE being thus reftor'd, *Vaca de Caftro* thought fit
to difperfe the Forces, and accordingly order'd Capt.
Vergara to return to his Conqueft of the *Bracamoros,*
which he did, as foon as recover'd of a Wound he
had receiv'd in the Battle; and Capt. *John Perez
de Guevara* then at *Lima,* to go fettle a Colony in
the Province of *Moyobamba.* He then went away
himfelf to *Cuzco,* being inform'd that *Almagro* was
gone that Way. The Battle here fpoken of having
been fought near the City of *Guamanga,* it will not
be improper, before we proceed, to fay fomething
of that Place. The firft Foundation of it has been
before mention'd. The Province is call'd *Bilcas,* lying between the Cities of *Cuzco* and *Lima,* the
Climate fo agreeable, that neither Heat nor Cold are
offenfive;

offensive; some Dew falls at the Beginning of the
Night, and in the Morning, but is not troublesome;
the Sky is serene most Part of the Year, the South
Wind prevailing most, and sometimes the North.
In the Neighbourhood there are cold and desert Hills,
which serve for Cattle to graze, and there are hot
Vales, with Rivulets, and Groves in them. Eight
Leagues from it is a Mountain cover'd with Snow
all the Year, from the Top whereof comes a sharp
Wind that occasions Colds, but not very dangerous;
all the Territory is uneven Land, and borders on
the *Andes*, which are eighteen Leagues Eastward of
the City, near which runs a good Brook, from
whence a Trench of Water is drawn to serve the
Houses and Orchards. Tho' the Province generally
wants Water, yet both *Spanish* and *Indian* Wheat
thrive well, as do *European* Trees, Clover-Grass, and
Vines, but subject to Damage by Frost, Hail, and
Fogs. The Natives are of a midling Stature, somewhat brown, their Wits low, inclin'd to mean Things,
flegmatick, and sloathful, in so much that the Magistrates must compel them to work for their own
Advantage. They are crafty, malicious, and have
little Charity among themselves, love to be sincerely
dealt with, but not to do so themselves. The Women dress Meat, and make Garments, and the Men
would willingly be always drunkening; every Clan
has a peculiar Language, but they all speak the general Tongue of *Cuzco.* The City of *Guamanga* is
seated in thirteen Degrees of South Latitude, and it
has been observ'd, that from the 15th of *October* to
the End of the same, the Sun makes no Shade at
Noon. In the Territory there are some notable
Springs; in a Farm belonging to *Peter de Ribera*, is
one that has several Sources, some luke-warm, and
others colder, where those bathe that are troubled
with gross Humours, and the Itch, and some Women

men that had no Children before, have been render'd fruitful by it, and the Water of it fertilizes a
Farm confifting of Vines and *Spanifh* Fruit. Ten
Leagues from the City, in a Defert Place, is another hot Spring, where Perfons troubled with feveral
Diftempers bathe, efpecially for the Pox and Itch;
and a League and half from thence is another very
hot Spring, which heals old Sores, the Itch, and
other Diftempers, and they fweat within the Water.
In this Territory likewife grows the Herb Coca,
fo much us'd by the *Indians,* and before fpoken of;
it affords very good Honey, Dantas like Calves,
Monkeys, large Snakes, which they call *Bobas,* that
is, Fools, Vipers, poifonous Spiders, Mofquitos, or
Gnats, and Pifmires. The Rivers on the *Andes*
produce Fifh, and fome large Crabs, and the Country is fubject to Rain. As for Birds, there are Parrots, Guacamayos, Turkeys, Ring-Doves, Turtles,
three or four Sorts of Partridges, Thrufhes, Felde-
fares, and other native Fowls, very beautiful, and of
feveral Colours, as alfo Hens, Eagles, Haggard Hawks,
Herons, Ravens, and Geefe. There are Abundance
of wholfome Herbs, and one poifonous, call'd *Mio,*
of which if the Cattle happen to eat they dye;
there are alfo Lions, Bears, and fome Tygers, Deer,
Tarugas, which are like Deer, Sheep of the Country, and *Vicuñas,* which have fine Wooll, Foxes,
and thofe Creatures whofe Urine is fo peftilential,
that it ftinks a Musket-Shot off, and the Stench never departs from any Thing it has once fallen upon, penetrating in fuch violent Manner into the
Noftils of Men, as to put fome into Fevers. Here
are many Mines of Gold and Silver, Mercury, Copper, Iron, Lead, Sulphur, and Loadftone. In this
Diftrict are the Quick-filver Mines of *Guancavelica,*
great Quarries of feveral Sorts of hard and foft Mar-
ble, wonderful Salt-Pits, and an Hill of Salt that feems
miracu-

miraculous, for whatſoever is cut off grows again. The City is in the Arch-biſhoprick of *Lima,* has three Pariſh Churches, one Monaſtery of *Dominicans,* and one of *Franciſcans,* with three Sodalities of the Holy Croſs, the Bleſſed Sacrament, and the Conception of our Lady, conſiſting of *Spaniards,* and another of *Indians* of the ſame Conception, and the Blacks have another of St. *Antony.* There is alſo another Monaſtery, which is of *Mercenarians,* and a Nunnery of *Poor Clares;* as likewiſe an Hoſpital for the Native *Indians,* one of the beſt in thoſe Parts.

C H A P. III.

Gonzalo Pizarro *returns from his* Diſcovery ; *his inſolent Behaviour* ; Almagro *put to Death* ; Peace, *and good*
Government reſtor'd in Peru, *by* Vaca
de Caſtro.

GONZALO *Pizarro,* of whom ſo much has been before, and is ſtill to be ſaid, returning at this Time into *Peru,* from the Diſcovery where we left him, enduring much Hunger, after Captain *Orellana* departed from him, it is requiſite here to conduct him back from thoſe Toils, to lay a Foundation for greater Troubles. Thoſe *Spaniards* in their Diſtreſs wiſhing to return into ſome Country among Chriſtians, *Pizarro* march'd ten Days up the River, to the Place where thoſe who had gone thither on the Water had left a Mark, whence he sent *John de Acosta* to view a Town the *Indians* gave Intimation of, which he found well fortify'd on an Eminence, and the Inhabitants in Readiness to oppose the *Spaniards*, charging them with mighty Cries, and tho' they wounded *John de Acosta*, and two others, yet were they repuls'd, and the *Spaniards* enter'd the Town with them, where, to their great Satisfaction, they found Plenty of Provisions, which recruited and comforted them all, but still they had many Days Journey to go through a Desert, in Order to return to *Quito*. In fine, setting out from thence, after many more Miseries endur'd, they came to the Town of *Coca* in a wretched Condition, bare-footed, ragged, and disfigur'd, and it pleas'd God, that the *Indians* receiv'd them in friendly Manner, giving what they had. There they rested ten Days, and then continuing their March, after many Difficulties arriv'd at *Quito*, two Thirds of two hundred and forty *Spaniards* that set out at first, having perish'd with Hunger; and yet they carry'd out with them five thousand Swine, three hundred Horses and Mules, and abundance of Dogs, and Sheep, all which were either eaten, or lost. At *Quito*, *Pizarro* heard of his Brother's Death, and then began to give some Tokens of what he afterwards did, for he blam'd those that had admitted of *Vaca de Castro*, as Governour, saying, that the Government belong'd to him, upon his Brother's Death, and the Victory gain'd at *Chupas* not being as yet known at *Quito*, he prepar'd to go away to *Vaca de Castro*, and having thus brought him into *Peru*, we will now return to what was doing there.

Almagro after his Defeat resolv'd to go take Shelter under *Mango Inga*, and was in the right, but *James Mendez* perswaded him first to go to *Cuzco* to provide Horse-shoes; but when he was gone out of that City he was pursu'd and taken. *Vaca de Castro* soon
after

after came thither, and was receiv'd in triumphant manner; he being very magnificent as well in his Houfhold Furniture, as in his Habit, and Retinue, which gave Occafion to rail at him. He went to the Prifon, to fee *Almagro,* and ask'd, what had mov'd him to rebel againft the King; to which he anfwer'd, that neither he, nor any of his had ever any Thoughts of Rebelling, but thought themfelves in his Service, as acting by his Commiffion. *Vaca de Caftro* reply'd, and concluded, that notwithftanding they were included under the fi ft general Sentence of Death as Tray-tors, he would leave them to the Tryal of the Law. He had began to divide the Lands among the Con-querors, and becaufe it was impoffible to content all Men, he thought fit to difperfe them, fending fome upon new Difcoveries, and Conquefts; and fome Account being then come of the Countries about the River of *Plate,* the Wealth whereof was cry'd up far be-yond the Truth, many were ambitious to go upon that Conqueft, which *Vaca de Caftro* granted to Capt. *James de Rojas* with the Title of Captain-General, and *Philip Gutierrez* as Chief-Juftice, who began to make the neceffary Preparations for that Enterprize. At that Time *Gonzalo Pizarro* was travelling from *Quito,* entertaining more haughty Thoughts than be-came him, and being come to *Lima,* talk'd audaci-oufly, pretending, that the Government belong'd to him, and charging the King with Ingratitude in ha-ving conferr'd it on *Vaca de Caftro.* Thefe Difcour-fes publickly bandy'd about among his Friends, came to the Ears of *Vaca de Caftro,* who immediately com-manded *Pizarro* to repair to him to *Cuzco,* and fent *John Velez de Guevara* to *Lima* to fupprefs any Com-motions there. *Pizarro* comply'd, and *Vaca de Caftro* order'd *Gafpar Rodriguez,* who was Captain of his Guard to have fome Men always privately in Readinefs for what might happen. Next for the Conveniency of

Travellers

Travellers, he ordain'd, that all the neareſt Caziques, and *Spaniſh* Landlords ſhould keep all Neceſſaries, and People in the Tambos, to ſupply all Paſſengers, that they might not be oblig'd to reſort to the *Indians*, and oppreſs them, as was often done on ſuch Occaſions, which he prohibited for the future under ſuch ſevere Penalties, that it was ſpunctually obſerv'd, to the great Benefit of the Country. Next he directed Capt. *Gabriel de Rojas* to go ſettle a Colony in the Province of *los Charcas*, becauſe he being a Man of Reputation, many follow'd him, and he thought it neceſſary to diſperſe thoſe unruly Soldiers, who were for any Novelty, eſpecially ſince *Pizarro* was return'd into the Kingdom, and it was reported abroad, that he talk'd audaciouſly, and uſing all means to gain Friends, and they on the other Hand encouraging him in his Folly. *John Velez de Guevara* was not admitted as Governour at *Lima*, but turn'd out of that Place, at which *Vaca de Caſtro* was juſtly offended, who at the ſame Time founded a Colony, call'd *Leon* at *Guanuco*, of which a few Words will be proper in this Place.

THE Situation of this City is good, and reputed very healthy, becauſe of the extraordinary Temperature of the Mornings and Evenings. The Country about it produces plenty of *Spaniſh* and *Indian* Wheat, Vines, Orange, Citron, Lemon, and other Trees carry'd over from *Spain*, beſides abundance of excellent Fruits of the Country, vaſt Store of Plantans, and ſundry Sorts of Pulſe, as alſo large Breeds of Cows, Goats, Horſes, and other Cattle, and no leſs Variety of Fowl; not to ſpeak of the wild Beaſts on the Mountains, all which Conveniencies have cauſ'd the City to thrive and increaſe very much. Add to all which that Great Roads croſs moſt of the Towns in its Territory, where were *Tambos*, or Publick Inns, and Store-houſes of the *Ingas*, well furniſh'd. At

Guanuco

Guanuco was a Royal Palace, of a wonderful Structure, being the Capital of the Provinces next the *Andes*, and near to it was the Temple of the Sun, with a Number of Virgins, and other Ministers, which was so great, that thirty thousand *Indians* were constantly deputed to the Service of it, and hither all the Provinces round about brought their Tribute. The Natives were very brave, and many bloody Battles were fought among themselves, upon trifling Occasions, before they were subdu'd by the *Ingas*, and they had Fortresses on the Tops of Hills for their Security in Time of War. As to Religion, they had Temples, in which they offer'd Sacrifices, and receiv'd Answers from the Devil, who convers'd with those that were appointed for the Purpose. They believ'd the Immortality of the Soul, and bury'd Women and Servants with their Lords, as was practis'd in other Parts, those People looking upon it as a great Happiness to go serve them in the other World, and thus being shut up in great Vaults made for that Purpose, they waited the dreadful Hour of Death, thinking those happy that dy'd first, to go to their Lord in the other World. There were many Fortune-tellers among them, who pretended to know what was signify'd by the Motions of the Stars. The *Conchuchos*, the great Province of *Guailos*, *Tamara*, and *Bombon* are within the Territory of the City of *Leon*, all of them Countries most fertile in Provisions, producing many pleasant and useful Roots, and the Number of Sheep is immense. The Houses were built with Stone, and thatch'd; the Men wore their Mark of Distinction on their Heads, like other Nations. The Sin of Sodom has never been heard of in this Nation, where there are rich Silver Mines.

THUS far in the Year 1542, we now proceed to what hapned in 1543. The Governour *Vaca de Castro* having none but *Almagro*'s Enemies about, the more to juftify his Proceedings, confulted them, what was to be done with him, who readily concluded, that he ought to be put to Death, and accordingly he pafs'd Sentence againft him, from which he appeal'd to the King, but to no Effect; whereupon he prepar'd for his End, with an undaunted Courage, and yet at the fame Time much like a pious Chriftian. In Conclufion, his Head was ftruck off in the Market-place, and his Body bury'd in the Monaftery of the *Mercenarians*, under his Father's, as he had defir'd. He was of a mean Stature, little above twenty-four Years of Age, virtuoufly inclin'd, very underftanding, brave, and a notable Horfeman; generous, and fond of doing good, tho' he was not quite exempt from Faults, as no Man is, but being fuch a hopeful Youth, he was much lamented. *Vaca de Caftro* having ridded himfelf of *Almagro*, apply'd himfelf to execute the King's Inftructions, both in Spirituals, and Temporals. In the firft Place, he took Care of the Converfion of the *Indians*, and by his Perfwafion the *Inga Paul*, Son to *Guaynacava*, and Brother to *Mango*, was baptiz'd, and took the Name of *Chriftopher*, and fome pious Servants of his became Religious Men, and went about *Collao*, inftructing the *Indians* in the Chriftian Doctrine. Befides the Governour erected feveral Schools to that Effect, and order'd the Sons of the Caziques to go to them. He publifh'd good Ordinances for preferving the Liberty of the *Indians*, and the regulating of them, by which they were eas'd of many Burdens, the Licencioufnefs of the Wars had brought upon them. He fupprefs'd all Vagabonds and idle Perfons, and prohibited quartering upon the Natives, whereupon many of them came to fettle at *Cuzco*, and in other Towns, by which means the Country was till'd, and the Roads render'd fafe. He fought out two Daughters of the *Inga Atahualpa*, and two of *Guaynacava*, whom he marry'd

to

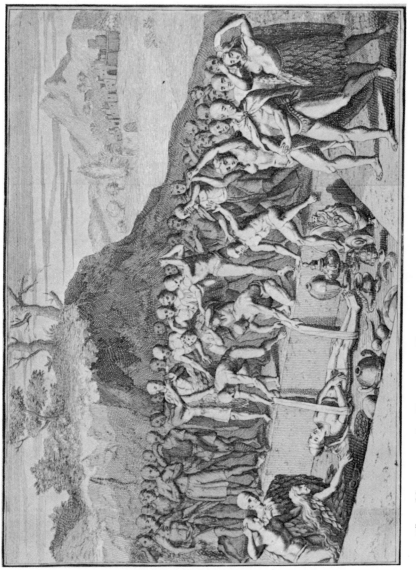

The Manner of Interring the Grandees of Peru

to *Spanish* Gentlemen, after inftrudting, and baptizing them ; retrench'd fome Diftributions of Lands, which he thought extravagant ; appointed the Limits of the feveral Diocefes ; made skilful Pilots afcertain the Latitude of the City of *Cuzco,* which had occafion'd fo many Confufions ; fequefter'd all the Marquefs *Pizarro's* Eftate, till what was owing to the King, and private Perfons were paid ; oblig'd many *Spaniards* to marry ; forbid bringing down the *Indians* from the Mountains to the Plains, becaufe of the Harm that Change of Air did them ; prohibited exceffive Gaming ; reftor'd to the *Indians* many Lands that had been taken from them unjuftly. Thefe Ordinances being executed with Severity, check'd the Licencioufnefs of the Soldiers, the *Indians* liv'd at Eafe, and Trade began to flourifh. Befides, he enquir'd into the Frauds in the Revenue of the Crown, which touching the King's Officers, who had extravagant Eftates, they refented it, and occafion'd fome Infolencies, that feem'd to threaten great Troubles, all which he redrefs'd with much Prudence and Celerity ; a Thing highly valu'd at that Time, when the Libertinifm till then practis'd in thofe Parts, was not quite fupprefs'd, thofe *Spaniards* being very unruly, as us'd to be under no reftraint, through the Fault of the Governours, and upon Occafion of the Civil Wars.

Gonzalo Pizarro was now travelling to *Cuzco,* by Order of the Governour *Vaca de Caftro,* attended by fome of the Soldiers that had been with him in his Expedition to the Province of *Canela,* and others that had join'd him fince, who always difcours'd him about paft Affairs, flattering, and puffing him up, with Perfwafions to fet a Value upon himfelf, and not to fuffer any Iniquity, or Wrong, but be fenfible of the Greatnefs God had rais'd him to, all which fuited well with his Ambition ; which thofe Soldiers, who were fond of Tumults and Mutinies to enrich themfelves,

and

and live lawlefs, perceiving, they proceeded, to put him in Mind, that he had been admitted as Governour of *Quito*, by his Brother's Appointment, which he ought not only to preferve, but to endeavour to be Governour of the whole Kingdom, elfe he would be look'd upon as a Man of a mean Spirit, who had little Regard to the Opportunity Providence put into his Hands, to reward his Friends, and promote himfelf, with what of Right belong'd to him. Hereupon they agreed, and confpir'd together to murder *Vaca de Caftro*, by that means to get the Government into their own Hands; but one *Villalva* being prefent, and abhorring the Defign, as foon as he could, went away before, and gave notice of the Project to *Vaca de Caftro*, who being of a fharp, and vigilant Temper, confulted with his greateft Confidents, refolv'd to keep a better Guard about his Perfon, and fince he had four hundred arm'd Men, that when *Pizarro* came to *Cuzco*, and any Token appear'd of the leaft Commotion, he fhould be immediately feiz'd, and his Head ftruck off, to prevent farther Troubles. When *Pizarro* drew near *Cuzco*, he receiv'd Letters from fome Friends, advifing him to take Care of his Perfon, for that *Vaca de Caftro* intended to kill him. Upon this Advice, he conferr'd with *John de Acofta*, and others, who agreed to kill *Vaca de Caftro* upon a Signal given. Being come into the City, where the Difcovery made by *Villalva* was publick, *Pizarro* affirm'd that he ly'd, and he ftood to what he had faid, naming the Confpirators, fome of whom fled, when they faw the Secret reveal'd. *Pizarro* went to vifit *Vaca de Caftro*, and found a good Guard of Musketeers, and Halberdeers at the Door, and in the Houfe, and *Don Martin de Guzman* had Orders to let none in but only *Pizarro* himfelf. *Vaca de Caftro* receiving him with all outward Demonftrations of Civility, and Affection, difcourfing him familiarly about his Expedition into

the

the Vale of *Canela,* thinking it convenient to deceive that haughty Man by Shows of Affability; and in Conclusion, by way of Advice, bid him to suspect nothing, and to live peaceably. Tales being still carry'd on both Sides, that they intended to murder one another. *Vaca de Castro* by the Advice of his Friends, concluded it was requisite to prevent Disorders that might ensue, and therefore in solemn manner, before a Notary, commanded *Pizarro,* to go away to *los Charcas,* an Inhabitant of which Place he was, and to stay there, without making any Assemblies of People, that might occasion Jealousies, on Pain of being reputed a Traytor, and Forfeiture of his Estate. When this Command had been notify'd, to avoid adding to the Scandal, when *Vaca de Castro* went abroad, *Pizarro* came to speak to him, and he honourably commanded his Guard to stand aside, saying, he had no need of it, where *Don Gonzalo Pizarro* was; who being still more puff'd up with this Honour, went away to live at the Town of *la Plata,* where he had a greater Revenue than the Archbishop of *Toledo.* Having thus brought the Affairs of *Peru* to some seeming Settlement, which yet lasted not long, they may remain in that Condition whilst we proceed to see what was acted in other Parts till the End of the Year 1543, which is the Period of the aforesaid Affairs.

CHAP.

CHAP. IV.

Difcoveries made by George Robledo, *in thofe they call the lower Provinces, which are about the Equinoctial; he founds the Town of* Antiochia, *and is fent Prifoner into* Spain; *other Difcoveries from the New Kingdom of* Granada.

IT has been before mention'd, that the Adelantado *Belalcazar* having taken Poffeffion of the Government of *Popayan,* and turn'd out *Pafqual de Andagoya, George Robedo* fubmitted to him, yet under the Reftriction of fome Proteftations, till the King upon farther Information fhould order otherwife; wherein *Robledo* acted not difcreetly, for that he having been put in Commiffion by *Laurence de Aldana,* and confirm'd by *Pafqual de Andagoya,* could not pretend to any Right to exempt himfelf from the Jurifdiction of the Government of *Popayan,* for having fubdu'd fome new Lands, and *Belalcazar* took fome Umbrage at it, looking upon it as a Defign to divide his Government, under Colour of his having difcover'd that Part which contains the City of *Cartago,* and the Provinces of *Quimbaya, Carrapa, Pucara, Paucura, Arma,* and fome others. *Robledo* after having thus own'd *Belalcazar,* went away into the Province of *Pucara,* where the Tributes laid up for the Lords were receiv'd, and the fame he did at *Paucura,* with eighty Foot, and twenty Horfe he had under him. From thence
he

he fent a Captain, with forty Horfe and Foot, to pafs the fnowy Mountains, and find a Way to the Vale of *Arby*. Thefe Men returning, faid, they had march'd feveral Days over defert Mountains, till at laft one Morning about Break of Day, they attack'd a Town in the Vale, and took fome *Indians*; but that being charg'd by a Multitude of thofe People, they had been forc'd to retire, for want of Horfemen, who could not pafs thofe uncooth Mountains. That Way being thus found impracticable, *Robledo* coafted along the Foot of the Ridge of Mountains, to the Province of *Arma*, and tho' he fent to fummon the Lords, only two came, one an old Man with a long Beard, and grey Hair, a Thing never before feen in the Country, the other an handfome Youth, his Face painted Yellow, Blue, and Black, and his Body fmear'd with fweet fcented Rofin of certain Trees, ftrew'd with a fort of Powder, call'd *Bixa*, which thofe People ufe to defend them from the Sun. The old Man carry'd a Gold Pottage Pot, for a Prefent, and the Youth a long Rod, with many Gold Plates hanging at it. This is a very craggy Country, fome Horfes fell Headlong; the Natives made feveral Excurfions, and took fome *Indians* that were in the Service of the *Spaniards*, whom they immediately kill'd, and either boil'd, or roafted. From *Arma* he went to the Towns *de la Pafqua*, and that they called *Blanco*, fubdu'd the *Indians* that were revolted, and finding that there was no croffing of the Mountains that Way, he travell'd fifteen Leagues through a Defert, till he came into a Province call'd *Zermefana*, which was in Arms, but fome *Indians* being taken, and kindly difmifs'd, they all came in peaceably. Thence he fent *John de Frades*, with fome Men, to difcover *Rio Grande*, or the Great River; who coming to fome Towns, the Inhabitants ran into the River, and pafs'd over to the other Side, fo that he return'd with a few

Prifoners,

Prifoners, and fome Cotton, which was welcome, as ferving to make Armour.

Robledo then proceeded to the Town of *Peras*, where the People being in Arms, the Enfign *Alvaro de Mendoza*, who was fent to reduce them, with fome Foot, becaufe the Horfe could do no Service by reafon of the Cragginefs of the Country, took fome Prifoners, and in his Return was met by four thoufand *Indians* carrying Cords to bind the *Spaniards*, their Flint Tools to cut them in Pieces, and Pots to boil them in ; but being fpoke to by the Interpreters, they concluded a Peace, and the Prifoners were difmifs'd. *Robledo* being inform'd that there were fome Towns at the Foot of the Mountain, fent *John de Frades*, with twelve Men, to find out the Way, who within a few Leagues difcover'd a Town, where the Natives having fpy'd him, affembled to about one thoufand, whereupon he fecur'd himfelf on the Top of a Rock, where fpeaking friendly to them by means of the Interpreter, and they admiring fuch ftrange People, for they had never feen any *Spaniards*, a prime Man came to him, with a Garland of Straw curioufly wrought on his Head, many Plumes of Feathers, and painted, and when he was grown more familiar by talking with the Interpreter, he call'd others, who carry'd the *Spaniards* much Provifion, and the next Day they all went away together to *Robledo*, who proceeded to their Town, which he call'd *de la Sal*, or of Salt, becaufe they found much of it there, made up like Sugar Loaves, fomewhat greyifh, and taken from Salt Springs. This Province being reduc'd, *Robledo* fent *Jerome Lewis Texelo*, with fome Horfe and Foot, to pafs through a Breach there was in the Ridge of the fnowy Mountains, as he did, and at Sun-rifing came into a Vale, where there was a Town, the Inhabitants whereof fpying him, beat the Alarm, and about one thoufand came out to ingage

the

the *Spaniards*, who were twelve Horfe and twenty
Foot, of which Number fix were wounded, and the
Indians admiring the Strangenefs of thofe Men, and
their Valour, fled, the *Spaniards* went into the Town,
and *Texelo* fent *Robledo* advice of what had hapned.
The next Day, the *Indians* return'd more numerous,
fought about an Hour and a half, and fuffer'd fo
much that they came no more. Their Weapons were
Darts, made of Palm-Tree Wood hardned at the Fire,
Macanas of the fame, Slings, and Eftolicas, which are
Rods they caft ftuck in a Stick, too Spears long, with
which they caft them out, and they fly like Arrows.
Robledo then came, having been inform'd, that there
was plenty of Provifions, as Mayz, Kidney-Beans,
Rabbits, dumb Dogs, and Fruit. This Province was
call'd *Aburra*, and the *Spaniards* gave it the Name of
the Vale of St. *Bartholomew.* In this Province fome
Indians hang'd themfelves in their own Mantles, as two
did in the Houfe where *Robledo* quarter'd, and being
cut down, and ask'd, why they did fo, they anfwer'd,
Becaufe they were frighted to fee the Countenances,
Beards, and Habit of the *Spaniards.* Several Horfe
and Foot were fent to difcover towards *Rio Grande*,
or the great River, and other Ways, ftill in Queft
of the Vale of *Arbi*, and *Robledo* finding nothing but
Deferts, on St. *Bartholomew*'s Day, this Year 1542,
departed that Province of *Aburra*, repafs'd the fnowy
Mountains, and after fix Days Journey through Deferts, they lighted on the River, the Defcent whereof was very craggy, and faw a Town in which there
were Salt Loaves as high as a Man; went down to a-
nother Town, where they took abundance of very
gay Cotton Cloth, with which the Soldiers were
cloath'd, and the Cazique fignify'd, that farther on
there was a very rich and populous Country, with
Graves that had much Gold in them, telling *Robledo*,
the *Indians* there were as thick as the Grafs in the Field,
and

and if he would go thither, he would furnish him
with Guides.

CAPT. *Vallejo* went with fome Men to fee fomething of it, and after travelling eight Days over fuch
cold Mountains, that they thought they fhould have
perifh'd, they came to a River, which was fo deep,
that there was fcarce feeing what was at the Bottom,
and the many Rocks were dreadful, as was the Noife
of the Water among them ; the Bridge over it being a Tree eighty Foot in Length, and thicker than
fix Men's Bodies, lying on a Rock, and from thence
forwards, Wattles made of Ofier, three Spans wide,
with Parapets of the fame, to which they held with
their Hands, but the Horfes not being able to pafs
were left behind. Two Leagues from thence, they
came to another Town on the River, and another
Bridge of Wattles, which being pafs'd, two Leagues
from thence they came to fome Cottages, where the
Inhabitants ftood upon their Guard. Having gain'd
them, from the Eminence they difcover'd large Vales,
and many Dwellings, and a few Hours after heard
much Noife of Horns and Drums, and faw feveral
Bodies of Men, whereupon the *Spaniards* thought
fit to retire to the Bridge, and juft came Time enough
to prevent the *Indians* hewing it afunder, to which
End they had Axes of Flint, yet they charg'd fo
fiercely, that the Bridge being fo narrow that they
could pafs but one by one ; *John de Torres* was kill'd
with the Arrows, and another thrown off the
Bridge, by fhaking it furioufly, and the Stream being
very rapid, and full of Rocks, the *Indians* took him
alive. Others were kill'd in paffing the Bridge, and
all the reft wounded, who made their Way to the
other Bridge, whence they fent to *Robledo*, for Blacks
to carry thofe that could not march, and Provifions,
without which they could not proceed any farther,
being oblig'd in the mean Time to eat the Horfes
that

that had been kill'd by falling. The *Indians* had fuffer'd fo much, that they did not think fit to purfue
the *Spaniards. Robledo* having heard the Account given by Capt. *Vallejo,* refolv'd to enter that Province
with all his Men, which occafion'd much muttering,
they alledging that it was expofing them to certain
Slaughter; whereupon *Robledo* difcours'd them, reprefenting the Honour they fhould gain, their own Po-
verty, how bafe it would be to turn back, the Want
they muft always live in, a Thing intolerable to Men
of high Spirits; that as for himfelf he had enough to
live on at home, and yet would expofe his Perfon,
therefore they might try to pafs another lefs dangerous Way, which, if not found, he would comply
with their Demands; as he afterwards was oblig'd to
do, refolving to crofs the River on Floats made of
thick Reeds, bound together with Withes, and they
fpent eight Days in paffing, becaufe there were only
twelve Swimmers, and thofe who could not fwim,
ty'd two Reeds, or Canes as thick as a Man's Thigh
together at the Ends, feated themfelves between them,
and then one Swimmer before and another behind conducted them over, which was look'd upon as a bold
and defperate Paffage; but by it *Robledo* was eas'd of
his Trouble, for having carry'd thofe Men into a
Place, whence the Retreat was fo difficult, and he
very well rewarded the Inventor of that Method of
carrying them over, being oblig'd to give a good
Account of thofe who had ferv'd him fo faithfully.

WHEN paft the River, they could not proceed
along its Bank, but were forc'd to crofs feveral fteep
Ridges, where two Horfes fell and were kill'd, which
furnifh'd Flefh for fome Days. From one of thofe
Hills, they difcover'd a Province call'd *Curane,* the
Natives whereof ftood upon their Guard in Places of
difficult

difficult Accefs ; but *Robledo* after having offer'd them
Peace, fell upon a great Number of them, killing and
taking many. The Prifoners, by means of the Interpreters acquainted him, that there were feveral Provinces farther on, with whom they were at War, and
us'd to eat one another. Having reprefented to them
how beaftly a Practice that was, and that they ought
to worfhip one only God, with more to that Purpofe,
he difmifs'd them, defiring that they might be Friends,
otherwife he would make War on them, and they pro-
mifs'd to return, with all the Lords. Some Days paffing, and none returning, *Robledo* fent out Capt. *Vallejo,* with fome Men, who took many Prifoners, and
fome of thofe that had been taken before being ask'd,
Why they would not accept of Peace? Anfwer'd,
That their Lord was very powerful, and would not
be a Friend to Chriftians. *Robledo* then advanc'd into
the Provinces of *Hebexico, Penco, Purruto,* and *Guara-
my,* and having been twenty Days in thofe Parts return'd to *Curame,* where he had left *Alvaro de Mendoza.* Thence he again went back to *Hebexico,* and
thinking he had difcover'd enough, propos'd to fettle
a Colony there, which being acceptable to all, becaufe
they were weary of going through fo many Hardfhips
and Fighting, the fame was perform'd with fome Difficulty, becaufe Provifions were to be got only by
Dint of Sword. The new Town was call'd *Antiochia,* and *Robledo* perceiving, that, tho' he had been
there two Months, the *Indians* would not be brought
to Peace, order'd Capt. *Robledo,* with forty Men to
go burn a Town they call'd *Guamas,* where the Inhabitants being upon their Guard, tho' he attack'd it
before Day, came out with burning Wreaths of Straw,
by the Light whereof the *Spaniards* defeated them,
killing many, and among the reft a Lord call'd *Zuza-
burruco.* The Place being abandon'd, the *Spaniards*
took

took much Gold, Cotton Cloth, and Prifoners, with which he return'd. *Robledo* told the Prifoners, that he did them Harm becaufe they would not accept of Peace. They anfwer'd, That their Lords were againft it, and not they ; becaufe other *Spaniards* had been at *Nori*, and *Buritica* thirty-four Leagues from thence, and done no Harm, and they meant thofe under *John de Badillo* that were in thofe Parts fome Years before. *Antony Pimentel* being fent to reduce the Province of *Pequi*, perform'd it by the Help of the Dogs, becaufe the Horfes were of no ufe by reafon of the Rough-nefs of the Country, and it was wonderful that thofe Dogs knew the *Indians* that were Friends from thofe who were Enemies.

Robledo having founded the Colonies of *Antiochia*, *Cartago*, and St. *Anne of Anzerma*, thought he had done enough to deferve being employ'd by the King, with-out any Subjection to another, and accordingly fet out with twelve Men for *Cartagena* on the 8th of *January* 1542, through the Vales of *Nori*, and the Pro-vince of *Guaca*, thirty Leagues from *Antiochia*, and two Days after over the Mountains of *Abile*, where they loft their Way, and travelling to the Weft-ward, a Black knew a River that falls into that of *Darien*, and being in want of Provifions, they kill'd an Horfe to eat, and fo proceeded till they came to a Field of *Indian* Wheat, which was a great Relief to them. Eight Days after, they found an *Indian* Fifh-ing, who becaufe they underftood not his Language, often repeated St. *Sebaftian*, St. *Sebaftian*, pointing with his Hand towards the Town of that Name, which was fifteen Leagues from thence at the End of the Bay of *Uraba*, and had been founded in the Ter-ritory of *Cartagena* by the Adelantado Don *Pedro de Heredia*. Other *Indians* came up afterwards with their Bows, and the Poifon for their Arrows wrapp'd up

386 The HISTORY of America.

in Leaves, that it might not take wet. They knowing *John de Frades*, who had been in that Country,
ran to embrace him, calling him by his Name, and
furnish'd Hens, *Indian* Wheat, and Fruit. At length
those *Spaniards* came in a very shatter'd Condition to
the Town of St. *Sebaftian de Buena Vifta*, where Capt.
Alonfo de Heredia, Brother to the Adelantado, was Governour, who tho' he admir'd that so small a Number
should pass through so many fierce Nations of *Indians*, inftead of ufing them kindly, feiz'd and robb'd
them of all the Gold they had ; and the Adelantado
coming soon after, form'd a Procefs againft *Robledo*,
pretending that the Town of *Antiochia* was within the
Territory of *Cartagena*, and fent him away Prifoner
into *Spain*. *Robledo*, to prevent farther Mifchief fent
Peter de Zieza to the Court at *Panama* to acquaint
them with what was doing, whence the faid *Zieza*
return'd to *Popayan*, and is the fame that writ the
Hiftory of the Provinces of *Quito* and *Popayan*,
with much Accuracy, and yet he was as unfortunate as many more, in receiving no Reward
for his Labours. When *Don Pedro de Heredia* had
fent away *Robledo* into *Spain*, he went away himfelf to the New City of *Antiochia*, where he feiz'd
the Magiftrates, and declar'd himfelf Governour ;
but *John Cabrera* coming in foon after from *Belalcazar* fecur'd him, and thinking that the Town
was not well feated among thofe craggy Mountains,
remov'd it to the Bank of a River, that runs through
the Vale of *Nore*, where it now is. That done he
carry'd away *Heredia* Prifoner to *Belalcazar*, who
fent him to the Court at *Panama*, to be punifh'd as
an Ufurper of another's Right.

THIS done *Belalcazar* perceiving that the *Indians*
of the Province of *Arma* were not otherwife to
be

be kept under, founded a Town there, which was alfo call'd *Arma*, and *Heredia* being difcharg'd by the Court at *Panama*, return'd with a Refolution to be reveng'd, and accordingly coming back to *Cartagena*, march'd from thence with Horfe and Foot, poffefs'd himfelf of *Antiochia* twice, and was as often turn'd out of it. Whilft thefe Things were in Agitation, Capt. *Ferdinand Perez de Quefada*, being inform'd that beyond the Mountains to the Weftward of the New Kingdom of *Granada*, which is adjoyning to the Parts we have been fpeaking of, there were extraordinary Treafures of Gold, Silver, and Emerauds, fet out from the faid New Kingdom of *Granada*, with two hundred and feventy *Spaniards*, and near two hundred Horfes, and all other Neceffaries for fuch an Enterprize. His firft March was through a very cold Defert, full of Moraffes, and Lands overflow'd, extending fifty Leagues, where fome Servants, and about twenty-five Horfes were loft. Being paft that Solitude, they came into a Vale, call'd of our Lady, where they got fome Provifion, which began already to fall fhort. When pafs'd the Vale, they advanc'd fifty Leagues Southward, along the Ridge of the Mountain, the fame Way *George de Efpira*, Governour of *Venezuela*, had gone before, becaufe the lower Land is apt to be flooded. Beyond that began the long Mountains, running to the Weftward; at the beginning whereof was a Race of *Indians*, call'd *Macos*, the moft agreeable of all that was then difcover'd there, tho' the Inhabitants were not very many, nor rich. Having found nothing to eat fince their coming from the Vale of our Lady, they ftay'd in this Place eight Days; and then came to the River *Papamere*, where is another Generation of *Indians* call'd *Guaipis*, faid to drive a Trade with

the

the People of the Country then fought after, and they gave fuch an Account as incourag'd the Men to continue their Hardfhips. Next they came to another Nation call'd *Choques,* Man-eaters, the Land fomewhat populous, and uneven, through which they travell'd nine Days, as far as *Rio Bermejo,* or the Red River, whence *George de Efpira* turn'd back, the fame being about five hundred Leagues from the North Sea.

WHEN paft this River, they enter'd upon a new Country, which the Guides faid they knew not, and being extraordinary craggy, Difcoverers were fent out, who could find no Way, but one that went up to the Mountain of *Tagaeza,* the fame that had always directed them. Thirty Leagues they travell'd along that uneafy Way, and not being able to proceed, were forc'd to return to the uncooth Plains, along which they march'd feveral Days, without finding any Provifions befides a few Roots, hewing their Way through, and being forc'd to make many Bridges. The Hardfhips continuing, and Food falling fhort, the Soldiers began to ficken apace, and fome dy'd, and thus they came to a Town call'd *del Sacramento,* whither the Difcoverers brought Samples of that Sort of Cinnamon, which has been faid to be carry'd to *Quito,* by which being put in Hopes of fome Eafe, they found themfelves drawn into greater Hardfhips, all that Country being full of Bogs, and Quagmires, without Provifions, and thofe call'd the Cinnamon-Trees extend forty Leagues, and there many Men perifh'd through Hunger. Departing thence, they proceeded to a Town they call'd *de la Fragua,* or of the Forge, where they crofs'd two mighty Rivers, and had fome Rancounters with the *Indians.* The Men being then much fatigu'd, and

the

the Place affording fome Provifions, it was thought
fit to reft there two Months, after which finding
themfelves inclos'd between the Mountains, they
return'd to a River they had pafs'd, not being a-
ble to go along the fame by which they came, becaufe the Lands were all flooded. This River led
them to a Vale within thofe Mountains, call'd *Mo-
coa,* where fome *Indians* that were taken, ᵹ ing a
good Account of what was farther on, fome were
fent to difcover the fame, whilft *Quefada* himfelf, with the reft of the Men, holding on his
Way, came to a Nation, that guarded all the moft
difficult Paffes, and made Stands in thofe Places
where the Horfes could be of no ufe. Thus, with
much Difficulty they went on, ftill hearing much
of a Country call'd *Achibichi,* and being come to
it with incredible Labour, found themfelves in the
Vale of *Cibundoy,* which is in the Territory of the
Town of *Pafto,* under the Government of the A-
delantado *Belalcazar,* having travell'd from their
firft Entrance into the Province of the *Macos* to
the faid Vale two hundred Leagues through Woods,
a Defert, poor, uncooth, and marfhy Country.
Eighty *Spaniards* dy'd in this Progrefs, and the
reft came off fpent, and fickly, it being look'd
upon as a Wonder that they did not all perifh
amidft fuch Hardfhips; cne hundred and ten
Horfes were loft, and almoft all the Servants.
The *Spaniards* were on their Journey from their
firft fetting out till their Arrival in the Vale of
Cibundoy, a Year and four Months, and from
the Entrance of the Woods, the Mountain runs
South to the aforefaid Vale, which they travell'd
on the oppofite Side to that where are the Towns
of *Guacacillo, Popayan,* and *Pafto,* whence Capt.
Quefada return'd to the New Kingdom of *Gra-*

C c 3
nada,

nada, all that heard of that long and dangerous March admiring, that thofe brave Men, in fo long a Time had not mutiny'd, but born all their Sufferings with fuch Refolution.

The End of the Eighth Book.

THE

THE
General HISTORY

Of the vaſt CONTINENT and ISLANDS of

A M E R I C A, &c.

DECAD IV. BOOK IX.

C H A P. I.

What was done at the River of Plate
by the Governour Alvar Nuñez Cabeza de Vaca ; *his Diſcovery up that
River, and ſeveral other Particulars.*

E concluded the laſt Book with the Affairs
of the Countries about the Equinoctial, and
muſt begin this in the Southern Regions
about the famous *River of Plate,* where we
left *Alvar Nuñez Cabeza de Vaca,* the new Governour, on the River *Parana,* haſting towards the City

of the *Affumption*. He arriv'd there on the 11th of *March* 1542, and it was obferv'd, that for fome Leagues before he reach'd it, many *Indians* met him on the Way with Provifions, bidding him welcome in *Spanifh*, and fome of them fo perfect in the Language, that they feem'd to have been bred in *Spain*. The City is feated on the Bank of the River *Paraguay*, in twenty-five Deg. of S. Lat. He was receiv'd with much Satisfaction by all the *Spaniards*, admiring how he had travell'd about three hundred Leagues among *Indians* in fuch peaceable manner, and having produc'd his Commiffion, he was receiv'd as Governour. He confidering that all the Ships which came from *Spain* would directly come to an Anchor at *Buenos Ayres*, where they ought to find a fuitable Reception, fent two Brigantines, with as many Men as was thought Requifite to fettle on that Harbour, the Diftance from which to the *Affumption* is three hundred and fifty Leagues up the River, a dangerous Paffage. Thofe Men fetting out towards the Middle of *April*, he next apply'd himfelf to reduce the Natives to Obedience, to which purpofe he affembled all the Priefts, to whom he caus'd to be read a Letter from the King, laying the good Ufage of the *Indians* on their Confciences. Soon after his Arrival the *Spaniards* made many Complaints againft the King's Officers, a wicked fort of People, who throughout all the *Weft-Indies*, under Colour of fecuring the Royal Revenue of the Crown, committed many Infolencies; however *Alvar Nunez* to take care firft of what was moft neceffary, fummon'd the *Indians* that were in Subjection, whom he difcours'd in the Prefence of the Clergy, and Religious Men, admonifhing them to give Attention to the Priefts, for their Inftruction in the Chriftian Faith, on which depended the Felicity of their Souls hereafter, and their good Ufage in

this

this World, declaring that the King's Will was fuch, and that he was much intent upon it; at the fame charging them to forbear eating Man's Flesh. They anfwer'd, They would readily comply with his Directions, and ever continue Loyal. This Nation of the *Guaranies* by their Language underftand all the other Nations along the *River of Plate,* they were wont to fatten Prifoners taken in War, to eat them, feeding them with all Dainties, and when fit for their Palates, kept great Feftivals with Dancing, as has been faid before of the *Brafilians,* and then devour'd them, with much Jollity. The *Agaces,* on the River *Paraguay,* are a People of a large Stature, and daring, went along the River in Canoes, like Pirates, neither tilling, nor fowing the Ground, making War continually on the *Guaranies,* to exchange Prifoners for Food. The *Spaniards* were firft at War with them, then they concluded a Peace, and broke it; but now being inform'd that *Alvar Nuñez* was come, and apprehending a War, they fent three prime Men, and Peace was again concluded upon good Terms, the chief Article being, that the *Agaces,* who were among the *Guaranies,* fhould ftay there if they pleas'd, and that fuch as of their own free Will defir'd to be Chriftians fhould not be molefted. Another Nation, call'd *Guaycurues,* had made War on the *Indians* that had fubmitted to the Crown of *Spain,* poffeffing their Lands and Fifheries, and the prime *Indians,* who were Chriftians, having made their Complaints againft them, the Governour order'd inquiry to be made into that Affair, and finding it to be as the Plaintiffs had faid, he fent three Priefts, with a Guard of fifty Soldiers, to require thofe People to reftore the Lands they had taken, to fubmit to the King, and give Ear to the Preachers, or elfe he would make War on them. They return'd eight Days after, and reported, that

the

the *Guaycurues* were fo far from complying, that they had committed Hoftil ries, and fome of the Soldiers fhow d the Wounds they had receiv'd. The Governour refolving, no longer to bear with their Infolence, drew together two hundred Musketeers, and Crofsbow-men, and twelve Horfemen, with whom he march'd from the *Affumption* on the 12th of *July,* and proceeded to the Town call'd *Zaguay,* on the Bank of the River, belonging to a Chriftian *Indian,* call'd *Laurence Mormocen,* where many thoufands of *Guaranie Indians* were drawn together, all well arm'd, and equipp'd, to take Part in that War, which was made in Favour of them. They all pafs'd the River by two in the Afternoon, in the Brigantines, and two hundred Canoes brought for that Purpofe.

THE Spies fent to difcover the *Guaycurues* brought word that they were hunting, and knew nothing of the *Spaniards* having pafs'd, whereupon it was refolv'd to march by Night, in order to furprize them when they were all together, which was accordingly done. In the Morning the Charge was given, and tho' thofe *Indians* were ftartled at the Horfes, they fought bravely, being large Men, active, and refolute ; however four hundred Men and Boys were taken, and for as much as it was the Cuftom of the *Guaranies* to return home into their own Country, if they had taken but a Feather from their Enemies, it was then thought requifite to retire, taking fpecial Care that the Prifoners might not be kill'd, the Enemy ftill making fome Attacks. In their return they kill'd abundance of Deer, the *Indians* very much admiring, that the Horfes fhould be fo fwift as to overtake them. Being come to the City of the *Affumption,* they found that *Gonzalo de Mendoça,* who had been left Governour there, with two hundred and fifty *Spaniards,* had fecur'd fix

of

of the *Yaperue Indians,* a Nation that neither fow'd
their Land, nor bred Cattle, and were extraordinary
Runners. *Mendoza* faid, that thofe *Indians* told him,
that their Nation underftanding there was War
made on the *Guaycurues,* defir'd to be at Peace with
the *Spaniards,* and affift them; but that he fufpecting
this to be a treacherous Defign, had detain'd them.
Alvar Nunez having difcours'd each of them apart,
gave them good Words, and fome Gifts, offering to
be their Friend, provided that they did not make
War on the *Guaranies,* who were the King's Subjects,
and fo they went away well pleas'd. *Mendoza* farther
inform'd, that the *Agaces,* with whom Peace had been
before concluded, had, during the Governour's Abfence advanc'd towards the City in Arms; but that
finding they were difcover'd, they had retir'd, and
fell upon the Country Houfes and Land of the Chriftian *Indians,* carrying away many Women; that they
made Inroads every Night, and that the Women they
had given as Hoftages were fled. The Religious
Men, the Commanders, and the Officers of the Crown
having been advis'd with about this Breach of the
Peace, all gave it under their Hands, that War ought
to be made upon thofe *Indians.* The Governour then
order'd all the Prifoners of the *Guaycurues* to appear
before him, and declar'd, it was the King's Will, that
none of them fhould be Slaves, and that thofe who
had any in their Cuftody fhould fecure them, and
conceal none; after which he fent one of them to
call the Prime Men of their Nation, faying, he would
conclude Peace with them. That Meffenger return'd
within four Days, with about twenty of them, who
fitting down upon one Foot, as is their Cuftom,
faid, they had been at War with the *Guaranies,* the
Imperues, the *Agaces,* the *Guatataes,* the *Naperbes,* the
Mayayes, and feveral other Nations, and vanquifh'd
them

them all, and fince they found that the *Spaniards* were braver than themfelves, they were come to fubmit to them. The Governour anfwer'd, He was come thither by Order of the great King of *Spain*, to endeavour to make them Chriftians, that they might be fav'd, and to keep them in Peace, and in cafe they would forbear making War on the *Guaranies* his Friends, he would look upon them as fuch, and difcharge all their Prifoners. They reply'd, that they then fubmitted themfelves to the King, promis'd to be Friends to the *Guaranies*, and would bring Provifions to the City, and obey what Orders fhould be given them. The Peace being concluded, they went away with the Prifoners, well fatisfy'd, coming afterwards in great Numbers once a Week to trade and barter, and never broke the Peace, but were very good Friends.

A few Days after the *Aperues* had been gone, many of them return'd to the Bank of the *Paraguay*; the Governour fent Canoes to bring them over, and they alfo being come in his Prefence, fate down upon one Foot, like peaceable People, which is their Cuftom, faying, That fince the *Guaycurues* had been vanquifh'd, they, and feveral other Nations were afraid, and willing to conclude Peace with, and fubmit to the Conquerors, to which purpofe they brought fome of their Daughters, whom they defir'd the Governour to accept of as Hoftages. *Alvar Nunez* anfwer'd, That he had been fent by the King of *Spain*, to fignify to all Nations, how much it concern'd them to become Chriftians, as the Religious Men would inftruct them; and that, if they would do fo, and be Friends to the *Guaranies*, he would defend them againft their Enemies, and they might come to trade in the City as the *Guaycurues* did. He then receiv'd their Hoftages, and their Act of Submiffion, whereupon

upon they went away well pleas'd; he giving them as he did to all others, Hawks-bells, Axes, Sciffors, Knives, Needles, and fuch like Things; for like a difcreet Man he endeavour'd rather to fubdue thofe Barbarian Nations by fair Means than by Force of Arms. The Affairs at the *Affumption* feeming to be in a peaceable Condition, the Governour fent two other Brigantines, with Supplies of Men, and Neceffaries to *Buenos Ayres* ; and becaufe *Dominick de Irala,* who had been Governour before his coming was a turbulent Perfon, he gave him good Words, promifing to acquaint the King with his good Services, and appointed him to go up the *Paraguay,* with ninety *Spaniards,* in three Brigantines, well furnifh'd with Provifions, for three Months and an half, to make Inquiry along the Shores of what was farther up the Country, and with them went fome chofen Chriftian *Guaranies,* to be fent with three *Spaniards* upon Difcovery. The Brigantines fail'd on the 20th of *November* 1542, and eight Days after gave Notice, that the three *Spaniards* had fet out, with about eight hundred *Indians* from Port *Piedras* ; and twenty Days after thofe three *Spaniards* return'd to the City of the *Affumption,* faying, that when they had travell'd four Days Journey with thofe *Indians,* they fir'd all the Fields they pafs'd through, which was giving Notice to their Enemies, and that befides it being contrary to the Cuftom of fuch as go upon Difcovery, the Captain of the *Indians,* whofe Name was *Aracare,* bid them go back, for the Chriftians were nought, and that feeing them go back, they alfo came away.

UPON this Advice, four Prime Chriftian *Indians* offer'd to go upon that Difcovery, provided that four *Spaniards* would go with them, which the Governour having accepted with Thanks, they gather'd fifteen hundred

hundred *Indians,* went up by Water to Port *Piedras,* and then travell'd thirty Days, through Defert Countries, with much Hunger, and Thirft, when not knowing how to proceed, they refolv'd to return, feeding on Herbs, and drinking the Juice of them. They return'd to the *Affumption,* quite fpent, having fuffer'd much from the *Indian Aracare,* who thereupon was try'd, condemn'd, and hang'd. At this Time arriv'd four Brigantines the Governour had fent to the River of *Parana,* to relieve the *Spaniards,* that were aboard the Ship he had fent from the Ifland of St. *Catherine,* and *Peter de Eftopinan* affirm'd, that all thofe Men had fuffer'd much, and been in Danger of perifhing, by reafon that the Port of *Buenos Ayres* was abandon'd ; that twenty-five Men had gone away to *Brafil* for Want, and all muft have perifh'd, had they not been fo feafonably reliev'd, for that after the Succour arriv'd, they had been attack'd, and five or fix Soldiers wounded, and that the Town of *Buenos Ayres* could not be built becaufe it was Winter, and the Wind and Water carry'd away the mud Walls.

THUS ended the Year 1542, and on the 4th of *February* 1543, a thatch'd Houfe in the City of the *Affumption* taking Fire, the fame was carry'd on by the Wind in fuch Manner, that only two hundred Houfes were fav'd, after which they were rebuilt with mud Walls. After this *Dominick de Irala* return'd with the three Brigantines he had commanded, and faid, he had gone as far as the Country of the *Indians* call'd *Cacones,* who till'd the Land, and bred Hens, that he had march'd three Days Journey up, and liked it, having feen fome Tokens of Gold and Silver ; calling that Province *de los Reyes,* or of the King's, becaufe he arriv'd there on the Feaft of the *Epiphany.* Upon this Relation it was refolv'd to make an Incur-

fion

fion that Way, and in order to it the Governour fent *Gonzalo de Mendoza,* with three Brigantines, to get Provifions among the *Guaranies,* directing him to pay for the fame, and ufe them well. When *Mendoza* was come to Port *Giguy,* the Governour was inform'd by the Interpreters, that two powerful *Indians* were revolted, and obftructed thofe who continu'd loyal from furnifhing Provifions, whereupon *Dominick de Irala,* went with one hundred and fifty Men to reduce them, as he did, partly by Force, and partly by fair Means, the Governour always adhering to the King's Inftructions, which enjoyn'd him to ufe all poffible Methods for gaining thofe People, without declaring War. Provifions were then purchas'd, and when all was ready to proceed on the intended Difcovery, the King's Officers privately induc'd F. *Bernard de Armenta,* and his Companion, to go away to the Sea Coaft, and bring over Letters to the King, complaining of the Government of *Alvar Nuñez,* whom they hated, becaufe he had deliver'd the Soldiers and Inhabitants from the Oppreffion, and Tyranny, and reform'd feveral Abufes, reducing them to Obedience, for which reafon they flander'd all his beft Actions. When *Alvar Nuñez* came to know of this Contrivance, the Friers were gone, but he fent after and fetch'd them back, and inquiring into the Matter, caus'd the King's Officers to be fecur'd, appointing a Judge, and when ready to fet out upon his Expedition, he took two of thofe Officers with him, leaving the other two in the City, but fufpended from the Execution of their Employments, till the King fhould order otherwife. Having thus fettled Affairs, he took four hundred Mufketeers, and Crofs-bowmen, two hundred whereof went in ten Brigantines, and the reft with twelve Horfe by Land, to the Port of *Guaybrañz,* and thus he fet out, leaving Capt.

John

John de Salazar de Espinosa in the City, with above two hundred Musketeers, and Cross-bow-men, and six good Horses. His Departure was on the 8th of *September* 1543, the ten Brigantines being attended by one hundred and twenty Canoes, aboard which were twelve hundred *Indian* Soldiers, very gay, with their Plumes of Feathers, and Plates of bright Metal on their Foreheads, which made a good Show, and they said, that when they fought, the Brightness thereof blinded there Enemies. In a few Days this Fleet arriv'd at the Port of *Guaybiano,* the Boundary of the Nation of the *Guaranies,* and the next Day proceeded to the Port of *Itabitan,* where he found those that went by Land, and there they all imbark'd, with the Horses, and sail'd up the River, very pleasantly, fishing, and landing to hunt, when they kill'd Abundance of Deer, and other wild Creatures. On the 12th of *October* that Fleet arriv'd at Port *Candelaria,* or *Candlemass,* where *John de Ayolas* had landed, and been treacherously kill'd, with eighty *Spaniards,* whilst he was waiting for *Dominick de Irala* to go fetch him off in the Brigantines. Here they made an Observation, and found the Latitude to be twenty Deg. forty Min. South.

To that Port came six *Paraguae Indians,* and ask'd, Whether those were any of the same Christians that had been before in those Parts? Being told, they were not, one of them went to speak to *Alvar Nunez,* and told him, He came from a principal *Indian* of that Country, who desir'd to be his Friend, and had preserv'd all he took from *John de Ayolas,* being about sixty-six Loads carry'd by *Indians* call'd *Chances,* being Plates, Bracelets, Crowns, Hatchets, and small Vessels of Gold, and Silver. *Alvar Nunez,* answer'd, he might assure his Lord, that he forgave all that was past, and would be his Friends, and having given him
some

some Toys, he went away, saying his Lord would
come the next Day. Four Days being past, and no
Body appearing, the Governour's Interpreter, advis'd
him, not to stay, for that they impos'd on him, to
gain Time to retire, and secure themselves, but that
he might follow and overtake them. After eight
Days sail, they discover'd the Track of the *Paragu-
aes*, and found the Bank of the *Paraguay* cover'd with
several Sorts of Fruit and Cassiafistula Trees, which
both *Spaniards* and *Indians* did eat. Having divided
the Fleet into two Parts, the Governour advanc'd
with one of them to the Country of the *Guaxarapos*,
leaving *Gonzalo de Mendoza* with the rest to follow
him slowly, for fear of alarming those People with
so great a Multitude. When come into that Country, some of the Natives appear'd, and Peace was concluded, and there an Observation was taken, and the
Lat. was nineteen Deg. twenty Min. The Natives,
when the River is low, draw near to it, to make
their Advantage of the Fishery, and when the Floods
come down, which is about *January*, they retire up
the Country, because the Water rises six Fathoms
above the Banks, and spread above one hundred
Leagues over the Plains, which happens every Year,
when the Sun departs from their Tropick towards
ours ; and those People when the Water rises a-
bove the Banks, have their Canoes ready, with
Hearths in them, and go away with the Water
whither they please ; and there they dress their Meat
for four Months, which is the Time the Floods
last, land where there is any dry Ground, and
hunt the wild Beasts that fly from the Water, and
as soon as the Water falls, they return to the
Banks of the River, where an infinite Multitude of
Fish remains, which occasions a Stench. *Alvar
Nunez* left those People peaceable, and well satisfy'd,

for they are Savage and Robbers, like Men living on Frontiers.

———————————————

C H A P. II.

Actions and Discoveries of the Gover-nour Alvar Nuñez *in the Province of the River of* Plate *continu'd; till the King's Officers mutiny, and send him Prisoner into* Spain, *where he is honou-rably discharg'd.*

PROCEEDING up the River, they came to a strong Current, that passes between upright Rocks, where they took a Multitude of the Fishes call'd *Dorados,* or Giltbacks, some of them weighing half a Quarter of an hundred Weight, very well tast-ed, fat, and so wholsome, that the Broth of them drank cures the Itch, and Leprosy. On the 25th of *October* they came to a Place where the River divides into three Branches, one of them forming a great Lake, call'd *Rio Negro,* or the Black River, which runs up the Country to the Northward. The other two Branches, meet again, something farther on ; and farther on again they found the Mouth of a River, which runs up the Country to the West-ward, where the End of the *Paraguay* is lost, because of other Rivers, and great Lakes, which are here di-vided, with so many Mouths, that tho' the Natives
are

are continually traverfing them, they can fcarce know all, and are fometimes loft. This River *Alvar Nuñez* now enter'd, is call *Yguatu*, fignifying good Water, and it runs into the Lake, and as before they had gone up againft the Stream, when once in it they went down the Water. *Alvar Nuñez* caus'd feveral Land-Marks, as Trees cut, and three Croffes to be fet up at the Mouth of that River he had enter'd, to direct the Ships which came after him. After eight Days failing, they came to fome Mountains ftanding in the Middle of the River, which are naked, red, big, and round like Bells, fuppos'd to contain much Metal, but no Tryal was made, for want of Tools, and becaufe moft of the Men were fickly. Advancing ftill along the River, they enter'd another Mouth of the fame Lake, that is above a League and half wide, and pafs'd out at another Mouth of it, along an Arm of the fame, clofe by the Continent, whence they proceeded to the Entrance into another Lake, where are the Towns of the *Xacocies,* the *Xaqueffes,* and the *Claueffes,* who receiv'd the Governour in peaceable manner, which was not acceptable to his Men, becaufe Soldiers never love Peace, but the Governor faid, that by means of the peaceable and friendly they were refpected by other Nations ; for if all were Enemies, it would be impoffible to penetrate fo far among thofe People, and keep them in Awe, for which reafon it was convenient to manage dexteroufly, without difcovering any Fear. It would have been requifite to unlade the Brigantines, that they might pafs to Port *Reyes,* becaufe the Waters were fallen, but the *Spaniards* and *Indians* lifted them over the Flat, which reach'd almoft a Musket-fhot and an half. Being come to that Port, they found Abundance of the Natives expecting the Governour, whom they receiv'd with much Joy. He then erected a Chapel to fay

Mafs,

Mafs, fet up a Crofs. took Poffeffion of the Country, and pitch'd the Camp, taking fpecial Care, that neither the *Spaniards,* nor the *Indians* fhould injure the Natives. The Country about Port *Reyes* is fruitful, abounding in Provifions, as *Indian* Wheat, Game and Fifh. The *Indians* there are of a middle Stature, go ftark naked, and have great Holes in their Ears. Here Idolatry was found among them, for they worfhipp'd wooden Idols, and the *Spaniards* were told, that farther up the Country, they had them of Gold and Silver. Upon preaching to them they burnt their Idols, tho' they were afraid of the Devil, yet, after the firft Mafs was faid, they refted fatisfy'd. The Governour inquiring about the Inland Country, in order to proceed thither, was inform'd that a Race of *Indians,* call'd *Xaraies,* five Days Journey diftant by Land, the way bad, and eight Days along the River, had fome Gold and Silver, which they got from the Inland Country, and that they till'd the Ground, and bred Hens, Geefe, and other Creatures. Hereupon he fent *Hector de Acuna* and *Antony Correa* the Interpreters, with ten, or twelve of the Native *Indians,* directing them to fpeak to the Chief of the *Xaraies,* acquainting him, that he would be his Friend, and giving them many Toys to prefent him, and to enquire particularly into the Nature of the Country.

THE next Day Capt. *Gonzalo de Mendoza* arriv'd with the reft of the Fleet, and faid, that the *Guaxarapo Indians,* notwithftanding the Amity concluded with them, had, without any Provocation attack'd the Brigantine commanded by Capt. *Auguftin de Campos,* and kill'd five *Spaniards,* and another endeavouring to make his Efcape had been drowned. Thofe *Indians* foon after went to perfwade their Neighbours at Port *Reyes* to break the Peace with the

Spaniards,

Spaniards, becaufe they were not brave, and had foft Heads, fo that they might eafily kill them. Eight Days after *Hector de Acuña* and *Antony Correa* return'd, faying, they had travell'd over Marfhy Lancs, with much Difficulty, till drawing near the Lands of the *Xaraies,* they met thirty *Indians,* who receiv'd them joyfully, and faid, their Chief had been inform'd of their coming, and fent them Meat ; that without the Towns they found about five hundred *Indians,* very gay, who advanc'd to receive them, and their Lord was fitting in a Cotton Net, encompafs'd by above three hundred *Indians* ftanding, who by means of an Interpreter of the *Guaranie* Language, bid them welcome, adding, that he was defirous to fee the Commander of the Chriftians, and to be his Friend, becaufe he had heard good Tidings of him. When they had deliver'd their Meffage, he anfwer'd, He accepted of the Friendfhip of the Chriftians, and would cultivate it with all the Kindnefs he could do them ; but as for the Inland Country, he knew nothing of it, becaufe it was all Subject to be overflow'd by the rifing of the Rivers ; but that the *Indian* Interpreter had travell'd the Country, whom they might take along with them, to give an Account of what he had feen, and fo they return'd. The *Xaraie Indians* are a People of a good Difpofition, the Men till the Ground and fow their Corn, which the Women reap, and carry Home, and are notable Spinfters of Cotton. Upon this Relation, and that which the *Indian* fent by the Lord gave, *Alvar Nuñez* refolv'd to go upon this Expedition, for which he chofe out three hundred Musketeers and Crofs-bow-men, leaving one hundred *Spaniards* and two hundred *Indians* to guard the Brigantines, under the Command of *John Romero.* The Governour march'd five Days through very thick Woods, till he came to a River, the Water

whereof

whereof was clear, but hot, where the Guide, faid, it was fo long fince he had been that way, and the Woods fo thick, that he knew not how to proceed. At this Time came ten or twelve *Indians,* who faid, they had ftay'd to live there ever fince the laft Wars, and knew nothing of what was farther on; but that in an Houfe hard by there was an *Indian,* who did, who being brought before the Governour, faid, there was fixteen Days Journey to the inhabited Countries they fought after, that the Ways were ftill worfe than thofe they had pafs'd, and that he would willingly guide them, as knowing the Way, tho' he fear'd the *Indians* of that Country would kill him. Having no Provifions for fo long a Journey, and confidering all other Difficulties, it was refolv'd to return to Port *Reyes*; but Capt. *Francis de Ribera* was order'd, with fix *Spaniards,* and fome *Indians,* to go along with the Guide, who knew the Way, as far as *Tapua,* which was the neareft Part of the inhabited Country they fought after.

THE Governour returning to Port *Reyes*; was affur'd by Capt. *John Romero,* that the Natives of that Country, being joyn'd in League with the *Getaxarapos,* had confpir'd to deftroy them, and take the Veffels, in order to which they furnifh'd no Provifions, nor perform'd any Acts of Friendfhip, as they were wont. Some of the Prime Men of that Country coming to *Alvar Nunez,* he admonifh'd them to ftand to their Ingagements, and he would be their Friend; for if they fail'd he would make War on them. They promis'd to continue faithful, and to quit the Alliance with the *Guaxarapos,* whereupon he gave them Caps, and other Things, and they went away well fatisfy'd. Some advis'd him to hang them, for a Terror to others, but he anfwer'd, that tho' they falfify'd their Words, he would not violate his Faith. Then
considering,

confid.ring, that he had there above three thoufand Men, between *Spaniards* and *Indians,* and that there was Provifion only for twelve Days, he fummon'd the Great Men of the Country, and demanded Provifions of them. They anfwer'd, That they had none, but that the *Arrianicocies,* who were nine Leagues from thence had Plenty, and would barter for *Spanifh* Commodities. It being refolv'd in Council, that the Effufion of Blood ought to be avoided, but that they might advance to get Provifions by way of Trade, which, if refus'd, the fame might be taken by Force, the Governour fent Capt. *Gonzalo de Mendoza* with one hundred and twenty *Spaniards,* and fixty *Indian* Archers to feek for Provifions, with ftrict Orders, not to wrong any Body, unlefs it were unavoidable, fuch being the King's Pleafure. Up the River went Capt. *Francis de Ribera,* to the Towns of the *Xarayes* to the fame Purpofe, and with like Inftructions. *Mendoza* fent the Governour Word, that the *Arrianicocies* were in Arms, and not only refus'd to give Provifions, but threatned in a very daring manner; and that having refus'd to give Ear to any Meffage he had fent them, they had been fo terrify'd by only feeing two *Indians* fhot by his Musketeers, that they were fled to the Woods, without hearkning to any thing he could fay, that all Endeavours were us'd to fignify, that he was for making Peace with them; that going then to their Houfes he found great Store of Food, whence he again fent to invite them to return to their Houfes, for as much as he defir'd their Friendfhip; to which they had anfwer'd, That they would not, and had fent for the *Guaxaropos* and the *Guatos* to come to there Affiftance. This is all that hapned there till the End of the Year 1543.

ABOUT the Beginning of 1544, Capt. *Francis de Ribera,* above-mention'd to have been fent to the

Xarayes,

Xarayes, with a Guide, and fix *Spaniards*, return'd,
having been as far as *Tapuaguazu*, where the Guide
faid the populous Country began; and tho' the fix
Spaniards were wounded, all the Men rejoyc'd, having concluded them to be loft, eight of the eleven
Indians that went with them being return'd before,
through the Dread of the Perils they were like to
undergo. *Ribera* faid, that he had travell'd twenty-
one Days, without ceafing, from the Wood, where
the Governour left him, the Way being fo impaffable
by reafon of the Briers, and Brambles, that fome Days
he had not advanc'd above a League, continually
holding on to the Weftward, feeding on Deer, Swine,
and Dantas, which the *Indians* kill'd with their Arrows; for there was great plenty of Game, as there
was Honey, which they found in hollow Trees, as
alfo of Fruit; that the 21ft Day they had crofs'd a
great River, where they caught a delicious Fifh like
an Olave, after which they prefently fell into a new
Track of *Indians*, and following the fame, found great
Stacks of *Indian* Corn, fhown them by an *Indian* that
came out to meet them, having a large Silver Chin
Plate hanging at his under Lip, and Gold Ornaments
in his Ears, who took *Ribera* by the Hand, and fignify'd by Signs, his Language not being underftood,
that they fhould go with him, and when come near
to a Cottage made of Timber and Straw, they faw
the Men and Women carry out what they had into
the Fields, and then from fome large Jars, in which
they laid up their Corn, they drew out Plates, little
Axes, Bracelets, and other Pieces of Silver. That
having caus'd them to fit down, they gave them fome
of their Liquor made of Mayz to drink, out of Ca-
labafhes, or Gourds; that fome Slaves, who ferv'd
them, faid, there were fome Chriftians three Days
Journey from thence among the *Indians* call'd *Payzu-*
zoes; and they fhow'd them *Tapuaguazu*, which is a
very

very large high Rock; after which some painted *Indians* appear'd with their Bows and Arrows; and the Master of that House, who had conducted them to it, taking up his Arms, and several Messengers passing to and fro, he perceiv'd they design'd to kill them, for which reason he advis'd his Comrades to return the same Way they came, not thinking they were safe there; that as they were so doing, tho' they said they were going to call more Christians, above three hundred *Indians* charg'd and pursu'd them into the Wood, all wounded; but the *Indians* durst not adventure any farther, as believing that there had been more Christians, that they return'd from thence the very same Way to Port *Reyes*, being about seventy Leagues; that he had observ'd those *Indians* call'd *Tarapecocies* had much Food, and bred Geese and Hens, like those in *Spain*.

Now all the Men that were at Port *Reyes* began to fall sick of Fevers, occasion'd by the Waters being spoilt by the Flood coming down. The *Socorine*, and *Xaquesse Indians*, seeing the *Spaniards* so sickly, began the War, in Conjunction with the *Guaxarapos*, and one Morning took five young Soldiers, who were gone out a Fishing, with some new converted *Guaranies*, carry'd them to their Town, where they kill'd and eat them, making several other Excursions, in all which they kill'd fifty-eight Christians, whereupon they were declar'd Enemies. At this Time Capt. *Ferdinand de Ribera* return'd with the Vessel he had been in, discovering up the River; and the Country being all overflow'd, there was no making War, or any Discovery, that Inundation continuing four Months. Hereupon he resolv'd to return to the City of the *Assumption*, not permitting any *Indians* to be carry'd away from Port *Reyes*, because the King had so order'd, and
therefore

therefore the *Spaniards* began to bear him ill Will, which would not have been, had he conniv'd at their Crimes, and Breach of the King's Commands, becaufe our corrupt Nature rather inclines us to e-vil than to good. Being come down to the *Af-fumption* in eight Days, whereas he had been two Months going up, he found that Capt. *Salazar*, whom he had left Governour there, had affembled above twenty thoufand *Indians*, with a great Num-ber of Canoes, to invade the *Agaces* both by Land and Water, becaufe they had broken the Peace, and made War on the Chriftians, and their Confe-derates, but all ceas'd at that Time. The Gover-nour had not been above a Fortnight at the *Af-fumption* before the King's Officers, who hated him, becaufe he would not connive at their Info-lencies and Frauds, confpir'd to remove him from the Government, perfwading the Men that had been left in the City, that he intended to take away their *Indians* and Lands, and give them to the fick that came with him, whereupon they broke into his Houfe, he being then fick, feiz'd his Per-fon, and plunder'd all he had. The next Day they appointed *Dominick de Irala*, who had been a chief Ring-leader in the Mutiny, Deputy-Go-vernour, becaufe being a Man of little Worth, he would do all that they fhould direct, and accor-dingly conferr'd all other Employments on their own Creatures, thus ufurping the Regal Authority. Next they gave out, that they would make an In-road, the fame Way *Alvar Nunez* had gone before, to get fome Gold and Silver to fend to the King, that he might pardon their Offence; but the Men would not confent to it, many crying out to have the Governour fet at Liberty, for which reafon, the King's Officers and their Adherents mifus'd them,

them, and took away their Eftates. However the
Mutiny ftill increas'd, many declaring for the Governour, fo that both Parties were in Arms, and
the Government being entirely off the Hinges, the
Soldiers went barefac'd about the *Indian* Towns,
robbing and abufing thofe People, and when they
complain'd to *Irala*, or the King's Officers, they
anfwer'd, It was not in their Power to prevent
it, which occafion'd many Chriftian *Indians* to with-
draw into the Mountains, where they could not
be inftructed. Befides thofe ufurping Magiftrates
and Officers ufing the *Spaniards* no lefs infolently,
fifty or fixty of them went away in a Paffion,
towards the Coaft of *Brafil*; and others who intended to have gone up the Country were fecur'd,
ftripp'd, and barbaroufly treated. They alfo imprifon'd three Clergymen, who reprov'd them for their
treafonable Practices, and proceeded to fuch Inhumanity, as to permit the *Indians*, who had already left
it off, to eat the Flefh of their Enemies. The Diforders daily increafing, thofe Rebels refolv'd to fend
away the Governour Prifoner into *Spain*, with formal
Informations drawn up againft him, as they thought
fit. Accordingly they put him aboard one of his
own Brigantines by Night, he being then fick and
weak, and yet he cry'd out, That he left in his
ftead, in the King's Name, Captain *John de Salazar
de Efpinofa*, and call'd Witneffes to it, whereupon
one of thofe Villains who acted as Treafurer, ran
to him with a Dagger, fwearing, he would ftab
him, if he mention'd the King. With him were
fent Prifoners, the aforefaid Capt, *Salazar*, and *Peter
de Eftopinan*. When at Sea there hapned a mighty
Storm, which continu'd four Days, and being in great
Danger of perifhing, the Infpector *Cabrera*, and the
under Treafurer *Garcivanegas*, who had been chief
Promoters

Promoters of all the Mifchiefs here mention'd, and were going into *Spain* to be the Governour's Acufers, and Profecutors, repenting of the horrid Crimes they had committed, looking upon that Storm, as a Judgment for their Enormities, took off the Governour's Fetters, and kifs'd his Feet, begging Pardon, acknowledging his Innocence, and their own Guilt in occafioning fo many falfe Oaths to be taken, and other heinous Sins to be committed. Being arriv'd in *Spain,* they return'd to their Vomit, forgot all their good Purpofes, and hafted to Court, to accufe the Governour, but upon his Arrival there they fcamper'd, pretending to go to their own Homes. *Cabrera* fell fick at *Loxa,* ran diftracted, and in that Condition kill'd his Wife. *Garcivanegas* dy'd fuddenly. The Council clear'd the Governour ; yet would not permit him to return to the River of *Plate ;* and thus Juftice was done him by halves. Having brought the Affairs of the River of *Plate* to this notable Period, it is Time to fee what was done in other Places.

C H A P.

CHAP. III.

The Expedition of the Viceroy of New Spain *to* subdue *the revolted* Indians *in* New Galicia ; *Voyage of two Ships of his to discover Northward on the* South-Sea ; *he sends Ships to the* Spice Islands.

DON *Antonio de Mendoza,* Viceroy of *New Spain,* understanding how haughty the *Indians* of *New Galicia* were grown, with the Success they had met with in their Revolt, and the killing of the Adelantado *Alvarado,* as has been said before in its Place, resolv'd to go in Person to reduce them, and in order to it commanded the *Indians* of *Tlascala, Cholula, Guaxocingo, Tepeaca, Tezcuco,* and others, to provide such Arms offensive and defensive as they us'd, granting leave to the Caziques and prime Men to buy Horses to ride, and to use *Spanish* Weapons, as Spears, Swords, Head-pieces, &c. and having thus drawn together fifty thousand *Indians,* they made a very agreeable Appearance, being all extraordinary well equipp'd; tho' there were some that said, it was not proper to arm the *Indians,* and accustom them to *Spanish* Weapons. He set out from *Mexico* on the 8th of *October* 1542, with three hundred *Spanish* Horse, among whom were many Persons of Distinction, and one hundred and fifty Foot Musketeers, Cross-bow-men, and Targeteers, under the Command

of

of Capt *Urbaneta*. He made fome Stay at *Mechoacan* for all the Men to join him, and thence proceeded to *Tazucalca*, which is the Boundary between the *Mechoacans* and the *Chichimecas*. Next he march'd three Days through a Defert to *Acuyna*, where was a ftony Mount defended by the Enemies, who having been fummon'd to fubmit, and perfifting in their Rebellion in Hopes of Relief, the *Spanifh* Infantry were order'd to poffefs themfelves of an Intrenchment, and to advance, if they found no Refiftance, being feconded by twenty thoufand *Indians*. Four of thofe Works were gain'd without any Oppofition, and the Enemy feeing the fifth attack'd, turn'd their Backs and fled, that the Paffes being fecur'd, the *Spanifh Indians* either kill'd, or took them all. A Squadron of Horfe had been order'd to mount as foon as the Foot had gain'd the fecond Intrenchment, and they were of ufe, becaufe the Top of the Hill was plain, and fit for Horfes. This was the firft Mount gain'd, where the friendly *Indians* behav'd themfelves very well, whom the Viceroy commanded, that fince no *Indians* were to be made Slaves, they fhould deliver up their Prifoners to have Juftice done on them.

NEXT the Army march'd in very good Order, fuch as did any Harm in the Country being punifh'd, and came to another Town call'd *Aquatique*, feven Leagues from the former, ftill in the Hollow of the Great River, where the Enemies were alfo fortify'd on a Mount, or Rock. The Defendants being fummon'd to furrender, anfwer'd, That if they were not reliev'd within fifteen Hours, they would fubmit, and come down to the Town, to pay the ufual Tributes. That Time being elaps'd, and the Rebels ftill delaying, the Viceroy order'd three Pedreros to be planted againft them, which having been

fir'd

fir'd fifteen or fixteen Times, fome chief Men, and
the Lady of the Town came down, with Croffes
in their Hands, in refpect to which holy Enfign, he
pardon'd, and bid them live peaceably in their Houfes. The next Day the Army march'd, at the Sight
whereof fome *Indians,* who were upon another Rock,
fled up the River, but being purfu'd, moft of them
were taken, yet the Viceroy would not make them
Slaves, but *Tamemes,* that is, Servants to attend the
Army during the War. From this Place to the
Rock of *Nuchiztlan* was twelve Leagues, and the
fame Diftance from *Guadalaxara,* and the main Strefs
of the War being in that Place, the Viceroy order'd
the People of *Guadalaxara* directing them not to be
there before him for Fear of any Misfortune, for he
was provident, mild, and good natur'd. The Commanders at *Guadalaxara,* took fuch good Meafures that
they arriv'd there exactly with the Army. When
the Army was incamp'd, no Enemy appear'd for
fome Days, till being rouz'd by fome Cannon-Shot,
they fell to work, and added two Intrenchments to
four they had before. Being fummon'd in the ufual
Form, they anfwer'd, That all the Country was their
own, and they would defend it. Some falfe Attacks were made to terrify them, whilft they made
Mantlets to cover the Men, The eighth Day
in the Morning the Artillery began to play, which
foon made Breaches in two of the Trenches, and
the Soldiers were for attacking the third, but the Infantry being a fmall Number, the Viceroy commanded all the Horfe, except twelve of each Troop, to
difmount, and give the Affault with Sword and Target, which being accordingly done, two Trenches
more were gain'd, and fo the reft, tho' with much
Difficulty, and the Cannon being brought up began to diflodge them, Capt. *Iñigo Lopez de A-*
nuncibay

nuncibay planted his Colours there. The Slaughter made by the *Tlafcallans, Mexicans,* and *Zarafcos* was very great, and would have been much greater had not the Viceroy prevented it, however the dead and living Prifoners amounted to eight thoufand, the latter of which the Viceroy declar'd Slaves, being above fourteen Years of Age, and diftributed them among the Forces, alledging, it was fit to be done for an Example, becaufe the Religious Men ftrenuoufly oppos'd him in that particular; and the reafon he gave for fo doing was, that thofe People were naturally Robbers, Murderers, and guilty of feveral other heinous Crimes. All the other ftrong Holds fubmitted, and the People came down from thofe Mountains to inhabit the Plains. The Viceroy, who had manag'd this War with fingular Conduct, having been now two Years from *Mexico,* return'd in triumphant manner, and applying himfelf to the Government, which he manag'd with much Difcretion, having among other good Things he did eftablifh'd a Council, or Court for Country Affairs, becaufe the Cattle had multiply'd very much, and ftill daily increas'd, which continues to this Day after the fame manner that it is practis'd in *Spain.*

NOR was the Viceroy only intent upon the Land Affairs, for tho' the two Ships he had fent before to difcover along the Coaft of *New Spain* to the Southward, had mifcarry'd, he fitted out two more, under the Command of *John Rodriguez Cabrillo,* the one call'd St. *Saviour,* and the other the *Victory,* which fail'd from the Port of the *Nativity,* on the 26th of *June* 1542, and the next Morning were at Cape *Corrientes* in twenty-two Deg. twenty Min. N. Lat. *Sunday* the 2d of *July* they came into twenty-four Deg. large, and had Sight of the Marquefs *del Valle's* Port, call'd *de la Cruz,* or of the Crofs, which is

on

on the Coaft of *California.* The 8th of the fame
Month, they were in twenty-five Deg. Lat. being
the Point of the *Trinity.* *Wednefday* the 19th they
difcover'd a Port, where was good Shelter, call'd it
of the *Magdalen*, in twenty-feven Deg. and water'd.
The 20th of *Auguft* they came to Cape *Engaño*, in
thirty-one Deg. Lat. *September* 14th, they anchor'd
at a Cape, which they call'd *de la Cruz,* or of the
Crofs, a good Bottom, the Land high, and naked, in
thirty-three Deg. *Tuefday, October* 10th, they difcover'd fome Towns of peaceable *Indians*, with whom
they traded, and call'd them the Towns of the Canoes, becaufe there were many, and they lye in thirty-five Deg. twenty Min. Having made little Way
for fome Days, by reafon of the Calm, on *Wednefday*
the 18th of the fame Month, they came to a long
Point of Land, which for that reafon they call'd *de
la Galera,* or of the Galey, in thirty-fix Deg. thirty
Min. when the Wind blowing frefh at N. W. they
ftood out to Sea, and difcover'd two Iflands, the one
eight Leagues in length Eaft and Weft, and the other
four, in which laft they faw a very good fmall Harbour, and both of them well inhabited, thofe People
and all the reft of the Coaft they had paft living on
their Fifheries, making Beads of the Fifh Bones to
barter with the People on the Continent. Thofe I-
flands are about ten Leagues from Cape *Galera* W.
by N. Staying eight Days in the Harbour, they
were kindly entertain'd by the *Indians*, who go naked,
their Faces painted in Checkers, and this they call'd
Port *Poffeffion.* *Wednefday* the 25th they fail'd from
that Port, with fair Weather, the Wind S. W. but the
next Day it blew hard at S. and S. W. with heavy
Showers of Rain, and Hazy, which put them in fome
Danger, becaufe that Wind was contrary, and they
near the Coaft, and that high. *Friday, Saturday* and

Sunday they had all forts of Winds, *Monday* and *Tuef-*
day heavy Rains, and clofe Weather. *Wednefday* the
1ft of *November*, they return'd to Port *Galera,* for
Shelter againft the N. W. Wind, which blew hard;
and *Thurfday* the 2d made into Port *Sardinas*, falling
off forty Leagues, the Country very populous, and
the Natives good natur'd. The Prime Men of a Town
near the Port went aboard the Ship, and danc'd to
the Mufick of a Tabor, and a Bag-pipe the *Spani-*
ards had, and lay aboard, the Boats in the mean Time
watering and wooding; thofe People's Houfes were
large and double, like thofe in *New Spain*, and their
burial Places were pal'd about. This Province was
call'd *Sejo*, the Natives fed on Acorns, Nuts, and
Fifh, and faid, that farther on there were People
cloath'd.

    Saturday the 11th they coafted along to the S. W.
feeking, but not finding *Our Lady*'s River, and faw
a vaft Ridge of high Mountains, which they call'd
the Mountains of St. *Martin*, in thirty-feven Deg.
thirty Min. Lat. and at the End of them towards
the N. W. is a Cape in thirty-eight Deg. which they
nam'd Cape St. *Martin*. At Night fuch a Storm
came up at S. S. E. and S. W. with Gluts of
Rain, that the Ships were parted, and one of them
threw over-board all that was upon Deck. *Monday*
the 13th the Commadore ftood in for the Land, to
feek the other Ship, and lay by all Night. There
a Cape runs out into the Sea, cover'd with very tall
Pine-Trees, which they call'd Cape *Pines*, and upon
an Obfervation found themfelves above forty Deg.
to the Northward, where they had a View of above
fifteen Leagues along the Coaft, high Land, bearing
North-Weft, and South-Eaft. *Wednefday* 15th, they
lay along the Coaft, the Wind North-Weft, the
Cold fo intenfe that they could fcarce Work, and faw
all

all the fnowy Hills, and in the Afternoon fpy'd the other Ship, in much Diftrefs, and leaky. *Friday* 16th, they came to a fpacious Bay, like an Harbour, and call'd it the Bay of *Pines.* The 18th they look'd out for an Harbour, feeing fnowy Mountains, with a Cape butting out from them, which they nam'd *Cabo de Nieve,* or Cape Snow, in thirty-eight Degrees forty Minutes Latitude, the Weather being all clear and fair along the Coaft, when the North-Weft Wind blows. From thirty-feven Degrees thirty Minutes, to forty, the Coaft bears North-Weft and South-Eaft, where finding no Harbour, they were forc'd to make for the Ifland of *Poffeffion,* which is one of thofe call'd of St. *Luke,* where they enter'd on the 23d of *November,* and the Harbour being good, re-fitted the fmall Ship, laying it a-ground, becaufe it was ready to fink. There they ftay'd till the End of *December,* the Weather continuing fo foul, that fome-times they could not go afhore in three or four Days. At length, on *Friday* the 19th of *January* 1543, with much Difficulty, they arriv'd at Port *Sardinas,* whence they fail'd again on the 14th of *Februa-ry,* and *Monday* the 26th to that they call'd Cape *Fortunas,* in forty-one Degrees Latitude. From the 27th of *February* till *Thurfday* the firft of *March* they had a dreadful Storm, and that Day took an Obfer-vation, and found forty-four Degrees Latitude, the Cold being fo exceffive, that they were almoft fro-zen. The 5th they return'd to the Ifland of *Poffeffi-on,* where the Sea breaking, they took Shelter on the South-South-Eaft of the Ifland of St. *Sebaftian.* At Night the Commadore vanifh'd, and in five Days they ran two hundred Leagues, under a Forefail Reef'd, having nothing to eat, but rotten Bisket, a Pound whereof was allow'd a Man. *Thurfday* the 8th the other Ship fail'd from Port St. *Sebaftian,* requiring

the

the Commander to return to *New Spain,* fince they had no Provifions, and on the 26th found the other Ship at the Ifland of *Cedars. Saturday, April* 14th, they return'd to the Port of the *Nativity,* their Commadore being dead. The Seamen faid that Voyage requir'd ftrong Ships, of two hundred Tuns Burthen, well rigg'd in all Refpects, and the Sails to be *Spanifh,* becaufe thofe of the *Weft-Indies* foon fplit; that they ought to carry much Store of Provifions, and no *Indians,* becaufe they were of no ufe on the Voyage, and only ferv'd to eat up the Stores. In fhort, thofe Ships reach'd to forty-four Degrees Latitude.

BESIDES the Enterprizes above-mention'd, the Viceroy of *New Spain* was intent upon trading to the *Molucco Iflands* in the *Eaft-Indies,* by way of the *South-Sea,* in Order to which he fitted out two Ships, one Galley, and two fmall Tenders, well furnifh'd with all Neceffaries, which fail'd under the Command of *Ruy Lopez de Villalobos,* from the Port of *Juan Gallego,* in *New Spain,* on the firft of *November* 1542. Having fail'd one hundred and eighty Leagues, in the Latitude of eighteen Degrees thirteen Minutes, they fell in with two Defert Iflands, twelve Leagues diftant from one another; the firft whereof they call'd St. *Thomas,* and the other *Anublada,* eighty Leagues from which they faw another Ifland, and nam'd it *Rocapartida*; fix Leagues beyond which, they difcover'd an *Archipelago* of low Iflands, all wooded, at one of which they with much Difficulty came to an Anchor, becaufe the Water is fo deep about them that they found no Bottom within a Musket-Shot of the Shore. They are inhabited by poor People, altogether unpolifh'd, where as foon as the Ships anchor'd at that call'd St. *Stephen,* the Inhabitants fled away on the oppofite Side, twenty-five Women remaining hid

hid in the moſt woody Part of the Iſland, who were
well us'd, and had Toys given them. Having water'd, the Ships ſail'd from this *Archipelago*, which
they call'd of *Coral*, having found ſome Tokens of
it. On the Feaſt of the *Epiphany* 1543, having run
thirty-five Leagues, they paſs'd by ten other Iſlands,
as agreeable as the others, for which reaſon they call'd
them the Gardins, the Latitude between nine and
ten Degrees. When they had proceeded one hundred
Leagues to the Weſtward, there blew ſuch a Storm,
that they expected all to have periſh'd, and actually
loſt the Galley, to their great Grief, as believing it
neceſſary for carrying on their Deſigns. The 10th
of *January*, when they had advanc'd fifty Leagues
farther, in ten Degrees Latitude, they paſs'd by a
beautiful Iſland, that was inhabited, and they not an-
choring, the *Indians* came out in Paraos, who made
the Sign of the Croſs, and were heard to ſay in *Spaniſh*, *Good Morrow Sailors*, for which reaſon they
nam'd it the Iſland *Matalotes*, or of Sailors. Thirty-
five Leagues to the Weſtward, they came to another
larger Iſland, and call'd it *de los Arracifes*, or of the
Ridges of Rocks, becauſe there were many about it.
The 2d of *February*, they anchor'd in a Bay, which
they call'd of *Malaga*, in ſeven Degrees Latitude, and
lay there a Month. *Ruy Lopez* would have ſettled
a Colony there, but did not, becauſe the Place was
unhealthy; yet he took Poſſeſſion for the Crown of
Spain, and call'd it *Ceſarea Caroli*, the Iſland being
three hundred and fifty Leagues in Compaſs, and it
is reckned to be above fifteen hundred Leagues from
the Port of the *Nativity* in *New Spain*. Departing
hence they coaſted ſixty Leagues along *Ceſarea*, and
diſcover'd two ſmall Iſlands about four Leagues di-
ſtant from each other to the Southward, where *Ruy
Lopez* thought to ſettle, and accordingly concluded a

Peace

Peace with the Inhabitants of one of them call'd *Sarragan*; yet the *Indians* foon repented, appear'd in Arms, and could not be perfwaded to fell Provifions, whereupon on *Monday* the 2d of *April,* the Town was attack'd, and taken, feveral *Spaniards* being wounded, fix whereof dy'd, and they nam'd this Ifland *Antonia,* being about fix Leagues in compafs, containing four Towns. All the Inhabitants retir'd to a fteep Rock, for which they were drove, and permitted to efcape, without being purfu'd, in order to gain them, but they fled over to *Cefarea.* On the Hill, or Rock was found much *China* Ware, Musk, Amber, Civet, Benjamin, Storax, and other Perfumes, both in Cakes, and Oyls, much us'd among them, which they bought of thofe that traded from *Mindanao* to the *Philippine* Iflands. There were alfo fome Tokens of Gold, and a Piece of Gold Mail ftudded through, but nothing elfe; becaufe all the Natives of thofe Iflands are wont to bury all they have in the Mountains. When the Booty was brought together, the General demanded the 7th Part, and any one Jewel he fhould choofe, which was granted. Then the Viceroy's Officers demanded his Dues, which provok'd the Soldiers; the King's Fifth was alfo requir'd, and the General anfwer'd, that it fhould be paid for Gold, Silver, and precious Stones, but not for any other Thing. He order'd *Indian* Wheat to be fow'd, for fear of wanting Provifions, which the Men refus'd, faying, Their Bufinefs was to fight, and not to till the Ground; however, he infifted on it, and they comply'd, which prov'd to their Advantage.

In that Ifland their Weapons were Hangers, Daggers, Spears, Darts, Bows and Arrows, and Trunks, all poifon'd. The defenfive Arms, Efcaupiles, or Armour of Cotton, down to their Feet, Corfelets of Wood,

Wood, and Buffaloes Skins, Cuiraſſes of Reeds, and
hard Wood, large Shields that cover them all over,
Helmets of hard Leather, and they had ſome ſmall
Pieces of Cannon, and Muskets. They are void of
all Sincerity, and notwithſtanding any Peace or Friend-
ſhip will break through all, when they have an Opportunity. Notwithſtanding what the *Spaniards* had
ſow'd, they were reduc'd to extreme Want, whereupon *Ruy Lopez* being inform'd that he might be
ſupply'd, if the Lord of *Mindanao* were his Friend,
being but fifty Leagues from *Ceſarea*, becauſe that
Iſland is very plentiful ; but he was there diſappointed, the Men he ſent thither narrowly eſcaping
the Treachery of thoſe People. *Ruy Lopez* having
got ſome Proviſions by Force at *Sanguin,* ſent away
one Veſſel back to *New Spain,* with Advice of what
he had done, and a Galiot to certain Iſlands afterwards call'd *Philippines,* to buy Proviſions.

C H A P. IV.

What hapned to the Spaniards *under the
Command of* Ruy Lopez de Villalobos *in
the aforeſaid Iſlands, the* Moluccos, *and
the* Eaſt-Indies, *till they return'd into*
Spain.

WHEN the aforeſaid Veſſels were gone, a Let-
ter was brought to *Ruy Lopez,* from Don
George de Caſtro, requiring him not to moleſt the
Indians of thoſe Iſlands, all which belong'd to the
King

King of *Portugal*, and offering him Relief, if he were in Diſtreſs. *Ruy Lopez* anſwer'd, That he had Orders from the King of *Spain* not to touch at the *Molucco* Iſlands, but to repair to all the reſt, which were within the Limits of the Crown of *Spain*. The *Spaniards* being in much Want of Proviſions, reſolv'd to remove from that Iſland, and were drove by the Currents to *Gilolo*, the King whereof being at War with the *Portugueſes*, concluded a Peace with *Ruy Lopez*, promiſing to ſupply him with Proviſions, and aſſign a Place for them to build a Fort. At *Gilolo* all the Goods were landed, and that King own'd himſelf a Subject of the Crown of *Spain*, and there came to the Ships one *Peter de Ramos*, who had been left there by the Ships of Don *Garcia de Loayſa*, and could never be induc'd to ſerve the *Portugueſes*, declaring he would rather dye than receive their Pay, and he had learnt the Language of the Country, and was well belov'd by the Natives. Soon after the King of *Tidore* came in Perſon to intreat the *Spaniards* to repair to his Iſland, and he would furniſh them with Proviſions, becauſe the *Portugueſes* were contriving to ſeize him. *Ruy Lopez* accepted of his offer, upon Condition, that he was not to make War againſt the *Portugueſes*, nor obſtruct them in their Trade of Cloves. It was ſaid before, that one of the Ships, call'd the St. *John*, had been ſent back from the Iſland of *Sarragon*, to carry Advice of all that had hapned till then, to *New Spain*. That Ship, in the Latitude of twenty-ſix Degrees diſcover'd a ſmall Iſland, and twenty-ſix Leagues farther on, two others, lying North and South from the Iſlands *Ladrones*, beyond that again they ſaw three more, one of them being a burning Mountain, that caſts forth Fire three ſeveral Ways. The 18th of *October* the Pilots found they had run ſeven hundred Leagues in a direct Line, in the

the Latitude of thirty Degrees bare, whence a violent North Wind drove them back to *Tendaya,* where
they anchor'd in a large Bay, on the North Side, the
Harbour good, the Country populous, with Plenty
of Rice, Swine, and Fowls; the Inhabitants well
fhap'd, wearing Gold in their Ears, Necklaces, and
fome Chains, and they faid the Land afforded much
Gold. There a Lord, whofe Name was *Herein,*
went three Times aboard, having about him above
the Value of one thoufand Pieces of Eight in Gold,
and the Slaves in his Boat had Gold Collars. They
went to another Town, the Lord whereof was call'd
Macabandala, where their Boat was ftolen, and they
feiz'd another Lord, whofe Name was *Turis,* that he
might caufe it to be reftor'd. They departed from
thence on the 3d of *January* 1544, and after much
driving backward and forward, at length arriv'd at
Tidore, where *Ruy Lopez* then was. At this Time
Jordan de Fletes came to Command at the *Molucco*
Iflands for the King of *Portugal,* and concluded a
Sufpenfion of Arms with the *Spaniards,* upon Condition that no *Portuguefes* fhould go to *Tidore*; that there
fhould be no Communication between the *Spaniards*
and the *Portuguefes,* and that the Cloves fhould be
fold them as they had been before, provided that they
went not thither to buy them, and this to hold till
the Kings of *Spain* and *Portugal,* or the Viceroys of
New Spain and *India* fhould order otherwife. The
Ship St. *John* that was mention'd above to have been
forc'd back from her Voyage to *New Spain,* being
now refitted, fail'd again for that Country on the
17th of *March* 1545, but with no better Succefs
than the firft Time, for after having been four Months
at Sea, it again return'd to *Tidore.*

ALL this Time many Meffages pafs'd between
the *Spaniards* and the *Portuguefes,* and between both
thofe

thofe Nations, and the Kings of *Gilolo*, *Tidore*, and *Ternate*, each being jealous of the other, and endeavouring to ftrengthen themfelves by Treaties, in which neverthelefs they plac'd no great Confidence. The *Portuguefe* Governour offer'd, in cafe the *Spaniards* would quit *Tidore*, and repair to one Side of *Ternate*, or to an Ifland clofe by it, that they would ferve them with all they had, which the *Spaniards* would not accept, as well knowing that the Defign was to fet the King of *Tidore*, and others againft them. Twenty *Spanifh* Soldiers, and three Clergymen having now deferted to the *Portuguefes*, the King of *Tidore* grew jealous, whereupon he fummon'd all the *Spaniards* into the Market-place, where he reprefented to them how much he had fuffer'd for adhering to the Crown of *Spain*, ever fince *Magellan's* Voyage, and how kind he had been in relieving them in their Diftrefs, praying that they would not forfake him, and offering whatfoever his Ifland could afford ; to all which *Ruy Lopez* return'd no other Anfwer, but that it was too late. However he privately treated with the *Portuguefe* Governour, without communicating what was in Hand, which all the *Spaniards* were concern'd at, being fully bent upon defending the King of *Tidore*, who had reliev'd them in their Diftrefs, and own'd himfelf a Subject to the King of *Spain*. On the 22d of *October*, *Ferdinand de Soufa*, a new *Portuguefe* Governour, fent from *India*, to the *Moluccos*, arriv'd at *Ternate*, with one hundred and fifty Men, in three Ships, and as many Foifts, with whom *Ruy Lopez* correfponded by Letter, and agreed to an Interview between them, contrary to the Opinion of all his Officers, and of the King of *Tidore*. But before his Departure, he ask'd their Advice concerning the Conditions to be ftipulated, and they unanimoufly agreed, that the Truce
ought

ought to be continu'd, till they had Orders from the King, or from the Viceroy of *New Spain*, and in Cafe of Refufal, that the *Portuguefe* Governour fhould give them a Ship well furnifh'd with all Neceffaries to carry them away, giving him Hoftages for Payment of all the Charges he fhould be at, and that the King of *Tidore* fhould no way fuffer for having entertain'd them. In cafe thefe Terms fhould be rejected, that the *Spaniards* fhould then ftand upon their Defence, being all ready to dye for the Honour of their Nation, and for their Friends and Benefactors. This Advice was given in Writing, and fign'd by all Perfons of Diftinction.

THE next Day *Ruy Lopez* and *Ferdinand de Soufa* met, and conferr'd together in private, the latter faid he would conclude nothing without communicating it to his Comrades, for fuch he reckned all aboard his Ships, and *Ruy Lopez* told his People, that he had deliver'd the Articles they gave him, and fhould have an Anfwer the next Day; but returning to *Tidore*, he declar'd, that the *Portuguefe* Commander having refus'd to confent to the Articles they had propos'd, he had left others with him, the Purport whereof was, That all the *Spaniards* fhould be carry'd to *India*, and there embark'd for *Spain*. This *Ruy Lopez* faid he had agreed to, and the prime Men intreating him not to conclude any thing, without the general Approbation of them all, fince they had always been punctually fubfervient to him, and that Complyance with the *Portuguefes* would render him contemptible; he anfwer'd, That no more fhould be faid of it, for he had pofitively agreed to thofe Conditions. Upon this pofitive Behaviour of his, all the Officers, and Soldiers, in Form intreated, and requir'd of him, not to conclude a Treaty fo difhonourable to himfelf and them all, efpecially at a Time
when

when there was fo little Neceffity to compel them to it, and in cafe he perfifted in his Refolution to conclude without, and contrary to their Opinion they protefted, that all the Lofs of Reputation fhould redound to himfelf, and he fhould be anfwerable for all other Loffes and Dangers that might enfue, fince he would act in that manner contrary to the Sentiments of fuch brave Officers and Soldiers. The next Day, being the 28th of *October*, he was told, that the Sailors complain'd that they had not a Ship allow'd them to fail to *New Spain*, which after fome Cavilling he pofitively refus'd to grant, alledging, that it was contrary to his Agreement with the *Portuguefes*. On the firft of *November* the Officers again demanded an Anfwer to their Remonftrance, and preffing the Matter home, fome harfh Words pafs'd, and *Bernard de la Torre* told him, That he would look upon him as his Superior, till they were in *Spain*; but that he might be affur'd he would profecute him there, and if that fail'd, he would call him to Account Man to Man. He anfwer'd, That the Challenge was very remote, and he ought to confider him as his Superior, and not ask any thing of him in a difrefpectful manner, and that he knew better what was for the good of them all, and for the Service of the King. At length *Ruy Lopez* return'd the following Anfwer to the above-mention'd Remonftrance, That they well knew they had pofitive Orders from the King not to touch at the *Molucco* Iflands, or any other Parts belonging to the *Portuguefes*, which he had fworn to obferve, among his other Inftructions, yet was fo far juftifiable in what he had done, that he had been compell'd to it by want of Provifions, yet could not continue there as a Chriftian, the fame being contrary to the King's exprefs Command, and muft give occafion to the

Slaugh-

Slaughtering of many Men, and other Mifchiefs, all which would be charg'd upon the Viceroy of *New Spain*, who had fent them, and he again would lay all at their Doors; many other Arguments he urg'd, very much to the Purpofe, and like a Man of Honour and Confcience, but too tedious to be here repeated at large. The Officers and Soldiers, having taken this into confideration, reply'd, That they had intreated the *Portuguefes* to relieve them in the great Want which had brought them thither, and fince thofe People had not done it, they might lawfully ftay there, without obftructing the *Portuguefe* Trade, till fuch Time as they could return to *New Spain*, which the *Portuguefes* would wiilingly have forwarded, had he not made the Propofal of going home by the Way of *India*; that it was uncertain, whether *Gilolo* belong'd to the Crown of *Portugal*, and therefore they ought not to give it up, efpecially fince the King of that Ifland, own'd himfelf a Subject of the King of *Spain*, and had always fhown fuch extraordinary Favour to all *Spaniards*, wherefore they intreated and requir'd him to infringe the Capitulation concluded with him upon Oath.

Ruy Lopez rejoyn'd, That he had never taken an Oath to, or contracted with the King of *Gilolo*, in the Name of his own King, and referr'd himfelf to the written Treaty; that he did not think himfelf fo much oblig'd to that King as they faid, nor had directed any to make War againft him, yet did not think it lawful to oppofe the fame; and in fhort, that he would juftify his Actions where there was an Authority to call him to Account. This was his Anfwer, and yet he affifted the *Portuguefes* with Men againft *Gilolo*, and fupply'd them with Gun-powder, becaufe that which they had was naught. The *Spaniards* having none to ftand by them, and being very poor,

at

ᵃt length comply'd with their Commander, and *Ferdinand de Soufa* offering them Cloaths, fome refus'd them, and ftay'd among the *Indians,* the reft took what was offer'd, and imbark'd aboard the *Portuguefe* Ships, which carry'd them to the City of *Malaca,* where they remain'd five Months, in very great Want, felling what little they had left. Thence they were tranfported to *Goa,* where the Viceroy kept them till the Middle of *May* 1547, when they again imbark'd and arriv'd at *Lisbon* the faid Year, having departed from *New Spain* in 1542. All this Relation has been here delivered together, tho' hapning in fo many Years, to avoid the frequent difmembring of fuch Accounts, which is inevitable in adhering to the Method of Annals.

The End of the Fifth Volume.